THE FATIMA PROPHECIES

AT THE DOORSTEP OF THE WORLD

THOMAS W.PETRISKO

CONSECRATION

AND

DEDICATION

This book is consecrated to Our Lady of the Rosary and dedicated
to my father, Andrew Petrisko. A man amongst men, always
faithful to his family and his God, dad put on the armor of
Christ each day and never failed to be anything less than heroic in
the eyes of his only son.

St. Andrews Productions
6111 Steubenville Pike
McKees Rocks, PA 15136

St. Andrews Productions
Phone: (412) 787-9754
Fax: (412) 787-5204
Internet: www.saintandrew.com
Printed in the United States of America

**Scriptural quotations are take from The Holy Bible —RSV: Catholic Edition.
Alternate translations from the Latin Vulgate Bible (Douay Rheims Version
—DV) are indicated when used. Some of the Scriptural quotations from the
New American Bible: St. Joseph Edition, The New American Bible— Fireside
Family Edition 1984-1985, The Holy Bible—Douay Rheims Edition, The New
American Bible— Red Letter Edition 1986.**

ACKNOWLEDGMENTS

I could never list all the people who helped with this work. I would like to say, however, that Christina Gallagher played, by accident or providence, an important part in the inception of this effort as did her spiritual director, Fr. Gerard McGinnity.

I wish to thank those most helpful to me during the writing of this book: Robert and Kim Petrisko, Dr. Frank Novasack, Fr. Richard Foley, Michael Fontecchio, Amanda DeFazio, Carole McElwain, Carol Jean Speck, Joan Smith, Jim Petrilena, Clyde Gualandri, John Haffert, Fr. Robert Herrmann, Joe and Sharon Ripper, Mrs. B. Laboissonniere, Sister Agnes McCormick, Mary Lou Sokol, the prayer group at the Pittsburgh Center for Peace, Fr. John O'Shea, Joe and Gerry Simboli, and Fr. Réne Laurentin.

Most importantly, I thank my family for the support and sacrifice they have made for this work; my wife, Emily; daughters Maria, Sarah and Natasha, and my son, Joshua. A special thank you to my mother and father, Andrew and Mary Petrisko, and my uncle, Sam.

ABOUT THE AUTHOR

D r. Thomas W. Petrisko was the President of the Pittsburgh Center for Peace from 1990 to 1998 and the served as editor of the Center's five "Special Edition" newspapers. These papers, featuring the apparitions and revelations of the Virgin Mary, were published in many millions throughout the world. He is the author of *For the Soul of the Family; The Story of the Apparitions of the Virgin Mary to Estela Ruiz, The Sorrow, the Sacrifice and the Triumph; The Visions, Apparitions and Prophecies of Christina Gallagher, Call of the Ages, The Prophecy of Daniel, In God's Hand; the Miraculous Story of Little Audrey Santo, Mother of The Secret, False Prophets of Today, St Joseph and The Triumph of the Saints* and *The Last Crusade.*

Dr. Petrisko, along with his wife Emily, have three daughters, Maria, Sarah, Natasha, and a son, Joshua.

The decree of the Congregation for the Propagation of the Faith (AAS 58, 1186 - approved by Pope Paul VI on 14 October 1966) rules that the *Nihil obstat* and *Imprimatur* are no longer required for publications that deal with private revelations, apparitions, prophecies, miracles, etc., provided that nothing is said in contradiction of faith and morals.

The author hereby affirms his unconditional submission to whatever final judgment is delivered by the Church regarding the events currently under investigation in this book.

St. Andrew's Productions
6111 Steubenville Pike
McKees Rocks, PA 15136
(412) 787-9735

CONTENTS

PART III
HIDDEN FROM THE WISE

PART IV
THY KINGDOM COME

PREFACE

BY FR. RÉNE LAURENTIN

D r. Thomas Petrisko is an efficacious man who has a passion for God the Heavenly Father, so forgotten and so neglected, and for the Blessed Virgin Mary.
This spiritual passion lead him to abandon his medical profession and to consecrate himself to the Pittsburgh Center for Peace, an organization that diffuses the apparitions of Mary and her messages and a special consecration to the Heavenly Father for the end of our millennium.

Dr. Petrisko possesses a prophetic charism that dares to present a synthesis and perspective of the numerous messages on the fight of the Virgin Mary against the demon, and of the finality of the triumph of the holy heart of Mary, which is the triumph of the Father Himself. This interpretation is proposed without dogmaticism and in a suggestive manner, because in matters of apparitions the Church itself is prudent in it's judgment and does not teach them as dogma. Indeed, the Catholic has no obligation to believe even in Guadalupe, Lourdes,and Fatima. But the Church encourages to the Christian, laymen or priests, the freedom of the faith, of inquiring to understand the design of God in the world where he lives. In fact, it is a freedom, even a duty for every Christian to seek the will and design of the plan of God in his own life and in the world where he is involved in the service of the Lord.

Many Christians will be happy to read this new book , remarkably informative on the message and promises of Fatima. They will see in it the awesome general view of the messages of Our

Lady for the end of our millennium.

The prophecies of Fatima are the exception to have been taken into consideration by several popes, from Pius XII to John Paul II, and they were welcomed and essential for the March 25, 1984, consecration of the world by Pope John Paul II to the heart of Mary. That was accomplished after one hundred million martyrs and the promise of Our Lady for the end of persecution in Russia. But we must still remember that the fulfillment of the promise of the full conversion of Russia still requires always our prayers and our constant cooperation in order to bring the Triumph of the Immaculate Heart of Mary and the Triumph of Our Heavenly Father.

Father Réne Laurentin
Paris, France
July 16, 1998

FOREWORD

BY JOHN M. HAFFERT

T wo years before this very important book by Dr. Thomas Petrisko went to press, a United Nations tribunal issued indictments for the massacres in Rwanda, where up to a million persons were systematically put to death. That would be the equivalent of the massacre of 50 million people in the United States! What the UN does not include in its report is that in a series of Marian apparitions in Rwanda, less than 10 years before the massacre there, the Blessed Virgin Mary had warned the country and offered specific requests for avoiding a **"river of blood."**

Her requests were not heard and the message she had given to Rwanda literally came true: "A river of blood ... people killing each other ... bodies without their heads."

The world was shocked by the almost incredible atrocities in Rwanda, a country more than 90 percent Christian, the majority of whom are Catholics. What must be chilling to the rest of us is that, in speaking to the youth of Rwanda, the Virgin Mary said that she came for the entire world: **"I am concerned not only for Rwanda or for the whole of Africa. I am concerned with, and turning to, the whole world. The world is on the edge of catastrophe."** One visionary, seeing Mary so sad, said: "I know what makes you suffer. It is because the day will come when we will wish we had listened to what you have been telling us about loving, serving and doing what you ask ... but it will be too late."

On March 27, 1982, the Bishop of Akita in Japan, announced that Mary had come in 1973 with a similar message for the entire world.

And here is where this book by Dr. Petrisko takes on world-shaking importance. It magnifies heavenly voices of warning from around the world. As you take this book into your hands, remember those prophetic words of the visionary of Rwanda speaking to Our Lady: "I know what makes you suffer ... the day will come when we will wish we had listened to you ... but it will be too late." If the message of this book is ignored, the Rwandan "river of blood" may engulf the world. In Rwanda, 22,000 people saw the visionaries crying out during eight hours of visions about the coming chastisement if people did not listen. Tragically, the critics turned people away from listening with the complaint: "They (the apparitions) are not approved."

In writing this book, Dr. Petrisko knows that God does not expect us to wait for a formal Church approval of all of its contents. When I was asked to translate the messages of Rwanda into English, shortly after they became known, I wrote to the local bishop for his opinion. He replied that he expected good fruit for souls from what was taking place and encouraged me to undertake the project. After due investigations, the bishop was of the opinion that the apparitions were authentic.

The same type of episcopal recognition applies to most of the apparitions and revelations of which Dr. Petrisko writes. And the most important have been formally approved in pastoral letters.

But because of the harm done by careless criticism, it is important to note that it is rare for any apparitions to be formally approved while they continue to take place, and sometimes even before many years have passed. In the case of the important apparitions of Pellevoisin, France, in 1876, the local bishop indicated "favor" but gave no formal approval. A shrine was built, pilgrimages began, and the bishop went personally every year to celebrate Mass there on the anniversary of the apparitions. However, formal approval by means of a pastoral letter took more than 100 years.

Canon Laurentin Affirms Journalistic Right

As journalists, we are not expected to wait a hundred years. Both common sense and the new policy of the Church (which explicitly permits publication of private revelations) indicate that we should publish if the local bishop so advises or at least raises no objection.

This has been a problem with the apparitions of Medjugorje, which despite all the good reported, were not approved by the local bishop. Many journalists and even theologians (perhaps the most noteworthy being the Rev. Réne Laurentin) seemed to defy the bishop's position. When I discussed this with Fr. Laurentin, he said that even when the bishop is negative, if there is sufficient evidence we have a right to investigate and to publish. He pointed out that most apparitions are initially refused any sign of episcopal recognition.

Some will always accuse those who take up the role of Jonah, as did the visionaries of Rwanda and those who published their story, of running after signs and wonders, of being too quick to believe and to sound the alarm.

Dr. Petrisko must have been well-aware of the risk of denunciation when he undertook the six-year long task of writing this book. Long after Fatima was recognized in 1942 by Pius XII, there were many, including clergy, who rejected it or vehemently emphasized that revelation stopped with the Apostles, implying that it was almost "un-Catholic" to emphasize private revelations, to frighten people with "Hell" and the idea that the alternative of reparation is the "annihilation of several entire nations" (the words of Our Lady of Fatima).

But we cannot be more Catholic than the Pope, and everyone knows how much the Popes since 1942 have affirmed Fatima and have accepted the discernment of local bishops in such matters.

The Great Sign

One would like to take the world by the shoulders and shake it into the realization that it faces a chastisement worse than the deluge if it does not listen.

Of all that Dr. Petrisko writes, perhaps nothing is more significant than the "Great Sign" of Jan. 25, 1938. Is it not at once stunning and frightening that God gave a great sign (and that is the very term used by Our Lady at Fatima) ... a sign of the world being destroyed by fire, a sign witnessed by millions ... and yet largely ignored? Is it any wonder that as this book goes to press, there are many wars being fought and tens of thousands of atomic weapons, at the ready, all over the world?

Through this book and many publications, at great personal sacrifice, Dr. Petrisko has felt the responsibility of giving voice to what God is saying to the world at the present moment. It is too late for Rwanda. And while Jonah could cover the city of Nineveh from end to end in three days, only with the help of discerning and courageous journalists like Dr. Thomas Petrisko can God's messages for the world of today reach the ends of the earth in time.

John M. Haffert
August 13, 1998

INTRODUCTION

In the beginning, God our Father created us in His own image—we were made for God's own Heart. But by free will, we chose to leave the home of our Creator. Over the course of our salvation history, however, God has intervened, calling His children back home.

Before Adam and Eve exiled themselves from God by choosing not to do His Will, God walked with them in Paradise "in the cool of the afternoon." After, God manifested Himself to His children in such ways as a burning bush, a pillar of fire, and through the voice of His prophets.

Two thousand years ago, Our Father sent His only begotten Son, Jesus, to redeem us—His children—from the bondage of sin and death. Scripture tells us that Christ is the Way, the Truth, and the Life—sent by God to lead us back home to Him. After Jesus' death, resurrection, and ascension into heaven, God sent His Holy Spirit to purify and refine us so that Presence could dwell in us. But for this to happen, we clearly needed to cooperate with His Grace.

So to aid us in this effort, He sent Mary, the Queen of Prophets, the Queen of Heaven, the Queen of Peace. She was not only the Mother of Jesus, the Mother of God—but she was also our Mother, given to all mankind at the foot of the cross.

If we look closely at the Christian era, we will see that Mary, our Mother, has been actively involved with God's children, her children, for a purpose—to return us to our heavenly Father. This is done not only through her role in our redemption, in mediating God's graces, and by serving as our advocate before God, but Mary also has a longstanding history of mystical interaction with her earthly children.

Indeed, Marian apparitions and supernatural manifestations have been reported since the earliest days of the Church. They have paralleled, in an almost complimentary fashion, the spiritual, social, and political needs of God's children. And Church history is filled with such stories.

Beginning in A.D. 40, just seven years after the death of Christ, Mary reportedly appeared to St. James on the plains of northern Spain at a place named "Saragozza." Just seven years later, she is said to have appeared again to a woman named Villa at Le Puy, France. After this, the rest is more than history. Throughout every century, in every land, there are stories of Mary coming from heaven to the aid of her children, often at the most desparate of times and in the most critical situations.

Since the Middle Ages there have been many efforts to gather such reports of Mary's apprearances. Many books have been written, including some very well written accounts that solidify and enhance the overall history of Marian interventions. But over the last fifty years, a series of scholarly studies have documented this phenomenon which have elevated the field of mystical theology to a new level. Especially noted is Robert Ernst's 1989 work titled *Lexikon der Marienerscheinungen,* which studied not only apparitions and visions but such phenomena as weeping and bleeding images, and was a look at all the reported apparitions he could uncover since the beginning of the Church. Although his work has been criticized, it also has been noted as a useful tool in charting the relative frequency and increase in the number of reported apparitions over the centuries. Ernst found that reports of Marian apparitions began to multiply significantly during the tenth century (except for a slight decline in the 14th century). He also found the 20th century alone (400 in his study) equaled the total number from all of the preceding centuries. This, of course, did not include the present decade (1990's) which continues to reveal more reports. A similar effort, *Les Apparitions de la Vierge*, was published by Sylvie Barnay for his doctoral dissertation in 1992. Barnay's study noted data from 2460 texts on apparitions.

Another highly referenced work is Fr. Bernard Billets 1971 study *True and False Apparitions in the Church*. This study found 210 apparitions reported between 1928 and 1971. A revised study published in 1976 continued to document the escalating number of reports. C.M. Staehlin wrote in his book *Apparitions*, that there were 30 apparitions of Mary "investigated" in Western Europe between 1930 and 1950, with some 300 cases of individual apparitions to children. And Yves Chiron's 1997 study *Enqu^te Sur Les Apparitions De La Vierge* reported over 300 twentieth century apparitions. Another study by W.A. Christian Jr., titled *Religious Apparitions and the Cold War in Southern Europe*, estimated as many as fourteen apparitions a year were reported to Catholic officials in the 1940's and 1950's in Europe.

While these studies are in no way considered by their authors to be precise, they do verify estimates and shed greater light on the entire field of modern day apparitions. It is a field that is mysterious in many ways, but one that is growing in interest especially among secular scholars and investigative writers. Some very accomplished scholars have published books on the subject over the last two decades, as have many professional lay Catholics who have developed strong interest in the field. In his 1998 book, *The Last Secret*, investigative journalist Michael Brown continued to reveal the vastness of this field of mystical theology. Brown writes that officials at the International Research Institute at the University of Dayton told him that at least eight thousand significant apparitions of the Virgin Mary have occurred since the earliest centuries. Father Johann G. Roten, director of the institute, estimated close to a thousand major, minor, and related apparitions have occurred between 1830 and 1981. Two other works, *A Guide to Apparitions of Our Blessed Virgin Mary* (1995) by Peter Heintz and *Erscheinungen und Botschaften der Gottesmutter Maria* (1995) by Gottfried Hierzenberger and Otto Nedomansky, also confirm the uniqueness of our times and the vast amount of interest in the subject by laymen.

Indeed, these studies document and confirm the apparitional woman's role in salvation history. But besides providing documented evidence of mystical phenomena over the centuries, the studies reveal something more. According to their authors, a documentable "outbreak" of Marian apparitions is discernable. This outbreak did not begin in the 20th century or even around 1830, the year many theologians note as the "official" onset of the Marian era because of the apparitions at Ru Du Bac, Paris. Rather, a careful examination of the past three centuries uncovers a more precise picture of the increasing phenomena of Marian apparitions.

From newspaper archives, as well as Church documents throughout Europe over the last 250 years, a wealth of data on reported apparitions emerges. Conclusions are difficult to make, but beginning somewhere in the mid to late 18th century, a trend of such reports began and continued throughout the 19th and 20th centuries.

The non-Catholic literature on Marian apparitions during the earliest part of this period is small but helpful. It consists mostly of local newspaper reports of the events and editorial commentaries. In some cases, major newspapers in larger cities became interested in the events and published stories. Often written in hostile language that was unsympathetic and agnostic, the reports paid little attention to the visionaries or their revelations but rather emphasized details of the events and the political and commercial interests served by the visions. Many newspaper accounts also explored the events in a style that sought to propagate the emerging psychological and philosophical movements of the day. For the most part, these accounts attributed the events to certain "afflicted types" or to the political, religious, and social aspirations of estranged groups during this period.

But beyond attempts by the secular press to marginalize the events in their reader's minds, another picture of the reported apparitions of this period can be found in these accounts. These events were considered great dramas, especially throughout Europe, and they drew millions of people to distant valleys and lofty mountains where the Virgin Mary was believed to be appearing. Likewise, according to historians, the apparitions were a tremendous source of religious revival and were clearly counterproductive to the emerging social and political movements of the day. Indeed, hostile government officials throughout Europe consistently blamed the

Catholic Church for orchestrating many of the events.

From the Church's standpoint, except for the great increase in the number of alleged apparitions, there was nothing different about the nature of the reports. The 19th century Marian apparitions were consistent with such accounts documented as far back as the 4th and 5th centuries. According to historians, by the 11th century the phenomena of Marian apparitions was well known. By then, studies of apparitions had been published and "classic" cases were already recognizable. Reports of such events continued throughout the late Middle Ages with documents revealing how accounts of visions contributed to the inception of shrines, pilgrimages, and stories of miracles.

However, immediately before the French Revolution (1789) a sharp increase in the number of Marian apparitions were reported. Some stereotypical changes occurred too, as records indicate more children and female visionaries. There is also a noted shift in the cults surrounding the events. The emphasis of such events seemed to move from being centered around the visionaries, as in the 15th and 16th centuries, to the reported "prophetic" messages the apparitions were giving to their messengers. But beginning around 1780, records show that there was an outbreak of miracles and that a growing number of priests, nuns, monks, and lay people began to prophesy about coming revolutions, wars, apostasy, droughts, food shortages, and persecution of the Church.

Indeed, from across Europe, the stories came from everywhere. Visions, miracles, prophecies, Eucharistic miracles, celestial signs, moving and weeping statues, and the stigmata were claimed in France, Germany, and the Papal States. Over the next hundred years, an endless stream of such phenomenon was reported. From the "Winking Madonnas" of Italy in the 1790's to the apparitions reported by a group of school children at Tilly-Sur-Seulles in the Calvados in 1896-99, an amazing picture of the late 18th and 19th centuries emerges. It is a picture that immediately sends a distinct message to believers of such affairs. God was trying to give the faithful a message. And His determination to do so was to be so visible and persistent as to be undeniable.

Most of all, these prophecies did what prophecies have

always done, they helped secure for believers tangible proof of God's existence and that God was concerned with the world and its cooperation with His Will. While opponents voiced numerous objections to these events at the time, the evidence reveals the prophecies were not for or against any political regime. Rather, they were surprisingly indifferent for the most part. Noted Notre Dame historian Thomas Kselman explores this in his book *Miracles and Prophecies In Nineteenth Century France*:

> The eighteenth century prophecies were not part of a reasoned argument intended to refute Enlightenment deism or atheism. Rather, they spoke directly to the emotions and satisfied the spiritual needs of the people who required not simply that God exists, but that He exists as a personality who could directly communicate His desires and plans to His followers.

Kselman also noted that whether the prophecy called forth opposition to the regime or attempted to support it, the function remained the same. The prophecies insisted that the "political order align itself with the supernatural order, and strive for the creation of a godly Kingdom of Earth."

Of course, the times at hand looked little like a striving for such a kingdom. And for the faithful, the prophecies only helped to confirm that something evil was in the air and that God was warning of danger.

According to Professor David Blackbourn of Harvard University, "the total number of alleged (19th century) apparitions ran to many hundreds." This estimate, arrived at by a secular scholar through research for his book on an 1876 apparition of the Virgin Mary in the German village of Marpingin, casts a bright light on the true history of 19th century apparitions. Blackbourn's work is helpful in looking at this emerging phenomena and its vastness. But with most of the reported miracles of the 19th century, the background information today is scant. However, we must remember that there is no denying these events occurred and that they tremendously influenced the times.

The turn of the 20th century witnessed more of the same. From throughout the world, apparitions were increasingly being reported. Again, the prophecies were often of a warning nature and seemed to be saying a climax in world history of some sort was approaching.

At Fatima in 1917, which the Church recognized in 1930, an impressive number of prophecies were given and later fulfilled. Most significantly, the apparitional woman spoke of an era of peace that was to come into the world. However, the prophecies also said that a great purging of evil would be necessary if her attempts to call the world to conversion failed. Over the next 80 years, a new level of genocide in human history was recorded as the message of the prophets was ignored, rejected and even ridiculed.

Since 1981, the world has witnessed what appears to be the approaching fulfillment of Fatima's remaining prophecies. Hundreds, if not thousands of apparitions have been reported. The end of an era is hurtling towards us, the prophets say. The errors of humanism, of what began with the French Revolution, are about to fall. Likewise, it is prophesied that a new dawn will now come into the world as the story of an age of evil passes by.

This book attempts to examine Mary's mystical intervention throughout this entire period beginning with the French Revolution, across the 19th and 20th centuries, into the new millenium. It seeks to focus on Fatima a great light and to document the events and mystical history of the era in a way that undeniably demonstrates God's great love and mercy for His people.

At Fatima, a commission of six experts appointed by the Bishop to interpret the message of Fatima rendered the opinion that the "Era of Peace" promised by Mary implied a true "reign of Christ" on the earth. This was because, they said, there "could be no other meaning of the word peace" on the lips of the Mother of Christ and "no other meaning to her words 'my Immaculate Heart will Triumph.'" This is not to confuse such a prophecy with heretical "millenarian" theories that the Church has condemned – theories that embrace a literal 1,000 year reign of Christ on earth. Likewise, this is also not to confuse the coming of a new era with other misguided prophecies associated with the belief that Christ will return at this time in history because of the approaching of the new millenium.

Rather, the prophecies of a new era given at Fatima, and all such prophecies of a coming "reign of the Father's Kingdom on earth" as described in this book and elsewhere, pertain to a future, glorious, grace - filled time on earth that is alluded to in Scripture and has written of by many great saints and Doctors of the Church. Indeed, by the fifth century, St. John Chrysostom was announcing a coming "golden era" of the Church, one to be dominated by greater peace and joy in God. Down through the centuries, many visionaries, popes, and mystics have echoed the arrival of such a spirit – filled time.

Is Fatima's Era of Peace this same prophesied time? Is the second Pentecost," the "new springtime for the Church," and the "definitive coming of the Kingdom" that Pope John Paul II continues to proclaim really near? I believe it is and I pray that all who read this book will share in this belief. I also pray that together we will hold fast to the truth that our forefathers lived and died for: a better world that promises to be filled with the light, peace, and the love of God.

PART I

THOSE

PROPHETS

OF OLD

*"I don't have to make you believe in this.
I have to let you know."*

-St. Bernadette Soubirous
Lourdes, France

CHAPTER ONE

SOMETHING IN THE AIR

"Can you penetrate the designs of God?"
— Jb 11:17

T here is no definitive time frame for the war we are going to describe. The parameters can stretch from the Garden of Eden to the 20th century with plenty of latitude for differing opinions. Moreover, even though this narrative prepares the reader for what is believed to be an impending climax that will be visibly manifested through the affairs of men and nations, succeeding generations may merely pick up the story and rewrite it with an entirely new time line and an entirely new, and perhaps more worthy, climax. This is because what we are talking about in this story is the great and final battle between the forces of good and the purveyors of evil, both visible and invisible. It is a story that Judeo-Christian teachings says began with two individuals, a man and a woman, and has moved across the world stage to now involve billions. It is already thousands of years old and holds within its history more memorable places, events, and characters than we will ever truly know. It also holds more drama, suspense, pain and joy that any writer could create in the caverns of his imagination. And, it must be realized, that no human history will ever record its ending. For by the mere fact that the conclusion has been realized, not only will the show be over but there will also no longer be an audience to view the last scene or even a historian to record the last chapter.

But for our purposes, a series of events that occurred in a little village in Portugal, named Fatima, from 1915 through 1917, permit us to frame our portion of this story in a more or less concise, defined period of history. And it is within this time frame that both human and reported supernatural events will be examined in order to present and to argue a fundamental premise: that the end of an era is descending upon the world as is the beginning of a new one, encased and revealed through the unfolding of a great spiritual war.

The events at Fatima in the early part of this century serve not just as our compass but also as a diorama for this story. For from Fatima, and specifically the Virgin Mary's apparitions there in 1917, we begin to understand how and why the world has gotten to where it is today and, just as importantly, how it got to Fatima.

Seven apparitions of the Virgin Mary to three shepard children occurred there from May 13th through October 13th of that year. And within this history lies the fact that some of these same children, as well as several others, said that they were visited by an angel in both 1915 and 1916. And this, then, is where our story begins.

It is with little fanfare that the account of the appearences of the angel at Fatima is noted in the history of the apparitions. Sister Lucia dos Santos, the lone surving visionary would later write in her memoirs that the angel looked so bright as to appear to be "wrapped in a sheet" and as white as "snow." This angel is believed by Church scholars who have studied and validated the events at Fatima in 1917 (The Catholic Church approved the apparitions of the Virgin Mary at Fatima on October 13, 1930.) to have been the legendary Archangel Michael, whose history is firmly recorded in the Old Testament and the New.

St. Michael the Archangel was revered as the guardian of Israel and the protector of synagogues and the Temple of Jerusalem. On the day of atonement, Jews concluded their prayers in a specific manner that invoked his intercession. "Michael, Prince of mercy, pray for Israel that it may reign in heaven." It is believed to have been Saint Michael who appeared to Abraham and forbade him to sacrifice his son Isaac. Likewise, according to Saint Gregory Nazianzen, St. Michael spoke to Moses and brought the plagues on Egypt. The great archangel is credited with leading the Israelites out of Egypt, across the Red Sea, and into the promised land and he fought with Lucifer (see the epistle of St. Jude 5-9) for the body of

Moses. St. Michael led Joshua across the Jordan and delivered the three young men from the fiery furnace. He sent Habacuc to feed Daniel in the lion's den and when a war broke our with Persia, it was St. Michael who met with that nation's guardian angel.

The New Testament upholds his vital and significant role throughout the unfolding of the Redemption, from beginning to end. Tradition holds that St. Michael announced to Saint Anne the Immaculate Conception of the Blessed Virgin Mary, freed St. Peter from prison, and escorted the Virgin to Heaven during her Assumption. Likewise his legendary call in the final battle as announced in St. John's Apocalypse is well known: "Who is like unto God?"

That Fatima's story, as authoratively documented and approved by the Catholic Church, begins with St. Michael is therefore not to be surprising for those who believe in what occurred there. Who other than Scripture's most celebrated defender of the faith could be expected to launch such a decisive fray? But with this understanding comes an equally important disclosure that may be surprising, for the story of Fatima does not begin in 1917 or 1915 for that matter, any more than the human events that led to the great prophecies given there by the Virgin Mary in 1917. Rather, a series of events in Fatima some 800 years before is where our time frame for this story begins to unfold, and once again it is with St. Michael.

Accordingly, theologians and historians alike agree that a new era in human history started to dawn around the 12th century. Indeed, a profound and visible line of demarcation is seen during this period, as scholars note it seemed like the world suddenly moved in a way that was decidedly in favor of dispelling with matters of faith. For a while, things became so bad that even the Church seemed forced to contemplate the possibility of its extinction. Such was the rebellious nature of the times. Division was everywhere in the affairs of men and most visibly in the Church, as a litany of controversial Popes came and went over the following centuries. Most significantly it was during the onset of this period of upheaval that we find a series of documented supernatural phenomena involving the Virgin Mary, St. Michael, the nation of Portugal and even the little village of Fatima.

In the year 1147, St. Michael reportedly appeared during the taking of the castle of Santarem from the Moors in Portugal by

3

Alfonsus Henriques and the Christians. The victory was won on May 8th, 1147, (the anniversary of St. Michael's most famous apparition in a cave at Monte Gargano in Apulia, Italy, in the year 490) and laid the way for a series of reported supernatural events in Portugal. On the same day St. Michael appeared at Santarem, a second battle began in Lisbon that led to its liberation from the Moors on October 25, 1147. During this siege, a miracle of the sun is documented to have occurred. (This miracle is credited by the historian A. Fernando Castilho to have occurred on October 13th, the same date 770 years later that the great miracle of the sun occurred at the last apparition of the Virgin Mary at Fatima).

One hundred years later, in the year 1247, the second most famous Eucharistic miracle in Catholic Church history occurred at Santarem. More and more miracles continued to be reported during this period as a string of leaders in Portugal moved to firmly solidify the nation under the protection of St. Michael and the Blessed Virgin Mary.

Throughout the country, hundreds of churches were built and dedicated to the Virgin Mary or St. Michael, massive triumphal arches were erected, statues and images adorned the greatest buildings and at every funeral a banner of St. Michael was carried before the coffin to demonstrate his protection of souls. New monastaries, abbeys, and orders arose as Portugal, inside and out, firmly proclaimed itself a nation consecrated to the faith.

In 1385, an army on the way to battle led by Nuno Alvares Pereira, later beatified by the Church, stopped in a church in a village named Ceica, in the country of Ourem. (This would be in the diocese of Leira-Fatima today). Nuno reportedly asked for the intercession of the Virgin Mary to bring his army victory. The following day the army passed through what is today the village of Fatima. There, the entire army experienced a miracle in which the soldiers claimed to hear angels singing and to witness St. Michael raising his sword in a sign of victory. Nuno himself is then said to have rode through what became known as the Cova da Iria (the future meadow where the Virgin would appear in 1917). There, he was reportedly divinely told the ground he knelt on was holy and that one day God would bring victory over evil on this very spot and an era of peace would be granted to the world. (This miracle occurred on August 13th, 1385).

Nuno achieved his victory the next day, opening the way,

even historians concur, for the great evangelization and exploration of the new world that would come from Portugal because of this significant event.

After this, more supernatural events are noted to have been reported in Portugal. Some fact, some legend, and many in the same diocese as the village of Fatima. Amongst the accounts were more reports of Marian apparitions which in retrospect perhaps signaled that the world was at a historical confluence. While not realized at the time, the medieval era was over and a new period, a renaissance age of esoteric ideas, laid simmering beneath the surface, about to boil over in a volcanic eruption of unparralled social and cultural change. And for our purposes, a great battle between the spirits of light and the spirits of darkness had now begun.

Indeed, by the 14th century, historians say the world experienced a radical metamorphosis. Civilization shifted away from the era of agriculture to a new era of human intellect—an era that was propelled forward by ideas and repelled even more by matters of faith.

This new period derived its roots from the same driving force civilization had always been driven by—the hunger for freedom. But now a different concept of freedom was at play, something beyond matters of foreign rule, but one that explored freedom of the individual and his potential. The word "Renaissance" was applied in retrospect to this new age by a French nationalist and historian named Jules Michelet around the year 1840. He embraced this term to describe the full range of opportunities that became available between the 15th and 18th centuries as a result of the phenomena of new ideas, innovations, and discoveries that had emerged during this period. The Renaissance of the late Middle Ages, argued Michelet, was a recovery of antiquity. But this term was not true to its intended meaning.

The word Renaissance actually implies a rebirth of the intellectual and artistic achievements of ancient Greece and Rome. This period had produced great administrators, philosophers, engineers, and lawyers. From the Parthenon to the Pantheon, the remnant architecture of these early societies are visible reminders of the extent to which individual freedom permits ideas to surface in all aspects of life.

However, the Renaissance was more than that. With the enlightenment came a realm of abstract thought devoid of the guiding principles associated with truth—something the Greeks and Romans attempted to recognize in most of their endeavors. The changes that occurred in Middle-Age Europe, however, were not viewed in association with the need for truth. Rather, they were exalted as an endless string of human successes that actually began and coincided with a philosophical movement that called for a redefining of truth based exclusively on man's objective experiences. This collateral movement, in turn, produced an effect on the world that exists to this day—the need by intellectuals to purge the world of its religious ties in order to attempt to perfect mankind through a continued unfolding of the new man—the renaissance man of idea, discovery, and accomplishment.

By the late Middle Ages, it became apparent to these philosophers that the new man needed an entirely new order to live by in a world that now included another hemisphere and was rapidly expanding in population. They believed society would have to be redesigned through a new system of government that eliminated ancient customs, especially religions, and installed, ironically, new limitations on liberties through the exercising of an ever-expanding range of laws. It was also recognized that men were going to be resistive to oppression by force, so consequently these changes needed to be gradually indoctrinated in accordance with the rationalistic approach of the new order.

Of course, regardless of how subtle, this new order still encountered resistance. The Church of Rome posed the greatest challenge, and there were plenty of other institutions that embodied faith in one form or another. But the seed of independent thinking had been planted. And if independent thinking caused changes in politics, science, art and learning, then why not religion? Couldn't, the world, by intellectual endeavor, find and agree upon one religion? Indeed, through such a compromising strategy, perhaps the new world order could be achieved faster and easier. The Protestant Reformation provided the gulf needed to begin the separation with Rome, and with it the slow dissolution of Church and state. Gradually, change was being implemented. Rationalists began to see that time and patience would build a new civilization—a civilization without a revealed God and especially without the God-Man, Jesus

Christ. For Christianity was considered the most serious threat to the new man.

The Reformation and Renaissance in northern Europe produced tremendous changes in an incredibly short period of time. A new era of commerce and travel began. And with the printing press, there were immediate changes in every area of life, especially nationalism and religion. Great armies arose along with great wars, as gun powder and new weapons produced violent confrontations. Advances in medicine and an increase in the birth rate saw world population increase at a dramatic pace. Throughout all of this, aggressive attempts to politically control the changes in Europe, and in its colonies, were gradually instituted. The elimination of the monarchies became the ultimate goal as the need for centralized government was seen as necessary for efficiency.

This history in itself is extensive. But it can be traced and found to reveal how intellectual organizations and secret societies began to gradually take over the local governments of nations, village by village, town by town. Combining repression with newer and greater methods of propaganda and control, Europe of the late 15th and early 16th centuries underwent a gradual political metamorphosis at this level. And while the monarchies and the Papal States were still in power, their "old" way of thinking was no longer popularly supported. Indeed, a revolution was inevitable. For the tentacles of humanism were deep and now spread far throughout the civilized world. Likewise, by the late 18th century, not only were anti-Semitism and anti-Catholicism evident throughout Europe, but much worse. Many people were becoming anti-religion, and almost anti-God. The conditions were right for a genuine, political revolution. And in France that's exactly what unfolded.

But approximately ten years or so before the storming of the Bastille in Paris on July 14, 1789, a counter-revolution began and was clearly revealing itself. Across Europe, humble, hidden voices forewarned of violence and chaos in the streets. There were also a growing number of reports of miracles and visions, including reports of apparitions of angels, saints, and the Blessed Virgin Mary. But unlike the scattered reports of visions and miracles that were heard in the 12th century down through the decades before the revolution. This was decidedly different. Together the reports of these supernatural events spanned the continent of Europe and into Asia and even the

7

Americas, adding to an atmosphere of tension and intrigue. Moreover there was a sense of something strange in the air, such a sense that if man was about to institute a new order in the world that didn't include God, then these extraordinary reports appeared to indicate that God Himself had heard the news and wasn't about to depart that easily.

CHAPTER TWO

THE FIRST WAVE

"Be warned, O Jerusalem"

— Jer 6:18

Historians have divided reports of the miraculous events of the last 225 years into waves and according to Professor Blackbourn, "The first great wave of visions in modern Europe occurred in the aftermath of the French Revolution." This wave produced visionaries and prophecies that can still be found in circulation today. However, it is important to note that some of the visionaries emerged about a decade before the revolution.

In Germany, a Westphalian woman named Anna Katherine Emmerich (d.1824) reported visions and revelations from the Virgin Mary beginning in the early 1780's. Emmerich was but a child when her experiences began, but her visions of an upcoming crisis in France were found to be uncannily accurate. Around the same time, a French woman from Brittany named Jeanne Le Royer (d. 1798), who took the religious name Sister Nativite, began to report visions that foretold France's woes spreading throughout Europe. A Poor Clare of Fougeres, Le Royer prophesied the coming of a great war and that judgement would come "by the year 2000." Another prophet of the times, Jacques Cazotte, predicted in 1788 that the death of the King of France was about to occur. The French Revolution saw this prophecy fulfilled. Two more pre-revolutionary prophets, Mille Le Normand and a farmer named Thomas Martin also had popular standing. Martin, a peasant known as the Prophet of Gallardon, based his prophecies on reported visits from the Archangel Raphael.

9

Of course, the French Revolution fulfilled many of these prophecies. On August 21, 1789, the National Assembly adopted a new document known as the *Declaration of the Rights of Man.* While acclaimed as a new charter on liberty, it wasn't really tolerant of religion. A second law called *The Civil Constitution of the Clergy* was passed in the 1790's which stated that priests and bishops were to be elected by the people—including non-Catholics—and paid by the state. Not long after, the state seized property of the Church, established a centralized government, checked the King's power, and enacted an entirely new National Assembly based on 83 new provinces. Persecution of the clergy and the Church produced extraordinary hardship and bloodshed in France. Democracy and nationalism are considered the result of the French Revolution, concepts on the surface that appear laudatory. But actually the revolution led to militarism and the founding seeds of socialism and communism. Moreover, the prophecies of revolution, persecution, and bloodshed were rather quickly fulfilled in the eyes of believers.

By the early 1790's, more and more prophecies emerged as visionaries and mystics began warning of even greater upheaval. The prophets were becoming, as one writer noted, "unabashedly apocalyptical." One visionary, Sister Marianne of the Ursulines foresaw the rise and fall of Napoleon and his brief return from Elba. Within France, a series of alleged miracles followed the French Revolution. Around the same time, weeping and moving statues, as well as Marian apparitions, were reported in Italy. In Rome in 1796, as many as 26 different pictures across the city were observed to have exhibited extraordinary characteristics. Witnesses swore under oath at a Church Commission of Inquiry that the "Winking Madonnas," so labeled by Protestant critics, truly displayed unexplainable actions. In that same year, the eyes on a painting of the Virgin Mary filled with tears on June 25th in Ancona, Markes, Italy. This was interpreted as Mary's sadness over the difficulties being inflicted upon the Catholic Church by Napoleon. Indeed, this was a reasonable assumption, for after persecuting Pope Pius VI, Napoleon's troops overtook Rome in 1797. The Pope died in exile in 1799 as the leaders of the French Revolution proclaimed that "the Papacy is abolished." But while massacres of nobles and clergyman brought great confusion to Europe, a new conclave was held in

Venice under the protection of schismatic Russia. Pope Pius VII was elected in March 1800, and his first gesture was to crown an image of Mary, proclaiming her Queen and Mother of the Church. Fourteen years later, Pius VII solemnly crowned the miraculous picture of Ancona on May 13, 1814.

More prophecies and phenomena were reportedly noted in the Papal States during the Napoleonic campaigns of the late 1790s, and a parallel "wave" was also seen in Germany at the time. How much of it was authentic no one knows. But after this, such reports became consistent and commonplace news items.

From this late 18th century period it is noted that only Anne-Catherine Emmerich gained lasting prominence. A sister of the Order of Augustine, Emmerich's pamphlets told of her miraculous visions and personal experiences including the stigmata. The pamphlets circulated throughout Europe and were popular in France. In 1818, a German romantic named Clemens Brentano began daily conversations with Emmerich concerning her visions, especially her accounts of the lives of Christ and the Virgin Mary. Brentano then transcribed and published these revelations. These works helped to support and confirm Holy Scripture for the public. Anne Catherine Emmerich was probably the least controversial of all the mystics of this period. Her work greatly defended the fundamental beliefs of Catholicism while introducing perhaps the first significant and trustworthy revelations surrounding something much bigger—the approaching of "the end times."

While this kind of talk had been heard by almost every generation before, never before had there been such a visible and credible spokesperson. The stigmatist, Emmerich, who reportedly lived only on water and the Eucharist for a dozen years, was a most compelling witness to such a radical prophecy. She was reportedly told in mystical visions that her gift of seeing the past, present, and future was greater than that possessed by anyone else in history. And there is one other extraordinary aspect to Emmerich's revelations. Besides receiving the most extensive private revelations of all time, Emmerich's work not only detailed the coming of the end times, but also specifically connected the events of the Old with the New Testaments. She was given to understand how from Adam and Eve through Noah, Abraham, Moses, the Prophets, and the Kings of Israel, all was related to Christ, and how in the end, the events of the end times directed themselves back to the beginning in a perfect plan to restore the Kingdom of the Father. This is significant, for the Triumph of the Immaculate Heart as revealed at Fatima is now understood, by some, to be very much in harmony with Emmerich's vast revelations.

One other mystic stood out during this period. A woman named Elizabeth Canori-Mora, (d. 1825) who too bore the stigmata, began reporting visions of great tribulation and, like Emmerich, the coming of the end times. Mora's revelations confirmed and illuminated another interesting piece of the puzzle: that there was to come an increase in the power of evil. "Great legions of devils shall roam the earth," Mora said. "The instrument of Divine Justice, they shall attack everything. They shall injure individual persons and entire families."

The beginning of the 19th century continued the first wave and saw it expand in number and prophetic force. In 1803, a little girl received her first Holy Communion at a Mass in Grandchamp, France, and reported that she then saw Mary. A chapel was erected and pilgrims flocked to the village. In 1804, a man in Russia named Seraphim of Kursk reported apparitions of Mary and the Apostles Peter and John. In 1813, there were visions reported in Leipzig. In 1814, a shepherdess named Marie-Jeanne Grave said Mary appeared to her. This led to the cult of Our Lady of Redon-Espic in the Perigord. In 1815, a woman named Mother Marie Rafola of Saragozza, Spain, reported urgent visions and that recourse to the Sacred Heart would forestall Divine Wrath. In 1816, a woman named Maria Catalini reported a series of apparitions in Rome that became most noteworthy after an ecclesiastical commission authenticated the events within four months of their inception. In 1820, apparitions were reported in Lescouet - Gouarec in Brittany.

During the 1820's, the movement gained even greater prominence through the emergence of more extraordinary prophets and the occurrence of several extraordinary events. One of most noted visionaries was an Italian wife, mother and mystic, named Anna Marie Taigi (.d 1837). Taigi was so well renowned that it was upon her urging that a seemingly recovered Pope Pius VII received his last rites. Four days later he died. Taigi, like Emmerich and Canori, reported visions that scanned the face of the earth. She saw individuals and nations, their diseases and what would heal them. For forty-seven years she was believed by almost all to have been raised up by God to "cast down the pomps of the world," especially in their "revolt of the intellect." Taigi saw the future too, and indelibly sealed the news that God was going to send a chastisement, unlike any before, if mankind did not convert.

In 1821, an apparition of Mary was seen on Tinos, an Aegean island, shortly after the onset of the Greek War of Liberation from Turkish rule. At Tinos, a nun in a convent said Mary inspired her to speak to her bishop about searching through the ruins of an old church before building a new one. In the remains of the Byzantine church, an Icon of Mary was discovered and it became recognized as a miraculous image. In 1831, a sanctuary was established on the island and by 1835 many pilgrims traveled to the church. The island is known today as Holy Island.

In 1825, many claimed to see Mary in Uruguay. This led to the cult of Our Lady of Treinta Y Tres. One year later, another major event occurred which added significant momentum to the mystical times at hand. On December 26, 1826, an apparition of a cross in the sky over Migne, France (diocese of Portiers) was given much attention, and was later seen by historians to have significantly increased support for the prophetic movement. The apparition appeared at the conclusion of a sermon preached at a mission, causing a violent and emotional reaction from the crowd. Two thousand witnesses reportedly fell to their knees and begged for mercy. In a report to the bishop, a letter was signed by the missionaries, the Cure and 41 witnesses. Immediately after the apparition and before the episcopal commission was formed, stories began to circulate. The Parisian press debated the miracle, but still 25,000 pamphlets were soon sold. The commission's report was released in February of 1827 and in November a decree officially approving the apparition was made public. Five bishops issued statements in support of the miracle which became a national and international event. In his decree, the Bishop of Portier stated, "O Divine Providence: it is in France which the devil regards as his conquest, that the sign of human redemption has suddenly appeared. It is the cross that has conquered hell, redeemed the world and subdued the universe."

Anne Catherine Emmerich

Anne Catherine Emmerich is considered the most credible prophet of the 18th century. Her visions foresaw the past and the future unlike any mystic in history.

CHAPTER THREE

PRAY FOR THE WORLD

"Yes, I know how many are your crimes, how grevious your sins."
— Am 5:12

A second great wave of apparitions is noted to have occurred right before the political upheaval in France of the 1830's. In 1829, a man named Antonius Maria Claret of Sallent was healed by Mary. He was a missionary preacher and went on to be Archbishop of Cuba. In Paris, a nun named Catherine Laboure reported a series of apparitions of Mary in 1830. From these visions came the Medal of the Immaculate Conception, better known as the Miraculous Medal (so labeled because of numerous miraculous healings), which circulated in the millions within a few years.

The medal was not without controversy, for the words on its back side declared, "O' Mary, conceived without sin, pray for us who have recourse to thee." The Church would eventually dogmatically proclaim Mary's Immaculate Conception on December 8, 1854. No sacramental of the Church had such an impact as the Miraculous Medal did on the Catholic world since the Rosary was said to have routed the Albigensians in the 13th century. Catherine Laboure's apparitions were eventually approved by the Church and became for Church scholars a line of demarcation for the beginning of the Marian era. Laboure was declared a saint by the Church on July 27, 1947, and after 57 years of internment, her body was exhumed and found incorrupt.

During the same year (1830), a 12th century statue wept at the Cathedral of Notre Dame in Paris and a woman named Maria

Latastic of Mimbaste reported an apparition of the Two Hearts. There were apparitions reported around this time in Bordeaux, Grandchamps, and Brittany. In 1833, a mystic named Anna Mues of Bous-Septfontaines reported a vision of Jesus, Mary, angels, and saints. She said she was told to sacrifice for the reformation of the Dominican Order. In 1836, a priest named Father Charles du Friche des Gennettes reported Mary spoke to him at Our Lady of Victories Church in Paris. Following the heavenly advice, the priest soon consecrated the historic church to the Immaculate heart of Mary. This led to the miracle of Our Lady of Victories and the almost instantaneous conversion of hundreds, if not thousands, of local Parisans who returned or joined the church. It also then helped to perpetuate a worldwide movement of devotion to the Immaculate Heart of Mary.

In America around the same time, an Indian orphan named Paul said Mary appeared to him in his tepee in Montana. The boy reported that, "The woman's feet didn't touch the ground" and that Mary was "thankful for the new reservation being named after her." A few years later (1841), Mary reportedly came again to Montana. This time she appeared to a Jesuit priest named Fr. Pierre De Smet in the Bitterroot Valley and requested devotion to her Immaculate Heart, a recurring theme that began to emerge in the many reported apparitions.

But Europe remained the center of the reports. In 1840, a woman in Ars named Mrs Durie said the Virgin Mary appeared to her as did a woman named Justine Bisqueyburu in Blangy, France. The Blangy apparitions led to the Green Scapular devotion which is still practiced today. In 1842, in a very famous apparition, the Virgin Mary appeared in Rome to a French Jew, Alphonse Ratisbonne, who practiced no religion. Ratisbonne was a noted liberal intellectual and his extraordinary conversion after receiving a Miraculous Medal caused the Church to ratify the vision just four months later. In that same year, a nun named Sr. Marie Stanislaus in Tournai, Belgium, reported that she saw Mary in a classroom of the poor. In 1845, a sister named Apolline Andriveau of the Daughters of Charity said Mary appeared to her in the Chapel House at Troyes, France. This led to the Red Scapular devotion.

One year later, two more children at La Salette, France— Melanie Calvat and Maximin Giraud, said Mary came to them. At La

Salette, the Virgin reportedly wept for the first time (Mary's eyes had welled with tears at Rue du Bac.) And not long after, the Church approved the apparition. It was to become, another mystical line drawn in the sand. For after La Salette, there is a noted increase in the apocalyptical theme of private revelations. William Christian, Jr., an acclaimed author, historian, and MacArthur Fellow, addressed the uniqueness and importance of La Salette's message and its significant effect. "The secrets Melanie divulged," wrote Christian, "addressed the division between Catholics and Rationalists."

On May 12, 1848, a man named Johann Stichlmayer reported that Mary appeared to him in a Bavarian pasture in the village of Obermauerbach. As at La Salette, the Madonna was sitting and weeping. Fifty six people eventually claimed to have seen Mary at Obermauerbach, where the Virgin foretold warfare and plague, saying she could no longer **"hold back the punishments of God."** By now Mary's apparitions, especially to children, were becoming more frequent. In the diocese of Valence during 1848-9, seven young children and farm servants reported apparitions of Mary. While in Dolina, Austria, Mary appeared around the same time to three more shepherd children.

During the 1840's, a young Carmelite nun in Tours, France, reported a series of revelations from Christ that were intended to establish a new worldwide devotion. Sr. Mary of St. Peter was told to spread devotion to Jesus' Holy Face. The devotion had a specific purpose, the nun said. It was to make reparation for the blasphemies of "revolutionary" men. It was also to be a divine tool given by God to "defeat communism." Curiously, the year Sr. Mary died (1848) saw the publishing of the *Communist Manifesto* of Karl Marx and Frederick Engels.

In the early 1850's, apparitions were reported in Rmini, Fossombrone, Alsace, Lugo, Sant'Arcangelo, Saint-Agate, and Montbarrocio. In Rome in 1850, the wife of a Protestant officer from France claimed that Mary appeared to her three times at the Vatican. She then converted to Catholicism. In Lichen, Poland, that same year, Mary appeared to beseech people to pray. One man at Lichen, Thomas Klossowski, said that Mary told him to call all people to pray the Rosary and to meditate on the life and death of Jesus Christ. The Church approved the visions at Lichen, where again some very powerful warnings were issued. In Riva, Italy, a young boy named

Dominic Savio (1842-1857) reported visions, ecstasies, prophecies, and the ability to read souls. He was a student of John Bosco of Turin, and reportedly even advised Pope Pius IX. Around the same time, again at Rmini, another miracle of great repute occurred when the eyes of a painting of Mary were seen to repeatedly open and close. This continued for several months, which permitted an independent investigation committee of four to unanimously agree on the phenomenon. There were also many other miracles claimed at Rimini.

In 1853, a shepherdess named Veronica Nucci claimed to see the weeping Virgin at Ceretto, Italy, and in 1855 a man named Simon Stock said Mary appeared to him in Bordeaux. That same year, a statue wept in Taggia, Italy. This miracle was approved three months later by the Archbishop. In Orero, Italy, in June of 1856, Mary appeared twice to a 20 year-old girl named Rosa Carbone. The Virgin reportedly mourned the sins of mankind and recommended to Rosa, as she would come to do at Medjugorje more than a century later, that the people pray seven Our Father's, Hail Mary's and Glory Be's daily to protect themselves. In Spoleto, Italy, that same year, an 18 year-old boy named Francesco Possenti said Mary spoke to him as a miraculous picture passed him by. He later became a priest. While in 1858, a woman in Israel named Mirjam Banardy said Mary appeared to her and healed her. Mirjam said that Mary warned her of Satan's "guile," a subtle hint of what many visionaries were intimating concerning a coming escalation in the power of evil, the roots of which were first discernable in Emmerich and Canori-Mora's revelations.

During this time there were reported visions in the Vosges and Valence and a cluster of reported miraculous events in Italy that were similar to the events reported there in the 1790's. But it was in the village of Lourdes, France, in 1858, where a fourteen year-old girl named Bernadette Soubirous reported eighteen (18) apparitions of the Virgin Mary, that the entire world would begin to take notice of Marian apparitions. Mary told Bernadette she was the **"Immaculate Conception,"** a declaration that set off a controversy. Four years later, the Church approved the visions, as millions from all over the world flocked to the shrine. As with Catherine Laboure, the Church would come to declare on December 8th, 1933, that little Bernadette Soubirous was indeed a saint. Likewise, when Bernadette's body was exhumed on September 23, 1909, thirty years after her death, it was found to be incorrupt.

In the same year as the apparitions at Lourdes (1858), Mary appeared near Green Bay, Wisconsin, to a Belgian woman named Adele Brisse, saying, **"I am the Queen of the Heavens. Offer your Communion for the conversion of sinners. If they do not convert, My Son will be obliged to punish them."** Like some of the other prevailing themes emerging in the revelations, the call for reparation was starting to be prominent. Three years later, Mary appeared again in America to a woman in St. Louis named Mary Wilson. Mary had been experiencing persecution because of her conversion to Catholicism.

The increase in mystical phenomena in America was certainly not without logical cause as the United States approached a crossroad in its history. The abolition of slavery was to come with a price, as 600,000 died in the Civil War. Indeed, even Abraham Lincoln reported that every time a momentous event occurred he appeared to be forewarned by a dream. His wife Mary felt that one dream, received right before their departure for Washington in 1861, meant he would not live to see the end of a second term.

Another extraordinary, but perhaps little known, statement by a prominent public figure during the American Civil War needs to be addressed for its extraordinary prophetic merit. Commenting on the rapid escalation in the science of warfare throughout the Civil War, a statesman named Henry Adams remarked, "I firmly believe that before many centuries more, science will be the master of man. The engines he will have invented will be beyond his strength to control. Someday science shall have the existence of mankind in its power and the human race could commit suicide by blowing up the world." As we shall later see, it is this very concern that Mary begins to address in her late 19th and 20th century revelations.

During the 1860's a Belgian girl named Louise Lateau reported visions and mystical experiences. After the stigmata appeared, over 100 doctors and two hundred theologians studied her. Lateau became known as the most famous stigmatist of the generation. There were also apparitions reported in 1860 at Francoules, France, and around the same time a statue moved in the Umbrian parish of Spoleto. On a farm in Loreto, Italy, in 1862, numerous witnesses attested to a weeping print of Mary on the feast of Corpus Christi. One year later there were apparitions reported in Vicovro, Italy, and at Anglet in France. At Anglet, Mary showed a man named Ludwig Cestac how the devil devastates the world and how God sends angels to protect people from evil spirits.

At Ilaca, Croatia, a farmer discovered a well in 1866 on his property. Healings occurred and in the following year, approximately 50 people reported apparitions of Mary. Soon after, a church was erected. Around the same time, Mary appeared to Theresa Steindel, a service maid in Kirchdorf, Australia, and to a 32 year-old prisoner in Tsuwanocho, Japan. Theresa reported messages that were eerily prophetic.

Most noted is the fact that with the outbreak of the first two waves of apparitions, there developed an understanding that the Virgin Mary was issuing warnings, warnings that became sterner and more sterner as time went by, sometimes surrounded by secrets that visionaries could not divulge.

Anna Katherine Emmerich said she was shown how a secret sect would seek to undermine the Church of Peter and how wars, bloodshed, and the "malice of Lucifer" would come against the world. Emmerich also said that rationalism would lead to liberalism and liberalism to (what became known as) Marxism. Sr. Jeanne le Royer said armies would "fill the earth with carnage," while Marie Taigi reported shocking visions of a "world empire of evil." Taigi saw Masonic conventions, Europe in shambles, cities on fire, thousands of soldiers dying, popes in prison, and a coming schism in the Church. Her famous prophecy of a coming world-wide chastisement is still often quoted and considered by some to be unfulfilled:

> God will send two punishments. One will be
> in the form of wars, revolutions, and other evils. It
> shall originate on earth. The other will be sent from
> Heaven. There will come over the whole earth an
> intense darkness lasting three days and three nights.

At Rue du Bac, Catherine Laboure reported that Mary had told her **"misfortunes will fall upon France"** and **"the entire world will be overcome by evils of all kinds."** Indeed, such harsh warnings were increasingly noted by the onset of the 2nd wave. At

Troyes, Sr. Apolline said Mary told her, **"The world is drawing ruin upon itself."** While at Obermauerbach, in 1848, the Virgin reportedly said, **"I can no longer hold back the punishments of God."**

In 1850 at Lichen, Poland, the approved messages were of the grimmest nature, as Mary foretold a bloody and worldwide conflict. Millions would die, the Virgin said at Lichen, in epidemics and bloodshed. However, there would come out of Poland, Mary foretold, **"the hope for all tormented mankind."** In Australia, Theresa Steindel's revelations during the 1860's continued this theme as she said Mary told her that if mankind did not convert **"a great affliction"** would emerge. The Virgin reportedly told Theresa that **"there will be terrible disease. Radiation will come from above and cover buildings with flames."** There would also come, Mary said, a **"sad darkness."** This revelation is carefully noted because subatomic science was still a half century away. Like Mary would do at Fatima in 1917 through her warnings and signs related to the coming of the atomic age in 1945, here was a disclosure linked far in advance of events that would later drastically change the world.

One almost completely unknown visionary is seen to have especially stood out during this period of the first two waves of miracles. This was because of the many prophecies of his that were fulfilled. Father Albert Sauvageau, who died in 1826, was the pastor of Montmouson in the diocese of Nantes in the west of France. He had been tortured in the French Revolution and was considered a very holy priest. Father Sauvageau prophesied that France would be invaded in the second half of the 19th century (Germany invaded France in 1870). Sauvageau further prophesied that France would be invaded twice in the first half of the nineteenth century. (Germany invaded France in August, 1914, during World War I and in May, 1940, in World War II). The holy priest reportedly saw that by the late 20th century there would be serious disorders in the family and society, religion would be lax, immorality would be scandalous and there would be a great increase in crime and violence. People, he said, would become addicted to materialism and creature comforts. His grave to this day is still visited by the faithful.

But perhaps Mary's message to Bernadette Soubirous at Lourdes in 1858 said it all. **"Pray for the world so troubled,"** Mary told the young girl. Indeed, if change did not come, Mary's messages prophesied woe to sinners and skeptics, believers and the indifferent. But one thing was clear, by the middle of the 19th century it was becoming a universal message.

CHAPTER FOUR

THE APPROACHING STORM

"Thus says the Lord of Hosts: 'Lo! Calamity stalks from nation to nation. A great storm is unleashed from the ends of the earth."
—Jer 25:32

Despite the gloomy forecasts, harsher prophecies were still to come. At La Salette, a secret message of extraordinary apocalyptical overtone, given only to the Pope on July 18, 1851, became known around 1860. Handwritten copies of the text had been circulated in religious communities and among the clergy for years but not to the public. Soon after this, many more apocalyptic revelations were being sounded. Critics viewed the warnings as copy-cat prophecies. By the 1870's in France, this was true in some cases. But quite often, unexplainable events would redeem beleaguered visionaries, such as the visions that occurred in the Bohemian village of Philippsdorf (now in the Czech Republic) on January 12-13,1866, at Pellovoisen, France on Feb. 19, 1876 and in St. Louis, Missouri on August 25, 1871.

At Philippsdorf, a 30 year-old unmarried weaver's daughter named Magdalena Kade developed a strong following. Magdalena had suffered a series of illnesses and persecutions which left her on her death bed. But when she reported that Mary promised to heal her and then did, thousands of pilgrims poured into the village. Magdalena's message was then taken seriously by priests and lay Catholics, even those of prestige and influence. A similar scenario occurred at Pellovoisen, France, in 1876, where a woman named Estelle Faquette reported apparitions of Mary and then a stunning healing. Estelle was thirty-two years old at the time and dying from consumption and an abdominal tumor. Doctors refused to see Estelle anymore since she was terminal and even her grave was purchased. Then the Virgin visited her 15 times, and she was healed. Estelle was given a special devotion to spread and lived until 1929. The apparitions were later approved by the bishop. In St. Louis, Mary appeared to a woman named Theresa Shaffer on her deathbed. Like at Philippsdorf and Pellovoisen, Theresa was healed and eventually entered a convent.

These apparitions and many more were part of another or "third" great wave of apparitions that especially shadowed the political upheaval in France and Germany of the late 1860's and early 1870's. It was an upheaval that led to a new map of Europe. But this "third wave" was fueled by additional factors: the railroad and the telegraph. These advances caused news of miracles to spread further more quickly, which, in turn, added to the global impact of such events. Indeed, records reveal an impressive list of well-documented and attended events that occurred during this period.

On December 8, 1870, a luminous cross was seen in the moon at Calvados and a vision of a serpent appeared over Lorraine with its tail facing Metz and its head toward Paris. More Marian phenomena was reported in Lorraine in the same year, where the eyes of a statue of Mary reportedly opened three times at a home for un-wed mothers. In 1871, a moving statue was reported in Soriano and again in Rome the same year. There were also numerous French and German apparitions around the time of the Franco-Prussian War, in villages named Kruth, Wittelsheim, Rohrbach, Leng, Blangy and several other Alsatian towns. At Wittelsheim, France, many people reportedly saw the Virgin in a church where a series of apparitions occurred that lasted for years.

In 1872 at Neubois, Alsace, four girls said they saw Mary in a forest. Just prior to the reported apparitions, the girls had agreed that they would refuse to convert to Protestantism, which was a fear associated with Prussian annexation of the province. At Vallensanges, France the Virgin appeared to a thirteen year-old girl named Jeanne Bernhard in a clover field. As at La Salette and Obermauerbach, Mary again came weeping over the sins of mankind and the "coming judgement." Around the same time in Lyons, the Virgin asked for a medal to be struck in honor of "the Forsaken

Mother."

At Valle di Pompeii, Italy, in 1872 a lawyer named Bartolo Longo heard the words, **"If you want to be saved, do something for the promotion or spread of the Rosary."** Longo had a church built and numerous miracles followed. His work and memory are still a part of Catholic popular devotion today.

In April of 1873, a series of Marian apparitions accompanied a miracle in the village of Buising, Germany, where Mary appeared to a thirteen year-old girl. After Buising, apparitions were reported in at least six other German villages, causing German officials to call in the army to disperse the many pilgrims. In Saargemund, and then Biding, a 25 year-old woman named Katherine Filljing reported that Mary appeared to her. Dressed in a blue dress and a white mantel, Mary's messages again reportedly called for the Rosary. In that same year, a woman in her mid-forties named Marie Bergadieu claimed a series of Marian apparitions. She became dubbed the "Ecstatic woman of Le Fontet" and her prophecies are still found in contemporary books that list more noted 19th century prophecies.

There were many more apparitions reported in 1873. In Dittrichswald, Poland, four visionaries claimed a series of 160 apparitions of Mary. Again Mary requested the Rosary, as Dittrichswald became a popular pilgrimage place. That same year, Mary appeared in Walbach, France, as "Our Lady of Rain." At Walbach, there were healings reported as Mary left "comforting words and prophetic visions."

In April of 1873, there were apparitions reported in the Lorraine village of Guisingen and a month later in the Palatine village of Medelsheim. At Medelsheim several children between the ages of 8 and 12 said they saw and spoke to Mary. In that same year, Mary reportedly appeared in Paris to an eleven year-old boy named Alfred Fontes.

In Rixheim, France, in 1873, Mary appeared in a cemetery to two girls returning from a pilgrimage. The Virgin was sitting on a tree stump and invited the girls to sit with her and discuss the coming times. To add credibility, heaven apparently added more miracles. The father of one of the children and the mother of the other were incurably ill. Mary promised to cure them both and did. This then attracted many pilgrims to Rixheim. Again in 1873, Mary reportedly appeared to August Arnauld in a vineyard at St. Bauzille de la Sylute,

France. The Virgin told August she wanted a statue, a cross, and a procession—which she got. On May 15, 1873, 25 children reported seeing Mary through a schoolhouse window in Samois, France. A second apparition occurred in the schoolyard as Mary appeared this time with the Baby Jesus in her arms. In England, a woman named Teresa Higginson reported visions, the stigmata, and messages from Christ beginning in 1874. That same year, Mary reportedly appeared to Jean Pierred La Boterff in Brittany.

On December 11, 1875, a woman named Josephine Reverdy reported that Mary appeared to her and healed her. Mary appeared to Josephine as the Sorrowful Mother and Queen of the Martyrs. After being healed, Josephine then reported mystical sufferings on Saturdays to atone for the sins of the world. At Villareggia-Turin, a 24 year-old named Rosina Ferro said that Mary appeared to her also as the Sorrowful Mother. The apparition occurred along a roadside and Rosina said Mary was surrounded by angels. Rosina later received the stigmata and suffered daily at 3 p.m. On Friday's, she would suffer the passion of Jesus Christ.

In Italy, there were a series of approved apparitions reported at Pompeii in July of 1876 and at the sanctuary of Santa Maria della Croce near Cremon. Around the same time, a Palestinian Carmelite nun named Marie of Jesus Crucified, who died in 1878, reported mystical experiences. Marie said she was told about "three days of darkness" and the perishing of "three-fourths of the human race."

In the Prussian village of Marpingen in 1876, three eight year-old and two six year-old girls were picking berries when they beheld a beautiful woman in white. Although never approved, Marpingen became known as the "German Lourdes" and developed a cult which lasted well into the 20th Century. There was numerous phenomena at Marpingen where Mary reportedly again declared, **"I am the Immaculate Conception."** That same year, a man named Thomas Fred Price, who later became co-founder of the Mary Knoll Missionaries, survived a ship wreck off the coast of Baltimore. Afterwards, Price insisted Mary had guided him to a ship plank and saved his life.

In late July, 1876, a group of children on an estate in Posen, Germany, reported an apparition of Mary along the road between Czekanow and Lewkow. Their claims were then supported by adults who also saw the vision. In 1877, another Bavarian village named

Mettenbuch reported apparitions. At Mettenbuch, a farm servant named Mathilda Sack and four peasant children claimed the Virgin Mary appeared to them. As at Marpingen, the authorities were hostile to the events. But again, a strong cult developed as numerous healings were reported. That same year, more apparitions were reported near Koblenz. The first apparition happened at Gappenach Mill near Polch, in the district of Mazen. Soon after, apparitions were reported in Germany at Mulheim, Gronig, Michelsberg, Muchweis, and Berschweiler. However, the visions at Gappenach and Berschweiler were later proved fraudulent.

But the most famous apparitions of this decade were at Pontmain, France, in 1871, and Knock, Ireland, in 1879. Both of these apparitions were approved as "worthy of the faith" by the Church. At Pontmain, four children described a beautiful lady in the sky who said the village would be saved from the invading Prussian army. Within eleven days the Prussians withdrew from France and an armistice was signed. At Knock, at least twenty-two people witnessed a vision of the Virgin Mary, St. Joseph, and St. John the Evangelist beside the village church on August 21, 1879. Soon, thousands flocked to the sight from all over Ireland. Curiously, theologians later concluded that the book St. John held in his hand at Knock during the apparition was most likely *The Apocalypse.*

These apparitions showed Mary's concern for her children in, what was now, very turbulent and difficult times. She was a mother, theologians said, who was coming in time of need, time of war, and starvation. Through prayer, she could be counted on to help.

At Pontmain, the Church recognized that a terrible war came to an abrupt end through the Virgin's intercession. Forty-two stars were seen at Mary's feet that night in Pontmain, and forty-two years of peace followed bringing France to 1914 and the First World War.

The apparition of the Virgin Mary in Pontmain, France.

Forty-two stars appeared below Mary's feet at Pontmain on January 17, 1871. France then experienced forty-two years of peace, causing some to believe the forty-two stars represented the forty-two years of peace.

CHAPTER FIVE

FORESHADOWING FATIMA

"There is an appointed time for everything and a time for every affair under the heavens."

— Eccl 3:1

During the 1880's, reports of Marian apparitions continued to mount and Mary's messages appear to have begun to prepare the way for her powerful revelations to come at Fatima in 1917 . In 1880, Mary reportedly appeared to an Anglican monk in Lanthony, South Whales, and in Blaine, France, a stigmatist named Marie-Juli Jahenny began to attract considerable attention throughout the continent. Jahenny's detailed visions of fire falling from the sky and holocaust scenarios are still cited today. Because of her credibility as a suffering victim, her Book of Revelation- type prophecies were well noted and stood out at the time. In Rouigo, Italy, in 1883, a seventeen year-old seamstress named Maria Inglese said Mary appeared to her in her room. In what may be considered a direct link to her later requests at Fatima, Maria said the Virgin requested **"atonement Communion on the first Saturday's of the month."**

A year later, the Virgin reportedly appeared as the Queen of the Rosary on March 3, 1884, to Fortuna Agrelli. Mary told Fortuna she would heal her grief if she prayed a "Rosary Novena." The girl was indeed healed on May 8th of that year. During the same month and year (March 1884), Mary appeared in the French Alps to Marie-Louise Nerbollier at Lyon and at Diemoz, France. The Virgin again recommended the Rosary and reportedly confirmed to Marie that she had appeared at La Salette. Marie Nerbollier received the stigmata and in 1939 her body was discovered to be incorrupt. Another apparition was reported in 1884 at Montligeon where again the Madonna came as the Sorrowful Mother, this time requesting prayers for the poor souls in Purgatory.

This entire period witnessed many foreshadowing elements of Fatima. Repeatedly, Mary was seen as the Sorrowful Mother, one of the ways she appeared in the sky to the visionaries at Fatima on October 13, 1917. There were also many requests to pray the Rosary and for acts of reparation, key elements of Fatima's message. It is especially noted how during this period Pope Leo XIII elevated the Rosary to the forefront of the Church and the family. He penned 12 Apostolic letters on the Rosary and transformed it from a mere popular prayer to what it is today—the spiritual weapon so many Church leaders and Mary herself say will eventually bring the collapse of evil. During the last apparition at Fatima, Mary announced she was the **"Lady of the Rosary."**

In 1886, two girls at St. Pierre-Eynac France, Francoise Prade, and Marie Grousson, reported 19 apparitions of Mary from July through November, 1886. The girls said the Virgin often wore a black veil and that they saw a cross overturned in the background of the vision, a reminder of her prophecies at Rue du Bac to St. Catherine Laboure. At Castelpetroso, Italy, on March 22, 1888, two country women looking for sheep reported seeing the Virgin Mary again as the Sorrowful Mother. Although doubts grew, so did the number of witnesses. Eventually, over a thousand people said they saw Mary and many healings were reported. Finally, on September 26, 1888, the bishop himself said that he saw the Virgin Mary three times. Pope John Paul II went on pilgrimage to Castelpetroso on March 19, 1995.

At Vallensanges France, Mary appeared 20 times in a clover field to a 13 year-old girl named Jean Bernhard. The apparition occurred from July 19 through September 29, 1888. The Virgin reportedly wept for "the sins of mankind and the coming justice." Several miracles confirmed the apparitions as Jean said Mary appeared in a "blinding white robe." Around the same time, the Virgin Mary appeared independently to three French Canadians in 1888 at the Church of Cap de la Madeleine in Quebec on the St. Lawrence River. A shrine commemorating the visions is still there today, and like Castelpetroso, was visited by Pope John Paul II.

During the early 1890s, the tidal wave of miracles continued. There were apparitions and a bleeding statue reported at Campocavallo, which the Church acknowledged, and at Sigy, France on August 5, 1890, where the Virgin reportedly appeared to two children named Alfred and Marie Cailleaux. Similar to Fatima, Mary was reported to come in a luminous cloud, with a long veil held by angels. The angels were silent but the children reported hearing a wonderful song being sung. In 1894, another 12 year-old girl reported that Mary appeared to her in Szezk-Bita, Poland. The girl's name was Julian Pezda and to this day a church sits on the site. Salesian priests from Auschwitz take care of the shrine. Around the same time at Luca, Italy, a young and beautiful girl named Gemma Calgani became the recipient of apparitions, visions, and the stigmata. Gemma was later declared a saint by the Catholic Church and is greatly admired because of the fact that despite her beauty she chose God over the world. In Flanders, a statue wept in 1893-94 and a Benedictine priest there named Father Paul of Moll reported apparitions of Jesus, Mary, and the poor souls. His story is still widely circulated today. During this period, a nun named Sister Louise Margaret Claret de la Touche began receiving revelations of Christ's Infinite Love in a convent at Romans in the south of France. To this day, her revelations are also circulated among the faithful.

From 1896 through 1899, in the French village of Tilly-Sur-Suelles in the Calvados, a 14 year-old shepherdess named Louise Poliniere and group of children reported apparitions of the Virgin Mary. At Tilly-sur-Suelles, the Virgin appeared to the children as they gazed out of their classroom windows across a field some twelve hundred yards away. In the distance, the youngsters said they could see an oval of a brilliant light containing the figure of Our Lady of the Miraculous Medal. The apparitions were also seen by dozens of nuns who taught at the school. Once more, Mary invited her onlookers to pray the Rosary and to do penance. Powerful visions of a coming judgement were reportedly given at Tilly-Sur-Suelles and signs in the heavens and a solar miracle were witnessed by many. There were also demonic influences.

In 1898, apparitions were reported at Aschaffenberg, near Frankfort in Germany. The visionary, Barbara Weigand reportedly received visions of Jesus, Mary, and many saints. The revelations called for frequent reception of the Eucharist and revealed that "hard times" were coming. In May of that same year, the Virgin reportedly told Barbara what was shaping up in the world and what could be expected as the 20th century dawned on the horizon. **"It is quite a bad time,"** Mary told Barbara. **"Mankind stands trembling in fully anxious expectation before the days of the future."** At Loretteville, Canada, that same year, a deathly ill girl reported a vision. She was then instantly healed. While at Campitello, Corsica, in 1899, two children, Cellesia Passi (14) and Perpetua Lorenzi (13) said that Mary appeared to them dressed in white with a blue veil. Later appearances were seen by many children and adults. At Corsica, the Virgin reportedly warned the people to pray **"so that you do not go to Hell."**

Ironically, perhaps the most supernatural event of the 19th century was really not very supernatural at all at the time. In Alencon, France, a girl named Marie Francoise Thérese Martin was born on January 2, 1873. She was raised in a home of comfort and surrounded by refinements which should have spoiled her, but through suffering and a supreme confidence in God, Thérese Martin rapidly progressed toward sanctity. At fifteen she entered a Carmelite convent at Lisieux, France, where before she died she penned her spiritual classic *Story of a Soul*. The little book quickly revealed her formula for sanctity, permitting all who read it to understand that the call to sainthood was readily available through all walks of life, even the most humblest and hidden. Thérese Martin died at the age of 24 on September 30, 1897, and was canonized by Pope Pius XI on May 17, 1925. "The Little Flower" revealed only one supernatural experience in her life, unlike the many visionaries in this narrative, but the fact that 100 years after her death over 2,000 churches throughout the world have adopted her name indicates that she was and remains perhaps the greatest supernatural force of the age.

Most significantly, by the early 1880's an almost universal apocalyptical theme had emerged from the apparitions, transcending most of the warnings associated with the local political upheavals and European clashes of the late 18th and the early half of the 19th centuries. More and more, the reported apparitions spoke of a danger that was approaching the whole world. Like the Secret of La Salette, which appeared to be in harmony with the more dire prophecies held in Scripture, revelation after revelation disclosed that a titanic, decisive struggle between good and evil would emerge. But the Secret of La Salette was literally terrifying. Great tribulations were announced to be coming, as its contents disclosed that Hell would now to be opened, and that wars, nature, and apostasy would come to shake the world:

God will strike in an unprecedented way. Woe to inhabitants of the earth! God will exhaust His wrath upon them, and no one will be able to escape so many afflictions together... . God will allow the old serpent to cause divisions among those who reign in every society and in every family... .Justice will be trampled underfoot and only homicides, hate, jealousy, lies, and dissension will be seen without love for country or family.... Physical and moral agonies will be suffered. God will abandon mankind to itself... .Churches will be locked up or desecrated... .A great number of priests and members of religious order will break away from the true religion... .There will be bloody wars and famines, plagues and infectious diseases... .Lucifer, together with a large number of demons, will be unloosed from hell... They will put an end to faith little by little... nature is asking for vengeance... .The earth will be struck by calamities of all kinds... .The seasons will be altered... .A general war will follow which will be appalling. For a time, God will cease to remember France and Italy because the Gospel of Jesus Christ has been forgotten. All the civil governments will have one and the same plan, which will be to abolish and do away with every religious principle, to make way for materialism, atheism, occultism, and vice of all kinds.

Many similar prophecies of a great spiritual war emerging are discernable from the records of the reported revelations during this period. Mirjam Banardy of Israel stated in 1858 that Mary had told her of "increased demonic activity" and how "Satan was growing in power." In Italy, in the early 1850's, a priest from Turin named Don Bosco reported powerful dreams that even the Pope recognized as having importance. Bosco's dreams seemed to read the future of Italy, France, Rome and Paris. Some of them, such as *the Two Columns*, were believed to be incredibly prophetic of the "end times."

In Ars, France, a saintly little priest named John Vianney, known as the Cure of Ars, reported a demonic infestation of verifiable proportion. Thousands were flocking to Ars during the 1850's to be confessed by the little priest and the dark side revealed its rage. "The devil has a very ugly voice," said Vianney. But he added that "one gets used to everything." The Cure's fellow priests insinuated to him that it was a figment of his imagination. "It's in your head that plays you tricks," one of them remarked. But just one night in Ars always brought swift retractions. As the priests would rush into his room terrified, they would often find the good Cure resting peacefully. With a smile he would remark, "I am sorry, I forgot to warn you beforehand. However, it is a good sign: there will be big fish tomorrow."

In 1866, a nun in the Congregation of the Daughters of Mary in Anglet claimed that Mary showed her a vision of demons let loose on the earth wreaking devastation. While largely unnoticed, the Bishop of Bayonne supported her revelations and ordered printed a half-million copies of a prayer she said Mary gave her to combat the evil spirits. Was this a forerunner to Pope Leo XIII's prayer to St. Michael the Archangel, which reportedly originated from a vision the Holy Father experienced on October 13, 1884?

Leo XIII's mystical experience reportedly included his overhearing of a conversation between God and Satan that disclosed the unleashing of Hell and a coming era in which God's people would be put to the test. Likewise, at Pellovoison, France, where the Bishop approved the apparitions, the devil again figured prominently. Estelle Faguette's messages revealed dire warnings of evil **"conquering"** the world. Soon would come, Mary told Estelle, **"a time of trials."** The same kind of apocalyptic message was heard at Medelsheim in 1873, where the children said the Virgin warned of a great **"bloodbath."**

The Church would especially come to feel the brunt of evil's invigorated campaign, the seers said. Indeed, another curious prophecy of the time emerges to bear witness to the truth of what the visionaries were saying. "In my time the devil is outside the Church," said John Henry Cardinal Newman (d. 1890). In about one hundred years, the devil will be inside." (Mary's Church-approved message at Akita, Japan, in 1973 fulfilled Cardinal Newman's prophecy: **"The devil will infiltrate even into the Church in such a way that one will see cardinals opposing cardinals, bishops against bishops. The priests who venerate me will be scorned and opposed by their conferees... churches and altars will be sacked, and the Church will be full of those who accept compromises. The demon will press many priests and consecrated souls to leave the service of the Lord."**)

Blackbourn noted in his study, upon review of an 1883 apparition at Hartervald, Germany, involving an adolescent visionary named Elisa Recktenwald, that "there is an apocalyptic tone here that exceeds anything to be found in 1876-77." (Elisa Recktenwald reported apparitions in which Mary bemoaned the "suffering and unrepentant" world. Mary reportedly said to Elisa, **"Have I not appeared already to so many of my children? Yet so few have believed."** The local bishop moved to discipline the child as well as the parents.)

Kselman recorded a similar observation concerning the rise in prophecy in his book *Miracles and Prophecies in Nineteeth Century France:*

> The popularity of prophecy in the early years of the Third Republic is evident in the increased attention given to it in the press and by the Church, and in the number of prophetic works published. The production of prophetic books and pamphlets increased more than fivefold in the decade 1870-1879 as compared to the previous ten years. Msgr. Dupanloup, in a decree of 1874, critical of the literature, related the popular interest in prophecy to the same political crisis referred to by Remond [a renowned 19th century social historian]: *Everywhere*

*there is talk only of miracles and prophecies, and to
our generation one can say what Our Lord said to
His: "This generation looks for a sign, Generatio ista
signum quaerit." (Mark 8:12)*

But not all the prophets emerging during this period were
delivering revelations of woe. Some were predicting the dawn of a
new era of peace and love for the world. One voice during this time
specifically noted such a coming time. Luisa Picarreta (1865-1947),
who became known as the Little daughter of the Divine Will, was a
stigmatist from Corato, Italy, and was confined to her bed for 64
years. A mystic of the highest order, her revelations comprised many
volumes and declared a new era of grace was coming. It would
begin, she said, after the earth was purged at the turn of the
millennium. Most of all, this new era of Divine Will would see,
Picarreta wrote, the coming of the Kingdom of the Father.

As noted, the total number of reported apparitions in the 19th
century ran into the hundreds. More were reported in France and
Italy, but there were reports from around the world. Little can be
learned about most of them because writers have concentrated on the
Church-approved ones, which, in turn, resulted in inferior
documentation on the unapproved ones. However, unless one
dismisses it all, there is plenty of evidence to conclude that something
unique occurred during the 19th century that had never occurred
before and which continues to this day.

A tidal wave of miracles and prophecies deluged the world,
warning of an exponentially growing danger that would cause great
suffering, bloodshed, and death for the human race. No one can say
how many of these reports were actually true. (There were reportedly
as many as 65 false visionairies at Lourdes after the onset of the
apparitions in 1858.) But considering their visible merit and the
hostile political times at hand, one should not be surprised if many of
these cases are not reopened in the future after the age of rationalism
has evaporated. Indeed, many of the apparitions deserve a just
verdict that is void of the political pressures and intimidation that
existed almost everywhere throughout the 19th century.

However, the greatest signs of authenticity for many of the
prophets and prophecies were the events that unfolded over the
century. Whether a devout atheist or a devout believer, who can deny

that by the end of the 19th century, the fulfillment of many of the revelations was discernable to a great degree. William A. Christian, Jr., noted that by the end of the 19th century even the Vatican realized the many apparitions could not be ignored. And although few were approved, a change in policy was to its advantage. Christian explains this shift in Vatican policy:

> Toward the end of the nineteenth century, however, when Catholicism was on the defensive, the Vatican came to realize that the Church should play to its strength. In southern Europe that strength lay in localized religion. By "crowning" Marian shrine images, the papacy associated them with the universal Church. Rome also endorsed a new series of proclamations of Marian images as patrons of dioceses or provinces. *And it regarded with increasing sympathy visions of Mary that led to the establishment of new shrines.* For by the nineteenth century virtually every adult in the Western world knew that there were profoundly different ways to organize society and imagine what happened after death. The industrialization of Europe in the eighteenth century had separated large numbers of rural folk from local authority and belief and many migrants to cities had found alternatives to established religion in deism, spiritism, science, or the idea of progress.
>
> The continued strength of Catholicism in nineteenth-century France was an incentive for intellectuals to challenge the idea of the supernatural radically and intensively. As a result, French Catholics needed all the divine help they could get. Throughout the century they sought and received innumerable signs that God and, in particular, the Virgin Mary were with them. An efficient railway system and press ensured that regional devotions could reach national audiences. *Secularization was a global problem, and the Vatican developed a global response to centralize and standardize devotion.*

France and Italy served as laboratories for devotional vaccines against moral diseases. Religious orders distributed these vaccines. Indeed, Our Lady of Lourdes became a new kind of general devotion, one with its origin in the laity. Replicas of the image entered parish churches worldwide.

Statistical documentation of the many millions who died during the wars and political upheavals of the 19th century would certainly be the most impressive confimation of the great turmoil prophesied and then fulfilled during this period. History clearly reveals the fall of the monarchies and the Papal States and the rise of modern socialism, which would lead to atheistic communism. The roots of so many other philosophical and political movements of this period that today hold great influence are also clearly discernable and, therefore, easily correlative to the prophecies of the 19th century. These range from the occult to communism, from materialism to sensualism, feminism to radical atheism. The 19th century saw the beginnings of so many modern day evils that many books are readily available for anyone seeking to research it all. But perhaps the greatest and most tangible evidence of the mounting danger the apparitions warned of is the evolution of weapons and warfare during this period. Moreover, the progress mankind made in its ability to wage war from the French Revolution to the early 20th century is stunning.

Indeed, the age of modern warfare had arrived and the changes were sweeping. Field guns undid fortresses. Artillery capability changed land and sea battles. Improved roads and canals made armies more mobile and the innovation of conscription, which requisitioned men by law, brought into existence armies that were reminiscent of the hordes of barbarians in the ancient world. By the mid-19th century some governments were mobilizing the youth of both sexes which brought whole nations in step with the military. Large battles were waged. In 1813 at Leipzeg, 539,000 fought. At Solferino in 1859, 300,000 men fought in a battle that ranged over sixty square miles. Before 1861, the U.S. army was 16,000. By the end of the Civil War the South had called up 90% of its men (approximately 1,400,000) and the North 45% (2,900,000).

The technological innovations of warfare were continuous

during the 19th century. Rifle accuracy went from 100 yards to 1,000 yards. Bullets became cylindrical in shape and revolvers and pistols were now mass produced. By the 1860's, some companies were making 1,000 rifles a week. Soon, rapid fire guns were developed and by 1900 machine guns could massacre infantrymen. In South Africa, machine guns were used for the first time that fired 2,000 rounds in three minutes.

Artillery had its own critical development. Large shells could now rip apart wooden ships causing the development of armored ships, wagons, and trains. Inventions such as land and sea-mines, torpedoes, and stream-driven battle ships further added to the science of killing.

The technological and organizational preparations for modern warfare seemed to be preparing the world for what some politicians feared to be approaching—a great war. This would be one that industry and government together could advance beyond anything ever before seen. One in which a nation could come to believe—because of its industrial-military capabilities—that it could wage to grab "world power," and maybe even more, "world control." But if not careful, as the American Civil War statesman Henry Adams observed, the rapid advance in military capability was also previewing a more dire possibility—the danger of "world destruction." And it was this idea that seemed to dominate the message Mary would continue to bring in her 20th century apparitions, especially in her plea at Fatima.

Pope Leo XIII

Pope Leo XIII penned 12 Apostolic Letters on the Rosary. He report-edly overheard a conversation between God and Satan that revealed a coming century (20th) of spiritual warfare unlike any before.

CHAPTER SIX

FLIRTING WITH ANNIHILATION

*"I set before you life and death, the Blessing and the curse, choose
life, then, that you and your descendants may live."*
— Dt 30:19

The early 20th century brought no reprieve from reports of the supernatural. Again, as in the 19th century, there were waves of apparitions before and during political upheavals. Likewise, growing numbers of visionaries reported that the Virgin Mary was warning of "mounting evil" and an approaching "storm."

In 1900, Mary was seen by several people in Luca, Italy and by crowds in Tung Lu and Peking, China. That same year, two women in Tanganika, Africa said Mary appeared to them. In 1901, a 4 year- old girl from Eppelborn reported an apparition of the Virgin Mary and a woman named Elizabeth Catez (better known as Elizabeth of the Trinity) entered the Carnel of Dijon, France, where she would reveal profound mystical writings on the Holy Trinity. In 1902, a woman in Esphesus named Helen said Mary appeared to her at Panama Kapulu, the house reportedly where Mary and St. John the Evangelist lived. In 1904, a teen age boy in Zdunska-Wola, Poland, said he received an apparition. In 1905, a eucharistic miracle occurred on the French island of Réunion in the Indian Ocean. Several thousand people witnessed the face of Christ on a host. The miracle attracted world-wide attention. On April 20, 1906, dozens reported seeing a weeping Madonna at a boarding school in Quito, Ecuador. In 1907, in the village of Porlow, County Waterford,

Ireland, a child known as Little Nelly of God attracted a stir. Nelly was said to experience ecstasies, utter prophetic statements and to be able to survive on just Holy Communion.

In France and Belgium, many new reports of miracles were made. At Angers, a nun named Sister Gertrude Marie reported visions in 1907 of a coming triumph of the Church and a great number of "saints to be." In Chambery, a sister of the Order of the Visitation named Mary Martha Chambon (d.1907) claimed that Jesus appeared to her and asked for a devotion to His Holy wounds. Christ also asked that sufferings be offered, she noted, for the "sins of the world." In Bordeaux, beginning in 1909, a woman named Marie Mesmin reported apparitions of Mary and messages that concerned the need for more prayer and a looming chastisement for "the world's sins." While in 1910 at Brussels, Belgium, a woman named Berthe Petit began having visions and apparitions. Berthe received the stigmata and prophesied two years in advance that the heir to the Austro-Hungarian empire would be killed. She also prophesied WWI and WWII. A year later, Brussels was the site of another apparition. Around the same time, detailed prophecies of "world wars" were given by a French priest at Le Pailley named Father Lamy.

At Foggio, Italy, another stigmatist, Francesco Forgione, known later to the world as Padre Pio, emerged at this time. Like other mystics, Padre Pio saw a world headed for ruin. He also reportedly foretold the rise of Pope John Paul II to the papacy. Over 100,000 people attended Padre Pio's funeral on September 23, 1968. It was a fitting tribute to a saintly man and mystic who reported so many unique qualities, such as bilocation, celestial perfume, reading souls, remarkable conversions, and prophetic insight. He remains to this day the most famous mystic of the 20th century. After World War I, around 1920, Padre Pio foretold that the League of Nations wouldn't survive and that a second world war would come. "I predicted that the League of Nations wouldn't last," he reminded a friend. "These nations are going to tear each other to pieces." By the time of World War II, his statements on the course of events were well known for their accuracy. Padre Pio saw that Germany's June 22, 1941, invasion of Russia would be rebuked ("Can a fly swallow an elephant?") and that Italy and its ally, Germany would be destroyed. "You can tell Mussolini," said Pio after messengers from the Italian dictator came to see him in 1943, "that nothing can save

Italy now! "

Not long before World War I, Mary appeared to a crowd of approximately 500 in Alzonne, France. Again, she warned of war. During this same period, there were a series of apparitions reported in Germany and Austria. In the Ukraine, Mary appeared at Hrushiv in 1914 to 22 people. The prophecies were dark as Mary foretold decades of suffering to come for the Ukrainian people. (Under Joseph Stalin, an estimated 10 million Ukrainians were murdered or deliberately starved to death. Millions more perished during World War II and after.)

During World War I there were more reports of apparitions. One of the most intriguing was at LaMaine, France. At LaMaine, Mary appeared to German troops from September 5 to 12, 1914. Because of the visions the Germans reportedly stopped their attack. Afterwards, soldiers were ordered under penalty of death to never repeat what they had seen. Of course World War I did nothing to deter belief in all the mystics, visionaries, and prophecies. Such a violent war had never before occurred and by its end an estimated 12 million lay dead, thereby fulfilling in the minds of many the numerous 19th century prophecies of the coming of "great wars and much bloodshed." There were other apparitions reported during World War I. In 1917, Mary was reportedly seen in Paris, Moscow, and Barral, Portugal. A year later, three children in Mazillac, France, claimed they saw the Virgin. But of course the most famous were the apparitions at Fatima.

Without question, the apparitions at Fatima in 1917 solidified heaven's more than century-long conversation with the world. Mary told three shepherd children the 20th century was moving rapidly forward toward an unpleasant date with its destiny, and that mankind was flirting with **"annihilation."** But if people changed, she added, it would hasten an **"era of peace."** Mary also promised to return to ask for the consecration of Russia and the Communion of Reparation on the first Saturdays. The Church was rather favorable from the beginning, as Pope Benedict XV wrote to the bishops of Portugal one year after the apparitions saying that he considered them "an extra ordinary favor from God." Fatima was a great call to conversion and was, perhaps more than any apparition in Church history, characterized by a series of prophecies that were fulfilled. At Fatima, Mary foretold the following:

1)   the October 13, 1917, great sign (the miracle of the spinning and falling sun) witnessed by an estimated 70,000 people

2)   the rise of an evil (communism) out of Russia

3)   a great sign on a night that lights up the sky

(This occurred on January 25- 26, 1938, when a bright light over the northern hemisphere illuminated the night and was witnessed by millions. Scientists said it was an aurora borealis but according to the lone surviving visionary of Fatima [Lucia dos Santos], it was the promised sign that would occur before the outbreak of the second world war which began a little more than a month later when Hitler took over Austria. Eight months later Germany invaded Czechoslovakia. Some note that this date is also the day on the Church calender that commemorates the conversion of St. Paul. Paul, as Scripture details, was confronted suddenly by a great light in the sky that flashed down upon him.)

5)   persecution of the faithful and especially the Holy Father

6)   the end of World War I

7)   a second great war

8)   Russia will scatter her errors throughout the world, provoking wars. (The Korean and Vietnam wars were Russian agitated as were the wars in several African nations, Afghanistan, El Salvador and Nicaragua. Numerous internal civil conflicts throughout the world can also be

linked to Russia.

9)   God was going to punish the world by means of further wars, hunger and persecution

10)   various nations will be annihilated

11)   Portugal would always keep the faith. (By this statement, some Fatima scholars have suggested that other parts of the world would not keep the faith and, therefore, a great apostasy was being prophesied to come.)

12)   The conversion of Russia. (Mary said at Fatima on July 13th, 1917, **"In the end...Russia will be converted..."**. The fall of communism in 1991 in Russia, which restored freedom of religion, is seen by some as being the fulfillment of this prophecy. Some Fatima experts refer to these events as the "Third Great Sign" that was prophesied at Fatima and then fulfilled.

13)   an era of peace

A few lesser known prophecies of Fatima can also be confirmed as having been fulfilled. Mary said the second world war would break out under the reign of Pius XI, which it did, and that Jacinta Marto and Francisco Marto, the two youngest Fatima visionaries, were soon going to heaven. Both died within several years of the apparitions. (Francisco died in Fatima on April 4, 1919 while Jacinta passed away in a Lisbon hospital on February 20, 1920.) The prophecies of Fatima took decades to fulfill and were not really known until the early 1940's. At that time, portions of the memoirs (five separate works, the last of which was published in Portuguese in March, 1990) of Sister Mary Lucia dos Santos, the surviving Fatima visionary and a nun of the Sisters of St. Dorothy, began to be released. But it is in what occurred one month after the apparitions at Fatima ended that the profound importance of Fatima is revealed and understood.

On July 13th, 1917, Mary spoke of the need for the conversion and consecration of Russia. The Bolshevik Revolution was still 6 months away when the three shepherd children at Fatima thought the Virgin's words concerning Russia that day were in reference to a person, not a nation. But time would quickly reveal the extraordinary reality of Mary's words to the three shepherd children. In November 1917, just one month after the October 13th apparition and "Miracle of the Sun" at Fatima, the Bolshevik communist Party seized power through a revolution in Russia. Led by Nikolai Lenin, the party replaced the ruling Romanoff family and set out to organize a world revolution based upon the communist Manifesto of Marx and Engels of 1848. This philosophy advocated seizure of power by the proletariat and the establishment of a transitional socialist state, with state control of labor, industry, distribution, and credit. Co-operation was not voluntary but mandatory and all classes of people had to be assimilated.

The philosophical concepts of modern communism actually stem from Sir Thomas More's 1516 work *Utopia* and 18th century French philosophers Rousseau, Robespierre, and Saint-Just. The conspiracy of Francois Baleuf in 1796 was intended to establish this system during the French Revolution but fell short. The Russian revolution was, however, financially sprung by the same secret societies that had fostered the French Revolution and that had been condemned by so many popes. Pope Leo XIII foresaw this evil approaching when he warned in his 1884 encyclical *Humanum Genus* that a danger brewed that intended to undermine the existing order of the world, and that the secret societies were behind it.

"Tear away the mask of Freemasonry," Leo wrote, "and make it plain to all what it is. It aims at the utter overthrow of the whole religious order of the world which Christian teaching has produced and the substitution of a new state of things—based on the principles of pure naturalism. Including almost every nation in its grasp, it unites itself with other sects of which it is the real inspiration and the hidden motive-power."

Marxist-Leninism embraced this same purpose, but to an even greater extent. It declared war on three fundamental institutions: the family, religion, and on the ownership of private property. Massive brutality, torture, and death came with the Bolshevick revolution in Russia, and in a short period of time it became evident that the

46

driving force behind communism was a profound, spiritual, literally demonic hatred for God and religion. (Historians note that Marx, Lenin, Trotsky, Engels, Stalin and Mao were spiritualists. Several were Satanists. Stalin, Marx, and Engels were Illuminati [secret society] recruits.) Tens of thousands of churches were closed and millions were imprisoned or murdered for their beliefs.

Over the decades, it also became apparent that Russia, because of its atheistic, militaristic principles, was becoming the threat it was foretold to be at Fatima: **"she (Russia) will spread her errors throughout the world provoking wars and persecution of the Church."** By the 1950's, the Soviet Union, which included Russia, was aggressively pursuing its world-wide communist agenda. And because of its weapons of mass destruction, Fatima's unfulfilled prophecy of the annihilation of nations now lingered over the world, suspended day to day for decades in what became a tug of war between the forces of good and evil, both visible and invisible.

Likewise, fire raining from the heavens was believed to have been symbolically represented in the great Fatima signs of both 1917 and 1938. Mary's last image in the sky at Fatima on October 13th, as Our Lady of Mt. Carmel, did nothing to diminish this understanding. This is because Mary's title of Our Lady of Mt. Carmel is related to the prophet Elias, who lived on Mt. Carmel and reportedly foresaw Mary in a vision centuries before her life on earth, and is most known for the miracle in which he called down fire from the sky, a fire that not only consumed the sacrifice but also the water in the trench around it. The vision of Our Lady of Mt. Carmel occurred at Fatima on October 13th just as the sun appeared to be falling from the sky. Then, as with Elias, immediately after the miracle the ground was dry as were the people's clothes. The Feast of Our Lady of Mt. Carmel is July 16th and it was that day, the following year, that proved to be the last full day of life for the last Tsar of Russia, Nicholas II and his family. The Romanoffs were executed by the communists on July 17th, 1918. (On July 17, 1998, the 80th anniversary date of their murder, the Romanoff family was buried in an official ceremony in St. Petersburg. The Vatican's Moscow-based ambassador to Russia, Archbishop Bukovsky attended the Orthodox burial service.) Twenty-seven years later, on July 16, 1945, fire did somewhat rain down from the heavens as the first atomic explosion was detonated at the Trinity site in New Mexico.

*The site where the angel
appeared to the children at Fatima.*

CHAPTER SEVEN

THE DESTINY OF NATIONS

"Son of Man, when a land sins against me by breaking faith, I stretch out my hand against it's staff of bread, I let famine loose upon it and cut from it both man and beast"

— Ez 14:13

Regardless of what occurred at Fatima and in Russia in 1917, by 1919 some theologians already had a clear understanding of what was developing on the global horizon. While the nuclear element remained hidden from the equation, as did the gravity of the Bolshevik revolution, it was clear liberalism was not molding the world into the image of God. Rationalism was becoming institutionalized, especially in government and education, and it was only a matter of time before generations were indoctrinated in humanism from their earliest childhood. Pope Pius IX's *Syllabus of Errors* in 1864 had sought to confront the emerging crisis of worldwide liberalism, but, unfortunately, his message was ignored and instead the enemies of the Church explicated the document as evidence of the Church's inflexible attitude toward modernism.

But, by 1919, the reality of the Pope's foresight was plain to all, as was the reality of so many "hard to believe" prophecies. Without question, World War I saw to this in a most undeniable way. "A great war" had truly been fought and the science and strategy of warfare had evolved to such a point (tanks, poison gas, etc.), that with the advent of the airplane and arial bombing, massive civilian slaughter was now part of warfare and even considered ethical because of a rival nations wartime industrial base. By the end of the World War I, most of the nations involved had armies of 5 million or more and weaponry that could "annihilate" whole nations.

Indeed, an imagination was not needed to see what was coming. And one visionary even reported where the danger would soon arise. Berthe Petit, the Belgium stigmatist, said that Jesus told her in July, 1919, that Germany, thought to be defeated, would rise again:

> **It will soon become apparent how unstable is a peace set up without Me, and without the intervention of him who speaks in My name (the Pope). The nation which is thought to be conquered, but whose strength is only temporarily diminished, remains a threat to your nation and to France. Trouble and danger will spread to all countries. It is because this peace is none of Mine that wars will blaze up again everywhere—intense wars, racial wars. What should have been so great, so true, so beautiful so durable, is delayed....Humanity is rushing toward a dreadful storm, which will divide the nations more and more.**

The Lord's words to Berthe Petit echoed Mary's words at Fatima almost to the letter:

> **All human plans will be annihilated; the pride of the lords of the moment will be broken. It will be clearly shown that nothing can subsist without Me, and that I remain sole Master of the destiny of nations.**

Berthe Petit's 1919 prophecies, though given decades before the second world war, were in retrospect revealing the supernatural chess game between heaven and hell that continued right after the first world war. In Italy, Benito Mussolini formed the first cell of his Fascist Party in 1919, and by 1922 his black-shirted bully boys had so intimated the government that he was able to seize power and become dictator. The German Nazi Party was also formed in 1919. It began that year as the minuscule German Workers Party and swiftly came under the control of the rabble-rousing orator, Adolf Hitler.

After World War I, Mary appeared at Limpias, Spain, near Santander in 1919. Here, a corpus of Christ on a crucifix wept tears and tears of blood as did several replicas. So many miracles were reported at Limpias that pilgrims from all over the world came to see, many of them Church hierarchy. From 1919 to 1926, over a quarter of a million pilgrims journeyed to Limpias. In 1920, residents in another Spanish village named Navarra reported that they too saw their crucifix move. These visions lasted more than a year, but were gradually suppressed by the Church.

Untolled and increasing numbers of Marian apparitions, especially in Europe, continued to be reported throughout the 1920's. In 1920, apparitions were reported at Templemore in County Tipperary, Ireland, and to an Ursuline nun named Sister Mangano in Catane, Italy. In 1921, a woman named Anna Marie Goebel reported apparitions and the stigmata in Beckendorf, Germany, as did Clare Moes in Luxembourg that same year. On February 25, 1922, a sister of the Society of Sacred Heart of Jesus named Josefa Menendez reported an apparition of Christ at the convent in Portiers, France. Jesus warned Josefa that many souls would go to Hell because of their sinful lives. The nun received the stigmata and also revealed extraordinary experiences involving her own visitations to Hell.

Another German mystic and stigmatist named Theresa Neumann of Konnersreuth also began to report shocking visions and detailed prophecies during this time. Hundreds of bishops and cardinals visited her and she retains the title "most visited mystic ever." Photographs of her bloody wounds are almost painful to look at as Neumann, like Padre Pio, developed an international following over the decades. In 1940, Neumann foretold, at the height of his power, the downfall of Hitler. The Gestapo did attempt to silence the mystic on one occasion but were literally horrified at what they saw when they arrived at her door. Adalbert Vogl, in his book *Theresa Neumann, Mystic and Stigmatist* relays this account:

The Gestapo did make one attempt to arrest

Theresa. It was decided to make this attempt during a Friday ecstasy. Two agents of the notorious police were detailed to make the arrest and they approached the Neumann home at noon. Therese, who was at the height of her suffering, suddenly sprang from her bed, walked down the stairs, and flung the house door open to confront her would-be captors just as they reached for the doorbell. Her pitiable figure, covered with blood, with the evidence of her ordeal vivid in every feature, so awed these harsh men that they turned and hurried away as fast as they could walk.

Around the same time, another stigmatist named Marthe Robin of Chateauneuf, France, began to attract considerable attention as did a woman in Mexico named Conchita. Robin would later see the threat of nuclear weapons for what they were in the simplest of terms. "This atom bomb—when one thinks that small nations will also have it and only two fools will be needed to ravage everything." Conchita was another victim soul and recorded 200 volumes of revelations.

In 1924, in the Portuguese town of Balasar, a young bedridden woman named Alexandrina de Costa not only bore the stigmata but lived on nothing but the Eucharist for the last 13 years of her life. Theologians say Alexandrina's message was the message of Fatima: do penance, sin no more, and pray the Rosary. In 1925, another religious reported a vision in Tuy, Spain, while a year later a child in Marlemont, France, claimed an apparition. In 1927, Mary appeared at Aichstetten, Germany, as Our Lady of La Salette and again reportedly near Grenoble, where she pleaded for penance. In Campina, Brazil, in 1929, a woman named Sister Amalia said that Our Lady appeared to her and asked for a chapel to be built. This became known as the "Chapel of Our Lady's Tears." While at Ferdrupt, France on March 2, 1928, two more children named Marcelle George, age 13, and Madeline Hingary, age 8, reported apparitions of the Virgin Mary.

At Tuy, Spain, on June 13th, 1929, one other apparition of this decade occurred worth noting. The lone surviving visionary of Fatima reported Mary appeared again to her, this time telling her, **"the moment has come when God asks the Holy Father, in union**

with the bishops of the world to make the consecration of Russia to My Heart, promising to save it by this means."

In the 1930's another wave struck. In Sillery, Quebec, a young girl named Dina Belanger reported visions, locutions and the stigmata as did a woman in Stenbergen, Holland, and a nun in Campinas, Brazil, named Sister Amalio of Jesus Scourged. That same year, on October 13, 1930, Bishop Jóse Correia de Silva granted official permission for the cult of Our Lady of Fatima. In Spain, in 1931, two children claimed to see the Virgin at Ezkioga in the Spanish Pyrenees. This led to a outpouring of apparitions throughout the northern part of Spain at places named Izurdiaga, Ormaiztegui, Zumarraga, Albiztur, Bacaicoa, and Iraneta. A negative decision was rendered at Izurdiaga and Ezkioga. Eventually there were hundreds of reported visionaries at Ezkioga, which attracted one million people to the apparitions in 1931 alone. According to William A. Christian in his book *Visionaries*, "Ezkioga attracted the most observers for any visions in the Catholic world until the teenagers of Medjugorje in the 1980's." These apparitions, noted Christian, were "the first large-scale apparitions of the old talking but invisible type in Spain since the sixteenth century."

In 1932, a woman named Mother Eugenia Elisabetta Ravasio, reported two apparitions, one in July and the second in August. But what made her account so unique was who she said appeared to her. It was not Mary or Jesus or an angel or a saint, but God the Father, she said. A Church commission took ten years to investigate and approved the visions as did the local ordinary, Bishop Alexander Caillot of Grenoble, France. The Eternal Father, said Eugenia, wanted a Feast day in the Church declared for Him, promising to save the world from a precipice and to consume it with His love and graces. But, He told her, it was urgent that this request be granted quickly—no later than the end of the century.

In Belgium, two apparitions in 1933, Beauraing and Banneaux, became very popular and were later approved by the Church in 1949. After this, a series of apparitions occurred in Flemish-speaking Walloon, Belgium. There were reports in Chaineux, Etikhove, Lokeen, Foy, Olsene, Herzele, Verviers, Melen, Onkerzele, Wilrijk, Wielsbeke, Berchem-Anvers Fory. Rotselaer and Tubise. The Church found against many of these reports. In France,

Mary was seen at Crollen by three children and in Metz. In Pradnik, Poland a nun named Sister Faustina Kowalska reported visions of Jesus and Mary that promised a period of *"Divine Mercy"* for the world. Her revelations would later become almost universally accepted and her diary is considered a spiritiual classic. One revelation especially revealed the seriousness of what was unfolding on the world stage.

> December 16, [1936] - I have offered this day for Russia. I have offered all my sufferings and prayers for that country. After Holy Communion, Jesus said to me, **I cannot suffer that country any longer. Do not tie My Hands My daughter. (209)** I understood that if it had not been for the prayers of souls that are pleasing to God, that whole nation would have already been reduced to nothingness. Oh, how I suffer for that nation which has banished God from its borders! (Diary 818)

The apparitions also now reflected the signs of the times, as warnings and prophecies about Hitler, the newly appointed German Chancellor in 1933, characterized many of the reported revelations. Fifteen (15) European locations cited apparitions in 1933 alone. In Germany, six apparitions were reported from 1933 to 1938 in the French Upper Rhine. In 1934, there were reported apparitions at Lucerne and Roggliswil, Switzerland, and again at Marpingen. Mary was seen in Rome in 1935 and at Valmontanal, Italy, that same year. Three more sites in Italy were reported in 1937, as were locations in France and Spain. In Ireland, an apparition of Mary was reported on January 11, 1939, at Kerrytown, County Donegal. While at Kerizenen, France, a woman named Jeanne Louise Ramonet claimed apparitions, visions, and prophecies that attracted attention for decades. Like at Fatima, the sun danced at Kerizenen. Ramonet revealed that the salvation of the world would come through the Hearts of Jesus and Mary. Once again, the key was said to be the Rosary.

By the late 1930's, war again exploded in Europe and a worldwide economic crisis had taken hold, causing great misery, starvation, and death. However, one victim soul, Sister Consolata

Betrone of Turin, Italy, revealed that Christ had told her that the crisis was an act of mercy, not justice:

> **"The distress which reigns in the world at the present is not the work of My Justice, but of My Mercy. For fewer sins are being committed because money is scarce, and many more prayers are being raised to heaven by people in financial straits. Do not think that the sorrowful conditions on earth do not move Me."**

Whatever importance these events had on local and national affairs is debatable. But the signs of the times clearly revealed that if God was trying to stop the dangers warned of in the prophecies from emerging into a world-wide conflagration, He hadn't succeeded. Bernard Billet's study reports only a dozen apparitions during WWII. But because of the very nature of war, it is safe to assume that conditions were not favorable for disclosures. However, some were very noteworthy, such as the apparitions in Girkalnis, Lithuania. In 1943, Mary reportedly appeared on three occasions to the townspeople of the little village of Girkalnis inside the Russian border. She was seen above the tabernacle of the local church with the Christ Child in her arms. According to records, everyone in the Church saw the apparition. She had come, Mary said, as the **"Mother of Mercy."**

By the end of World War II in 1945, the final pieces of the puzzle were in place. Atheistic communism was on the scene and spreading and a nuclear confrontation potentially loomed on the horizon. Indeed, the many apocalyptical prophecies had, almost overnight, become close to fulfillment with the dropping of the atomic bombs in Japan. Anything was now possible.

Sadly, for believers, more than a hundred and fifty years of divine warnings had done little to impede mankind's march toward, as General MacArthur noted at the end of World War II, the coming of Armageddon.

And although the world made peace in 1945, another wave of apparitions began to be reported at the end of the war, almost as if on cue that things truly were as bad as they seemed.

JESUS I TRUST IN YOU

The image of the Divine Mercy, based upon the revelations to Sr. Faustina in the 1930's. The Polish nun's diary is considered a spiritual classic for our times.

CHAPTER EIGHT

ARMAGEDDON?

"They went out to the Kings of the whole world to assemble them for the battle on the great day of God Almighty."

— Rv 16:41

A rmageddon.
It would be "Armageddon" if the world went to war again, predicted General Douglas MacArthur.

In Tokyo Bay, at 9:04 a.m. on Sept. 2, 1945, MacArthur finished his mission. World War II was over. Two atomic strokes finished it. But ironically, although over 50 million people had died, the world was an even more dangerous place. After the war, communism submerged Eastern Europe, and a few years later it surfaced in China. Around the same time (1949), the Soviets began to test nuclear weapons and with this capability the whole world was now facing the Red Menace. "Every nation," as one writer put it, "was now as vulnerable as an island."

All of this presented an extraordinary reality. Were these two ghastly horrors of the 20th century, communism and nuclear weaponry, now nestled together, destined to fulfill the more apocalyptical prophecies recorded in the Book of Revelation? Could the heavens rain fire as St. John and St. Peter foretold in Scripture and as so many visionaries had prophesied since the mid-19th century? Had theology and human history finally intersected in such a visible manifestation of fulfillable prophecy as to be undeniable? Perhaps, General MacArthur's words possessed a striking truth beyond their sensational value.

The post-war nations of the West quickly discovered they could not slip into complacency. The agreements reached at Potsdam and Yalta with the Soviets were flawed and held the potential for renewed hostilities. From Eastern Europe to South Korea, the world was a powder keg. Stalin realized the deck was stacked in his favor and he was not the kind of leader to discard opportunity. By 1946, the despot had wasted no time tightening his hold on Eastern Europe. To counter the situation, the United States hoped that financial aid could loosen the Soviet grip. But it produced no success. Only Western Europe accepted help under the Marshall Plan. Meanwhile, communist insurgencies in Greece and Turkey began to signal trouble as did the growth of strong communist parties in Italy and France. And while their numbers were small, their influence wasn't. President Truman, recognizing the threat, proclaimed in March 1947 what later became known as the "Truman Doctrine." The essence of the document was the "containment of communism through military and economic support." But with the Russian blockade of Berlin in the spring of 1948, which provoked a massive allied airlift of food and supplies into West Berlin for over a year, and with the fall of China to the communists in 1949, it became evident the world was again sliding toward serious trouble. The Cold War was at the door.

To make matters more interesting, immediately after WWII, dozens of apparitions of the Blessed Virgin Mary began to be reported in Europe. While attracting little attention in the secular press, these supernatural encounters brought another curious factor to the table. Almost in harmony, visionaries insisted the apparitional woman from Heaven brought urgent, almost unbelievable warnings to them. But unlike Mary's apparitions of the 19th and early 20th centuries, these revelations, the visionaries said, reflected a growing concern for the very survival of mankind.

The Virgin's words were loud and clear, the latter-day prophets repeated. People needed to change. Nations had to change. It was the only way the world could survive, the Virgin reportedly insisted to her messengers. Atheistic communism and the atomic awakening had conceived a new danger that threatened to truly lead to an Armageddon. "War" and "fire from the sky" were repeated over and over in the messages and nowhere was that danger said to be greater than in Europe. It was a potential battlefield between the superpowers of the East and West. Indeed, Europe had nowhere to go, it was caught in the middle of a nuclear vice.

Perhaps this is why so many apparitions in Europe continued to be reported immediately after World War II. According to theologian Bernard Billet's 1976 study, 232 separate apparitions were reported in 32 countries from 1928 to 1975, of which 114 occurred from 1945-1955. Most of them were in Europe. In fact, a total of 190 of the 232 apparitions in Billet's study were reported in Europe. It was a telling statistic.

From 1945 to 1960 there was a flood of reports from all over Europe. Beginning at Codosera, Spain, on May 27, 1945, just weeks after the surrender of Germany, a hundred people claimed to see Mary. This was the beginning of another and even greater wave of apparitions and prophecies. In Germany, Mary was seen in Tanhausen, Heede, Pfaffenhofen, Forstweiler, Pingsdorf, Rodalben, Niederhbach, Fehrbach, Munich, Dueren, Wurzburg, Heroldsbach, Remagen, and Marienfried. She reportedly appeared at Lublin. She was seen at Ardhee, County Tyrone in Ireland right after the war, at Belmuttet in 1950, and at Windy Gap in 1954.

Blackbourn noted eighteen apparitions in Europe in 1954 alone at places named Newcastle, England; St. Tropez, and Bodenneov, France and Tinos, Greece. There were reported apparitions in Amsterdam and in many little towns and villages in Italy such as Montichiari, Astuna, Marina de Pisa, Liceta, Ribera, Casa Cicchio, Rombia, Arluno, Cimigliano di Venarotta, Marta, Cisterna, and Balestrino.

Many of the reports were special. In Portugal, at a village named Vilar - Chao in 1946, a woman named Amelia de la Natividad Rodriques said she saw Our Lady of Fatima. Thirty thousand gathered as healings and solar wonders were reported. At Angri in Italy in 1954, a 31 year-old named Sultana Ricci claimed visions and a healing from paralysis. Likewise, as in the past, a number of the apparitions involved children: at Vorstenbosch in Holland in 1947, three children; at Grottamore, Italy in 1947, a child; at Ille Napoleon, France in 1947, three little boys; at Marina di Pisa, Italy in 1948, three children and many adults; at Tor-Pignattaira in 1948, a thirteen year old boy named Bruno Bolotte; at Maria Bolsena, Italy in 1948, four little girls and some adults; at Zischowicz, Czechoslovakia in 1948, two girls; at Ribera, Italy, two children; at Cossirano, Italy, in

1953, several children; and in Jerusalem in June of 1954, a child reported an apparition in a church. Country by country, the breakdown from 1945 to 1960 in Western Europe read like this: Holland, 2, France, 12, Italy, 55, Germany, 12, Spain, 3, England, 2, Portugal, 1, Luxembourg, 1, and Belgium, 2. But of course, there were apparitions all over the world, not just in Europe.

Behind the Iron Curtain, Mary was seen at Turzovka and Turomestice in Czechoslovakia, and at Ile Pasman, Yugoslavia, in 1946. She was seen at Mont-Saint Emeric, Hungary, in 1947. In Lublin, Poland, in 1949, a statue reportedly wept blood for 2 days while in that same year a large crowd gathered for a miracle at Hanos in Hungary. At Cluz, in Romania in September, 1955, revelations from "the Immaculate Heart of Mary" were reported. In 1957, Mary was seen in the town square in Cracovie, Poland. And in Warsaw in October, 1959, many people said they saw the Virgin on the roof of St. Augustine's Church.

Across the Atlantic, it was much of the same. In Brazil, there were apparitions reported in Uracaina, in 1947 and Tangua, in 1951. Mary was seen in Palmira and Bogata, Columbia, in 1949. In Canada, she was reported in Trois-Rivieres in 1947, in Montreal in 1949, and at Saint-Eugene de Gambry in 1950. In the United States, five apparitions were reported from 1945 through 1957. The most famous one at Necedah, Wisconsin, was eventually condemned.

Some of the events of this period became very well known. A weeping statue in Syracuse, Sicily in 1953, that was unanimously approved by an episcopal conference held in Sicily, and by the bishop in little over three months, attracted world-wide attention. After this, from 1953 to 1954, thirteen weeping pictures representing the same image of Mary as at Syracuse were reported. More attention was focused on a statue of the Sacred Heart of Jesus that wept blood in Trenzano in 1957 and one that wept tears over 100 times in Roca Corneta that same year.

Of all of these reports, Mary's most famous appearance was north of Rome at a place called Tre Fontane in 1947, where she appeared as the "Woman of Revelation" to a man named Bruno Cornacchoia, who planned to kill Pope Pius XII.

On April 12, 1947, Cornacchio, a former Catholic who had come under the influence of communists, took his children to a field north of Rome called Three Fountains. Bruno's plot to kill the pope was already planned and as his children played ball, he recorded notes for an anti-Catholic speech he would give the next day. But when his children lost their ball, he tried to help by following them into a cave. There, he suddenly discovered his youngest son Gianfranco (4) kneeling and whispering, as if in a trance, "Beautiful Lady! Beautiful lady!" Soon his daughter Isola (10) and oldest son Carlo (7) were also kneeling. Then, Cornacchio saw two hands touch his face and remove something from his eyes. A small light then grew brighter and brighter, lighting up the grotto, until Bruno saw her; the Madonna standing before him, materialized. The Virgin gave Bruno a secret for the Pope and warned him that his friends would tell him the vision was satanic. Church investigators confirmed the veracity of the experience and approved the apparition. Thirty-three years later to the day, April 12, 1980, a "miracle of the sun" was reported at Tre Fontane. There were 3,000 in attendance for the annual commemoration of the apparition. Then, on August 12, 1986, a second miracle of the sun was witnessed at Tre Fontane. *Il Tempo*, the largest newspaper in Rome, reported the story and how the miracle was captured on film and shown on Italian television.

However, despite the miracles at Tre Fontane and at so many other locales around the world, there was still plenty of room for skepticism and suspicion. Psychological and sociological explanations were again being offered for the "mass hysteria" of the times. It was noted how previous generations had also claimed to see "signs" of the end. Therefore, critics argued that this kind of talk was nothing new. Likewise, the fact that Israel had suddenly come into existence in 1948 was also something that few placed much significance, despite the prophetic implications of such a developement.

But for the majority who believed in God, the condition of the world by the mid-twentieth century was enough to at least command some concern. With or without the many signs, apparitions, and weeping statues, General MacArthur was not alone in his opinion of where the world was headed. And, the many reported "signs of the times" did nothing to soothe the gravity of the situation. "Will men understand," said Pope Pius XII in reference to the weeping Madonna of Syracuse, "the mysterious language of those tears?"

By now, Pius XII certainly understood the meaning of the tears and continuously tried to do something about them. On October 31, 1942, he suddenly consecrated the world to Mary's Immaculate Heart, with a veiled reference to Russia. However, he was not accompanied by the bishops as Mary had requested. By 1943, Sr. Lucia had already noted that the consecration was incomplete, although there would be benefits, she said. In 1944, the Pope led the way in imposing the Feast of the Immaculate Heart upon the universal Church, to be celebrated August 22nd. Two years later, on May 13th, 1946, Pius XII sent a legate *'a latere'* (Cardinal Masella) to Fatima to crown the statue of Our Lady of Fatima as "Queen of the World" in the Pope's own name. (The crown was a gift from the women of Portugal who contributed their wedding rings and jewelry for its construction. It weighed 44 pounds.)

Then on November 1, 1950, Pius XII declared the dogma of Mary's Assumption into heaven. It was the fourth Marian dogma and the second to be proclaimed in a little less than a century. In 1951, Puis XII broke a precedent by having the Holy Year conclude at Fatima rather than in Rome. In 1952, he formulated what some say was the only explicit consecration of Russia, but it was again not considered valid. Finally, in 1954, Pius issued an encyclical on the Queenship of Mary in which he referred to Mary's miraculous appearance at Fatima. On November 12th of the same year, he raised the Church of Our Lady of the Rosary at Fatima to the rank of a minor basilica. The work of this great Pope must have pleased God, for Pius XII revealed that on four occasions he personally experienced in Rome the miracle of the sun and other reported solar phenomena:

> At a certain moment, having lifted my eyes above the papers I had in my hand, I was stuck by a phenomenon I had never seen before. The sun, which was fairly high, looked like a pale, yellow opaque globe completely surrounded by a luminous halo, which nevertheless did not prevent me at all from staring attentively at the sun without the slightest discomfort. A very light cloud was before it.
>
> The opaque globe began moving outward, slowly turning over upon itself, and going from left to

right and vice versa. But within the globe, very strong movements could be seen in all clarity and without interruption. (The same phenomenon repeated itself on the following day, October 31, Pius XII wrote in a note to one of his cardinals. And there was one other fact worth noting: The statue of the Pilgrim Virgin of Fatima was in the Vatican at the time.)

Pius XII's entire reign can be viewed as one in which God was directly and visibly working through him to combat Russia, the evil of communism, and to spread the message of Fatima. Many odd coincidences also reflect this truth. At the hour of Mary's first appearance at Fatima (noon, 13 May 1917), Pope Pius XII was consecrated a bishop and at the same hour blood was shed in a Moscow church. In May 1946, when Stalin held his greatest May Day parade, with a million uniformed marchers, Pope Pius XII sent a Cardinal Legate to Fatima, and in the presence of a million pilgrims, crowned Our Lady of Fatima, "Queen of the World." Finally, Stalin was struck down on the anniversary of the election of Pope Pius XII, which was also the Pope's birthday. Indeed, Pius XII always referred to himself as the "Pope of Our Lady of Fatima."

By now, the surviving visionary of Fatima understood the seriousness of the Madonna's tears too. On May 22, 1958, Father Augustine Fuentes, a Mexican priest who had been appointed vice-postulator of the causes for the beatification of Francisco and Jacinta Marto, the two deceased visionaries of Fatima, interviewed Sister Lucia. The conversation set off a stir for many reasons, the most prevelant being the publishing of many distorted versions of the interview. But the authentic dialogue, as published in Fatima historian Father Joaquin Alonso's book *The Secret of Fatima,* revealed a clear, mystical picture of the times. Sister Lucia said that a "terrible chastisement" was about to "befall" the world and was imminent: "Many nations will disappear from the face of the earth, and Russia will be the instrument of heaven's chastisement for the entire world. Father, the devil is carrying on a decisive battle ...we are living in the last epoch of the world...we are going through a decisive battle ...there will be no middle way ...the last means God will give to the world are the Holy Rosary and the devotion to the Immaculate Heart of Mary."

But despite the efforts of Pius XII and Sister Lucia, the situation got worse. In Germany, a wall was erected in Berlin in 1961 to separate the East from the West and along the Iron Curtain hostilities flared. Throughout the world, from Africa to South America from Southeast Asia to the Middle East, communism was on the move. More and more, insidious theoretical atheism and its deadly effects were spreading. Likewise, modern weaponry continued to advance, as the 60's became known as the decade of the intercontinental missile.

Unrelentingly, Mary's apparitions to visionaries during the '60s emphasized the gravity of the situation. Communism was a tyrannical slavery of body and soul, she reportedly declared in her messages, and it was demonically conceived. The philosophical errors of the previous centuries were now ingrained in civilization and this was the fruit of a world order conceived without God. But soon the Virgin Mary's messages began to say even more. Communism had been forewarned long before, she disclosed, as symbolicly being the Red Dragon in the Book of Revelation. And these truly were, she said, the times foretold in St. John's Book of Revelation.

The Church's long and strong condemnation of communism indicated something serious was at hand too. From Pope Leo XIII through John Paul II, the denunciations for over one hundred years were clear and powerful. Most noted are the harsh condemnations of Popes Pius XI, Pius XII and Paul VI. Pius XI wrote the following condemnation of communism in *Divine Redemptores* on March 19, 1937:

> For the first time in history we are witnessing a struggle between man and 'all that is called God,' that is cold-blooded in purpose and mapped out to the least detail. Communism is by its nature anti-religious... See to it, Venerable Brethren, that the faithful do not allow themselves to be deceived! Communism is intrinsically evil, and no one who would save Christian civilization may collaborate with it in any undertaking whatsoever.

Pope Pius XII echoed his predecessor in his Christmas message of 1942:

> The Church has condemned the diverse systems of Marxist Socialism. She always maintains this condemnation because it is her duty and her permanent right to preserve men from the influences that put their eternal salvation in danger.

Almost twenty years later, Pope Paul VI, who was the first reigning pope to visit Fatima on May 13, 1967 and who renewed the consecration in 1964, wrote similarly in *Octogesima Adveniens*:

> He (the Christian) cannot adhere to the Marxist ideology, to its atheistic materialism, to its dialectic of violence and to the way it absorbs individual freedom in the collectivity, at the same time denying all transcendence to man and his personal and collective history.

During the 1960's, apparitions continued to be reported throughout Europe. In Spain, Mary reportedly appeared in Barcelona, El Palmar de Troya, and on a mountainside called Garabandal. Along the Mediterranean she was seen in Malta, Corsica, and in Athens, Greece. In France, she was seen at Thierenbach and again at Maille where four children were the visionaries. By now, her messages and visions were more intense. In Spain, extraordinary ecstasies were captured on film and the visionaries reported frightening visions of fire everywhere. There was coming a "global warning" the seers insisted, to be followed by an horrendous, fiery, chastisement if people did not convert. Despite the extraordinary supernatural qualities of Garabandal, the Church was not convinced enough to give approval. In Vietnam, where a terrible war would cost over a million lives, Mary appeared at a convent in Saigon from 1963 through 1965. The Virgin reportedly pleaded for peace, and like at Fatima, a miracle of the sun was witnessed to help the faithful to believe.

Like before, the sightings in Italy in the 1960's were

continuous. Mary was seen in San Damiano, Ostie, Cavati Tirenni, Ulzio, Fontanelle, Ventebbio, Cafala Diana, Raccuia, Acqua Voltri, San Vittorino, Quix, Florence, Craveggia, Ventebbio, Porto San Stefano, Maropati, and Rome. At Casapulla a statue wept. While at Milano in 1968, a woman named Mama Carmela Carabelli began to receive apparitions of Mary and the saints, one of whom, she claimed, was Sister Faustina, perhaps signifying that God's time of Divine Mercy had descended on a world bent on destroying itself. Sister Elena Aiello of Constanza, a stigmatist, revealed a similar understanding of the times and said Mary warned her of the growing threat: **"If people do not recognize in these scourges of nature the warnings of Divine Mercy and do not return to God with truly Christian living, another terrible war will come from East to West. Russia with her secret armies will battle America, and will overrun Europe."** One must ask why Italy had by far the most reports. That answer, perhaps again lied in the revelations of Fatima, where a great apostasy was foretold. Italy, being the home of the Catholic Church, perhaps deserved in heaven's eyes a preponderance of attention.

In Skemonaia, Lithuania, in 1962, Mary reportedly foretold the coming of her great apparitions in Cairo in 1968. While in Ain-El-Del, Libya, in 1966, ten thousand people gathered at an apparition to a 14-year old girl named Wardi Mansour. As in the previous two decades, Mary continued to appear to many children the world over. At St. Bruno De Chambly, Mary appeared in 1968 to two children, Manon St. Jean, 13, and Danielle Vincent, 10. At Anse Aux Gascons in Canada of the same year, she appeared to Julien Roussey, who was also ten. And at Fort Kent in the U.S., another ten year-old named Gerald Pelletier claimed to see the Virgin.

Because of improved communication and reporting techniques, by the 1960's, reports of apparitions from all over the world were able to be accumulated and assessed. There were reported apparitions in Fribourg, Switzerland; Cabra, Philippines; Liege, Belgium; Nativitade, Brazil; Quebec, Canada; and Mexico City. The messages were almost always the same: God was calling His people to repentance and conversion. And sin was pushing the world, the visionaries echoed each other, to a point of no return. Nothing emphasized this point stronger than the growing number of images and statues that continued to weep and shed blood. A good example of this was the hundred year old crucifix at Porta das Caixas in Brazil which dripped blood in 1968 onto a church altar for two hours. Doctors confirmed it was human blood and cures of cancer and blindness were verified.

In her apparitions, Mary promised hope for the world, but it had to change its heart and it had to pray more. Prayer was the answer to the danger that threatened all humanity, Mary reportedly told visionaries. Nothing human could succeed without prayer.

At the close of Vatican II, Pope Paul VI's message was not much different. "Be converted and believe in the Gospel," Paul VI wrote on February 17, 1966 quoting St. Mark's Gospel (Mk 1:15) at the introduction of his apostolic letter *Paenitemini*. Indeed, the Council had embraced Pope John XXIII's prayer for "a new Pentecost" in the Church, but it recognized that justice and peace would come only when people and nations recognized the urgency of penance, conversion and forgiveness.

The Weeping Madonna of Syracuse, Sicily.
"Will men come to understand," said Pope Pius XII,
"the mysterious language of those tears?"

CHAPTER NINE

HER TIME OF VISITATION

"The Kingdom of God is at hand. Repent, and believe in the Gospel."

— Mk 1:15

In America, the United States was still the land of the free. It was the country many people the world over came to admire after World War II. Indeed, "civilization at its highest point" was a tag easily applied to a nation rich in everything a country could want. And of course, America's greatest commodity *was* its incredible freedom, which was the envy of the world. But this freedom revealed to be a two-edged sword. Moreover, by the 1970's, an increasing number of apparitions were being reported in America, too. As in Europe, visionaries warned that the nation was headed for trouble. People were following the wrong road and listening to the wrong message, the seers reported. Used incorrectly, freedom and prosperity had become toxic to the souls of the people and to the nation as a whole. But how could this have happened?

After World War II, America set out to turn its war-time production into the manufacture of goods for peace-time use. Business boomed. Labor prospered. A scientific revolution followed, brought about by the atomic research. There was a baby boom. It was an exciting time to live.

A new medium of communication—television—brought entertainment to millions of homes. With the development of super highways, international airlines, and mass transportation, factories churned out new lines of products that could be taken from one end of the world to the other. Typewriters, telephones, and plastic devices of every kind turned life into an unending quest for convenience and pleasure.

Twenty years later, something occurred that could not have been foreseen. The post-war generation, who had everything, had been transformed into a new breed of malcontents. They were disgruntled souls. Large on talk, they propounded radical philosophies and opinions on everything from sex to politics. Everyone had an opinion, but they were generally unenlightened opinions.

Over the next two decades, television brought the philosophies of the 60's into every home in America, and the erroneous ways of this generation were made to seem normal. What had once been socially taboo was now portrayed as socially acceptable. Out went religion, the traditional family, decency, and God. In came a variety of lifestyles, beliefs, and movements that sought to redefine society. From pro-choice to political correctness, from radical feminism to New Age, from homosexual rights to white collar crime, the economic and intellectual fruits of the post World War II era backfired. By the 1970's, the free West had become the wild and dangerous West. Like communism, the people were becoming slaves to a tyranny, not of the body, but of the mind and soul just as Mary foretold. In short, the fruits of humanism and the enlightenment were reaching their peak. To one of her chosen ones, a humble little Italian priest named Fr. Stefano Gobbi, Mary clearly laid out how the spiritual war had evolved to an entirely new level of understanding:

> **He [Satan] has succeeded in seducing you through pride. He has managed to pre-arrange everything in a most clever fashion. He has bent to his design every sector of human science and technique, arranging everything for rebellion against God. The greater part of humanity is now in his hands. He has managed by guile to draw to himself scientists, artists, philosophers, scholars and the powerful. Enticed by him, they have now put themselves at his service to act without God and against God.**

Make no doubt about it though, death and the physical destruction of the planet, were still at the center of the war against God, visionaries said. The period between 1955 and 1975 saw a huge escalation in the production of weapons, especially nuclear weapons. And while the Virgin Mary warned at Fatima of the errors of Russia, the visionaries said that America and the rest of the free-world, with its unholy practices, were now as much a potential source for world destruction as for world peace. This was because wherever sin darkens the mind, danger exists. And now, the entire world faced the consequences of hatred and atheism mixed together with modern science and its Pandora's box of ungodly weapons of mass destruction.

This was a worldwide spiritual crisis at the core, Mary now said in her apparitions. And the free nations were now submerged in much of the same darkness as the people in Communist countries. The Virgin called it "practical atheism" and said that in the long run this danger could do even more harm than communism. To one Italian locutionist, the Virgin Mary went so far as to reveal that **"practical atheism was the greatest evil of the 20th century"** (The Virgin Mary to Fr. Stefano Gobbi, September 2, 1996). In simple terms, the apostasy of faith warned of at Fatima had arrived, and this time it was a worldwide apostasy. And again, its cause was the same; it was the result of the spiritual war being waged on the mind of man.

While gradually seducing mankind with materialism, intellectualism and the pleasures of the flesh, Mary explained how over time the forces of darkness had also conducted an onslaught against God, His Commandments and belief in His very existence. This onslaught was against all religion, but especially Christianity. It began during the Renaissance, but starting with the Protestant Reformation, the erroneous philosophies that gave exclusive value to science and reason gradually but effectively, began to dismantle all Christian truth. This happened, the Virgin said, through the misguided belief that human intelligence alone was the sole criteria of truth and through the exaggerated importance of reason, which in turn led to the Protestant rejection of tradition as a source of Divine Revelation. Then, with Scripture established as the sole source of Divine Revelation, an assault on its interpretation was mounted. This resulted in more error, more confusion, more schism and eventually the great apostasy of the late 20th century. Thus, all of this has contributed to another form of atheism, "practical atheism", which, as Mary noted, is worse than the theoretical atheism of communism. This is because it is not forced on people, but chosen through free will.

Perhaps this was what Sister Lucia Santos of Fatima was implying when the distinguished author and historian William Thomas Walsh asked her in a 1946 interview about the "spread of communism." Walsh asked Lucia if communism would take over the whole world. "Yes," Lucia replied. "Even America?" inquired Walsh. "Even America," Lucia answered.

The West, Mary cautioned visionaries, was at a crossroads. It needed to choose God, not Satan, if it were to survive. It needed to confess its sins. It needed to become holy again if it were to continue to be blessed. This was especially true for America. America had always prided itself on being a "nation under God," but by the late 1970s, the prophets insisted this was no longer true. Contraception, abortion and sins of the flesh were especially calling God's justice down upon the nation and soon, it would be too late.

Just as General MacArthur had warned, something had to be done or else Armageddon would be at the door. Perhaps Bishop Fulton Sheen said it best: "We live in apocalyptic times. Our Western world has not denied Christianity, it has refused Christianity. We are not Christians, but post-Christians. We should sacrifice so that the love of God may spread to all peoples before the day of wrath."

Was this day of wrath near? God seemed to be saying so. There were reports of apparitions in the early 70's at Dozule, France; El Mimbral, Spain; and Bonn, Germany. In Italy, nothing changed. Four new apparitions were reported, while many of the previous ones continued to occur. In Monterrey, Mexico, a village to the north of Mexico City, a statue of the Infant Jesus was said to be "breathing, perspiring and weeping". The bishop advised prudence, but crowds as large as 15,000 a day soon came to the home of Aurea Martinez Sifuentes. Teresa Musco, an Italian stigmatist who lived in Caserta, opened her home to reveal in 1975 an array of weeping images, crucifixes, and statues, many of which shed blood. There were more weeping statues reported during the 1970's at Maropati, Porziano di Assisi, Cinquefrond, Lendinarara, Naples, Porto San Stefano, Ravenna, Firenzam and Vertora. In Greece, in 1979, an icon of Mary was seen weeping at Thessaloniki. In just a short time, thousands gathered for all-night vigils. In Haite, the government television station filmed a weeping statue of Mary in 1976, as throngs gathered at the church to see for themselves. While in Damascus, Syria, a Fatima Pilgrim Virgin statue weeped in 1977 with even the bishop promoting the evidence.

The visionaries seemed to be saying God's day of wrath was closer too. By the mid-1970's, two more Italian stigmatists, Mother Elena Leonardi and Sister Elena Aiello, were reporting phenomenal visions about a world in distress and fire falling from the sky. So were two eastern European mystics/stigmatists: a woman named Julka in Yugoslavia and a Hungarian visionary named Sr. Maria Natalie. At Akita, Japan, in 1973, Mary told stigmatist Sister Agnes Sasagawa that fire falling from the sky would **"wipe out a greater part of humanity."** The apparitions at Akita were approved by the Church ten years later. The message of Akita was, many theologians and Church hierarchy agreed, the "full" message of Fatima. A wooden statue of Our Lady of all Nations also wept 101 times at Akita and in its left hand appeared the stigmata. Like elsewhere, the messages at Akita spoke of war, destruction, "fire from the sky," and a world filled with massive death.

By the late 1970's, this scenario, according to the prophecies, began to reveal several other elements. There was coming, visionaries said, not just a major chastisement from the hands of men, as foretold at Fatima, but an overall, world wide upheaval in society and nature. Wars were still threatened, but because of the massive amount of sin, especially sins of the flesh, God intended to bring a purification of the whole world. The prophets noted celestial signs and wonders were soon to come as well as a change in weather patterns. Along with a worldwide economic crisis, there was talk of a cosmic disturbance of some form and the rise of an antichrist figure, perhaps even Scripture's long awaited Antichrist. God would control all of this to insure the outcome and the faithful were being invited to understand the 'signs of the times', but the catastrophic events the prophets described sounded like something out of the Gospel of Matthew (Mat 24) and the book of Revelation. All in all, there was to come a massive cleanup of the world in order for it to be able to enter into a true era of peace. But the severity of these events, visionaries reminded, was still in people's hands. The destruction could be prevented.

It must have been clear to those who heard him, that General Douglas MacArthur wanted no more destruction. And he, too, could foresee that mankind was challenging God. As he accepted the surrender of Japan on August 15, 1945, and then again before Congress on April 19, 1951, MacArthur said what many were already thinking:

> Men since the beginning of time have sought peace. Various methods through the ages have been attempted to devise an international process to prevent or settle disputes between nations. From the very start workable methods were found in so far as individual citizens were concerned, but the mechanics of an instrumentality of larger international scope have never been successful. Military alliances, balances of power, leagues of nations, all in turn failed, leaving the only path to be by way of the crucible of war. The utter destructiveness of war now blocks out this alternative. We have our last chance. If we will not devise some greater and more equitable system, ARMAGEDDON WILL BE AT OUR DOOR. The problem basically is theological.

According to religious writers, what MacArthur was saying was that it all came back to Scripture. Throughout the world, Mary's visionaries said it all came back to Scripture, too. Jesus wept over Jerusalem. He wept because He knew it would be destroyed. And He wept because he knew why it would be destroyed—It was no longer holy, the Lord said. The Gospel of Luke phrased it this way: **"He saw the city and wept over it, saying, 'If this day you only knew what makes for peace, but now it is hidden from your eyes'"** (Luke 19:42).

That scriptural passage, some visionaries say, is the same message Mary brings today to the world. It is the same message she brought in the 19th century and throughout the early 20th Century. It is the message the Church approved when it approved Fatima and Akita. It is not a new revelation. Indeed, at Fatima in 1917, Mary clearly foretold a troubled future and warned of disaster.

Fatima, which gave the world the fulfillment of prophesies unlike any before, is where we must look to truly understand what God began to tell the world right before the French Revolution and what He continues to tell the world to this day. This is especially true because of the two great signs Mary promised at Fatima, both have taken place.

On Oct. 13, 1917, the sun hurtled toward earth as 70,000 people watched transfixed in terror. At the last second, it stopped and returned. Many believed it was the end of the world. Three months before, Mary had promised the children a sign, and this was the sign. According to the front page report in Lisbon's leading newspaper, *O'Seculo*, the following day, even unbelievers witnessed the extraordinary celestial phenomenon.

Many Marian experts have long speculated that the sign was a symbolic message of what could happen in the world someday. A sign, they believe, that fire could fall from the sky. The falling sun that day was just that, they say—a sign foreshadowing man's errors falling down upon himself.

In 1938, another sign was given that was foretold at Fatima in 1917. (**"When you see a night illuminated by an unknown light, know that this is the great sign that God is giving you that he is going to punish the world for its crimes..."**) The sky lit up on January 25-26 over Europe and the northern hemisphere. Scientists reported an aurora borealis, but in a convent in Spain, Sr. Lucia of Fatima said that it was actually the second sign Mary had promised in 1917. "God made use of this," Lucia would later write, "to make me understand His justice was about to strike the guilty nations." Lucia knew that this sign marked the prophesied coming of World War II, and today, some nuclear physicists believe Sr. Lucia was correct about its true nature. It was not an aurora borealis. It appeared to be, the scientists say, something like "the false aurora created by an atomic explosion only recently discovered."

Theologians emphasize that Mary didn't just come to Fatima to prophesy the approaching dangers of the nuclear age. Rather, her warnings came hand in hand with a package of solutions – spiritual solutions, especially for Catholics and all Christians, Prayer, especially the Rosary and the Scapular, were mystical weapons of defense, she revealed. And she promised to return at the right moment to ask for something more from the faithful: the Communion of Reparation of the first five Saturdays. This she did in 1925 and 1929.

But in 1929, Mary asked Lucia to ask the Pope for one more thing. The Virgin wanted Russia collegially consecrated to her Immaculate Heart, as she had also spoken of in 1917. Russia had been mysteriously identified by Mary then as a danger to the future of the world, and by 1929 it was understood why. Communism had taken hold in Russia and its death grip was clearly visible.

Mariologists note the similarity of this request for the consecration of Russia with the Sacred Heart revelations given to Saint Margaret Mary Alacoque about a century before the French Revolution. On June 17, 1689, St. Margaret Mary reported an apparition of Jesus that requested the King of France consecrate France to the Sacred Heart of Jesus. This request was never carried out and one hundred years to the day, June 17, 1789, the King of France was stripped of his power by the Third Estate. Four years later King Louis XVI was beheaded on the guillotine. The similarity of these requests was later revealed to be no accident. In 1931, Sr. Lucia reported that Jesus told her that failure to consecrate Russia in a timely fashion could lead to the same tragic end that came to France and its King. In August 1931, at Rianjo, Spain, Christ told Sister Lucia, **"Make it known to my ministers that given they follow the example of the King of France in delaying the execution of My command, that they will follow him into misfortune."** Yes, Russia had to be consecrated to her, Mary repeatedly told Sister Lucia, if true peace was to come into the world.

On May 5, 1917, Pope Benedict XV, after fruitless appeals to end World War I, added an invocation to the Litany of Loretto: "Queen of Peace pray for us." Eight days later, Mary appeared at Fatima (May 13, 1917). Today, throughout the world, visionaries say that Mary has declared in some of her apparitions that she has come as the "Queen of Peace." It is a pronouncement that she makes for a reason as the 20th century comes to an end. Peace, the Virgin proclaims, peace is what God wants for this world, and peace is what God promised through her at Fatima when she prophesied a future **"era of peace."** It is one of two remaining unfulfilled Fatima prophecies.

The other is her prediction of **"the annihilation of nations,"** which appears to be directly related to the many prophecies of "fire" falling from the sky and to the two signs at Fatima that both symbolically forewarn, say experts, of the coming nuclear age.

Today, just as Jesus wept, so does Mary. The apparitional woman is often crying, say visionaries everywhere. Throughout the world, statues, icons, and paintings of the Virgin also weep. Not just in churches but in hundreds of homes.

Why does Mary weep? Visionaries say because the people and nations of the world, much like ancient Jerusalem, are no longer holy, and she knows what this unholiness will bring. Mary has been warning of it since before the French Revolution and she keeps repeating that her warnings are now urgent.

The Virgin foretold at Fatima the annihilation of nations on July 13, 1917. In March 1939, Jesus reportedly told Sr. Lucia almost the exact same words in a vision at Pontreveda: **"The time is coming when the reign of my justice will punish the crimes of various nations. Some of them will be annihilated."**

Theologians say that when Jesus wept over Jerusalem, He did not say God would destroy the city. Rather, men would bring this about themselves. Peace could have been possible, but instead men chose destruction.

> **If only you had known the path to peace this day, but you have completely lost it from your view! Days will come upon you when your enemies will encircle you with a rampart, hem you in, and press you hard from every side. They will smash you to the ground and your children within you, and they will not leave one stone upon another because you did not recognize the time of your visitation** (Lk 19:42-44).

By the early 1980's, what began to happen in Europe wasn't surprising. Reports of Marian apparitions began to escalate even more. On the tiny island nation of Ireland, there were over thirty different reports of apparitions alone during the decade. While many were dubious in nature or just plain corrupt, some were unmistakable divine in origin. Elsewhere, throughout the world, it was the same.

A plethora of the supernatural was being reported.

But in the recent revelations, another disturbing disclosure emerged. The fulfillment of Fatima's remaining prophecies, the visionaries said, was now at the doorstep of the world and all of Mary's words would soon be fulfilled. Likewise, the times at hands were times foretold in Scripture. Before the end of the century, either something extraordinarily good or terribly bad would befall the world. It was up to mankind, visionaries said they were told, to decide once and for all its fate.

According to so many reports since 1981, the apparitional woman has been trying in a special, more urgent way than ever to help the world with its conversion. Visionaries say she won't give up, she won't stop trying to prevent annihilation. She appears and appears. She weeps and weeps.

"Because of such cases even many men of the Church ought to weep," remarked Cardinal Ratzinger on April 2, 1995. Indeed, the many documented accounts seem to support that the Virgin has intervened everywhere one can imagine. (According to one source, the French periodical *Le Monde* there have been an estimated 21,000 apparitions of Mary between 1976 and 1986.) And Mary has chosen literally dozens more since 1981 to be her messengers. Thousands of miracles have been reported and visionaries have repeatedly linked her words and actions with the fulfillment of the prophecies of Fatima, prophecies which reportedly Sister Lucia herself said can be found in Scripture.

Some Mariologists say that the events of the last two decades are unparalleled in history. They are an account of what is perhaps the final hour of an era and they are a story in themselves.

PART II

A

TIME

FOR ALL

SEASONS

"That which is being prepared is so great that its equal has never existed since the creation of the world. Prepare yourselves with humility, with faith, with intense prayer."

-The Blessed Virgin Mary
to Father Stefano Gobbi
Mexico City, Oct. 13, 1990

CHAPTER TEN

THE HOUR HAS COME

"But woe to you, earth and sea, for the Devil has come down upon you! His fury knows no limits, for he knows his time is short."
—Rv 12:12

It would be difficult, but Estela Ruiz knew what she had to do. Even though she held a master's degree and had written a highly acclaimed educational text for bilingual children, this was something her training and experience hadn't prepared her for. But the Texas born Mexican-American abandoned her fear and addressed the crowd gathered in her backyard.

"First of all, "Estela began, "I should explain that earlier today, after the cleaning, I kind of tried to relax. I always try to do that, and as I was preparing to take a shower and freshen up and go to my room, I heard her [the Virgin Mary] call me. She said, **'I need for you to come and talk to me!'** So I went into my bedroom and closed the door, and she told me, **'This evening I want you to write the message, which I will give you for today.'** She must have known that we were going to have such a big crowd.

"She gave me the message, and she asked me to write it down, and she said, **'When I do talk to you throughout the prayers, it will be mostly conversation between you and me ... like comadres!'** This is what she told me, and you know what it is from our culture. ... It is two women that have great rapport with each other!

"So this pretty much is what happened," Estela continued. "But she did say this evening as we prayed here, that she wanted to welcome all the new people that are here, and for me to explain that she is here in the Americas and that she is doing many, many things with many, many people! She's here to stomp on the head of Lucifer, and that he does know that she is here, and that she is **"going to show him what a victory is!!!"**

Eight years later, as Estela Ruiz and her husband, Reyes, soared 35,000 feet above the earth on another cross-continental excursion, neither could have imagined so much was in store for them that December evening in 1988. Much had transpired since that first day when the Virgin Mary unexpectedly appeared in an apparition to this middle-aged, mother of seven and grandmother of a couple dozen. She had experienced dozens of visions, recorded countless messages. Some profound, some cloaked in mystery. Estela's life now took her on the road; places like Los Angeles and New York were becoming as commonplace as her own hometown of Phoenix. Overall, it had been a fast five years, and there was a great deal to ponder, a lot to absorb.

But according to the Virgin's revelations to Estela Ruiz, there wasn't time. She was telling Estela that a great victory over evil in the world was near, very near, and that every trip she made was critical because the great prophecies given at Fatima in 1917 were about to be fulfilled. The world was going to change, Mary assured Estela. It was going to change in a radical way.

Indeed by 1990, the evidence was accumulating that some sort of metamorphasis was underway and perhaps more change was imminent. A stunned world witnessed pieces of the Berlin Wall being sold as souvenirs, while in just a few years a half-dozen communist dictators were dead, on the run, or behind bars. In South Africa, apartheid had crumbled, and the Soviet Union was no longer on the map.

Meanwhile, another wave of reported miracles was sweeping over the world. Hundreds of apparitions and thousands of heavenly messages were being reported. From all four corners of the globe, people like Estela Ruiz claimed they heard voices and witnessed visions, often in homes that revealed weeping icons and bleeding statues. Even in Nepal, Hindus had alleged to see towering apparitions in the sky, apparitions of a man nailed to a cross. For believers, it was perhaps like the 1780's all over again—God was trying to desperately tell the world something, just as He had in France before the French Revolution.

Yet apparently, if He was, all this was still not enough. According to news reports, the world remained a troubled, dangerous place regardless of how hard the prophets tried to hammer home their urgent message. Murder, divorce, crime, abortion, and every evil under the sun was still on the rise. And by the mid 1980's, violent crime in America was reaching epidemic proportions. Around the world, the century of genocide continued. According to a 1994 report published by the Pontifical Council for Justice and Peace, titled, *The International Arms Trade: An Ethical Reflection*, "Never before has our earth known so many armed conflicts." The report concluded that the world's arms industry (estimated at $20 billion annually) had grown "out of control." Thus, for many throughout the world, it would be hard to say that hope prevailed.

But more and more, reports of the miraculous were starting to attract attention. Major news organizations such as *CBS, CNN,* and the *Wall Street Journal,* were reporting on the outbreak of miracles. And around the world, there were stories of new apparitions almost everywhere, with the number of incidents on the rise. Indeed, by 1998, Estela Ruiz was perhaps just one of many "everyday people" who were now circumnavigating the globe, taking their message of conversion to anyone who invited them.

But the truth of the matter was that Estela Ruiz , and others like her, were no longer everyday people. Not by a long shot. They were now seen as chosen ones like Catherine Laboure, and Bernadette Soubirous, Estelle Faguette, Lucia Santos, and so many more from a simpler time gone by—they, too, had claimed to see and speak to invisible friends from the world beyond.

Moreover, out of the 1980s and 1990s came scores of new visionaries, mystics, and prophets, all like Estela Ruiz and almost all talking about visions of the Virgin Mary and the fulfillment of the prophecies of Fatima.

There was Christina Gallagher of Ireland, whose life radically changed after she visited a grotto to pray in 1985. Within just a few years, Christina reported that she had experienced almost every type of mystical phenomenon—including the sacred stigmata.

81

Then, there was Josyp Terelya, a Ukrainian Catholic dissident whose life unfolded and was about to end in the Soviet Gulag—until, he said, the Virgin Mary appeared to him in a freezer cell moments before he was about to die. Years later Terelya would foresee in a vision, a half decade in advance, the exact unfolding of the 1991 attempted coup of Mikhael Gorbachev in the Soviet Union.

There was Mirna Nazour—a beautiful young Syrian housewife living in Damascus, who found herself chosen by God to be the instrument of a string of incredible miracles, miracles that left hierarchy in both the Orthodox and Catholic Churches in awe. Witnesses gasped as oil poured from Mirna's hands, and blood oozed from the center of her head.

And then there was Fr. Stefano Gobbi, a most unremarkable priest who suddenly experienced an "interior locution" while on pilgrimage at Fatima. Like the others, within a few years, Fr. Gobbi was traveling to almost every country of the world, exhorting his fellow priests about the approaching fulfillment of Fatima's prophecies. Mary's messages to him, perhaps more than any before, revealed new insight into the Book of Revelation.

These fascinating individuals and others like them had all been ordinary people, living quite ordinary lives. But by the 1980's, they were being referred to as "prophets" and "visionaries." Like so many before, they were chosen ones whom the world not only sought to touch but flocked to hear, and they all were spreading the same urgent message: "Change your life now, before it's too late." The fulfillment of the prophecies of Fatima was at hand, they repeated everywhere. And the world needed to listen while it still had time.

Fatima had provided many prophecies, but the remaining ones concerned an era of peace for mankind. The consensus among these visionaries was that this era was fast approaching. But before the Era of Peace would occur, they cautioned, the world would pass through a painful purification, one that could witness **"the annihilation of nations."** It was a purification some believed was foretold at Fatima, and even long before. But this prophecy was never really grasped by mankind. It was ignored by a world that was captivated by 20th century technological progress and embarrassed by such antiquated ideas.

This purification would be instigated by a great apostasy of faith, and propelled forward by an atheist Russia, Mary foretold at Fatima. First, a second World War would occur if mankind did not return to God, and then even more upheaval of every kind. But World War II came and went and the world got worse, literally embracing evil for good by the 1980's. Thus, according to these new visionaries, God was now sending one last urgent call to His people, one last wave of prophets. It was to be one final appeal to conversion before all of Fatima's remaining prophecies would be fulfilled.

Not surprisingly, Church leaders and theologians were puzzled. In light of all the revelations and miracles over the past two and a half centuries, who could have foreseen that so much more would unfold at so late an hour? Beginning in 1981, there were so many new reports of apparitions, visions, locutions, weeping statues, and miraculous phenomena that some experts began to suspect that it was either a dangerous, deceptive trend or something unprecedented in the history of salvation was occurring.

In part, the many new apparitions echoed the revelations and legacies of past visionaries, mystics, saints, and popes. Repeatedly, the experiences of contemporary visionaries struck familiar chords, and their alleged messages and visions touched on many of the Church-approved apparitions of the past two centuries, apparitions such as Rue du Bac, La Salette, Lourdes, Knock, and Fatima.

However, the new prophets who came from remote places on every continent of the world echoed one another concerning the immediate future in an almost uncanny way. Indeed, whether the messages came from a middle-aged housewife in Spain or from grade-school children in a remote rural village in Czechoslovakia, their prophecies and warnings rang out in almost perfect harmony with each other, even more so than their predecessors.

Overall, the contemporary revelations seemed to condense and parallel everything visionaries and mystics had been saying for so long to so many. Yet it was all so much in such a brief period of time that no one, not even Marian experts, knew what to think.

But according to some Mariologists, would it not be like God to recognize a need to summarize His prophetic messages? Theologians point out that over the last two centuries God's generous outpouring of light and truth had led to an almost endless accumulation of prophetic writings and histories, much more than anyone can review, absorb, and interpret. In fact, the sheer quantity of so much private revelation has led to uncertainty and debate, and created confusion and doubt over whom to believe and what God is really saying to His people. It was noted that in the Old Testament, God Himself spoke specifically of this predicament. The divinely inspired author of Maccabees (2 Maccabees 2) cited the compelling need for "abridgment in reporting the narrations of God's history," for often the full matter has become "a multitude and difficult."

Similarly, today's ongoing revelations reflect this very concern. Joseph Cardinal Ratzinger, the Catholic Church's Prefect for the Doctrine of the Congregation of the Faith, considered the avalanche of reports as being a "sign of the times." Therefore, some theologians conjectured that perhaps God was now sending many visionaries to give the world an abbreviated, concise review of how generous He has been in directing his people toward the right path, the path of love, hope, and salvation. Perhaps in the summary of His love, manifested through these chosen souls, God hoped mankind would finally come to see the whole picture more clearly and accept with confidence what was previously revealed. Perhaps in the lives and messages of these modern day prophets, the world would discern the truth, and turn away from its present evil course, a course that Pope John Paul II described as having led to "a culture of death."

1981. This was the year Marian experts say this final thrust, this final wave began.

According to visionaries, a countdown had begun, and a great, climactic spiritual battle would now erupt in full force through a series of mystical as well as historical events. On the international scene, a thermo-nuclear stalemate between the United States and the Soviet Union was barely holding. But one lapse could easily turn the Cold War into the hottest war in the history of the world. In fact, the relationship between the super powers was at its lowest in 1981, creating a palpable tension not experienced since the Cuban Missile Crisis in 1962. The Soviets had invaded Afghanistan and the United States had boycotted the Olympic Games in Moscow. While there was talk of disarmament there was also talk of nuclear winters and star wars defense systems. At Medjugorje, a little hamlet nestled high in the hills of Herzegovina, a province of what was once Yugoslavia, the Virgin Mary reportedly appeared to six children and defined for them the moment: **"The hour has come when the Demon is authorized to act with all his force and power."**

According to some theologians , this was an extraordinary revelation, for it surely accounted for why evil had spread like a plague. However, Mary further disclosed to the visionaries that this authorization came from God, and the Lord promised it would soon conclude with the new era, an era of peace, regardless of evil's present reign of terror. The question remained though—at what price would this new era come?

It had now been more than a century since Pope Leo XIII's 1884 vision of a final confrontation between God and Satan. In that startling account, Satan was said to have been granted a century to wreak havoc upon the world, and as foretold so often, to accompany evil's elevation in power, Hell would be emptied and a flood of demons would converge upon the earth. However no one knew exactly when Satan's sanctioned time had begun, and no one was sure when it would end. But Mary told the children at Medjugorje that the end of this allotted time was near, and confirmed to one of them that Pope Leo's vision of the 100-year reign was true.

This prophecy of evil's reign coming to an end was now also being heard over and over at other apparition sites throughout the world much the way its beginning had been repeatedly foretold. In Argentina in 1985, the Madonna reportedly confided to the stigmatist Gladys Quiroga, **"the Evil One knows there is only a little time left."** At Oliveto Citra, Italy, in 1986 the Virgin stated to several visionaries that Satan's final hour **"had started a century ago."** And to Father Stefano Gobbi Mary emphasized that Satan's grip on the world would now be broken. The world at the close of the 20th century was in for some kind of spiritual meltdown that would be visibly manifested in a string of extraordinary events.

Nevertheless, important questions remained. Where exactly in the eschatological order of events was mankind now? How much time remained before all would be fulfilled? And what was going to happen?

From theologians to lay people, there was an abundance of opinions. People speculated about the world living in certain chapters of The Book of Revelation. Others argued that the end times were really just beginning. Some protestant ministries even spoke of the end of the world and Second Coming of Jesus Christ by the year

2000.

Fr. Gobbi, the Italian locutionist and founder of the Marian Movement of Priests, reported a message that disclosed a 10-year interval beginning in 1990 that would be the decisive period. It would be the period, the revelation indicated, when the **"Great Tribulation'** would unfold and events concealed in the Secret of Fatima and Scripture would be revealed. This period of 10 years, the Madonna's message detailed, would occur when **"there will come to completion that fullness of time which was pointed out to you by me, beginning with La Salette (1846) all the way to my most recent and present apparitions!"**

Thus, if all of this were true, then these apparitions were those now being reported on every continent of the world, apparitions the world was starting to hear about through the media, apparitions that Mary said at Medjugorje would be her last in the history of the world.

So with all of this in mind, let us take one final, sweeping look at what has unfolded since 1981. Let us travel the globe. Let us go to all the continents. Let us search out these prophets of peace. Let us ponder the miracles and try to comprehend their visions. Most importantly, let us examine their revelations and see what they are attempting to tell us about the end of one era and the beginning of the next.

CHAPTER ELEVEN

THE SILLY SEASON

"When the fool walks through the street, in his lack of understanding, he calls everything foolish."

—Eccl 10:3

It began in February 1985. Out of nowhere, newspapers in the Republic of Ireland began to report scattered incidents of moving statues of the Virgin Mary. The phenomena reportedly began at a village named Asdee in County Kerry, where a seven year-old girl saw a statue move. Thirty-four other little girls soon agreed and one girl even reached out to feel it. "I don't know what it was like," she said, "but it wasn't like stone. It did not feel like a statue at all."

At first there wasn't much of a stir in Ireland over Asdee or the other incidents, but as sightings of Mary multiplied and swept across the country, no province was left untouched. Like a fire out of control, reports came from churches and grottos, mostly in the southern part of the country. These mysterious events continued into the spring and summer. Then, in July an incident occurred that was widely publicized and attracted a considerable crowd. Several women claimed that a statue of the Virgin at a roadside grotto south of Cork was rocking back and forth while raising and lowering its hands, and that images of saints and popes could be seen on the statue's face.

As preposterous as this seemed, similar reports continued to gain public attention, and by September 1985, locations throughout the country claimed such phenomena. From Gortnadreha to Inchigeela, from Grantstown to Mayfield, from Bessbrook to

Ballinspittle, from Melleray to Dublin, the Virgin Mary was reported to be appearing. Almost everywhere, the events began to attract throngs of the faithful and the curious. At Ballinspittle in the summer of 1985, up to 40,000 persons a week were estimated to be visiting the grotto.

The dozens of visionaries were of every age and background—grandmas, grandpas, mothers, fathers, housewives, teachers, farmers, children, the educated, the simple, men and women alike. And they all seemed to agree on one thing—it was the Blessed Virgin Mary they saw with their very own eyes, and for most, it didn't matter who believed them.

But just as unusual was the fact that many *did* believe the fascinating reports. Indeed, the stories enchanted the public as throngs of curious onlookers followed almost every new incident. But such was not the case with the Irish press. Reporters at the *Cork Examiner* treated the accounts with cynicism, amusement, and doubt. Some journalists labeled the reports as a product of *"the silly season"* and attempted to make them a national joke. "It was a confirmation," one scribe wrote, "that the Irish people had finally done what they had threatened to do for generations—lost their national marbles."

Radio talk shows took delight in the mockery. Wisecracks, innuendoes, and sarcasm flew freely over the airwaves about their Irish kinsmen who were "head cases" or just plain crazy. But when the *Cork Examiner* enlisted a dozen eyewitnesses to observe a rocking statue, seven came back puzzled, saying they too saw odd movements. It was an unexpected twist; more people, including the skeptics, were apparently losing their marbles.

On August 2, 1985, within weeks of the reported events at the Ballinspittle Grotto, Kevin D. O'Connor, a reporter for the *Irish Independent* newspaper, was assigned to investigate the events because of his "objectivity." Ironically, what he found didn't lend credibility to his reputation.

"The features (on the statue) went out of focus," wrote O'Connor, "and when they resumed the hands were up to the side of the face, as if she (the statue of Mary) had received a blow." Stunned by what he saw, O'Connor twice inquired of a neighboring girl if she too saw any movements. "No," she replied, leaving him to anguish over the experience.

Jim O'Herlihy, a professional photographer, suffered a similar dilemma. After positioning his camera on a tripod for "fixed" shots, the pictures somehow revealed the statue with hands in different positions. This was, of course, exactly what people had said was happening in the first place.

According to American investigative journalist Michael Brown, the accumulated evidence was compelling. The initial reports described the statues as smiling, frowning, or turning. It wasn't the kind of blurring or twitching one would expect to see in an optical illusion, said Brown. It was as if the statues were somehow alive! The movements were pronounced, continuous, and nearly violent at time. Even self-proclaimed disbelievers witnessed the statues quaking.

This turn of events apparently poured cold water on the jesters. Over time, twenty or more sites reported moving statues. But soon, much more startling claims were publicized. Strange fog, lights, and wind were reported at one grotto; others reported seeing pillars of light, angels, and demonic animal-like creatures. In the south of Ireland, the statues now appeared to be talking and moving around. Then, they began disappearing and transforming into living apparitions in which the Virgin Mary gave urgent messages, prophetic declarations that warned people all was not well and that troubled times lay ahead. Without a doubt, the Madonna's roadside warnings were serious admonitions. Brown observed that "anyone who wanted to hear forecasts of coming events was in the right place along Ireland's winding roads."

And many took to the roads. The silly season wouldn't end. At one grotto on an early evening, Brown reported that a hundred spectators witnessed the sun come down and rest over the grotto. It grew pale and pink and then assumed the shape of a huge heart. After pulsating, it burst, and miraculously spread a purple mist over the stunned onlookers.

As hard as it may be to believe, there were many more such reports:

- After witnessing 81 apparitions, a woman named Mrs. Casey said she could even tell you about the dimples on the Virgin Mary's cheeks.

- Ten year-old Marie Vaughan, who had become friends with Mary, said she couldn't get over how a little boy in a long white robe with blond hair, who accompanied the Madonna, looked so remarkably like herself. The beautiful child, Marie said, eventually told her he was her guardian angel but asked her to keep his name secret.

- Everyone thought Mike O'Donnell was drunk when he fell down as he hurriedly backpedaled in fear. However, the Irish farmer, who swore he didn't smoke or drink, insisted he had good reason. He was simply trying to escape from a statue of the Virgin Mary that had sprung to life and was heading straight toward him.

- On the evening of September 4, 1985 more than three thousand people came to an empty field in Carnes, Sligo County. They had heard about the apparitions to four girls just two nights before and were anxious to see Mary themselves. But at about 11 p.m., they got a lot more than they expected. Suddenly, an orange ball sped across the sky, witnesses said, as lights flashed and a cross formed out of a cloud. Then, as many remained mute, the Virgin Mary was seen walking towards the crowd. She eventually disappeared, people said, but a fragrance of roses remained in the air.

In keeping with the history of such events over the last two hundred years, many of the stories continued to also reveal a more serious side to the events. At Melleray Grotto in southeastern Ireland, the Virgin again introduced herself by miraculously springing to life from a statue. Although no one fell over, people laughed. But when two young cousins, Tom and Barry Cliffe, insisted the Virgin was sad and begging for prayer, the laughter stopped. Indeed, strange stories from the children about profound biblical visions of Jesus and His Apostles, and Noah and his Ark left everyone alarmed and puzzled. But most curiously, the two boys insisted Mary told them the world had **"only ten years left to improve."**

Across the island, another urgent message emerged when a young housewife named Christina Gallagher reported a life-changing experience. While visiting a grotto in County Sligo, Ireland, in the fall of 1985, Christina unexpectedly witnessed with her own eyes the Head of Jesus crowned with thorns. Unknown to her, this apparition would actually begin a series of miraculous events in her life, events she could not have imagined. Before long, besides encounters with the Virgin Mary and apparitions of Christ, the simple Irish homemaker said she was being shown extraordinary, mystical, and heavenly sights. From awesome glimpses of the Face of the Eternal

Father in Heaven to terrorizing experiences with the Prince of Darkness in her own home, Christina's breathtaking accounts were beyond words. Within a short time, a considerable number of messages for the Church and the world were reported by Christina. She was to be, the revelations indicated, a **"fearless witness"** to a **"misguided and sinful generation."** Soon the young woman's body would also reveal the stigmata and all the world would come to hear her story. But it was a story few were ready to fully embrace, for Christina Gallagher said she was told a time of divine justice was near, a frightful time of purification. The fulfillment of the age approached, Mary told the Irish woman, and by the end of the century God would cleanse the world.

These reports were baffling and intriguing, for a nation known for shamrocks and leprechauns was having a difficult time convincing the world such events were not just more Irish folklore. Fortunately for the Irish, they weren't the only ones having trouble with their eyes in the early 1980's.

In Eastern Europe, millions flocked to the tiny mountain village of Medjugorje in the former Yugoslavia, where six children had reported visions of the Gospa (Madonna) since June 24, 1981. Down the road in the rural Herzegovina hamlets of Izbicno and Gala, more people were seeing the Virgin—as were folks in Kureschek, Slovenia; Litminova, Czechoslovakia; Chotyneu, Poland; and in villages and hamlets from Hungary to Rumania.

Western Europe was no different. Crowds flocked to rural places like El Escorial, Spain, and Oliveto Citra, Italy, and to major metropolitan areas including London, Paris, and Madrid, where apparitions, weeping statues, and unexplainable phenomena were attracting attention.

Even in the Soviet Union, reports of strange sightings of the Virgin Mary began to leak out. In a little Ukrainian village named Hrushiv, where Mary had appeared once before in 1914, an estimated half-million people reportedly witnessed the Madonna floating above a church. Some of them were allegedly KGB and high-ranking communist military officers. Shooting at the visions did little good, as one assailant was struck unconscious, reportedly stunned by an invisible force.

By the mid-1980s, the "silly season" was on the way to becoming the "silly decade," as reports were flooding in from all over

Europe, from France to Switzerland, from Germany to Croatia, from Lithuania to Malta—every week brought another surprise. Brown estimated at least 40 different countries since 1985. As in Ireland, people throughout Europe were claiming they saw visions and unexplainable phenomena. And like the Irish, they were also extremely animated and concerned, not just because of what they saw, but most of all because of what they heard. For almost everywhere, visionaries said the Virgin Mary was talking about history taking a surprising turn.

"This is my year, and my times have come!" the Virgin Mary told nine year-old Andrijana Bocina on March 18, 1988 in Split, Croatia. Like little Andrijana, those who claimed to see and hear the Virgin Mary in the 1980's said she brought important news. It was news about the future of the world as had been revealed at Fatima in 1917.

It was a future, visionaries throughout Europe repeated during the 1980's, that included surprises and startling events. Some of them were secret events, the visionaries in Medjugorje said. So secret that Mary told them that what was to come, the world "**could not even imagine**."

CHAPTER TWELVE

THE MOTHER OF GOD IS VISITING EARTH

"Behold, the virgin shall be with child and bear a son."

—Mt 1:23

When the apparitions began in 1981, few had heard of Medjugorje or where it was in Bosnia, Herzegovina. The passing years have made a big difference. More than 25 million people have traveled to Medjugorje, making it one of the most visited Marian sites in the world. Now, most everyone knows of Bosnia, where a violent clash of religions and ethnic groups has also captured the world's attention. It has become the Holocaust of the 90's, tragically characterized by war, rape, ethnic cleansing, genocide, and fratricidal hatred.

According to the visionaries there, it is the reason Mary has come now. Forces of evil seek to control the world and bring misery to places like Bosnia. This is what people must realize, the visionaries say Mary explained, that what is occurring in Bosnia could quickly spread.

All this is taking place, the Virgin Mary also told the children, because Satan has enticed the world to love sin over God. And the price of that choice is misery, suffering, and death. Through deception, the devil has also convinced the world that he and his demonic followers do not exist. As a result, the world is falling deeper and deeper into the abyss as the decisive confrontation between good and evil draws near. Pope John Paul II has cited this reality several times in his talks, hoping as Mary does through her apparitions, to awaken the world to the reality of the invisible dimension of evil and to the spiritual war that is unfolding.

Indeed, those who studied the Virgin Mary's messages of the last two centuries are probably the only ones who appreciated the title, *The Land of the Demons,* for the 1993 ABC News documentary on the Bosnian war. This is because the whole world *is* at war with demons, not just in Bosnia. And Mary began to immediately explain this years ago when she first appeared in Medjugorje. In fact, Marian apparition followers will tell you without reservation: if you want to know the real message the Virgin Mary now brings to the world through her miraculous interventions, if you want to know what 200 years of apparitions and heavenly revelations have been all about, then set your attention on the story of Medjugorje.

It was June 24, 1981. Grandmothers walked through the village streets alongside their ox carts, scattering farm animals in their path. It seemed like any other day, even though at 1 o'clock that morning, some thought Judgment Day had arrived in Medjugorje.

A violent rainstorm brought hail stones, lightning, and fires. It was the talk of the village later that morning as people hurried along their way. No one could have imagined what was about to happen. That evening, events would unfold in Bijakovici, a rural hamlet like Medjugorje, which sits at the foot of a mountain named Krizevac.

The day was tranquil despite the previous night, but for two young girls it would be a day like no other. Fifteen year-old Ivanka Ivankovic and 16 year-old Mirjana Dragicevic were on summer vacation at their grandparent's house. As was their habit, the girls went for an evening walk on a small hill named Podbrdo. Suddenly, Ivanka looked up, and there in the distance she noticed something odd, something luminous that looked like the figure of a woman.

"Mirjana, look, there... .It's the Gospa [Madonna]!" she exclaimed.

"Don't be idiotic," Mirjana replied.

A second later, fear gripped them both, and they raced down the hill. After spotting their friend, Milka Pavlovic, they regained their strength and returned. Again, they saw the mysterious shimmering figure. After a while, it beckoned to them, along with several others who arrived, including two 16 year-olds, Vicka Ivankovic and Ivan Dragicevic. No one dared approach.

That night, word spread through the village, which was ablaze with talk. Iva Vasilj, the wife of a peasant farmer, offered a personal interpretation: "Ahhh, so that's why all that thunder and lightning last night. The Mother of God is visiting earth."

She probably was right. There were many different reactions. Some favorable, some not. However, the presence of Ivan Dragicevic added credibility to the story because he was known as being trustworthy and straightforward. Marenko Ivankovic, a mechanic who lived next door to one of the children, noted, "Ivan's a sensible boy. I'd trust his word."

The next day, after much discussion, the young people decided to return. Something, they said, beckoned them back. Mirjana and Ivanka were there, along with another girl, Marija Pavlovic, who was Milka's sister. Milka did not return. Vicka Ivankovic returned with a 10 year-old boy named Jacov Colo.

Suddenly, the glowing apparition appeared, and the figure beckoned them. This time, instead of fleeing, the children raced towards it, "as though we had wings, in spite of the sharp stones and brambles," recalled Marija.

The children seemed to fly up the hillside toward the Virgin, who appeared in a mist. When the vapor cleared, all six could clearly see her, all of her. To each of them, she was breathtaking! Mary wore, they said, a long shimmering gray dress and a white veil. She glowed like the sun, and she didn't hesitate to speak to the children, answering their questions and allaying their fears.

"Dear Madonna," said Mirjana, "they won't believe us, you know. They'll say we're mad." The Virgin reportedly smiled; as if she knew what was to come.

Indeed, the response was unprecedented. By the third day, several thousand people were climbing Podbrdo. The curious and the pious. People who had nothing better to do. The children returned, too.

Once again, the six visionaries raced up the hill and stopped suddenly. Together, at the same time, they dropped to their knees. In keeping with a plan they had devised, Vicka threw salt and holy water at the apparition and said, "If you really are the Madonna, please stay with us. But if you are not, go away and leave us alone."

Mary smiled. She didn't move.

"Who are you?" the children asked.

"I am the Blessed Virgin Mary."

"And why have you come here?"

"I have chosen this place specially because there are many faithful believers here."

Then, the visionaries said the Madonna told them to stand and join her in prayer. The children recited seven Our Father's, seven Hail Mary's and seven Gloria's. At Mary's request, they added the Creed.

The entire crowd joined them. Before leaving, the visionaries said Mary told them she would return the following day at the original location farther down the hill. **"Go in the peace of God,"** she reportedly said, and with that, the Virgin vanished.

After the third apparition, Marija Pavlovic, acting on an impulse, descended by a separate path, and Mary suddenly appeared again to her.

"Peace. Peace. You must seek peace," Marija said the Madonna said to her, **"You must be reconciled with God and with each other. Peace, Peace, Peace."** Then, as she has at so many other places, Mary cried.

"It was an overwhelming experience," said Marija. "I saw the Madonna weeping, and the sight drove me to commit myself totally to her request."

Perhaps it was a fitting request and response because in 1981, the world was more dangerous than ever. Mary Craig, in her book *Spark from Heaven*, shows that the Virgin's request to Marija reflected the political feeling of the times:

> Thus was the essence of the Medjugorje message revealed. The Madonna's desperate plea for peace would go echoing round a world which, in that summer of 1981, seemed to hover on the brink of self-destruction. Relations between the superpowers were at their lowest ebb; and there were real fears of a Soviet invasion of Poland—they had invaded Afghanistan the previous year—that might engulf the world in nuclear war. In those dark days, few people would have rated the chances for peace as being very high. Though the very idea chilled the blood, the time for building fallout shelters seemed to be at hand.

CHAPTER THIRTEEN

THE EPICENTER

"The woman herself fled into the desert, where a special place had been prepared for her by God."

—Rv 12:6

To Marian experts studying it all, it was clear. Besides leaving warnings, the Virgin Mary had come to help build something: a new world, she told the children at Medjugorje. It was to be a world, she reportedly said, that would witness her Triumph as foretold at Fatima. But what remained to be seen was how radical the coming changes would need to be. This was because the entire planet was a cauldron of brewing hostilities between people and nations and, as Mary said at Medjugorje, Yugoslavia was a microcosm of it all.

Far from a melting pot, Yugoslavia was a tragic example of the conditions the Virgin Mary said in her visions that God deplored in the world. Serbs. Croats. Muslims. Three ethnic groups whose history had been a chronicle of constant animosity toward one another. Indeed, World War I had broken out in Yugoslavia. And by late 1994, geopolitical analysts were constantly reminding the world that this scenario could be repeated. The Balkans were still a tinder box as the war in Herzegovina so perfectly illustrated.

But the Medjugorje visionaries said that the Virgin kept reminding them that the world, itself, was also a tinder box and it was because of this she had come to Medjugorje in the first place. Peace in the world was threatened, and it was in Medjugorje, and places like this Herzegovina hamlet where Mary was also now appearing, that the world's fate could be determined. The Gospa wanted to make this little village, the visionaries said, an example of how true peace could, indeed, reign in all hearts.

So began the epicenter apparition of the late 20th century. For of all the apparitions of the 1980s and 1990s, Medjugorje, Marian experts concluded, was revealing itself to be the central apparition because it was so significant in every way. Medjugorje was unparalleled and incomparable, many said. Something beyond words.

In the history of Marian apparitions, there has never been anything like Medjugorje. Of the hundreds of apparitions since Fatima, none has had the power and impact of the events in Bosnia. Professor Frederick Copleston, the celebrated author of the nine-volume *History of Philosophy* declared that the apparitions in Medjugorje manifest "a pattern that is consistent with the activity of the Divine in human history."

Indeed, and Mary reportedly set the tone from the beginning: **"I am here to call the world to conversion for the last time,"** the visionaries said the Madonna proclaimed. **"After this period, I will not appear anymore on earth."**

In his book *The Final Hour,* author Michael Brown summarized the extraordinary events of Medjugorje:

> It was like the end of a long day, an hour before midnight. It was our spiritual entrance into a new era and time to break the power of Satan. She had come, along with the most extraordinary supernatural signs she'd ever displayed, to renew the diminishing faith not just of Catholicism but of all religions.
>
> Pray, she implored pilgrims, pray for as long as possible every day. Prayer is the manna that will sustain mankind, and the Rosary should be said by everyone no matter what religion or beliefs they hold.
>
> She called for Judeo-Christian unity and said that while not all religions are equal, all people are equal before God. It is not God but mankind who created religious divisions. **"You are not true**

Christians," she said, **"if you do not respect other religions."**

Moslems, Jews, and Protestants were equally touched by Medjugorje. Bring harmony, Mary begged, peace and harmony. She made clear that she wasn't there to usurp the power of her Son. **"There is only one mediator between God and man, and it is Jesus Christ,"** she said, adding that Jesus preferred His people to address themselves directly to Him.

But in the meantime, she'd come as a confidant and protector. She also came as a spiritual advisor. **"Keep the faith, fast, and pray. Advance against Satan by means of prayer. Satan wants to work still more now that you know he is at work. Dear children, put on the armor for battle and with the Rosary in your hand defeat him!"**

Especially it was in the Book of Revelation. Unless it was all a grand hoax, we were nearing the end of Chapter 12 and approaching Chapter 13. Mary, persecuted by the dragon, had flown to her place in the wilderness, and the war, engaged by her and the Archangel Michael with Satan, was reaching a critical juncture. The chastisements, warded off, were now looming larger than ever. **"You must warn the bishop very soon, and the Pope,"** she said in 1983. The war's greatest battle was about to unfold. The visionaries were given secrets, secrets that pertained to the future of the Church and mankind in general.

But the apparitions at Medjugorje haven't been all smooth sailing. Opposition and controversy have persisted every step of the way. The local bishop, Bishop Zanic, the communists, and various forces have contributed to the situation. Add to this, the war in Bosnia, and it is apparent that Medjugorje has been tested, coming precariously close to destruction in more ways than one.

Somehow, however, it has survived and flourished. Bishop Zanic and his investigative commission were dismissed. Likewise, the communists. And the war stayed away from Medjugorje. Even Serbian pilots reportedly said that the village mysteriously disappeared from their radar screens during bombing missions.

And despite the war, pilgrims traveled there. Even at its height, people continued to go to Medjugorje. It has been that way since the beginning. Millions trek there, including thousands of Americans during the 1980's who never dreamed of visiting a communist nation, yet alone one that was a dangerous war zone. Most significantly, St. James church in Medjugorje has over 50,000 priests registered on its rolls as having been there since 1981.

Author Mary Craig writes about this phenomenon:

> But nothing seemed to deter the people from coming. They came by car, by public transport or on foot. Long-distance coaches were coming in, not only from other regions of Yugoslavia—and with many Orthodox and Muslims among them now—but also from Italy, where priests connected with the radical youth movement Comunione e Liberzione had begun organizing pilgrimages. Hard on their heels came groups from Austria, Germany and Switzerland. They were given a warm welcome by the villagers. "They came morning and night," said Vicka.

While the Madonna and Medjugorje are the story, so too are the six visionaries. Not since the three children at Fatima has the world been so taken with such personalities. Four of the six seers claim to have seen the Virgin Mary daily for almost two decades. Theologians say it has been an unprecedented occurrence. Consequently, what these young people see and experience is something the world cannot get enough of. Like celebrities, the visionaries of Medjugorje are in constant demand. Marian experts believe this is because they have an understanding of Mary's words which many hunger to hear.

From the very beginning, the message of Medjugorje has been evangelical and centered around the Virgin's call to peace in people, families, nations, and the world. Mary's messages acknowledge that humanity has fashioned weapons of immense destruction. They also acknowledge that mankind has forgotten and neglected its alliance with God and obedience to God's laws. They point to the reality that most of the world denies the spiritual dimension of humanity. Likewise, the messages indicate that natural and moral values have disappeared. Materialism and sensuality and technological progress have become the world's focus, all to the detriment of millions who are suffering and dying both physically and spiritually.

The messages of Medjugorje address all these themes; the Virgin Mary, for many years, has reportedly pleaded for a change of heart, often as she first did at La Salette, with tears. At Medjugorje, the visionaries report that Mary pleads for love, for forgiveness, and for repentance. They say the Virgin tells her children about the reality of evil, Satan, and Hell. Most of all, they say the Gospa tells the world about her Son, Jesus Christ, and how He, and only He, is the hope of the world's future—that He is the key to it all. That is why she has come, and that is what people want to know as they flock to hear the visionaries speak.

Nothing is conclusive about the future, the visionaries say at Medjugorje. Nothing is etched in stone. However, **"Evil will come if the world does not convert,"** Mary reportedly told the visionaries, **"Call the world to conversion."**

Indeed, there is extreme urgency in the messages of Medjugorje. Even though miracles abound in the stars and sun in the Bosnian hamlet, and numerous healings and conversions continue to be reported, the seers say that Mary cautions that only so much time will be allotted.

"It is necessary for the world to be saved, while there is still time, for it to pray strongly, and for the world to have the spirit of faith" (Nov. 29, 1981).

The "time factor" in so many of the Virgin Mary's messages everywhere in the last two decades is a mystery—for the urgency revolves around 10 secrets Mary is revealing to the visionaries concerning the future of the world, secrets that remind us of the Secret of Fatima and especially the message of Fatima. It was at Fatima that Mary urged the faithful to **"say the Rosary every day to obtain world peace."** But now, Mary is said to be asking for people to recite all 15 decades of the Rosary each day. Is it an ominous sign?

In fact, thousands of messages have been reportedly given by Mary at Medjugorje, where she pleads for conversion and begs for prayer, penance and peace. According to bishops and cardinals, and even Mary herself, these apparitions are the fulfillment of Fatima. Moreover, the apparitions provide the greatest apocalyptical messages of all times—messages that remain hidden in the 10 harrowing secrets to be unveiled in the future.

But for now, only the six visionaries at Medjugorje know what is to come—and when.

On March 18, 1989, the visionary's birthday, Mary reportedly told Mirjana Dragicevic Soldo, the oldest of the six visionaries: **"One more time I beseech all of you to pray, to help by your prayers the unbelievers, those who do not have the grace to experience God in their hearts with a living faith. I do not want to threaten again! My desire is just to warn you all as a mother. I beg you for people who do not know about the secrets...."**

CHAPTER FOURTEEN

THE FULFILLMENT OF FATIMA

"In the right hand of the One who sat on the throne, I saw a scroll. It had writing on both sides and was sealed with seven seals."

—Rv 5:1

The secrets. The visionaries at Medjugorje say the 10 secrets involve warnings, signs, and chastisements. And most curiously, their unfolding centers on the third secret about a great sign to appear in Medjugorje.

"Hasten your conversion," the Virgin reportedly told the visionaries, **"Do not await the sign which has been announced, for people who do not believe, it will be too late. You who believe, be converted and strengthen your faith"** (Spring 1983).

The sign, the secrets, the urgency is difficult to summarize adequately. In a way, though, one need not try because it has already been done. On Nov. 30, 1983, visionary Marija Pavlovic urged a letter be sent to the Pope. It was written by a Franciscan priest in Medjugorje, Fr. Tomislav Vlasic, on Dec. 2, 1983. Its purpose was to emphasize the urgency of the message of Medjugorje. The following is the full text of the correspondence:

> After the apparition of the Blessed Virgin on November 30, 1983, Marija Pavlovic came to see me and said, "The Madonna says that the Supreme Pontiff and the Bishop must be advised immediately of the urgency and great importance of the message of Medjugorje."

This letter seeks to fulfill that duty.

1. Five young people (Vicka Ivankovic, Marija Pavlovic, Ivanka Ivankovic, Ivan Dragicevic, and Jakov Colo) see an apparition of the Blessed Virgin every day. The experience in which they see her is a fact that can be checked by direct observation. It has been filmed. During the apparitions, the youngsters do not react to light, they do not hear sounds, they do not react if someone touches them, they feel that they are beyond time and space.

All of the youngsters basically agree that:

* We see the Blessed Virgin just as we see anyone else. We pray with her, we speak to her, and we can touch her.

* The Blessed Virgin says that world peace is at a critical stage. She repeatedly calls for reconciliation and conversion.

* She has promised to leave a visible sign for all humanity at the site of the apparitions at Medjugorje.

* The period preceding this visible sign is a time of grace for conversion and deepening of the faith.

* The Blessed Virgin has promised to disclose ten secrets to us. So far, Vicka Ivankovic has received eight. Marija Pavlovic received the ninth one on December 8, 1983. Jakov Colo, Ivan Dragicevic and Ivanka Ivankovic have each received nine. Only Mirjana Dragicevic has received all ten.

* These apparitions are the last apparitions of the Blessed Virgin on earth. That is why they are lasting so long and occurring so frequently.

2. The Blessed Virgin no longer appears to Mirjana Dragicevic. The last time she saw one of the daily apparitions was Christmas, 1982. Since then, the apparitions have ceased for her, except on her birthday (March 18th). Mirjana knew that this latter would occur.

According to Mirjana, the Madonna confided

the tenth and last secret to her during the apparition of December 25, 1982. She also disclosed the dates on which the different secrets will come to pass. The Blessed Virgin has revealed to Mirjana many things about the future, more than to any of the other youngsters so far. For that reason I am reporting below what Mirjana told me during our conversation on November 5, 1983:

Before the visible sign is given to humanity, there will be three warnings to the world. The warnings will be in the form of events on earth. Mirjana will be a witness to them. Three days before one of the admonitions, Mirjana will notify a priest of her choice. The witness of Mirjana will be a confirmation of the apparitions and a stimulus for the conversion of the world.

After the admonitions, the visible sign will appear on the site of the apparitions in Medjugorje for all the world to see. The sign will be given as a testimony to the apparitions and in order to call people back to faith.

The ninth and tenth secrets are serious. They concern chastisement for the sins of the world. Punishment is inevitable, for we cannot expect the whole world to be converted. The punishment can be diminished by prayer and penance, but it cannot be eliminated. Mirjana says that one of the evils that threatened the world, the one contained in the seventh secret, has been averted thanks to prayer and fasting. That is why the Blessed Virgin continues to encourage prayer and fasting: **"You have forgotten that through prayer and fasting you can avert war and suspend the laws of nature."**

After the first admonition, the others will follow in a rather short time. Thus, people will have some time for conversion.

That interval will be a period of grace and conversion. After the visible sign appears, those who are still alive will have little time for conversion. For that reason, the Blessed Virgin invites us to urgent conversion and reconciliation.

The invitation to prayer and penance is meant to avert evil and war, but most of all to save souls.

According to Mirjana, the events predicted by the Blessed Virgin are near. By virtue of this experience, Mirjana proclaims to the world: **"Hurry, be converted; open your hearts to God."**

In addition to this basic message, Mirjana related an apparition she had in 1982 which we believe sheds some light on some aspects of Church history. She spoke of an apparition in which Satan appeared to her disguised as the Blessed Virgin. Satan asked Mirjana to renounce the Madonna and follow him. That way she could be happy in love and in life. He said that following the Virgin, on the contrary, would only lead to suffering. Mirjana rejected him, and immediately the Virgin arrived and Satan disappeared. Then the Blessed Virgin gave her the following message, in substance:

"Excuse me for this, but you must realize that Satan exists. One day he appeared before the

throne of God and asked permission to submit the Church to a period of trial. God gave him permission to try the Church for one century. This century is under the power of the devil, but when the secrets confided to you come to pass, his power will be destroyed. Even now he is beginning to lose his power and has become aggressive. He is destroying marriages, creating division among priests and is responsible for obsessions and murder. You must protect yourselves against these things through fasting and prayer, especially community prayer. Carry blessed objects with you. Put them in your house, and restore the use of holy water."

According to certain Catholic experts who have studied these apparitions, this message of Mirjana may shed light on the vision Pope Leo XIII had. According to them, it was after having had an apocalyptic vision of the future of the Church that Leo XIII introduced the prayer to Saint Michael which priests used to recite after Mass up to the time of the Second Vatican Council. These experts say that the century of trials foreseen by Leo XIII is about to end.

Holy Father, I do not want to be responsible for the ruin of anyone. I am doing my best. The world is being called to conversion and reconciliation. In writing to you, Holy Father, I am only doing my duty. After drafting this letter, I showed it to the youngsters so that they might ask the Blessed Virgin whether its contents are accurate. Ivan Dragicevic relayed the following answer: "Yes, the contents of the letter are the truth. You must notify first of all the Supreme Pontiff and then the bishop."

This letter is accompanied by fasting and prayers that the Holy Spirit will guide your mind and your heart during this important moment in history.

Yours in the Sacred Hearts of Jesus and Mary,

Father Tomislav Vlasic

Father Vlasic's letter succinctly summarized the message and urgency of Medjugorje as did the Virgin in a reported message at Medjugorje on Aug. 25, 1991, when Mary reportedly stated to the visionaries she had come to fulfill what she began **"through the secrets at Fatima."** Whether or not Pope John Paul II received or ever responded to Vlasic's letter is unknown. But on May 13, 1981, just six weeks before the apparitions at Medjugorje began, a Turkish man named Mehmet Ali Agca attempted to assassinate Pope John Paul II in St. Peter's Square. The fact that this dark event occurred on the anniversary of the first apparition at Fatima (May 13, 1917) immediately brought to attention Fatima's message (**"The Holy Father will have much to suffer."**) and according to the Pope himself, the importance of Mary's warnings there.

As he recovered in the hospital, Pope John Paul II called for the "Third Secret of Fatima" to be brought to him and subsequently, this led him to consecrate the world to the Immaculate Heart of Mary on May 13, 1982, and then again on March 25, 1984, this time in union the bishops. The 1984 consecration, according to several published interviews with Sr. Lucia, "fulfilled" Mary's 1917 announcement at Fatima for the consecration of Russia and her specific request for this act to Sister Lucia in 1929. Just one month after the 1984 consecration, Mikhail Gorbachev came to power in the USSR and his policies of Perestroika and Glasnost led to the collapse of communism and the dissolution of the Soviet Union. Not surprisingly, many believe that perhaps the message of Medjugorje had its effect in some way on this issue.

But Medjugorje is more. More than its message. More than the secrets. More than the supernatural. Medjugorje is the experience, people say, the unbelievable experience.

Indeed, the experience of Medjugorje is legendary. Most pilgrims who go there are convinced it is unlike any other place in the world.

A professor from Dusseldorf said, "I have traveled the whole world, and I have never seen people like this. They are alive."

Others agree. Eminent theologian Fr. Rene Laurentin reported the following comments in one of his books on Medjugorje: "At Medjugorje, I did not see the face of the Virgin, but I saw her reflection in the face of the people there. I do not know if Our Lady appeared to the young people, but I see that she has appeared to the world." And "if Our Lady has not appeared there, the receptive atmosphere will make her appear."

Millions appear to concur with these types of statements. That's why not even Bosnia's war could stop the people from coming to Medjugorje. The village, Marian experts say, is an oasis of peace. A peace, according to the visionaries at Medjugorje, that the people of the world are desperately searching for and that God desperately wants to help them find through the prophets of our times.

One such other prophet, a little Italian priest named Father Stefano Gobbi, reported in 1973 that he was receiving messages through interior locutions from Mary, too, about the "end times." The messages, he disclosed, were at the heart of what Mary revealed at Fatima. They involved the secrets and mysteries behind our times and even the Book of Revelation.

Over the next 25 years, Fr. Gobbi was sent to almost every continent, every nation, to sound the alarm. And those who have studied private revelations believe, that like Medjugorje, the messages of Fr. Gobbi hold the key to understanding what lies ahead.

St. James Church in Medjugorje, Hercegovina

*Over 25 million people are estimated to have gone
to Medjugorje since 1981. Ten secret messages
are to be given to each of the six visionaries there.*

CHAPTER FIFTEEN

AN APOCALYPTIC MESSAGE?

"Will not the day of the Lord be darkness and not light, gloom from any brightness?"

—Am 5:20

If Mary came to Medjugorje in 1981 to "conclude the end times" and to bring fulfillment to the message of Fatima, it is equally clear God sent her to an unremarkable priest in Italy eight years before to firmly reiterate just exactly what Fatima's message was.

Like bookends that go together, experts in private revelation agree that to understand the times at hands, one must view these two supernatural interventions of the late 20th century together. Together they tighten the tapestry of God's work throughout the world, allowing a picture to emerge that is easy to understand even for the most novice of the faithful.

The extraordinary messages to Father Stefano Gobbi began in the summer of 1973. Many say it's hard to imagine how God could have chosen such a soul for His work since the sedate, bald cleric hardly conjures up images of what would typify a visionary of such prominence. Rather, Fr. Gobbi appears to resemble a passive spectator, rotund and seemingly frivolous, unlikely to be involved with anything so serious. But those who understand the ways of God say it was probably these characteristics and a few more like them that led God to choose this jovial priest from north of Milan, Italy.

Indeed, of all God's present day prophets, Fr. Gobbi has received messages from heaven that are among the most profound ever given.

Fr. Gobbi was 42 years old when he received his first "interior locution." He entered the priesthood late in life and was ordained in 1964 after jobs in real estate and insurance. Then, in 1973, his life radically changed. After the priest received a sign, he was led to understand the Virgin Mary's messages to him were intended especially for priests. Consequently, the Marian Movement of Priests was born, and in 20 years, the organization has attracted tens of thousands of priests, bishops, and cardinals, as well as millions of laity worldwide.

For years, Fr. Gobbi traveled the world continuously, holding cenacles and prayer retreats. He was tireless. He visited almost every country in the world, moving constantly forward toward the approaching fulfillment of the times. It is a fulfillment that appears to have unfolded step by step in Mary's messages to him.

Fr. Gobbi's messages are considered extraordinary, far beyond what most visionaries receive. Most of all, the messages were directly linked to the Virgin's words at Fatima. It was in Portugal at Fatima's Chapel of the Apparitions where Fr. Gobbi first experienced an "interior force" and then the inspiration to begin his work. Soon, Mary was giving him messages that were profound, startling and immensely prophetic.

The times at hand, Mary's messages to Fr. Gobbi explained, are described in the Book of Revelation. Other messages foretold with astonishing accuracy the unfolding of human events over the last three decades, events such as the fall of communism in Eastern Europe and the dismantling of the Soviet Union. From AIDS to a coming conversion of Japan to Christianity, Mary's prophecies to Fr. Gobbi are overwhelming in their detail. Mary has even reportedly revealed in her messages the contents of the Third Part of the Secret of Fatima to him (see Chapter 41), something the world anxiously awaited until 1960, but which was never disclosed.

But more than anything else, Mary's messages to Father Stefano Gobbi have significantly defined how the invisible world is wreaking havoc on the visible world, how the tragic events of this century can only be correctly understood in spiritual terms, and how the foretold climax of this period, the apostasy predicted at Fatima in the revealed portion of the Third Secret, is now visible for all to see.

Indeed, the very basis for the messages appears to be this apostasy, especially in the priesthood. Curiously, Father Gobbi had gone to Fatima on pilgrimage that first day and was praying for some priests who, besides having personally given up their vocations, were attempting to form themselves into associations in rebellion against Church authority.

Noting her revelations at La Salette to Melanie Calvat and Maximin Giraud in 1846, the Virgin Mary's messages to Fr. Gobbi explained that the world has truly witnessed over the last two centuries what was foretold at La Salette. The many wars and the great genocide, the messages state, speaks for itself as confirmation. Likewise, the gradual escalation of the power of evil in the world, as foretold at La Salette, is undeniably visible for anyone who has any spiritual sense.

According to Marian writers and theologians, Father Gobbi's messages also crystalize the story of the century long reign of Satan. The following message from the Virgin Mary to Father Gobbi illustrates this point:

This is a plan which embraces this century. In 1917 at Fatima, I anticipated it, as in a prophetic announcement, at the moment when the great struggle between the Woman Clothed with the Sun and the Red Dragon became evident, a struggle which was to last throughout the whole century, as a proud challenge to God on the part of my Adversary, who was certain that he would succeed in destroying the Church and in bringing all humanity to a universal rejection of God. The Lord has granted him this space of time, because in the end the pride of the Red Dragon will be broken and conquered by the humility, the littleness, and the power of your heavenly Mother, the Woman Clothed with the Sun, who is now gathering all her little children into her army, drawn up for battle.

In lieu of this understanding, Mary's messages to Fr. Gobbi have defined what had to and what must still occur. They reveal how human events are unfolding in fulfillment of prophetic portions of Scripture, especially the long awaited "Great Tribulation" described in Luke and Matthew. The messages also illuminate the spiritual basis of all human conflict and intimately reveal how Masonic forces, communism, and Mary's many apparitions are all part of the Book of Revelation's symbolic account of the great struggle long foretold to come between the forces of good and the forces of evil, both visible and invisible. Mary's messages also explained to Father Gobbi the meaning behind some of the Book of Revelation's great symbolism.

The huge Red Dragon described in Revelation, one message stated, was atheistic communism. It's goal was to spread the error of the denial and of the obstinate rejection of God. Through theoretical and practical atheism, it seeks to lead humanity to disobey the Ten Commandments of God and to build a new civilization without God. It would be a hedonistic, materialistic, egoistic, and cold civilization which carried the seeds of corruption and death. The Red Dragon's color was red because it used blood and war as instruments of its numerous conquests.

The Beast like a Leopard in the Book of Revelation was Freemasonry, Mary's messages revealed. This beast acted in the shadows to obstruct souls from God. Its aim was to blaspheme God, his dwelling place, and all who dwell in heaven. It also sought to deny God his worship and to prevent souls from being saved. Mary even explained to Father Gobbi how through Freemasonry, the Beast had set up laws completely opposed to the Ten Commandments:

> To the Commandment of the Lord: 'You shall not have any other God but me,' it builds other false idols, before which many today prostrate themselves in adoration.
>
> To the Commandment: 'You shall not take the name of God in vain,' it sets itself up in opposition by blaspheming God and his Christ, in many subtle and diabolical ways, even to reducing his Name indecorously to the level of a brand-name of an object of sale and of producing sacrilegious films concerning his life and his divine Person.
>
> To the Commandment: 'Remember to keep holy the Sabbath Days,' it transforms the Sunday into

a weekend, into a day of sorts, of competitions and of entertainments.

To the Commandment: 'Honor the father and your mother,' it opposes a new model of family based on cohabitation, even between homosexuals.

To the Commandment: 'You shall not commit impure acts,' it justifies, exalts, and propagates every form of impurity, even to the justification of acts against nature.

To the Commandment: 'You shall not kill,' it has succeeded in making abortion legal everywhere, in making euthanasia acceptable, and in causing respect due to the value of human life to all but disappear.

To the Commandment: 'You shall not steal,' it works to the end that theft, violence, kidnapping, and robbery spread more and more.

To the Commandment: 'You shall not bear false witness,' acts in such a way that the laws of deceit, lying, and duplicity becomes more and more propagated.

To the Commandment: 'You shall not covet the goods and the wife of another,' it works to corrupt in the depths of the conscience, betraying the mind and the heart of man.

It was in this way, the messages revealed, that souls become driven along the perverse and wicked road of disobedience to the laws of the Lord, become submerged in sin and are thus prevented from receiving the gift of grace and the life of God. The messages also explained how the Beast like a Leopard (Freemasonry) opposes the seven theological and cardinal virtues:

To the seven theological and cardinal virtues, which are the fruits of living in the grace of God, Freemasonry counters with the diffusion of *the seven capital vices,* which are the fruit of living habitually in the state of sin. To faith it opposes pride; to hope lust; to charity, avarice; to

prudence, anger; to fortitude, sloth; to justice, envy; to temperance, gluttony.

Whoever becomes a victim of the seven capital vices, said Gobbi, is gradually led to take away the worship that is due to God alone in order to give it to false divinities, who are the very personification of all these vices. And in this, he said, consists the greatest and most horrible blasphemy.

CHAPTER SIXTEEN

A SIGN FOR ALL

"Woe to those who are wise in their own sight."

— Is 5:21

But although communism and Masonry have wreaked havoc throughout the world over the last two centuries, the element of this mystery that brings the world nearer to its date with destiny, the messages to Fr. Gobbi reveal, is another symbolic creature contained in the Book of Revelation. This is the Mystery of the Beast like a Lamb.

This beast represents Ecclesiastical Masonry, which has spread, according to Fr. Gobbi's messages, among the members of the hierarchy of the Church. This masonic infiltration in the interior of the Church was warned of, Gobbi says, in Mary's message at Fatima. Its purpose is singular: to destroy Christ and His Church and to build a new idol, namely a false church and a false christ. Initiated centuries ago by the atheist philosophers of the Renaissance period, it seeks to do this by slowly dismantling the foundation of the unity of the Church through an insidious attack on the Pope. It weaves, the messages disclosed, plots of dissension and contestation against him, and it supports and rewards those who vilify and oppose the Holy Father. This is done, said Gobbi, by disseminating the criticisms and the contestation of bishops and theologians.

All of this, Mary's messages to Gobbi reveal, has contributed to the apostasy foretold at Fatima. Yes, a great apostasy is at hand, however, this is not just another apostasy, the messages explained. Rather, it was Scripture's "Great Apostasy," long expected by every generation. If one understood the "signs of the times," Gobbi said, then this truth would be undeniable.

This leaves us at a very argumentable state, for many theological experts argue that this reality of the "end times according to the signs" has been misunderstood many times before throughout history. But before, said Gobbi, not all the signs were present together. This is the defining ingredient now, for "all" the signs are present, just as Scripture promised.

Indeed, many Christians of different denominations concur. In a world-wide telecast on February 5, 1998, Billy Graham, the international Protestant evangelist, noted that he believed the reality of the fulfillment of this Scriptural prophecy was presently at hand: "For the first time in history," said Graham to CNN host Larry King, "all the signs are happening together—right now."

No words more adequately summarize this than Mary's message to Father Gobbi on December 31, 1992. In this message, Mary explained all the signs and why they are now present. Most significantly, the message noted the extraordinary significance of Fatima, and how Fatima's message is to be fulfilled. Here is the complete text of Mary's message to Father Gobbi on that day. It is the quintessence of her revelations, summarizing all that has been revealed and foretold, and is titled *The End Times*:

With docility, allow yourselves to be taught by me, beloved children. On this last night of the year, gather together in prayer and in listening to the word of your heavenly Mother, the Prophetess of these last times.

Do not spend these hours noisily in dissipation, but in silence, in recollection, and in contemplation.

I have announced to you many times that *the end of the times* and the coming of Jesus in glory is very near. Now, I want to help you understand the signs described in the Holy Scriptures, which indicate that his glorious return is now close.

These signs are clearly indicated in the Gospels, in the letters of Saint Peter and Saint

Paul, and they are becoming a reality during these years.

-*The first sign is the spread of errors*, which lead to the loss of faith and to apostasy.

These errors are being propagated by false teachers, by renowned theologians who are no longer teaching the truths of the Gospel, but pernicious heresies based on errors and on human reasoning. It is because of the teaching of these errors that the true faith is being lost and that the great apostasy is spreading everywhere.

See that no one deceives you. For many will attempt to deceive many people. False prophets will come and will deceive very many. (Mt 24, 4-5)

'The day of the Lord will not come unless the great apostasy comes first." (2 Thes 2,3)

"There will be false teachers among you. These will seek to introduce disastrous heresies and will even set themselves against the Master who ransomed them. Many will listen to them and will follow their licentious ways. Through their offense, the Christian faith will be reviled. In their greed, they will exploit you with fabrications.' (2 Pt 2, 1-3)

-*The second sign is the outbreak of wars and fratricidal struggles*, which lead to the prevalence of violence and hatred and a general slackening off of charity, while natural catastrophes, such as epidemics, famines, floods and earthquakes, become more and more frequent.

'When you hear of reports of wars, close at hand or far away, see that you are not alarmed; for these things must happen. Nation will rise against nation, and kingdom against kingdom. There will be famines and earthquakes in many places. All this will be only the beginning of greater sufferings to come. Evil doing will be widespread that the love of many will grow cold. But God will save those who persevere until the end." (Mt 24,6-8.12-13)

-*The third sign is the bloody persecution* of those who remain faithful to Jesus and to his Gospel and who stand fast in the true faith. Throughout this all, the Gospel will be preached in every part of the world.

Think, beloved children, of the great persecutions to which the Church is being subjected; think of the apostolic zeal of the recent popes, above all of my Pope, John Paul II, as he brings to all the nations of the earth the announcement of the Gospel.

'They will hand you over to persecution and they will kill you. You will be hated by all because of me. And then many will abandon the faith; they will betray and hate one another. Meanwhile, the message of the kingdom of God will be preached in all the world; all nations must hear it. And then the end will come.' (Mt 24,9-10.14)

-*The fourth sign is the horrible sacrilege,* perpetrated by him who sets himself against Christ, that is, the Antichrist. He will enter into the holy temple of God and will sit on his throne, and have himself adored as God.

'This one will oppose and exalt himself against everything that men adore and call God. The lawless one will come by the power of Satan, with all the force of false miracles and pretended wonders. He will make use of every kind of wicked deception, in order to work harm. (2 Thes 2.4.9)

One day, you will see in the holy place he who commits *the horrible sacrilege.* The prophet Daniel spoke of this. Let the reader seek to understand.' (Mt 24,15)

Beloved children, in order to understand in what this *horrible sacrilege* consists, read what has been predicted by the prophet Daniel: 'Go, Daniel; these words are to remain secret and sealed upright, but the wicked will persist in doing wrong. Not one of the wicked will understand these things, but he wise will comprehend.

'Now, from the moment that the daily sacrifice is abolished and the horrible abomination is set up, there shall be one thousand two hundred and ninety days. Blessed is he who waits with patience and attains one thousand three hundred and thirty-five days.' (Dn 12,9-12)

The Holy Mass is the daily sacrifice, the pure oblation which is offered to the Lord everywhere, from the rising of the sun to its going down.

The sacrifice of the Mass renews that which was accomplished by Jesus on Calvary. By accepting the protestant doctrine, people will hold that the Mass is not a sacrifice but only a sacred meal, that is to say, a remembrance of what which Jesus did at his last supper. And thus, the celebration of Holy Mass will be suppressed. In this abolition of the daily sacrifice consists *the horrible sacrilege* accomplished by the Antichrist, which will last about three and a half years, namely, one thousand two hundred and ninety days.

-*The fifth sign consists in extraordinary phenomena,* which occur in the skies.

'The sun will be darkened and the moon will not give its light; and the stars will fall form the sky; and the powers of the heavens will be shaken.' (Mt 24,29)

The miracle of the sun, which took place at Fatima during my last apparition, is intended to point out to you that you are now entering into the times when these events will take place, events which will prepare for the return of Jesus in glory.

'And there the sign of the Son of Man will appear in Heaven. All the tribes of the earth will mourn, and men will see the Son of Man coming upon the clouds of heaven, with great power and splendor.' (Mt 24, 30)

My beloved ones and children consecrated to my Immaculate Heart, I have wanted to teach you about these signs, which Jesus has pointed out to you in his gospel, in order to prepare *for the end of times, because these are about to take place in your days.*

The year which is coming to a close, and that which is beginning, form part of the great tribulation, during which the apostasy is spreading, the wars are multiplying, natural catastrophes are occurring in many places, persecution are intensifying, the announcement of the Gospel is being brought to all nations, extraordinary phenomena are occurring in the sky, and the moment of the full manifestation of the Antichrist is drawing ever nearer.

And so I urge you to remain strong in the faith, secure in trust and ardent in charity. Allow yourselves to be led by me and gather together, each and all, in the sure refuge of my Immaculate Heart, which I have prepared for you especially during these last times. Read, with me, the signs of your time, and live in peace of heart and in confidence.

I am always with you, to tell you that the coming about of these signs indicates to you with certainty that *the end of the times,* with the return for Jesus in glory, is close at hand.

'Learn a lesson form the fig tree: when its branches become tender and sprout the first leaves, you know that summer is near. In the same way, when you see these things taking place, know

that your liberation is near (Mt 24,32-33).

In 1996, when Father Gobbi visited Zagreb, Croatia, not far from Bosnia and Medjugorje, he reported a message that told him the world needed to take notice of what happens when Scripture is ignored, when hate rules over love, and violence dismantles peace. When this occurs, Mary's message to Fr. Gobbi revealed, **"what has taken place in this country** (Bosnia) **becomes a sign for all"** (Sept. 20, 1996). The message also revealed that it was through Mary's intervention that peace was obtained in Bosnia. (Curiously, the Dayton Peace Accord, which brought to a close the fighting in Bosnia, was negotiated at Dayton University in Ohio, the site of the largest Marian Library in the world.) But Mary's message warned the holy priest, **"still graver tribulations are awaiting."** What are those tribulations? One of them is none other than what Mary has been warning of since Fatima in 1917—nuclear destruction.

On October 18, 1996, in the city of Nagasaki, Japan, where the second atomic bomb was dropped on August 9, 1945, another message from Mary made it clear to Father Gobbi that this danger, this threat, was still alive despite the fall of the Iron Curtain, despite the collapse of communism in the USSR and Eastern Europe. And it was at this time in history that the world desperately needed to recognize the looming presence of such a threat:

> *In this city (Nagasaki)* **there also exploded the atomic bomb, causing tens of thousands of deaths in a few brief instants, a chastisement and terrible sign of what man can do when distancing himself from God—he becomes incapable of love, of compassion and of mercy. This is what the whole world could become if it does not welcome my invitation to conversion and return to the Lord. From this place, I renew my anguished appeal to all the nations of the earth.**

Mary's anguished appeal through her interior locutions to Fr. Gobbi has, indeed, been unprecedented. But on December 31, 1997, another event occurred that was just as disconcerting as many of the messages given to the stoic little priest. The Virgin Mary announced

123

to Father Gobbi on that day that she had concluded her public mission through him and that all that could be said was now said.

CHAPTER SEVENTEEN

"I NEED YOUR PRAYERS"

"First of all, then, I ask that supplications, prayers, petitions and thanksgiving be offered for everyone."

— 1 Tm 2:1

As the sun is at the center of the solar system, many theologians believe Medjugorje is at the center of God's plan for the future of world. However, as in previous decades, there have been many more reported apparitions. Many of these "satellite" apparitions began to arise not long after Medjugorje began in 1981. Many of them also appear to support and echo the message of Medjugorje, while often revealing a local or national theme perhaps specifically designed to enhance God's call to all His people. This was true throughout the world in the 80's and 90's and especially in Europe.

Across Europe, apparitions and supernatural phenomena everywhere reinforced the century long build-up that was now reportedly headed to a climax. In Maasmechelen, Belgium, a head of Christ shed tears and tears of blood in 1984. In England, apparitions were reported to a woman in Subitron in 1983, and a statue of the infant Jesus wept on August 4, 1985. The visionary, a woman named Patricia, said that Christ and Mary were revealing to her that abortion and all merciless persecutions, which the revelations called "crucified innocence," were calling for God's justice. At Ohlau Poland on December 8, 1985, a village not far from Wroclaw-Breslau, a great miracle of the sun was reported to have occurred in the presence of 40,000 people who had gathered there. The visionary, Casimierz Domanski said that Mary requested a chapel, and also warned of **"three days of darkness."** Mary was reported in France at La TalaudieËe (1981), Kernequez (1984), Montipinchon (1984), Beaumone-du-Ventou (1990) and Holving (1991). In Belgium, visions were reported at Verviers (1986) and at Arc-Watriponx (1993). There were reports in Spain. At Granada, another statue of Mary reportedly shed tears of blood. Rosario, the visionary, said Mary told her, **"It is not my blood; it is the blood of the world."** A similar event occurred in Madrid.

But one apparition in the early 1980's in Spain attracted thousands. It began Nov. 13, 1980. The visionary's name was Amparo Cuevos, and she was born on March 13, 1931. Amparo lived in El Escorial, Spain, where King Philip of Spain erected a monastery-palace in 1559 in honor of Saint Lawrence after the Spanish defeated the French. El Escorial is 30 miles from Madrid in a place where King Philip also ordered the monks to sing Ad Te Deum, a hymn of praise to God, after the defeat of his Spanish Armada in 1587.

Similar to many other visionaries, Amparo had a childhood plagued by cruelty and misfortune. Her mother died when she was 6 months old. Her stepmother was vicious and would send the child into the streets to sell goods for money. If Amparo did poorly, she could not come home. At night, Amparo often slept under trees covered with snow. On one occasion, the young girl had to be resuscitated while she lay at the point of death.

Her home life was no better. Amparo owned no bed and had to sleep in a cupboard. There was no room for her legs. At 10, she was arrested for begging. She lived on flour and water in her cell. Somehow, despite it all, she survived. There was one more thing: Amparo Cuevos reported she had a friend, a friend from heaven named Mary.

"Dear Mother in heaven," Amparo says she would plead, "I would like to see my own mother. Tell me where she is."

According to several accounts, the child had no doubt that God heard her. Amparo's faith was strong, but her miserable childhood was soon followed by a miserable adulthood. Her husband was an alcoholic who was abusive. As his wife, she raised seven children with little income. But Amparo Cuevos overcame it all. Despite her poverty, she rose up, and then her experiences reportedly began.

But in the early 1980's, Amparo reported apparitions of Mary and then Jesus, and shortly after she received the stigmata. Miracles were reported and even her husband converted. Yet like at Medjugorje, it was the messages she received that drew the most attention, for they often foretold "a cataclysm without precedent" that would soon be at hand. Indeed, Amparo's reported revelations were increasingly foreboding. Mary's and Jesus's words warned of war and a precipice that humanity was approaching.

In the early 1990's, another event began to emerge in Eastern Europe, another significant one. This time, at a place called Litmanova, Slovakia, near the state's borders with Russia and Poland. The onset of the visions in Slovakia coincided with the fall of the Iron Curtain and the liberation of Eastern Europe.

In the foothills of the Tatras, Mary appeared on a mountain top named Mt. Zvir. In August 1991, a reported 500,000 people climbed the two-mile high mountain for the first anniversary of the apparitions. Two Slovakian children, Ivetka and Katka, were the visionaries, although Katka did not hear Mary. Both visionaries were about 12 years old when the events began. Mary came to Slovakia, the children said, as the "All Pure Sinless One." The Virgin spoke to them in the Carpatho-Rusyn language and announced that a new world of joy and peace was approaching. Mary also reportedly called for a medal to be struck and revealed a miraculous spring.

The many effects in Slovakia have been incredible. Before climbing the mountain, pilgrims go to confession, for they believe they should carry no sin before the "All Pure Sinless One." In the winter, some climbed the mountain barefoot as a penance while singing hymns and reciting the Rosary. On Nov. 7, 1993, the apparitions were moved to the bishop's chapel at Presov as 20,000 pilgrims followed and prayed outside. There, an investigative commission observed the children, while the Church moved to study the events. A month later, on Dec. 5, 1993, a cloudy, wintery day filled with ice and snow, 100,000 pilgrims again gathered on Mt. Zvir for a special apparition.

At Litmanova, the Virgin's message called for prayer and penance, conversion, and reconciliation, and also reflected the times at hand. **"You don't know how much I need your prayers,"** Mary reportedly told the visionaries. But on July 3, 1993, they said Mary warned that if a renewal fails, the result will be **"worse than war."** The Litmanova apparitions, say pilgrims from afar, are touching in their simplicity and faith. People of all ages and all backgrounds were said to have journeyed there from throughout Europe.

But as in previous decades, Italy reported the most apparitions. There were reported apparitions at Gargallo di Carpi (1984), Schio (1985), Sofferitti (1985), Bisceglie (1985), Belluno (1985), Floridia (1985), Casavatore (1985), Mazzano (1986), Cardito (1986), Sezze (1986), Belpasso (1986 & 1987), Campobasso (1986), Giubasco (1986), Borgosesia (1987), and Crosia (1987). At Schio, the apparitions drew huge crowds as a 14 year-old girl displayed fervent and sincere ecstasies. The weeping Madonnas were reported across Italy, too. More than a dozen were reported in 1995 alone, in towns and villages named Terni (March 20th), Tivoli (March 22nd), Camaiore (March 25th) and Catania (March 25th).

In May 1985, in Oliveto Citra, Italy, reports of Marian apparitions began to circulate. Over one hundred people signed documents in a parish office that they saw Mary at the gate of an old castle. Others saw her, too. Tourists, pilgrims, and people from nearby towns reported to have seen her. Oliveto Citra is south of Naples and has a population of about 3500. Since then, the apparitions of Oliveto Citra have continued, with the visionaries receiving extraordinary messages.

These apparitions, both in style and content, according to Father Robert Faricy, S.J., a professor of theology at the Pontifical Gregorian University in Rome, are truly apocalyptic. Faricy said the apparitions emphasize secrets, hidden things, divine judgement, chastisement for sins, and the catastrophic consequences of sinfulness. However, the message is also a message of hope. Mary also calls, said Faricy, the world to conversion, prayer and penance. She especially calls people to pray the Rosary. The Oliveto Citra apparitions also hold one special note. These visionaries, like those at Medjugorje, say Mary told them her real birthday is August 5th.

On February 2, 1995 another major supernatural event rocked Italy. At a small town named Civtavecchia, a terracotta statue of the Virgin of Medjugorje began weeping tears of blood. On one occasion, local bishop Girolamo Grillo was present. Even the Vatican was moved to respond, as tens of thousands came to see for themselves. A commision was formed and its conclusion was favorable.

Throughout Europe during the 80's and 90's millions visited the many reported apparition sites. The pilgrims were of all ages, nationalities, and backgrounds. Curiously, they were not just Catholics, but of every faith and denomination. There were especially many Moslems, who like Catholics, hold great devotion to the Blessed Virgin Mary.

Indeed, the Blessed Virgin Mary is mentioned in five Suras (chapters) of the Koran, the book of Islam. Moslems believe the Koran to be the literal word of God, as given to Mohammed in the 7th century. One of these chapters even bears the Virgin's name. In fact, Mary's name is the only personal name of a woman found in the Koran. It is mentioned 34 times and Mohammed explicitly affirms Mary's virgin birth (Sura 21, 23, and 66). The Koran (sura 3) is especially explicit about the Annunciation and how the angel Gabriel told Mary that she was favored by God. Therefore, because of the words in the Koran, Moslems hold great devotion to Mary. Indeed, they have a genuine love of her and offer prayers in her name. This love for Mary was demonstrated before the whole world during the 1991 war in Kuwait. In Iraq, western television news media captured footage of Iraqi women beseeching Mary (a statue of Mary was shown in the scene) to intervene before God for protection of their men in the military and to help bring an end to the suffering caused by the bombing of Baghdad.

The "Moslem - phenomenon" is of great interest to Marian theologians as our era reportedly winds down. This is because ever since Mary's apparitions at Fatima, Portugal, a village named after the prophet Mohammed's daughter *Fatima*, Mariologists have suspected God was using the Virgin Mary as a bridge for unity between the two faiths. It is a unity that some believe is on the near horizon. Bishop Fulton Sheen said that he believed Mary came to Fatima because "the Mohammedans are to be intimately involved in the triumph and in the era of peace mankind was promised there."

Several decades ago, in 1968, another sign of this surfaced on the other side of the Mediterranean Sea. And this time, so many Moslems and people of different faiths witnessed the supernatural event that to this day it is still considered unprecedented and extremely relevant to the message of today's apparitions.

The gate of the old castle at Oliveto Citra, Italy, where Mary appeared in 1985 to over one hundred witnesses. The messages of the apparitions, according to Jesuit theologian Fr. Robert Faricy, were extremely apocalyptical.

CHAPTER EIGHTEEN

WE BELIEVE IN YOU

"See, I am laying a cornerstone in Zion, an approved stone and precious. He who puts faith in it shall not be shaken."
—1 Pt 2:6

The continent of Africa rises out of the waters of the Atlantic and Indian oceans, stretching 5,000 miles from the sunny northern tip of the Mediterranean Sea to the storm-lashed Cape of Good Hope in the south. At 12 million square miles, it is the second largest continent and holds perhaps the most misunderstood collection of people on earth. To the rest of the world, Africa is still a mysterious continent of secrets, a land of legends that recalls brave explorers, who trudged through jungles and swamps, confronting ferocious animals and primitive tribes. But Africa is also known for its beauty, for its mountains, lakes, great plains, and deserts. Some claim that civilization began in Africa. The pyramids on the Nile outside of Cairo bear witness to an early advanced culture. Joseph and Mary fled there with the Christ Child, Scripture says, and Egypt is no stranger to God's unfolding revelation. A famous 10th century apparition of Mary is also noted for the conversion of a Moslem caliph named Almuizz Ledeen Allah.

But now, out of Africa, the Virgin Mary has reportedly come once again. In a series of stunning and dramatic manifestations of the supernatural, apparitions of Mary are being reported in every part of the continent. But the 1968 apparitions in Cairo should first be addressed.

The apparitions in Cairo were unprecedented. Mary's public

appearance above a Coptic Church from 1968 to 1971 was unlike any of her previous apparitions. And this phenomenon reportedly began with a dream.

The family's name was Khalil. They were Coptic. In the early 1920s, one of them was considering what to build on a piece of property the family owned. To his surprise, the Virgin Mary reportedly appeared to him and gave him special instructions that the Khalil family was to build a Coptic Church in her honor. In 50 years, the Virgin promised, she would bless it in a singular manner.

Mary's Coptic Orthodox Church on Khalil Lane was completed in 1925. It still sits in a Cairo suburb called Zeitoun, which is close to the reported route taken by the Holy Family during their flight into Egypt. On Tuesday, April 2, 1968, at 8:30 p.m., a group of Muslim workmen employed by the transportation system arrived at the gate of their garage, which was opposite the church. It was a routine change of shifts. The same as any other day. Suddenly, two workers put down their cups of tea, stood up, and stared in disbelief at what they saw.

Across the street, above the dome of the church, a "white lady" appeared. The lady was kneeling beside the cross at the top of the dome. Motionless. Whispers. Then a rising tremor of alarm.

Farouk Mohammed Atwa, a Muslim, quickly pointed at the lady with his bandaged, gangrene-infected finger, which was to be amputated the next day, and cried out, "Lady, don't jump! Don't jump!" Desperate, Farouk ran for help along with his companions who found a priest, Fr. Constantine.

Meanwhile, above the church, the shimmering luminous lady rose to her feet, revealing a stunningly recognizable figure.

"Our Lady, Mary!" a woman screamed. With that, a flight of glowing white doves suddenly appeared, which hovered around the apparition. Then, with the apparition, they faded upward into the dark sky.

The spectators were speechless. Most of them were stupefied. The next morning when Farouk Atwa arrived for surgery, his doctors removed his bandages and got a shocking surprise. Farouk's finger was completely healed. It was the first known miracle of the Virgin of Zeitoun, an apparition reportedly foretold by the Virgin herself in her 1962 appearance in Lithuania, behind the Iron Curtain.

A week later, the apparition came again. And again and again.

With Mary came a celestial shower of shooting stars, mysterious lights and luminous doves. As with the first apparition, the doves appeared and flew around the flood-lit church and then disappeared. The people were amazed. One witness said it was like a "shower of diamonds made of light." Others thought they saw "strange birdlike creatures made of light" that flew with astonishing swiftness, yet these birds had wings that never fluttered. The doves always came and then vanished like snowflakes.

After the apparition of birds came a blinding explosion of light, bathing the roof of the church. Refocusing, the light gradually formed into a brilliant radiance of the Madonna, which revealed her long white robe and a veil of bluish light. Often Mary's garments would flutter, as if a breeze were blowing them.

Above the Virgin's head was a glowing halo, giving her an unearthly and majestic aura. The halo's radiance was so intense Mary's facial features were discernible. Overall, the shimmering luminescence of the Virgin was said to mimic the sun, in much the same way she had appeared at Guadalupe.

As throngs gathered each day, Mary could be seen gliding effortlessly around the four domes of the church, bowing and greeting the crowds below. Occasionally, the apparition would appear lower, above a palm tree in the church courtyard or in one of the church's arches. Several times the Virgin came with the Christ Child or with Joseph.

News of the apparitions spread quickly. Across Egypt, multitudes flocked to Cairo, including Christians, Jews, Muslims and atheists. Within weeks, crowds as large as 250,000 were gathering, causing traffic jams that paralyzed the city.

Each night, the crowds would yell, "We believe in you, Mary! We believe in you!" Muslims knelt on their mats and sang hymns from the Koran to her while Christians offered their prayers and petitions. Eventually, the crowds grew so large the government had to demolish the transportation garage and cut down trees to make more space available for the Virgin's audience.

Throughout it all, the apparitional woman would acknowledge the sea of humanity with a special gesture of her arm. Triumphantly, she would even occasionally hold out an olive branch to an ecstatic response from the multitudes. Sometimes, huge red billowing clouds of incense-smelling smoke rose around the vision.

Many photographs and movies were taken to document the apparition, and miracles were reported, most of them physical healings. Countless testimonies were made from people of all religions and all races. Indeed, it was the Madonna whom the people swore they saw, and no one could tell them anything different.

Bishop Athanasius of Beni Soueiff, who was sent personally by the Coptic Pope to Zeitoun to make a detailed investigation, gave the following account:

> Suddenly, there she was standing in full figure. The crowd was tremendous. It was too difficult to move among the people. But I tried and worked my way in front of the figure. There she was, five or six meters above the dome, high in the sky, full figure, like a phosphorous statue, but not so stiff as a statue. There was movement of the body and of the clothing. It was very difficult for me to stand all the time before the figure, as human waves were pushing me from all sides. ... Our Lady looked to the north; she waved her hand, she blessed the people, sometimes in the direction where we stood. Her garments swayed in the wind. She was very quiet, full of glory. It was something really supernatural, very, very, heavenly. ... Some people were reciting verses from the Koran. Some (Greeks) were praying in Greek; others were singing Coptic hymns. It was something really above human experience that attracted and captivated me.

> I stood there and tried to distinguish the face and features. I can say there was something about the eyes and mouth I could see, but I could not make out the features. That continued until about five minutes before dawn. The apparition then began to grow fainter, little by little. The light gave way to a cloud, bright at first, then less and less bright until it disappeared ...

> On another night I visited the church. I took the door keys and entered, locking the doors from the inside. As I stood on the ladder that led from the

second floor to the top, my eyes turned to the ceiling or inner dome. No one could see me. I was shaking all over. I took hold of the ladder. I felt there was something unusual there. I prayed: 'If you are there, Holy Mary, let me see you. I just want to give witness to you.' Then I heard people shouting. I hurried outside and saw the Virgin standing one meter from where I had been. There was no message ... but definitely faith in God, in the supernatural, has been strengthened. Christians and non-Christians reported that what they saw in Zeitoun brought them back faith in God. Hundreds of missions could not do what the apparitions have done. People are beginning to think of Christianity in a new way, especially those who were antagonistic ... (*Our Lady Returns to Egypt*, by Jerome Palmer, O.S.B.).

By the time it ended, an estimated 15 million people witnessed the apparitions at Zeitoun. The Coptic Church, after official investigation, granted full approval of the events. In Rome, Pope Paul VI sent two investigators who also studied the apparitions, but no ruling was rendered since the events were not under Catholic jurisdiction.

On Sunday August 21, 1981, the Virgin Mary appeared again in Cairo at a church on Massarra Street in the Shoubra section. This time she appeared floating above the worshippers at the Sunday liturgy. A full-sized carved image of Mary was later found on the arch, but since it was a one-time incident no investigation or research was made. In 1986, a similar report surfaced when a 16 year-old girl named Hermane Sami reported seeing Mary standing on the minaret of St. Demiana Church on March 25th at 2 a.m. in the morning. Crowds gathered, and by the break of dawn, the news had spread throughout the entire area. The local bishop, Bishop Ana Bola, witnessed the ongoing apparition himself and wrote that there was "positive evidence that the apparition was unnatural phenomenon." Accounts of the apparitions later appeared in The *Pittsburgh Press,* The *San Francisco Chronicle,* The *St. Louis Dispatch,* The *New York Times,* and The *Washington Post* on April 14, 1986 and April 26, 1986. During this same period, a Rosa Mystica statue in Egypt was reported exuding oil. This miracle continued for several years.

For Mariologists, mystery still surrounds the Cairo apparitions and their apparent connection to the Moslem people. But there have been other mystical events that have revealed ties to the Middle East and the Moslem faith. At Medjugorje, the Virgin Mary once responded to a question put forth by one of the visionaries (under orders from the local bishop) in a way that continued to reveal God's love for the Moslem people. When asked who was the holiest person in Medjugorje, Mary disclosed it was a little old "Moslem" lady. Some critics wailed since they could not conceive a non-Christian as worthy. Some even deliberately distorted the revelation into a point of argument against the authenticity of the apparitions. The Virgin's reply, they said, meant that Mary was saying all religions were equal. But theologians countered that Mary had said no such thing, nor did she imply it in her response. And for those attuned to the higher implications of the revelation, it was clear. God was sending another sign that "unity" amongst all God's peoples is part of his plan.

Indeed, with the apparitions at Cairo, millions of Moslems witnessed the visions of Mary, providing another clue that perhaps the time was approaching for this unification to unfold. It was another tie to what Mary began at Fatima and to what St. Louis de Montfort prophetically foretold when he declared centuries ago:

> The power of Mary over all devils will be particularly outstanding in the last period of time. She will extend the Kingdom of Christ over the Idolators and Moslems, and there will come a glorious era in which Mary will be the ruler and Queen of human hearts.

CHAPTER NINETEEN

A RIVER OF BLOOD

"I will water the land with what flows from you, and the river beds shall be filled with your blood."

—Ez 32:6

On the other end of Africa, deep in Northern Zululand in the nation of South Africa, there were more reports of Mary, stunning reports. Like at Zeitoun, one of them began in the 1920s, when a mission was founded at Ngome, some 20 miles from Vryheid. And since it's effects are still being felt, it is important that it be addressed.

The Ngome area is classic Africa with natural forests and striking scenery unlike anything in modern civilization. It contains only tea farms and backland and animals. For 40 years, a hospital was run at Ngome by the Benedictine Sisters. But from 1955 to 1971, the hospital reportedly had one periodic visitor, who never complained—the Blessed Virgin Mary.

The apparition would come to Sr. Reinolda May, O.S.B., sometimes standing on a globe with her hands and feet out of sight, and glowing with a dazzling radiance. During the first apparition, the nun reported a large host surrounded by a brilliant corona rested on Mary's chest, radiating light. Sister Reinolda said the Virgin resembled a living monstrance.

For days after the apparitions began, the nun was preoccupied with this brilliant light and, she says, the Virgin's beauty. Nevertheless, Sr. Reinolda still had doubts, and she asked for a sign so that others would believe. This she received when a picture of Mary came to life before a group of women.

Over time, the nun also reported that Satan attacked her, and that Saint Michael appeared. The apparitions culminated when a spring was found on the property where the Virgin requested a shrine be built. The local bishops blessed the shrine, and in 1990 a commission found the messages and visions to be doctrinally sound. At Ngome, the Virgin's messages centered on a call to conversion and the Eucharist. But Mary reportedly warned, **"Fearful things are in store for you if you don't convert."**

By the early 1980s, many apparitions were being reported throughout Africa. In 1980, an apparition was reported in Ede Oballa, Nigeria. In 1986, images of Mary were seen in lamps and torches in Magomano, Kenya. There were reports of apparitions in Kinshasa, Zaire, where nine people saw Mary and at Chatsworth, South Africa, a small town near Dubun. In Mulevala, Mozambique, a throng witnessed a vision. And in Mozambique, on January 18, 1983, a crucifix on the wall of a home wept tears of blood. The tears flowed all day and left a pool of blood on the floor.

There were also apparitions reported in Kenya. A nun named Sr. Anna Ali reported startling visions during which Jesus reportedly came to her and gave messages that were subsequently approved by her bishop. Christ warned Sr. Anna of the coming abolition of the Mass and of Satan's growing influence, and He said chaos in the Church would develop. **"The world has lost its senses,"** He reportedly told the nun.

Farther west, Mary appeared again. On May 13, 1986, the anniversary of the first apparition at Fatima, in the territory of Cameroon, West Africa, at about 1:20 p.m., the Virgin Mary appeared above a gable of a chapel in Nsimalen, illuminating the surrounding forest. Even though there was no message, two miracles occurred. A 6 year-old girl who had been deaf and mute from birth instantly spoke and pointed to the Virgin. Jacqueline Atangana then cried out, "Maria! Maria!" At the same time in Burundi, Pierre Zang Nvonda, a 41 year-old blind chemist claimed he regained his sight when he stood under a tree above which the Virgin appeared.

Meanwhile, there were similar reports in other villages in Burundi. A vision was reported at Mushasha in 1984 and in that same year, a seriously ill woman was miraculously healed and a Mystica Rosa statue shed tears of blood. Several years later, on Feb. 8, 1987, the Archbishop of Gitega approved the events and called for a sanctuary to be built. "On many occasions, Our Blessed Mother has given us signs of her presence to help us through our difficulties and to help us overcome them with faith and hope," he wrote in his opinion.

That same year (1984), more apparitions were reported in Burundi. This time, to a 19 year-old boy named Cyril Mararhirsha. Huge crowds gathered, and again the bishop called for a sanctuary to be built. Mary was showing signs of her presence, the bishop said, and calling for "conversion." Apparitions were also reported at Bujumbura-Bubanz.

Some speculated that all of the mystical reports in Burundi was because of the danger that lay hidden in this nation. Even though Burundi had suffered persecutions, the visions were perhaps intended as a sign to the Hutus and the Tutsis, the warring tribes, to not follow the path taken in neighboring Rwanda where a terrible war had broken out between them.

Rwanda is the site of what is considered among the worst cases of genocide in the past 50 years, provoked by a civil war between the Hutus and the Tutsis. The country lies in the center of Africa, 750 miles from the Indian Ocean. The original natives were pygmies, who were followed by the Bahatu tribe, which sought to escape the advancing Sahara. By the 16th century, the Nicotes arrived with great herds of cattle. Eventually, the territory was colonized by Europeans, and by the turn of the century, Rwanda passed from German to Belgian hands and finally achieved independence. Today, it is home for 5.5 million people, mostly Christians, who live on 16,100 square miles of land. The capital is Kigali, which has a population of more than 180,000 people. Over the years, Rwanda became known as the "Switzerland of Africa" because of its vegetation and mountainous regions; 97 percent of the population are farmers.

In the Rwanda tragedy, 500,000 or more were killed. Hundreds of thousands were maimed. Countless died of disease. Millions became refugees. As in Bosnia, the media could make no sense of it and even stated that the events seemed demonic and right out of Hell. The cover of Aug. 1, 1994, issue of *Newsweek* magazine declared "HELL ON EARTH" while on May 16, *Time* magazine proclaimed, "THERE ARE NO DEVILS LEFT IN HELL. THEY ARE ALL IN RWANDA." The *Time* writers concluded, "Rwanda serves as a modern laboratory for anyone trying to figure out which factors will matter and which will not in the pursuit of peace."

Indeed, but one factor the media ignored was the reported apparitions that had foretold the coming crisis.

Apparitions of Mary began to be reported in Rwanda in 1981, the same year the Virgin first appeared in Medjugorje. According to Church sources, it was an incredible apparition that received approval in the first stage by Rwanda's Bishop Gehany on Aug. 15, 1988.

The Virgin came to a region named Kibeho, which is 18 miles from Butare. From 1979 to 1981, Kibeho had been racked by violence. It was an almost demonic violence. Religious pictures, images, and statues were destroyed and many believe these events precipitated the apparitions.

Mary's apparitions in Rwanda were distinctive. They were almost always in public, with the time and place announced in advance. Some lasted as long as 80 hours and took place before crowds as large as 10,000 people.

The events seemed to begin out of nowhere. On Nov. 28, 1981, Alphonsine Mumureka, a 16 year-old girl, was serving a table at a boarding school, when she heard a voice speak her name. As she turned, she said the Virgin Mary suddenly appeared, and the girl fell to her knees in awe. Wearing a white dress, the Virgin floated above. "She had incomparable beauty," the girl said. After the Virgin departed, the girls' teachers said the apparition would have to happen to someone else for them to believe.

Alphonsine became the object of ridicule until Mary did, indeed, appear to someone else. On Jan. 12, 1982, a stunned Anathalie Mukamazimpaka also beheld the Virgin and after this apparition, she was left blind for 15 days. Two months later, another girl, Marie Claire Mukanganjo, who had been a critic of the events, saw Mary.

Over the next six months, three more girls received apparitions—Vestine Salima, who had been raised a Muslim, on Sept. 15, 1982; Stephanie Mukamurenzi on May 25, 1982; and Agnes Kamagaju on June 4, 1982. Agnes saw Mary and Jesus. There was one more visionary, but he was different. Emmanuel Segatashya was not a student; he was a 15 year-old field hand, who was pagan. In

July 1982, while Emmanuel was picking beans, a teenage Jesus appeared and taught him how to pray the Our Father. Before that time, Emmanuel had never entered a church and lived in an area with no radio or television.

The Kibeho apparitions were a unique phenomenon. Strange lights, spinning suns, and even two suns were reported, but the other stories were more incredible. The visionaries reported trips to Heaven, Hell, and Purgatory. While they were gone, their bodies would go into coma-like states for days. "I will be like a dead person," Alphonsine warned Sister Superior. "But have no fear, and do not bury me."

During these states, the African visionaries exhibited pronounced behavior, often hurling themselves to the ground at the end of an apparition. Witnesses said they prayed with great fervor and reported seeing flowers and trees in place of people, along with visions of fire.

The Virgin, the visionaries insisted, was neither white nor black. She had no color, but she was beautiful and sweet, dressed in white with a blue veil. Mary usually stood with her hands joined at her breasts or down at her side much like her image on the Miraculous Medal. Jesus appeared in white with a white or red mantle, they said.

The warnings at Kibeho are particularly important.

"I am talking to the world, but you do not understand," Mary reportedly told Anathalie on May 5, 1982. **"I want to raise you up, but you remain down. I am calling you, but you do not hear me. When will you do what I'm asking you?"** Emmanuel Segatashya, said that Jesus told him, **"Tell them to purify their hearts because the time is near."**

While most of the messages at Kibeho called for prayer, love and reconciliation, the visionaries reported a shocking vision that lasted eight hours. In it was a river of blood. People were killing one another. They saw abandoned corpses without heads. Dead babies lay everywhere. Trees were aflame. Throughout the vision, there was screaming and tens of thousands of people overwhelmed by fear and sadness. After it, the visionaries said they understood Mary's pain.

Anathalie reported that she said to the Virgin, "I understand that what makes you suffer is the fact that the day will come when we will like to follow what you are saying about loving, serving, and doing God's will ... but it will be too late. The day will come when we will long for you, and we will not find you. We will want to listen to you, but we will not hear you, the day when we will want to run to you, but will not be able to. Have mercy on us."

After the holocaust in Rwanda, at least three of the visionaries were reported slain.

Today, the world prays for God's mercy on Rwanda as it struggles to recover from the war and to make sense of it all.

"They were beset by a biblical array of pestilence, of cholera, dysentery, bubonic plague and measles," reported *Newsweek* magazine on Aug. 1, 1994. "By last Friday, they were estimated to be dying at the rate of one a minute, and the pace seemed sure to rise."

CHAPTER TWENTY

ASIAN WONDERS

*"The hand of our God remained upon us, and He protected us
from enemies and bandits along the way."*

—Ezr 8:31

There have been apparitions in Asia. Everywhere from
the Carpathian foothills to the jungles of Vietnam.
Across a stretch of 5,000 miles, the reports have
poured in.

Asia. The world's largest continent. Billions of people.
Almost endless expanses of land. Mountains that scrape the heavens.
And great dark evergreen forests that seem to smother the northern
part of the continent. Farthest north are the frozen arctic plains where
only lichen and moss grow and a few wandering nomadic tribes live
with their herds of reindeer. South of the frozen tundra are miles of
grassland and forests. This is where millions of bushels of wheat are
grown, and farther south lie the hot rainy jungles with rich fertile
farm soil and millions of people. To the east and south of this great
continent are the islands of Japan and the Philippines, islands so
crowded every available inch of land is needed for food. Life in Asia
can be difficult, even cruel, for life here has been subject to the
whims of either island dictators or communist demagogues.

Not surprisingly, visionaries report that the Virgin Mary says
she has seen and understands it all. They say the Madonna knows the
pain of her Asian children, so shackled, so devoid of life and truth.
Fed pagan religions and oppressive philosophies, the persecution here
has been great. But by the early 1980s, signs of the Virgin Mary's
intercession began to appear, and people from one end of the

continent to the other started bearing witness to her manifestations. Against the backdrop of suffering caused by political, social, and environmental upheavals, numerous miracles, and supernatural phenomena were being reported everywhere.

By 1985, the sightings began to multiply from the far western reaches of the Soviet Union to the mountains of Nepal. Apparitions. Numerous reported miracles. Even in remote and restricted nations like China and Vietnam, reports struggled to the surface. Communism or not, people could not deny what they were seeing. Dictators or no dictators, the hearts of the people were on fire, on fire for God the stories disclosed.

In the Philippines, an estimated 1.5 million people were present at an apparition of the Blessed Mother in the early 1990s. As in Ireland, experts say her mark was evident. Elsewhere throughout this country of more than 7,000 islands, stories abounded of weeping statues, spinning suns, and visions, visions, visions. Just as was occurring everywhere, reports revealed that visionaries were receiving urgent messages, calling the Filipino people to a conversion of heart.

One report was especially noted. In 1986, just moments from a bloody showdown in the streets of Manila between the forces of former dictator Ferdinand Marcos and the supporters of newly elected President Corazon Acquino, the Virgin reportedly suddenly appeared, stood between both sides, and boldly proclaimed she was the Queen of Peace. Surrendering helplessly to the unbelievable sight, the combatants laid down their arms, along with their anger, and went home. Even Cardinal Jaime Sin has spoken of this miraculous episode which occurred at the corner of Oritigas and Epifanio de los Santos. A church named *Queen of Peace* now stands on the site.

This was not the first time an apparition of Mary had healed a conflict in the Philippines. In 1948, Mary reportedly appeared at a Carmel monastery in Lipa, the former site of a World War II holocaust. It was a wonderful story. Miraculous phenomena included rose petals portraying images of Christ and Saint Joseph, which materialized in the sky and fell to earth. And as had occurred at Fatima, Communion reportedly emanated from the hands of angels. (Although disavowed by the Church in a 1951 decision, these apparitions are under investigation again and may soon be approved, according to reports.) And on Jan. 24, 1991, rose petals again fell at Lipa, where Mary had announced to Terasita Castillo that she had come, as at Knock, as the **"Mediatrix of all Graces,"** bringing the **"message of Fatima."**

By 1994, Lipa was just one of many towns and villages across the Philippines reporting apparitions and miracles. Towns with names like Agoo, Cebu, Tagbilaran City, Sacobia Lake, and Angeles City. Towns like Kaunlaran and Quezon and Bagvio City. The Church struggled to respond and everyone wondered where Mary would appear next.

Off the coast of Red China, the news was captivating. On Jan. 11, 1980, six mountaineers in Eastern Taiwan near Wu Fung Chi reported that the Blessed Virgin Mary appeared to them out of nowhere. It was, they said, a miracle.

It happened suddenly, after a group of climbers had become frightened on a hazardous mountain path and begged God for help. Instantly the apparition appeared, they said, and Mary led them to safety. The apparition took place in front of a hut where a Camillian brother had built a statue of Mary that many now flock to see.

A year later in Red China, another extraordinary apparition of Mary was reported. According to a June 2, 1995 article in *The Washington Post*, apparitions of Mary occurred at the illegal pilgrimage site of Dong Lu, a poor region near Peipiing. Dong Lu is in the Hebei Province of northern China and was the site of a reported apparition of Mary and St. Michael in 1900 during the violent Boxer Rebellion. Since then, Chinese tradition has continued to honor Mary at Dong Lu for protecting the people from an army of invading warriors.

The apparitions began during the Vigil of Our Lady of China on May 23, 1995 and continued into the next day. *The Washington Post* reported that as many as 10,000 people, attending an underground Mass, saw the Virgin in Dong Lu. Some reports put the crowd as high as 30,000. The Mass was concelebrated by 4 bishops and 110 priests in an open field. The miracle began during the opening prayers and recurred during the consecration of the Eucharist. The people reportedly even broke into applause and song as the Virgin Mary hovered over them on what was a hot afternoon day. Witnesses claimed that besides the apparition of Mary, the crowd, including Bishop Su Zhimin of the Baoding Diocese, saw the sun move and give off different colors. "Rays of various colors emanated from the sun," said a report from the Cardinal King Foundation in Connecticut. "With the passing of the minutes, the sun changed colors, first to yellow, then to red and blue, followed by other colors. Subsequently people saw different apparitions in the core of the sun: a Holy Cross, the Holy Family, Holy Mary, and the Holy Eucharist. At times, the sun would approach the crowd and then retreat. People were heard crying out, 'Holy Mother, have pity on us, your children,' and 'Holy Mother, please forgive my sins.' The people were all seeing similar things because they shouted out similar observations. ("Yellow! Red! Blue!") This lasted about twenty minutes until a sudden white ray came and the sky returned to normal. The people also saw a white dove and the Lord raise His hand to bless the congregation."

While reports of this nature are rare in China because of the great secrecy imposed by the state, occasionally events of this nature are leaked to the West. In 1949, Mary reportedly apeared in Zose, China, to a woman named Mother Van Sarten. In 1953, a statue of Our Lady of Zose wept in Shanghai for three days. There were reports that this phenomena had occurred again in the 1970's.

There were also accounts of another recent apparition of Mary in China. According to *Soul* magazine, Father Peter Hsiang, C.S.J.B., Director of the Chinese Catholic Apostolate, reported that, "Our Lady, appeared in China in 1978, in an apparition in Chiang Si province, near Shanghai." In 1981, *Soul* magazine quoted the *Wall Street Journal* as again reporting an apparition of Mary at Zose. "A mysterious light appeared in a hilly wooden area on the outskirts of Shanghai," the account read, "for reasons difficult to fathom, word spread that the Virgin Mary had made an appearance." The light reportedly shone for 3 days over the Church of Our Lady of Zose.

CHAPTER TWENTY-ONE

MAMA WILL SAVE VIETNAM

"His mercy is from age to age to those who fear him."

— Lk 1:50

In Vietnam, desperation and an urgent call for help reportedly also brought the Virgin Mary in an apparition. It was for this reason the Madonna appeared at the Binh-Trieu Fatima Center to Stephen Ho Ngoc Ahn, a former soldier in the South Vietnamese Army. Stephen was a paralytic who could not speak, but in the mid-1970's Mary reportedly came and spoke to the young man. **"Tomorrow is the anniversary of my appearance at Fatima,"** she reportedly told Stephen. **"I will cure you so that you can walk and talk again."**

Indeed, Stephen was healed and word of the miracle spread among the Vietnamese people. Unfortunately, the story generated a tragic response because Stephen's communist oppressors arrested him and refractured his spine, leaving the young man worse than before. Ironically, Stephen says he had not fully comprehended the Virgin's original warning that his healing would bring new suffering. However, it would also, Mary promised him, eventually lead to a second healing. This occured in 1993. Most significantly, Stephen says Mary told him she wanted people to **"pray the Rosary"** to escape **"destruction."** And that **"the end"** was near.

Vietnam, some say, has been chosen by God to be a victim-nation in the latter days. This means that like a victim soul, who suffers for the sins of his brothers and sisters, Vietnam is suffering for the luxuries and sins of other nations. And so, some believe God is visiting this nation in a special way. There have been reported apparitions throughout the country, such as the apparitions at Thu Duc to a girl in 1993. A Fatima pilgrim Virgin statue reportedly also wept there. But because of the danger imposed by the communist authorities, these events are not well publicized.

Other reports from Vietnam include apparitions to a woman named Rosa Marie at a convent outside of Saigon, messages received by a woman named Theresa from the Eternal Father, mystical experiences given to two children in North Vietnam that corroborated each other, and one truly amazing story. In a communist military camp that held a large blackboard in the yard, an invisible hand reportedly wrote out before the eyes of many stunned onlookers: MESE CUU VIETNAM, which means: "MAMA WILL SAVE VIETNAM."

Meanwhile, on the other side of Asia, the reports were just as compelling. In the sky—way up in the upper atmosphere—people reported seeing things, all kinds of stange things. Even UFO sightings seemed more explicable than this—words formed from clouds and huge, glowing crosses. Strange rainbows, odd lights and giant angels were said to have soared through the air. In the Ukraine above a city of 100,000, a hand reportedly appeared in the heavens, according to a secular press account, and wrote a message: "SOON THE JUST WILL BE SEPARATED FROM THE UNJUST." A similar report came from Tombow, a city 25 miles south of Moscow where another "white hand" wrote in the sky for a half-hour. Onlookers said the message remained readable for 3 hours.

In Hrushiv, a small Ukrainian village, it was no different. Many curious phenomena were reported in the sky, especially above a small Byzantine church named Blessed Trinity. People saw pulsating lights and dark silhouettes, and on some nights, onlookers said they witnessed the Virgin floating in the air. Some heard Mary speak. Others say the light was so strong and iridescent that their fingernails glowed, leaving them in awe and wonder.

Eleven more locations in the Ukraine reported apparitions during the 1980's, places named Buchach, Ozerna, Kaminkobursk, Pochaiv, Lviv, Bilychi, Berezhany, and Zarvanysta. At Pochaiv, Mary appeared "wrapped in flames." While at Zarvanysta, people spoke of a huge glowing mass that, twice the height of a tree, moved north over quiet meadows. People reported strange celestial spheres often near missile silos. At Hoshiw, in Western Ukraine in 1987, two men taking a short cut through a forest saw a young woman in radiant white. They followed her until she reached a monastery's church. There the radiant woman rose and disappeared over top of the domes.

In Pidkamir, a village between Pochaiv and Lviv, hundreds came to see the radiant Virgin at a stone church named St. Paraskovey's. While at Grushevo in 1987, a city near Chernobyl (the site of the nuclear accident, April 26, 1986), Mary reportedly appeared to thousands as a silent, glowing figure. It is especially noted that the outbreak of apparitions in the Ukraine and throughout the Soviet Union began not long after Pope John Paul II conducted what is considered by many to have finally been an adequate consecration of Russia and the world to the Immaculate Heart of Mary in 1984. The almost immediate change that occurred within 6 months of the Consecration is extraordinary. According to Orthodox sources, more than 5,000 churches were reopened in the Soviet Union, 106 in Moscow alone. Baptisms tripled. Marriages increased ninefold. The number of monasteries went up from 18 to 121. Said Patriarch Aleksy II of Moscow, "I never thought this moment would come." This was also around the time of Mikhail Gorbachev's rise to power. Gorbachev, although a communist had been baptized.

Chornij Zrnovia, a woman who spent years at a Soviet Concentration camp in Siberia and was a witness to Mary's apparitions in the Ukraine, especially at Buchach (a sight of many KGB atrocities), describes her encounter with the Virgin Mary:

> One day on my way to cut wheat, I stopped to see why there was a crowd around the well. The people said they were seeing the Holy Mother. I knelt and started praying very hard and suddenly instead of the well I saw a big glow, like a mountain, and in it I saw a lady holding a baby in her arms. The light was like silver. The lady was in blue clothes with a white sash, and a barefooted baby was in her arms. On her head Mary had a white shawl. I saw this for about half an hour. The glow was seen very often for two to three weeks in 1987, I think during the autumn. The Holy Mother warned us to return to the Church and

love one another. Personally I took it as a sign that communists would soon disappear from the face of the earth.

Three years later communism did collapse and on October 13, 1991, forty million former Soviet citizens watched a live broadcast of ceremonies at Fatima where almost a million pilgrims prayed and pledged themselves to the conversion of Russia and the West.

There were more apparitions reported in Lithuania, Iraq, and Sri Lanka in the 1980's and 90's. In the U.S.S.R., there were apparitions reported in Rostov, Kharkhov, Girkalnis, and Leningrad. There was one even in Moscow in 1992.

At a village named Mozul near the ancient ruins of Nineveh in Iraq, a fourteen year old girl named Dina Basher reported apparitions in 1991 and even exhibited the stigmata. The young girl was Syrian Orthodox and the Bishop of Baghdad ruled that the events were "miraculous." Dina said our period, according to what Jesus reportedly told her, was a period of transition and that the "second coming was near." Not far from Iraq, Mary appeared in 1984 to a young girl at Jallel-Dib in Lebanon and on a wall at Beit Sahour in1983 in Bethlehem, a city filled with Palestinians. This wasn't the first time the Virgin was seen in Israel. In 1979, Mary reportedly appeared during the war in various villages in Israel and Lebanon with words of consolation. At Mutival in Sri Lanka in 1987, more apparitions were claimed and a statue of Mary was seen to move.

In India there was apparitions reported in Ajmer, southwest of Delhi, and in Goa, south of Bombay. At Poondy in T. Nady a statue reportedly wept. While in a village named Little Mont in Madras, India, the Roche family, who had prayed the Rosary for 25 years before an Our Lady of Lourdes statue, saw the statue's eyes fill with tears on May 29, 1985. The mother of the family saw it as a sign to permit her two daughters to enter a Carmelite convent. She had been opposed. Like elsewhere, reports of Mary's presence in India wasn't anything new. In 1952, she had apeared to a Jesuit priest named Father Louis M. Shouriah, pleading for devotion to her "sorrowful heart."

In neighboring Nepal, another extraordinary report emerged in 1992. According to a November 12, 1992 *Catholic News Service* release from Katmandu, many people, mostly Hindus, reported seeing the image of a man on a cross in the sky over a hill in midwestern Nepal.

According to witnesses, the apparition near Palpa village began around 5:30 p.m. and continued for about an hour. Witnesses saw a bright light in the sky, which then became a figure of a crucified man, said *UCA News*, a church news agency in Thailand. Nearly all those who saw the vision, which reportedly occurred on Sept. 11, 1992 were Hindus. Many, however, identified the figure as that of Jesus Christ.

A Protestant minister in Katmandu described the Hindu and Christian communities of Plapa as close-knit. He said several Hindu families had recently been baptized. The area is Protestant mission territory, although most of the inhabitants are Hindus. A member of a Protestant Congregation in Katmandu went to the site of the incident and recorded statements by witnesses.

"I saw a human figure, hands stretched, head leaned down, who had a piece of cloth wrapped around his waist," said villager Moya Devi Thapa. "I looked at it for some time."

Villagers who said they observed the phenomenon report they saw light in the sky and a human figure visible from the waist up with hands stretched out as if on a cross. Some of those who said they saw the vision also said they knew nothing about Christ.

"Mostly non-Christians reportedly saw it," said the Rev. Robert Karthak, a Katmandu Protestant minister. "It must be authentic." A Jesuit priest who was head of the Catholic mission in Nepal declined to comment.

This apparition deserves to be noted, however, in lieu of Mary's consistent appearances where extreme danger lurks, especially where nuclear or fraticidal tension exists and is mounting. The May-June 1998 undergound atomic detonations of both Pakistan and India add a curious footnote to the place where this vision occurred.

Likewise, the makeup of the apparition is significant. Christ's appearance on a cross in the sky can be directly connected to what many believe was another supernatural image of Christ on a cross that appeared in photographs of the French testing of an atom bomb in the Pacific in 1968.

From pictures taken of the explosion by a professional photographer, it can be clearly seen in the center of the atomic mushroom cloud the undeniable image of Chist crucified on the cross. To the right of Christ, an image of Our Lady is seen glowing in all white silhouette. This radiating image of Mary is distinctly visible in contrast against the background of the red mushroom cloud. It even appears to be the same likeness as Our Lady of Medjugorje. Both *Newsweek* and *U.S. News* and *World Report* magazines ran the photograph in the summer of 1989. Thus, both visions can be understood to be warnings of nuclear danger.

But from all of the reports throughout Asia over the past two decades, two incredible stories emerged that were characterized by miraculous events and urgent messages. They were events and revelations that reportedly pointed back to Fatima and by the mid-1980's accounts of these two apparitions had spread throughout the world.

Since the 18th century, hundreds of Marian apparitions have been reported. Some believe this photograph to be an authentic picture of the Blessed Virgin Mary at a late 20th century apparition site.

French revolutionaries demanding the surrender of the Bastille in 1789. The beginning of the prophesied coming of "great bloodshed?"

Bl. Anna Marie Taigi foretold a two-fold purification of the world. One punishment would come from God and one from the hands of man.

The Virgin Mary appeared to St. Catherine Labouré at Rue de Bac, Paris in 1830.

Alphonse Ratisbonne, a prominent Jewish agnostic who experienced a miraculous conversion.

Maximin Girard and Melanie Calvat, the two visionaries at La Salette, France, where Mary appeared on September 19, 1846.

The Basilica at La Salette, seated high in the mountains. The Church approved the apparition there in 1851.

St. Bernadette Soubirous of Lourdes (1858). Bernadette received 18 apparitions of Mary.

The shrine at Knock, Ireland where an apparition occurred on August 22, 1879.

St. John Vianney of Ars reported extraordinary confrontations with demonic spirits.

St. Thérèse of Lisieux is considered the greatest Saint of the modern era. In 1997, Pope John II declared her a Doctor of the Church.

The Basilica at Lisieux, France. Although St. Thérèse recounted only one supernatural experience, she remains perhaps the greatest supernatural event of the 19th Century. Today over 2,000 churches are named after her throughout the world.

CHAPTER TWENTY-TWO

THE MADONNA OF THE GULAG

"But who am I that the Mother of my Lord should come to me?"
— Lk 1:43

S ecretly he prayed. It was January 1964, and Josyp Terelya had just been transferred to another prison in the Soviet Gulag, one of the more than 210 concentration camps and 36 prisons in the Ukraine, where 450,000 people were detained. This camp was in the Donbas Komisarovka region. It was known as PJA-128-22.

And being caught in prayer here meant one thing—solitary confinement.

In the Gulag, solitary confinement meant horror—forced containment in a closet-size room. No windows. Barely enough air. And dripping moisture everywhere that left a man sick and miserable. Salt was placed on walls to retain moisture as an added misery. There was one meal a day, which consisted of a small portion of bread and fish and two cups of water, and the challenge in this state of intense hunger is not to lick the salt off the walls because along with the cold, it could produce fatal results.

Prayer was the only survival kit that inmate Terelya trusted. As he traveled from prison to prison, he kept God close to his heart and always in his mind. As a religious and political prisoner, this dissident knew trust in God was something the system could not strip him of.

Terelya was born Oct. 27, 1943, in the Carpathian Ukraine. Both his parents were communists when Stalin's reign of terror was at its peak. Terelya's family was predominantly Catholic, and after the fall of Nazi Germany, some of them worked in the underground to keep the Church alive.

Raised by his grandparents, Terelya was nurtured in the faith, and his personal role in the underground Church became so strong that by age 18, he was branded an enemy of the state. It was the height of irony since Terelya's mother had been employed by the party to eradicate Christianity.

In the summer of 1947, when Terelya was 6, the Soviets decided to liquidate the Ukrainian Catholic Church. At the time, according to Terelya's father's records, there were 700,000 Eastern Rite Catholics in the Carpathian region, 450 churches and chapels, 281 parishes, and 359 priests. Throughout the Ukraine, there were 2,772 parishes and 4 million faithful. When Stalin died in 1953, the Church had already been decimated, and by the mid-1960's, there was nothing left. More than 10,000 churches throughout the Soviet empire had been destroyed, and most of the faithful were incarcerated or silenced or dead.

On Sept. 4, 1962, they came for Terelya. Even his parents, who were communist party prima donnas, couldn't help. Charged with inciting nationalism, he was sent to the Gulag. It was the beginning of three decades of imprisonment.

The Soviet prison system stretched from the Ukraine to Siberia to Moldovia, and Terelya visited much of it during three decades of subhuman living, beatings and attempted escapes. Yes, Terelya would escape, but each escape was followed by recapture and a longer sentence. Soon he wasn't just a nationalist—he was an enemy of the Bolsheviks and was classified as a high-risk prisoner. Special camps were built for such prisoners, and Terelya soon found himself in the middle of swamps and bogs, places that made escaping virtually impossible. For inmate Josyp Terelya, death was all but a certainty.

In prison, the beatings were horrific. Blood loss and broken bones often left him certain that death was imminent. Still, Terelya kept praying. And he kept surviving. "Glory be to Jesus Christ," he would proclaim, serenading his jailers. Our Father's, Hail Mary's, and Creeds would flow from his lips. Over time, he survived riots, starvation, psychiatric wards, and even crucifixion.

Like Alexander Solzhenitsyn, Terelya became a living legend in the Gulag system. The KGB officials and communist hierarchy tried everything short of shooting him, but as his reputation grew, direct termination of his life became an unwise option because officials feared civil retribution or political embarrassment.

Meanwhile, Terelya kept escaping any way possible, even through tunnels. But his attempts were always fruitless because there was nowhere to go but back to prison. To isolation cells and surveillance camps. And finally to a special cell, where his destiny would unfold.

On Feb. 12, 1970, at Vladimir Prison in Special Corpus 2, the supernatural intervened in an event the whole world would learn about.

Vladimir was a cold, stark prison that epitomized the strange horrors of the Gulag. Twenty to 30 people would be crammed in 10-by-10-foot cells. No sunlight. No heat. Only artificial light that was kept on all day and night to induce terror and mental deterioration. Twenty-four hours a day. Day after day.

By then, Terelya was down to 120 pounds, his athletic boxer physique reduced to a shell of his former self. He ached and developed rheumatism. His kidneys and liver often faltered, while his many broken bones left him in chronic pain.

Vladimir meant pain. All kinds of pain. Constant beatings and psychological torture. The unending cold. But even here, Terelya was a renegade. He kept on praying and kept on agitating the officials. That was what his life was like until Feb. 12, 1970, while he was lying prostrate in prayer.

Suddenly, without warning, he felt an unusual warmth that flowed through his body. And then, shortly after 10 p.m., Terelya says a brilliant light filled his cell. It was an unusual light, something Terelya had never seen before. It was "like moonlight," he later wrote, but it almost seemed to be a "living light." Gradually, this aureole settled next to his bunk bed. And within seconds, Terelya says the Blessed Virgin Mary materialized. It was a brief appearance but an unfathomable experience, recalled Terelya.

Instantly, Terelya remembers that the Virgin filled his distraught body with peace. All his fears dissipated and were replaced by an intense feeling of security that was emancipating. Mary's blue eyes penetrated his soul, he said and she was beyond beautiful in human terms, unlike anything he had ever known. She appeared, he would later write, like a "huge jewel in shimmery light—majestic beyond imagination."

In this apparition, Mary came as s young peasant-looking woman wearing a blue veil and light clothing, despite the cold, damp cell. And, most of all says Terelya, she was real—very, very real!

Josyp said the Virgin spoke and to him and told him some of his future. She instructed him to pray to "The Angel of the Ukraine" and then Mary admonished him. He recorded her words to him:

You must learn to forgive those who persecute you the most. I will always be with you. But you're not ready. You doubt. You question. You must go through all of this. You must change your life and learn to forgive the Russians and learn to understand yourself so you won't be like Cain. There are difficult years before you, of trial and humiliation, but from today on you'll never have fear. I shall be with you. I have shed many tears. Many people are denying the future life. They are denying my Son. Around us is a very intense intolerance. Russia continues to remain in darkness and error and to spread hatred for Christ the King. Until people sincerely repent and accept the love of my Son, there will not be peace because peace comes only where there is justice. Pray for your enemies. Forgive them, and before you there will be a very bright road.

With this suddenly, Josyp said that the Virgin showed him a spectacular vision. It was a vision of war! "I saw fire," Josyp recalled. "I saw fire and tanks and knew there would be war between Russia and some other country." With that, the Virgin vanished.

Two years later to the day—Feb. 12, 1972—it happened again. This time, Mary reportedly intervened to save Terelya's life.

By this time, the Soviets had had enough. There were rumors of a new type of confinement that Josyp discovered to be true. Deep in the bowels of Vladimir, a hellish torture had been devised. In a dungeon-like room, the Soviets had constructed a system to ventilate frigid air into a cell, which in no time could kill anyone who was exposed to it, as Terelya was. Officially, it was Cell 21, but it had been converted to a freezer cell. Ironically, this was the same cell the Virgin visited two years before, and now he was back.

Surrendering all resistance, Terelya was resigned to his fate and his certain death. His lips and eyelids froze, and he could feel his head splitting from the cold. He couldn't move his limbs or his jaw. In little time, he knew His entire body would soon be frozen. While he waited for death, he prayed.

Then, says Terelya, it happened. An intense flash of light suddenly engulfed the room. Even though he couldn't move, Terelya could see the room being miraculously illuminated and then he felt heat and a woman's hand upon his frozen eyelids. A sweet smell filled the air, he recalled.

As the hand lifted, Terelya opened his eyes and heard.

"You called me," the Virgin said, **"and I have come."**

Terelya said that Mary was wearing a heavily pleated dark blue dress, and she looked like a Carpathian mountain woman. **"You don't believe it's me,"** Mary said to Josyp as he wrestled with the thought that he was hallucinating. But it was her, she assured him.

Terelya recalls that Mary's light poured over his frozen body, and that he went from extreme cold to being uncomfortably hot, and as one can only imagine, his spirits soared.

Josyp Terelya and his three children

Josyp and his family now live in Ontario.
He still experiences visions and apparitions.

CHAPTER TWENTY-THREE

A CHOSEN NATION

"For you are a people sacred to the Lord, your God; He has chosen you from all the nations on the face of the earth to be a people particularly his own."

— Dt 7:6

With a Rosary in her hand, Terelya says the Virgin Mary stood next to him for two hours. She instructed him. His future, Josyp says he was told, would unfold with God's plan for this part of the world, especially the Ukraine. More importantly, Mary foretold to him some of the the future of mankind. She then showed Terelya some startling visions:

"Now look," she said as a vision of a map unfolded. It was Russia. But this time, fire was everywhere, igniting the country. Other parts of the world appeared the same, and Mary told Josyp mankind's fate if it did not soon return to God:

> I saw entire landscapes. I saw a river I recognized, the Amur. I don't know how I knew it was that river. I saw many islands there. I saw tanks on the Soviet side—but not the Soviet type—and a city in flames. Siberia was on fire to the Ural Mountains. I saw Moscow, and the people there had faces that were twisted and deformed. Moscow was sinking, and throughout the city were strange creatures running down the streets. Their faces were those of rats, and their tails were long and fat with scaly skin and hairs sticking out like spikes. They were as big as a dog and

whoever the creatures spat at would fall to the ground, as if by venom. There was a tremendous fear that filled Moscow, and the city was falling into the earth. I saw hills, forests, cities, walls. The whole countryside was aflame. And all these explosions were taking place. ...

And then, Terelya says he understood another part of the prophetic vision. Red China would be involved in the war. He could see the tanks in the vision were Chinese. It could occur, Josyp understood, before the year 2,000.

By supernatural intuition, Terelya says he now understood his role. He was chosen, as was the Ukraine, for an important mission to assist in the salvation of the world in the time that remained. Mary explained to Josyp that the world desperately needed prayers:

The Ukrainians should also repent. You're an unfortunate people because you love each other so little. You've dedicated your better forces to ungodly goals. God punishes a nation as he punished Cain for the slaughter of Abel. You have to follow that road that has been set for you. There shall be many builders, but many are without my Son and without His love. There will be many who use His name to aggrandize themselves. But do not fear. They are not the builders. The builders are those who are humble before my Son. Without love and without faith, people can attain their own desires, but not that which has been foretold by the Lord Jesus Christ, my Son. I shall always be with you. Pray and work for the conversion of Russia to Christ the King. Do not lose faith. The world is cold and spiritless, as it was before the Flood.

Josyp says Mary urged him to repent quickly. Likewise, this was what the world must do or the future could be filled with horror. Then, in a powerful flash of light, the Virgin was gone, and only a sweet aroma lingered, confirming the reality of the experience.

Just as Terelya began to remove his shirt, guards burst into his cell. Shocked and confused, the soldiers could only ask, "What are you doing?"

"The Mother of God was here with me, and nothing has happened to me," he recalls telling them. Stunned, the soldiers removed him from the freezer cell.

Days of interrogation produced nothing but confusion and dismay. The KGB was dumbfounded and puzzled. For Terelya, the episode led to a new series of psychological studies and interrogations in even worse detention centers, such as Serbsky Institute in Moscow and prisons named Lubyanka, Butyrka, and Lefortovo. They were infamous torture houses that were the pride of Brezhnev's regime.

Even though Terelya was serving a life sentence, the Virgin's prophecy to him was fulfilled, and he was released on April 7, 1976, through a series of incredible state blunders and miraculous events. Not for long, however. A year later he was arrested again for "anti-Soviet agitation."

On Dec. 26, 1983, Terelya was released once more, only to be re-sentenced on Aug. 20, 1985, and sent to camps in the Perm area, which many considered the worst in the Soviet system. These were more than prisons, they were death camps. Perm is situated on the western side of the Ural Mountains near Siberia, where sub-zero temperatures are typical of the winter months. Once again, solitary confinement was to be Terelya's fate.

But he continued to pray, and he somehow survived. By now, Terelya was known in the West, and a petition for his release, signed by 151 U.S. Congressmen, was sent to the new Soviet General Secretary, Mikhail Gorbachev. In February 1987, Terelya was transferred and released for good.

By this time, the world was a different place. The communist Soviet Union was changing, and Terelya quickly learned something else: The Virgin Mary was said to be appearing in the Ukraine at a place named Hrushiv. For Terelya and his fellow religious dissidents, the enthusiasm was difficult to control. They recalled how Mary had reportedly come to the Ukraine before, once during the 19th century and twice before in this century.

But according to some, Mary first appeared in Hrushiv almost 350 years ago during a turbulent period of wars and invasions. Then, in 1806, a miraculous spring of water surfaced at a spot where an

Icon of the Virgin had been hung on a tree. This led to a Chapel, which was later destroyed around 1840. Not long after this, the area was hit with a plague. Seeing divine retribution at work for the destruction of the chapel, the local residents turned to despair until one woman reported a dream in which Mary reportedly told her, **"Clean the desecrated well and have a Mass celebrated in dedication of Our Lord, so that death will cease throughout your village."**

After the new chapel was erected more stories emerged. People reported visions of tongues of flames burning above the rededicated well and more dreams and visions of Mary bringing assistance. Ukraine has always prided itself on such stories of the miraculous, for it is said to have consecrated itself as a nation to Mary in the year 1037.

In 1914, 22 peasants from the same region were said to have witnessed an apparition in which Mary foretold 80 years of suffering for the Ukraine. But she promised, the story goes, freedom would come to the first nation ever to consecrate itself to the Immaculate Heart of Mary.

Several decades later at a place in the Ukraine called Seredne the Virgin reportedly appeared to a woman named Hanya on 20 occasions between December 20, 1954, through November 22, 1955. Hanya said that Mary predicted a fiery future for the Ukraine and its people. The Virgin reportedly told Hanya:

> **Disaster is upon you as in the times of Noah. Not by flood, but by fire will the destruction come. An immense flood of fire shall destroy nations for sinning before God. Since the beginning of the world, there's never been such a fall as there is today. This is the kingdom of Satan. I shall dwell on this hill from which I see the entire universe and the many sinners, and I shall distribute my graces through this well. Who comes to repent of his sins and receive this water with faith, him shall I heal in soul and body.**

Then, the Virgin is said to have added:

> **Rome is in danger of being destroyed, the Pope of being killed. Rome must be renewed and raised through the hill of Seredne. The Catholic faith shall spread throughout the entire world. The sinful world with its sinful people is in desperate need of renewal.**

When Mary departed, Hanya says she was left with an intriguing question: "How shall this renewal come? Through *whom* and *when?*"

A religious procession in Ukraine in 1993. After decades of suffering because of atheistic communism, the people now publicly celebrate their religious freedom.

CHAPTER TWENTY-FOUR

THE CONVERSION OF RUSSIA

"It was not because you are the largest of all nations on the face of the earth to be a people particularly his own."

—Dt 7:7

According to confidential sources, the KGB did all it could to discredit Hanya's reported message from the Virgin Mary. And it became evident in 1987, with the new apparitions at Hrushiv, that the same misinformation and suppression was inevitable. But by then, excitement was building among the people. The 80 years were all but past, and the remnant of the faithful knew it. A climax was approaching, and they appeared to be ready. KGB or no KGB, the crowds converged on Hrushiv.

According to the Ukrainian publication, *SVITLO*, 45,000 pilgrims arrived daily in Hrushiv in early 1987. Others estimated the crowds to be as large as 80,000. The apparitions began on April 26, 1987, exactly one year to the day after the nuclear accident at the eastern Ukrainian city of Chernobyl.

A small hamlet of perhaps 2,000 houses, Hrushiv is about 35 miles southwest of L'viv, a large western Ukrainian city of several million. To the west is Moscow, approximately 700 miles away.

His fate and destiny unfolding, Terelya hurried to Hrushiv to see for himself. There, above the cupola of a small Byzantine chapel, the Madonna stood, silently floating and giving off a sublime luminescence and letting throngs of people observe her. Even the KGB and communists, who were busy photographing the crowds, could see the apparition.

Day after day, it was the same. The Madonna would

materialize and float about the church. While silent at first, Mary soon began to speak to some, giving messages that requested prayer and conversion.

For Terelya, it was as unbelievable as the times he saw the Virgin in prison. He says that Mary awaited him at Hrushiv, for he was to convey a message given there to the entire world, an important message that echoed Mary's words at Fatima, only with greater urgency. Indeed, Terelya was about to be given more insight concerning the future.

At Hrushiv, he also received a truly prophetic vision, one that a few years later would be almost totally fulfilled before the eyes of the whole world. And his vision could not have been more accurate—it was of the attempted coup against Mikhail Gorbachev, which eight Soviet military leaders undertook in Moscow in the summer of 1990.

In the book *Witness*, he described the 1987 vision:

Again I saw the ocean and floating in it was the globe of the earth. Billows of black and red smoke were spreading over the horizon. Over one part of the earth I saw the inscription 'SOCIALISM.' It was written in Russian and was like blue on red. A mass of people were walking along the heads of Marx, Lenin, and Engels—again, yellow and not alive. This man became as a statue. I heard his voice. 'It has been given to me to take peace from the earth.'

I experienced and felt the earth shaking. I was filled with fear. It wasn't really fear but something deeper and worse. The woman said, **"Do not fear. You see the Antichrist in three persons but he can no longer do anything to you. He will not bother you anymore."**

I saw a map of the Ukraine and the bloody river began to dry up. The earth in many places was scorched and took on a black-gray color. This was the color of death. But amid the black-gray ashes, I saw grass sprouting. It was very tall. I saw the people kneeling and crying, but I knew these were the tears of joy and salvation. I saw the new Babylon, the red city, that was falling into the earth. In that city, under a Christian temple, was a secret hiding place. There were eight men there—eight rulers, all eight waxen yellow. They laughed horribly and bared their teeth.

Gorbachev told me it wasn't he who was in charge of the state. I saw the real leader of the USSR behind a yellow screen: It was Lucifer himself in the figure of Yeltsin, his eyes red and his face blushed. I looked and from the earth of that city, immense dull red rats, large as dogs, began running. These animals were awful. I knew they were poisonous.

While Terelya's vision came to fulfillment, most of what Mary told and showed him has still not. Echoing her words at Fatima in 1917, the Virgin made it clear to Josyp that the fulfillment of Fatima's remaining prophecies would occur. An era of peace approached, but first, Russia had to convert or the world would suffer the consequences.

At Hrushiv, Mary explained the following to Terelya:

You have seen the godless East and West. The difference is that in the West godlessness is not officially recognized. But the goal of godlessness in the East and West is the same. In order to save Russia and the whole world from godless hell, you must convert Russia to Christ the King. The conversion of Russia will save Christian culture in the West and will be a push for Christianity throughout the world. But the kingdom of Christ the King shall establish itself through the reign of the Mother of God.

Hrushiv's message is clear. Great events were said to be approaching, events related to the fulfillment of Fatima. While 13 other places in the Ukraine reported supernatural signs and apparitions, the message given at Hrushiv was the most significant, for it was to be delivered to the world.

By 1989, Terelya, who once had been a prisoner of a hateful system, was now free to proclaim God's love. The freed dissident traveled to America and began to share with the West what Mary told him, and to describe his days of captivity in the Gulag.

But he says he was told that time was short. Terelya, like so many other chosen ones, began traveling throughout the world. Fatima's fulfillment was near, he would tell people, and all mankind needed to know and believe and to respond:

> We must always think back to Fatima. The miracle of the sun—when it seemed to come crashing toward the earth—may have been a warning of nuclear warfare. The bombs dropped in Japan were later described as flashing with the force of the sun.
>
> It also brings to mind the prophet Elijah, who called down fire from heaven to consume the pagan altar and end drought and idolatry. Elijah lived in the Mount Carmel region of Israel, and at Fatima, the Mother of God appeared as Our Lady of Mount Carmel.
>
> What was the date America tested its atomic bomb? The test was on July 16, 1945, the feast day of Our Lady of Mount Carmel.
>
> The bomb was later dropped, looking like the falling sun, and on August 15—the Feast of the Assumption—Japan surrendered. I believe we are all a part of a cosmic plan. When I look back at it now, I see the long series of coincidences, not only in our lives but in events of the world. For example, on Oct. 13, 1960, there was an all-night vigil for peace at Fatima, and just days later, a secret super-missile under manufacture by the Soviets was destroyed in an accidental blast.

Around the same time in the early 1980s, on the other side of Asia, 6,000 miles away, another unlikely voice emerged. Another unsuspecting soul was plucked out of nowhere to be a visionary, a modern day prophet. And again, the triumph promised at Fatima would become the recurrent theme of the apparitions, along with some of the more terrible dangers that Mary says she had come to prevent.

CHAPTER TWENTY-FIVE

"MY GOD, WHAT HAVE WE DONE?"

"Then the angel of the Lord spoke out and said, 'O Lord of Hosts, how long will you be without mercy for Jerusalem and the cities of Judah that have felt your anger these seventy years?"
—Zec 1:12

The 13th U.S. Marines, one of the regiments of the 5th Marine Division, was redeployed in Hawaii after being removed from Iwo Jima in March 1945. The division was getting ready for its next assignment: the assault landing on Kyushu, the southernmost of the Japanese islands. Planners estimated initial casualties of 100,000 or more, which was a conservative estimate.

Around the clock outside Tokyo, a crew of Japanese professional radiomen monitored all signals emanating from U.S. transmitters. Early on Aug. 6, 1945, they monitored a call sign they had just heard three weeks earlier. It came from the island of Tinian. By late July, it was heard daily. The Japanese named it "New Task Company."

Throughout that day, they continued to hear it, but what they didn't know was that New Task Company, indeed, had a new task. It was the highly secret 509th Composite Group. Its ultimate mission: drop the atomic bomb on Japan.

After months of soul-searching, the decision was made to drop atomic bombs on Japan. Ethically, the experts concluded there was nothing new in the bomb that was not already available in TNT or the fire bomb. All that remained was determining where these bombs would be dropped. That decision was shaped by a consensus of where it could make the deepest impression—preferably a city hitherto untouched by bombing. Four names came up—Kyoto, Kokura, Niigata, and Hiroshima. A fifth was considered at the last minute: Nagasaki.

Around midnight on Aug. 6, 1945, the chaplain of the 509th said a brief prayer. Seven B-29 crewmembers ate breakfast, and an hour or so later, they were airborne and headed toward Hiroshima, the beautiful city of Hiroshima, which was known for its spectacular willow trees and which had received only twelve bombs throughout the war.

At 8:15 a.m., plus 17 seconds, the "Enola Gay" arched upwards and to the right on a 60-degree angle. Now, it was 10,000 pounds lighter. Below it, an atomic bomb was now hurtling towards Hiroshima. In 45 seconds, it would hit.

First Lieutenant Morris R. Jeppson, who was in charge of console monitoring the bomb circuits, started his own count, "40 ... 41 ... 42 ..." He stopped the count. A thought raced through his mind, "It's a dud!"

But an instant later, Jeppson thought he had gone blind. The world turned purple as an immense flash of light stunned his brain. Below, a ball of fire stretched across 1800 feet, with a temperature at its center of 100 million degrees!

Seconds before, people on the ground had observed falling parachutes that carried radiation instruments. The Japanese cheered because they thought the enemy planes flying overhead were in trouble.

Suddenly, without a sound, there was no sky over Hiroshima. Those who survived said the first instant of the atomic explosion was pure light. Blinding and intense, yet beautiful and awesome.

One witness said the flash turned from white to pink and then to blue as it rose, and the mushroom cloud blossomed. Others said they saw fire in six colors. Some gold and some white. It reminded them of a huge photographic flashbulb popping over the entire city.

But most of them saw nothing at all. They were completely incinerated, exactly where they stood. Radiant heat literally melted them. Others were shredded by blast waves that carried glass, bricks, beams, and solid objects.

The drop had been perfect, only 200 yards from the designated aiming point. Seventy-thousand instant casualties; 2.5

miles from Ground Zero, the heat still burned skin. At 1.5 miles from the point of detonation, a printed page exposed to the heat had the black letters burned completely out of the white paper.

In the sky, the "Enola Gay" arched upward. A minute after the explosion, tail gunner Bob Caron could see a shimmering light rushing toward the plane and braced to be hit by the shock waves. It resembled, he thought, a heat wave rising from an asphalt road surface.

After two shock waves, it was over. The crew looked back to scan what they wrought. By now, a perfect mushroom cloud had risen four miles into the sky. Below, Hiroshima was gone. It had "collapsed."

"My God!" said Capt. Robert A. Levis, who was Col. Paul W. Tibbets, Jr.'s, copilot. "What have we done?"

Indeed, all that remained of Hiroshima was an atomic desert. Within the innermost one-mile radius, everything was leveled. Almost everything. Eight blocks from the epicenter of the blast was the Jesuit Church of Our Lady of the Assumption. Inside were four Jesuit priests with four others. Even though flaming death surrounded them, they had not been affected. Not even by the radiation. And although they were wounded and the church was in ruins, the eight survived. "In that house," Fr. H. Shifner, S.J., would say on American television, "we were living the message of Fatima."

Over the years, some 200 scientists examined the survivors to discover what saved them from the incineration. No conclusions. No objective leads. What do the survivors say themselves? To a man, they agreed with Fr. Shifner. They were living the message, they insisted, the Virgin delivered at Fatima in 1917. They had been praying the Rosary.

It took two atomic bombs to end World War II. Three days after Hiroshima, a second bomb was dropped on Aug. 9, 1945. It destroyed Nagasaki.

On Aug. 15, the war was over. Emperor Hirohito addressed his people and said, "It is our desire to initiate an 'era of peace' for future generations."

On Aug. 15, 1549, the feast of the Assumption of the Virgin Mary, Saint Francis Xavier landed in Japan for the first time. He

175

immediately consecrated the country to Mary's Immaculate Heart. But martyrdom followed for many, especially at a place named Akita.

Sr. Agnes Katsuko Sasagawa always had a weak constitution. She had been born prematurely, and by age 19 she was stricken with paralysis of the central nervous system, a condition brought on by a mistake during an appendectomy. For the next 16 years, her life was a series of trials. Surgery followed surgery. Hospitals followed hospitals.

Nurtured back to health by a Catholic nurse, Agnes decided to become a nun. Shortly after, she was admitted to the Community of Sisters of Junshen in a convent in Nagasaki.

Four months later, Sr. Agnes again succumbed to illness. She lapsed into a coma and was near death when the sisters of Nagasaki rushed her some water from Lourdes. The water hardly entered her mouth when she regained consciousness, and her limbs became mobile. It was a miraculous healing.

Not long afterward, Sr. Agnes Sasagawa entered the Institute of the Handmaids of the Eucharist. And once again, the nun was stricken with tragedy. Without prior warning, on March 16, 1973, she found herself plunged into a state of total deafness. She could not hear out of her left ear, and an exam revealed the exact same disability in her right ear. To convalesce, Sr. Agnes accepted an invitation from her order to live at a convent on the hill of Yuzawadai in the outskirts of Akita. And that is where her amazing story began.

CHAPTER TWENTY-SIX

NO MORE HIROSHIMA'S

"As that city rejoiced at your collapse and made merry at your downfall, so shall she grieve at her own desolation."

—Bar 4:33

On the evening of June 12, 1973, Sr. Agnes Sasagawa, who was all alone, was given permission to open the door of the tabernacle for adoration of the Blessed Sacrament. Suddenly, a brilliant light appeared, which seemed to be coming through the tabernacle. The nun flung herself to the ground, partly in fear. An hour later, after the light vanished, she still couldn't determine whether God was enlightening her soul to her sins or she had experienced a hallucination. But the next morning it happened again. And again two days later.

The experiences continued and became more mystical. A week later, Sr. Agnes said she saw a multitude of supernatural beings similar to angels surround the altar in adoration before the Eucharist. And then, another mysterious event occurred.

While praying in the chapel, Sr. Agnes reported that she felt as though someone had pierced the palm of her hand. It happened twice. After the second incident, the nun looked at the center of her hand and saw two scratches in the form of a cross. The pain was intense, and when she examined herself, she found what looked like a cross engraved in her skin. The wound was two centimeters wide and three centimeters long. The pain was continuous ... and more was to come.

The following Thursday, the nun reported that an angel appeared to her, and they prayed the Rosary together. Suddenly, the palm of her left hand felt as if a pick had been thrust into it. The pain was so intense, it took all her strength to keep from crying out. Then, when Sister Agnes opened her hand, there was a hole in it from which blood flowed.

But the most overwhelming events were yet to come. The night of July 5, around 3 a.m., Sr. Agnes' guardian angel appeared again and urged her to go to the chapel. There, as she prayed, she says she witnessed a wooden statue of the Virgin Mary come to life. Bathed in spectacular light, the Virgin Mary addressed the bewildered nun and said, **"My daughter, my novice, you have obeyed me well in abandoning all to follow me. Is the infirmity of your ears painful? Your deafness will be healed, be sure. Be patient! It is the last trial. Does the wound in your hand cause you to suffer? Pray in reparation for the sins of men ...."**

Before leaving, Sr. Agnes said Mary told her, **"Pray very much for the Pope, bishops, and priests."**

With that, the Madonna and the angel vanished, and the statue returned to its normal appearance, and a small wound appeared in the right hand of the wooden statue and just as with her own hand, blood was flowing from it. All in the convent were witness to the events.

When this news was first published in Japan, a potpourri of explanations surfaced. Some even proposed that Sr. Agnes Sasagawa had ectoplasmic powers. According to this theory, the nun mentally transferred her wound into the wood along with her blood. However, an analysis of the statue's blood differed from Sister Agnes'. But this was, an irrelevant fact for those who had dismissed the events as sheer nonsense.

As it turned out, theologians say the stigmata in Sr. Agnes' left hand and the stigmata in the wooden statue's right hand were meant as signs. On Aug. 3, 1973, the Virgin Mary appeared again. This time she brought another message. A serious message. One that would evoke memories of Nagasaki and Hiroshima. The Virgin instructed Sr. Agnes to tell the world about events that loomed on the horizon. Just as she had with Josyp Terelya, the Virgin delivered a dire message about God's justice. The time for "signs" was passing, Mary reportedly told the nun:

It is very important. You will convey it to

your superior.

Many men in this world afflict the Lord. I desire souls to console Him to soften the anger of the Heavenly Father. I wish, with my Son, for souls who will repair by their suffering and their poverty for the sinners and ingrates.

In order that the world might know His anger, the Heavenly Father is preparing to inflict a great chastisement on all mankind. With my Son I have intervened so many times to appease the wrath of the Father. I have prevented the coming of calamities by offering Him the sufferings of the Son on the Cross, His Precious Blood, and beloved souls who console Him, forming a cohort of victim souls. Prayer, penance, and courageous sacrifices can soften the Father's anger.

A chastisement can take many forms, and Sr. Agnes indicated that Mary told her it would come from the hands of men.

Then, on Oct. 13, 1973, the 56th anniversary of the great miracle at Fatima, Mary appeared again and delivered one final message. As at Hiroshima and Nagasaki, fire would rain upon the world. The chastisement, the Virgin warned Sister Agnes, would come from the sky:

My dear daughter, listen well to what I have to say to you. You will inform your superior.

As I told you, if men do not repent and better themselves, the Father will inflict a terrible punishment on all humanity. It will be a punishment greater than the deluge, such as one will never have seen before. Fire will fall from the sky and will wipe out a great part of humanity, the good as well as the bad, sparing neither priests nor faithful. The survivors will find themselves so desolate that they will envy the dead. The only arms which will remain for you will be the Rosary and the Sign left by my Son. Each day recite the prayers of the Rosary. With the Rosary, pray for

the Pope, the bishops, and the priests.

The work of the devil will infiltrate even into the Church in such a way that one will see cardinals opposing cardinals, bishops against other bishops. The priests who venerate me will be scorned and opposed by their conferes ... churches and altars will be sacked; the Church will be full of those who accept compromises and the demon will press many priests and consecrated souls to leave the service of the Lord.

The demon will be especially implacable against souls consecrated to God. The thought of the loss of so many souls is the cause of my sadness. If sins increase in number and gravity, there will be no longer pardon for them.

With courage, speak to your superior. He will know how to encourage each one of you to pray and accomplish works of reparation.

The Virgin Mary added that the Rosary and confidence in Christ would save many souls. It was the last time Mary addressed the nun in an audible voice. With that, the events at Akita were over. Even though other signs appeared and Sister Agnes continued to experience supernatural graces, heaven's work was concluded.

As at Medjugorje, as at Kibeho, theologians said the message was critical. Sr. Agnes would also stress over and over its importance. Likewise, Marian experts concurred that with the events in Akita the world was entering the conclusion of the times foretold at Fatima. Indeed, many Marian followers agreed something monumental was approaching.

Eleven years later in 1984, the Church approved the events in Akita as supernatural, and in 1993 at the Akita International Marian Convention on the occasion of the 75th anniversary of the Fatima apparitions, Marian cardinals, bishops and priests the world over met and published their opinion: *The message of Fatima is repeated and completed at Akita.*

The conference emphasized that the world must respond with reparation and prayer in order to prevent tragedy. Indeed, chosen souls from one end of Asia to the other repeated that they weren't wasting words. Visionaries Terelya and Sasagawa, and many more throughout Asia, were insisting there was no more time to give excuses for not believing. Someday, they said, excuses would not be enough. If people wanted to discover the truth, the formula was apparent. With just a little faith and prayer, the Virgin Mary was showing the world the light.

It was a light, the Virgin's apparitions indicated, that was coming from everywhere. Every nation was being given notice. And if the world wanted no more Hiroshima's and no more Nagasaki's, the visionaries insisted it needed to heed the message of so many extraordinary divine interventions.

The wooden statue of Our Lady of Akita.
The statue wept 101 times and the stigmata
miraculously appeared in its right hand. After this miracle
was reported in the Japanese press, pundits theorized Sister
Agnes Sasagawa had "ecloplasmic powers".

CHAPTER TWENTY-SEVEN

"DO MY WILL"

"He encouraged them all to remain firm in their commitment to the Lord."

—Acts 11:23

Europaean cartographers were aware of the approximate location of the "Island Continent" in the early 16thcentury. With the help of Italian explorer Marco Polo, they outlined it in 1542, and while the French and Portuguese claim to have gone ashore, the Dutch are the ones who made it official in 1606 and ended up in the history books for discovering Australia.

Now the former penal colony "down under," which is known for aborigines, kangaroos and a myriad of other oddities, can also claim something else. Since the 1980's, a series of extraordinary reports of divine encounters have manifested themselves, leaving many Australians surprised by so many unique and curious unfoldings.

Yes, even in Australia, there are apparitions, visions, weeping statues and crucifixes. From coastal cities like Melbourne and Sydney to the mountains of the great dividing range, reports of the supernatural are surfacing. Since the mid-1980s, they have been accompanied by urgent messages.

From February 4 to May 21, 1986, in the Blue Mountain region, a small statue of Our Lady of Lourdes issued oil from its hands and feet. Not long afterward, there were reports of a bleeding crucifix followed by apparitions that became known as "Our Lady of the Blue Mountains." Mary also reportedly came as the "Mother of

Charity" and pleaded for faith and prayer. She warned that Lucifer had been **"loosed from the pit."** To the south in the coastal city of Melbourne, another report of the supernatural occurred about 1990. It was not just Mary, but also Jesus who reportedly began to speak to a young woman named Josefina-Marie, a school teacher who had always tried to live a simple life of prayer. The messages centered on devotions to the Sacred Heart of Jesus and Immaculate Heart of Mary, and called for a renewal of the world through suffering and divine justice. **"The times at hand are those foretold in Scripture,"** Josephina said Jesus told her.

Throughout the late 1980's and early 1990's, more reports emerged. Everywhere, visionaries said that God was calling Australia to conversion and prayer. But according to many, one prophetic voice stood out.

New South Wales is British in name and character. It is a region with a notorious history. Largely because of its preoccupation with American colonial affairs, the British government is said to have made no attempt to colonize New South Wales for more than a decade. British explorers and mariner James Cook had landed on this southeastern corner of the continent in 1770, but it wasn't until 1788 that the first British penal settlement was founded. By 1830, more than 75,000 convicts were transferred from England to New South Wales. It was there that William Bligh, the naval officer of the ship Bounty, governed and played a role in the famous mutiny. And it was here in 1808, that the so-called Rum Rebellion occurred. New South Wales had earned a reputation for lawlessness and vice. It was a reputation that spread around the world.

Whether or not its reputation for sin was a factor, no one will ever know, but in 1993, a young man who lived there reported that he heard a voice. Not just any voice, but a powerful, loving voice. A voice that stirred his soul and brought him to his knees. It was God who spoke to him, the young man said. God the Father. The Eternal Father. The First Person of the Most Holy Trinity. And those messages from the Eternal Father are now being spread throughout the world.

Matthew Kelly is now 26, tall and handsome. He is personable and energetic. He possesses humility and charisma. He has charm and intelligence. Most importantly, he possesses

184

wisdom—not just human wisdom, but supernatural wisdom. It is a gift, the young man says, that the Eternal Father gave him.

At his age, with his looks and intelligence, Matthew Kelly could now be making the world his oyster—if not, he says, for what occurred on that special night of April 7, 1993.

That evening, Matthew was preparing for bed. He had been up since 5 a.m. and was exhausted. But it had been worth it because his life at that time seemed perfect.

"Everything was going brilliantly in my life," he recalled, "work-wise, study-wise, family-wise, friendship-wise. Everything was going brilliantly."

Born in Sydney, Matthew Kelly grew up in a large family of eight brothers, of which he was the fourth. His mother, Jenny, managed the home while his father, Bernard, supplied catering equipment to restaurants and bakeries. By 1993, Matthew was on a path to success. He was studying commerce and majoring in marketing at the University of Western Sydney. He enjoyed sports and music. He liked all the things people his age everywhere like. Thus, perhaps it is revealing that on that first night, the voice he heard intervened only after Matthew reluctantly removed the Walkman radio headset from his head.

It all began that night with a feeling, an intense feeling. Matthew says he had planned to listen to music before falling asleep, but moments after putting on his headphones, a strong sensation overcame him. It was an uncontrollable urge. After a few moments, he fell to his knees in prayer by his bed. It was something he wasn't prone to do.

Then, as he knelt in the darkness slightly before midnight, the feeling intensified. Suddenly, he says, there was a voice, a clear voice. Even though it wasn't audible, Matthew remembers that he could "hear" it.

"KEEP DOING WHAT YOU ARE DOING AND BELIEVE IN YOURSELF AND IN ME," he says the voice commanded.

With that, the incident ended. The voice said no more, and the urgent feeling disappeared. The next morning, Matthew was not sure what had happened. However, something started to erase his anxiety. It was a "peace," he says. "A tremendous peace had filled me at that moment, and it remained with me," he said.

The supernatural events in Matthew Kelly's life began during Holy Week. Four days later, on Easter Sunday, April 11, 1993, something happened while he was at Mass. At the moment of the consecration of the bread and wine, he says the voice spoke to him again.

"LISTEN TO ME, HEAR MY WORDS, AND DO MY WILL."

Now, Matthew knew. He says he knew the voice was real beyond a doubt. And he knew the events of the first night had been genuine. Two days later, the voice revealed its identity: **"I AM YOUR HEAVENLY FATHER."**

After that, Matthew Kelly's life would never be the same. He began to receive locutions and messages from the Eternal Father, an extraordinary number of them, sometimes 10 a day.

He says the Eternal Father made it clear to him that he was to keep his mind open and trust God. The Father requested he visit a church three times a day; morning, afternoon, and evening. He was to write down everything he received because the messages God the Father would give him were not just for him—they were for the world.

During the dictation process, Matthew says he would hear the Eternal Father's voice only as long as he wrote. When he stopped writing, the voice would cease. When the Eternal Father began a message, His voice would repeat it three or four times, until Matthew realized he was to record it:

> The first night it was engraved in my mind. I was very tired. I wrote it down, and then the next ensuing days, as the messages got longer, He, (God the Father) started saying just the first three or four words and He would repeat them over and over until I would start writing. And then He told me that I had to write them; if I didn't write them, He wouldn't continue the message. And He would repeat the three or four words, and as I would write, He would then dictate. If I'd stop, He'd stop. If I'd run out of ink, if I'd run out of paper, have to blow my nose, He'd stop and repeat the next three or four words over and over.

Matthew says it didn't take long for him to learn the process. And it didn't take long, the revelations reveal, for God the Father to confirm once more that the prophecies of Fatima were *at the doorstep of the world.*

Time, Oct. 28, 1996

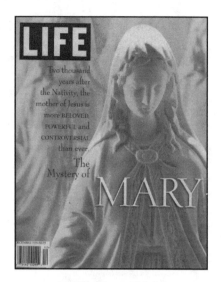

Life, Dec. 1996

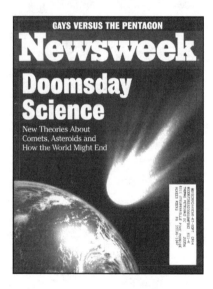

Newsweek, Nov. 23, 1992

U.S. News and World Report, Dec. 15, 1997

Is God trying to tell us something? The mainstream media has become increasingly more aware and more involved with religious matters, especially those involving miracles and prophecy.

CHAPTER TWENTY-EIGHT

AT THE DOORSTEP OF THE WORLD

"Father, the hour has come. Give glory to your son, so that your son may glorify you."

— Jn 17:1

According to some Marian writers, the Eternal Father's messages to Matthew Kelly were profound in their simplicity and filled with a wisdom that revealed their divine authorship.

As months passed, the messages revealed God's ways during lessons that covered many subjects, ranging from the Virgin Mary to life itself. Matthew reported that Christ also began to speak. Overall, the revelations presented a mosaic of divine knowledge:

> **May is Mary's month. The Mother of God, the most beautiful creature I ever created. In Mary, you will find care and concern for even the smallest details. Mary is a mother; she knows what you need. You are her son; she loves you as she loved Jesus. When she wept for Jesus, she also wept for you. She is the 'Mother of the World' and is greatly disturbed that her household has strayed.**
>
> **But in any household, there is one or two that keep the faith and in time bring the rest of the**

family back to My love. ... Bringing her family, the world, back to your Heavenly Father's love, little by little.

She has revealed to others the way in which this should be done: prayer, the Mass, the Rosary, and fasting. Her love is stronger than all the love and attention you have ever been shown put together.

All this love will come to you every moment of every day if you open yourself to her.

In this month of May, try especially in the area of devotion to Mary. ... Love, Love, Love is the answer.

Mary is your mother, and she loves you dearly; consecrate yourself to her each day, and the graces of love will flow through your work, prayer, and relationships. (May 14, 1993)

On Saturday, May 15, 1993, Matthew said that God told him he needed to trust in Him alone: **"You, My son, have a path to follow. You don't know where the path is going; that is one of the major parts of your faith journey. You must trust in Me, your Heavenly Father."**

The following day, a message from the Eternal Father revealed how important the family was to civilization and the future of the world:

Family. Family. Family. You must push and emphasize the importance of family. If the family unit and family morals had not been broken down by Western Society, the world would not be in the dark pit of sin which it is.

The return of family importance and family values and morality are the secret to bringing the world out of this pit, the secret to the world's finding the light, My Son, Jesus Christ. You must touch people by your deep concern for them, especially your family; you must show them that they are precious and very important in your

life. Other people may or may not see your love for your family, but they will not be able to help feel it by the way you live your life, doing the little things well.

Work endlessly and untiringly at this task of family. You tell Me that you encounter opposition to your love for Me. ... and I tell you, wasn't it written that no prophet, no one that loves Me and keeps My Son's way, will be loved in his home town? Love them and their hearts will melt, and they will find Me.

Your family is important; even if you feel you are getting nowhere, don't be discouraged, be patient. You must be careful never to tire in loving them because one tired moment could cost you a month's work; if you are tired say nothing, it is too dangerous.

Love all, but especially love your family selflessly, and you will bring My love to them without their even recognizing it. (May 16, 1993)

Matthew says that Jesus also imparted to him messages that were deeply profound and revealing, and confirmed that Mary was appearing in Australia:

Today, you must tell the world that time is short. Before long, I will be with you again. ... You, My brother, carry My cross and do My work, prepare My way. My mother has specially formed and selected Pope John Paul II for this time in the world. The evil one is not happy at this. The Pope is a great instrument of your Father in Heaven and in a single day, in a single address, can return many hundreds, even thousands of hearts, to a fuller love of Me. You must pray for the Pope.

In these times, persecution will occur. Throughout time since I left the earth, Christians have been persecuted, but it will become worse than ever. People will shed blood, people will lose their lives. Share My cross. No servant is greater than his master. I, your Lord, Jesus Christ, suffered. As My servant, how do you expect you will escape this suffering? But more than this, you must suffer lovingly. Do it for love and suffer acceptingly.

Many who are close to Me don't understand these times. There are many manifestations of the Holy Spirit taking place to warn you, but due to the increasing level of apostasy in the world, many of the faithful are not interested in these many warnings and won't be until the Church approves them. Mary is appearing to many and speaking to many more. She is appearing right here in Australia. If you are relying on people to believe you, I'm sorry; you will be sadly disappointed. You must seek refuge in the Immaculate Heart of Mary from the attack and pain that will come from nonbelievers.

On your own, you are dust, but I have taken you and done great things for you; I have led you through a conversion. Your love for Me has never been stronger or more complete, but be wary that you don't become lazy or lukewarm. I will vomit the lukewarm from My mouth. You must continue to pray, especially the Rosary, go to Mass daily, go to confession regularly (at least once a month), fast, and work on bringing your friends to a greater love of Me.

Above all, trust. Do My will and all will be provided. You will have all you need and more. You will have peace and love.

Most importantly, Matthew reveals that the Eternal Father confirmed reports about the coming times, revealing that great warnings and miracles were to come:

The mini-judgment is a reality. People no longer realize that they offend Me. Out of My infinite Mercy, I will provide a mini-judgment. It will be painful, very painful, but short. You will see your sins; you will see how much you offend Me every day.

I know that you think this sounds like a very good thing, but unfortunately even this won't bring the whole world into My love. Some people will turn even further away from Me; they will be proud and stubborn. Satan is working hard against me.

Poor souls, all of you, robbed of the knowledge of My love. Be ready for this judgment of Mine. 'Judgment' is the best word you humans have to describe it, but it will be more like this: You will see your own personal darkness contrasted against the pure light of My love.

Those who repent will be given an unquenchable thirst for this light. Their love for Me then will be so strong that united with Mary's Immaculate Heart and the Sacred Heart of Jesus, the head of Satan shall be crushed, and he will be detained in hell forever. All those who love Me will join to help form the heel that crushes Satan.

Then, as you all die naturally, your thirst for this light will be quenched; you shall see Me, your God. You shall live in My love; you will be in Heaven.

Now, do you see how important these times are? Don't wait for this mini-judgment; you must start to look at yourselves more closely so that you can see your faults and repent. You are fortunate to have the faith needed to believe. Read and accept this message; you must not go away indifferent to it. You must examine yourself more every day and pray in reparation.

All of you, be like the blind man. Each day you should cry, 'Lord, open My eyes,' and My son will open your eyes so that you can see your wretchedness and repent.

Pray now more than ever, and remember the world's standards are a false indication of My justice. I am your God, and while I am perfectly merciful to those who repent, I am perfectly just to those who do not.

Many people think that I, your God, won't mind; it's only little, they say. But it's not a matter of minding. I want people to love Me. Love respects little things as well as the big things, and in the most cases, these little things are not so little.

Do not judge your actions or other's actions; you are unable to judge; you are incapable of judging because you cannot read a man's heart.

You must love Me with your whole heart, with your whole mind, with your whole soul, and with your whole strength.

Today is the day; do your best to renounce yourself and let Christ reign in your lives. You will never be ready for the mini-judgment, but some will be more prepared than others. You must aim to be one of those and bring as many others as you can to be prepared, or as prepared as possible.

Above all, do not fear; I don't tell you all of this to become scared. No, simply try to become better people each day; more than this I could not ask. I am your God; I am perfectly just and perfectly merciful. You are sons and daughters of Mine; does not a father look after his children? I send this message to spare you from any pain I can, but the pain that you experience by seeing the darkness of your soul is an act of love on My behalf. Do you not see that this will return many, many souls to a fuller love of Me? This will save many souls from the fires of hell.

This is the most important of all My messages: I am the Lord, your God; you are My sons and daughters whom I love very much, and My greatest delight is in being with you, and I want to be with you for eternity. Anything I do is

done out of love for you, My children. Trust in Me, your Heavenly Father.

Although Matthew Kelly reveals the messages he receives, he does not discuss visions, apparitions, or other gifts he may have been given. His personal mystical experiences are not part of his mission, he explains. He says the Eternal Father made this clear to him. "The purity of the messages is only *infected* when I get involved," Matthew said.

Across the world, the same can be said for numerous reported apparitions and supernatural phenomena. Fr. Rene Laurentin, the world's foremost Marian scholar, says many events he investigates are being contaminated by Satan or by visionaries' pride.

By early 1998, the events in Australia were attracting incredible attention. Over 100,000 copies of a book that contained the revelations to Matthew Kelly were distributed. Matthew Kelly, like many visionaries, was now traveling around the world, bringing the Eternal Father's messages to all who invited him. He was on an urgent mission because like the others, he is aware of a divine schedule.

Indeed, the revelations to Matthew expecially confirmed that all is to be fulfilled. Formally announced at Fatima more than 75 years ago, Mary's work throughout the world, is now, with all her chosen messengers of the 1980's and 1990's, approaching its climax:

My children, I am the breath of fresh air in the new day. I am the light sent forth to remove all darkness. I am your Mother Mary, Queen of Peace, and peace is what I want for all my children. May the peace of the Lord be with you always.

My children, don't let anything take this peace away from your souls. As persecution begins to mount, you must keep firm in your mind your aim: To do the will of God so as to achieve your sanctification.

I am your mother, Queen of Heaven, I will bring you all you need. You have an abundance of

human qualities already, my children, take care of spiritual matters, and do everything you can in temporal matters, and leave the rest up to me. My children, I will bring to you all you need, just keep firm in your path to do God's will.

Yes, time is a factor, and Matthew says the Eternal Father explained to him that soon His justice would come upon humanity:

You are called today to accept My words and live in My love; many have rejected My love, and many will. They will feel the whole force of heaven against them when fires come from heaven, when My justice comes to those who abuse their freedom, which has been entrusted to them by Me, your Heavenly Father, so that they may pursue eternal happiness for their souls and assist others in doing the same. (June 21, 1993)

And like Mary reportedly has revealed so often, Matthew says God the Father told him that this was the world's call to change:

This is the only preparation for the times that await at the doorstep of the world.

My son, tell the world to pray and return to the Sacraments. I am the Lord your God; I come to you out of My infinite mercy in these words, but before long I will come to you out of My infinite justice, and the world will feel the wrath of My justice through natural disasters worse than those ever experienced. Now is the time to respond, My children.

Seek My Will in each moment and live not for pleasure in this life but in hope of Heaven.

Seek first the Kingdom of God, and His justice and all else will be given in addition.

My children, spread these messages; deny no one the opportunity to heed My warning one more time.

I have spoken to this young boy, but I speak to you all; he is merely the instrument I have chosen to use.

These messages are to each and every one of My children throughout the world. These messages will show you how to live My Will in the midst of these times. (July, 1993)

As in Europe, Asia and Africa, the revelations emerging from Australia bore witness to this final wave of apparition's dominant theme of "urgent conversion" in order to escape "chastisement".

However, according to visionaries, Australia like elsewhere, was free of communism and therefore, its sinful indulgences seemed to carry with them a greater "responsibility" and a greater "accountability." This reality, seers noted, held its basis in Scripture. God's justice would not avoid this truth, they implied, for "to whom much is given, much is to be expected."

Indeed, this chilly reminder is revealed when many of the messages of today's visionaries are examined "between the lines." And for America, perhaps unlike anywhere else in the world, some say the debt was seriously mounting.

Bishop Fulton Sheen

A great believer in the message of Fatima, by 1950, Bishop Fulton Sheen had already written that the great miracle of the sun at Fatima in 1917 was a foreshadowing sign of the choice mankind faced in the near future because of atomic weapons. Many of the Bishop's words can now be seen to reveal that he had extraordinary insight and was a great prophet of the times now at hand.

198

CHAPTER TWENTY-NINE

A CHOICE

"He called them and immediatly they left their boat and their fathers and followed."

— Mt 4:21-22

From sea to shining sea, there have been numerous reports of apparitions of the Virgin Mary everywhere in America since 1981. From Canada to Texas, from California to Massachusetts, from Alaska to Florida, the Madonna is constantly being seen and has even appeared on the covers of *Time, Newsweek* and *Life* magazines. Throughout America, almost every state has reports of something.

These reports are not just from Catholics. There are also Orthodox and Protestant claims. Even major newspapers are covering the events. *The Atlanta Constitution, Arizona Republic, Wall Street Journal* and the *Los Angeles Times* have featured front-page stories, and television newscasts and shows such as *Geraldo, Joan Rivers, 20/20, Sally Jessy Raphael*, and *Oprah* have interviewed witnesses and visionaries.

Across America, however, the sheer number of reported visionaries has led to a wave of skepticism—a fear of false manifestations and a fear of angels of darkness and a fear of fraud and a fear of psychopaths. Many believers are confused in their search for truth. Surely all these visionaries and apparitions can't be authentic, they reason correctly.

Nevertheless, the authentic events can't help but stand out because they are often graced with signs from God. From the Snow Belt to the Wheat Belt, from the Rust Belt to the Beltway, Mary is being encountered all across America, many experts say. One need only to look carefully—without fear.

In Lakeridge, Virginia, a priest bears the stigmata, and statues seem to weep wherever he goes. *U.S. News and World Report* was so impressed by his account, they ran it as a cover story.

In New Orleans, beginning in 1975, a Cuban exile reported numerous apparitions of Mary. The revelations reportedly concerned Fatima and the evils of communism. And again, weeping images accompanied the reported visions.

In Canada, an 80-year-old Belgian stigmatist named Georgette Faniel claims the Eternal Father speaks to her. Her humility overwhelms even the greatest skeptic, and incredible events surround her. One time, Georgette even offered to bear the suffering of a woman's pregnancy in order to prevent her from having an abortion. The woman agreed, and her pain vanished, even during her delivery. Meanwhile, not only did Faniel endure the suffering, but her abdomen steadily grew in proportion each month to the real mother's pregnancy. It was a suffering not without purpose, for Faniel reports that both Jesus and the Eternal Father have asked her that it be offered specifically for Mary's apparitions at Medjugorje to be officially recognized. The intention is significant because through Medjugorje, many believe will come "the fulfillment of Fatima."

Nearby in Toronto, more miracles are claimed. In one house, statues of Jesus and Mary weep in every room while just outside the city in a place called Marmora, countless pilgrims report that Mary appears and speaks to them, even to a relocated Ukrainian seer named Josyp Terelya.

In Chicago and Houston, statues and icons weep, and crowds stand in line for hours to witness the phenomenon. In Lubbock, Texas, a woman tells of incredible conversations with angels, while across town, thousands gather at St. John Neumann Church to witness a series of solar miracles promised to occur by several visionaries.

The phenomena of weeping statues has especially seemed to dominate such reports in America since the 1960's. It's as if the Virgin cries for an unknown danger the country is approaching, for everywhere in America there have been reports of weeping pictures, statues, and icons, perhaps the likes of which can only be found in

Italy. In 1972, a Lourdes statue wept in a small town in New York State. That same year, a Fatima statue wept over 50 times on Long Island. The same statue wept in Chicago, Pittsburgh, and Washington, D.C. Since 1970, there have been reports of Mary weeping in New Orleans, Las Vegas, Cathage N.Y., California, Brooklyn, Chicago, Atlanta, Connecticut, Wheeling, and dozens of other places. The Rev. Albert Herbert, S.M., who has written two books on Mary's many weeping images, conjectured the Virgin Mary appears to be weeping in Italy and America more than anywhere else in the world because of the danger these countries must face:

> But, why so many weeping images centered about Italy and the United States? Italy almost renegade in the practice of the Catholic Faith for millions of its children, a once glorious daughter of the Church, the land area of the Spouse of Christ, the Church, is given over, in many of her so-called Catholic children, to the harlotry of much immorality and association with atheist Communism. For Italy, and for the Church housed there, the warnings seem clear enough as do the messages.
>
> Why the United States? Already this nation has held a glorious place in history. It has been a refuge for all the good aspirations of mankind and has been a home for liberty-loving people from over the entire world. It still continues to be so, although many rights are trampled on. Liberty has been turned into permissiveness and immorality flourishes among many.
>
> That nation, America, which should be the major political and spiritual bastion against atheistic Communism, is becoming more and more degenerate in many areas of its moral and spiritual life: abortion, sexual immorality of all kinds, Sodoms and Gomarrahs of homosexuals and lesbians, pre-marital sex (plain fornication), adultery, divorce, broken families, child abuse and pornography, political corruption, disregard of holy days, cursing, disobedience, drunkedness, drugs, murder, etc.

It would seem that Mary and Christ are calling America to reform, to renewal, reparation, holiness, at least to normally good lives; to the restoration of America to a true place of world leadership; and perhaps the political and military defeat of atheism.

What was—and is!—the great significance of so many remarkable weepings as we have seen, that have occurred since 1972?

There does not appear to be moral certainty now that all the prophecies of Fatima will be fulfilled, and that the Third Secret will continue on its unfolding course translating into action. And it seems events forecast in the Twelfth Chapter of *Apocalypse* or the *Book of Revelation* can well be in motion now, as it is claimed by Mary.

In Worchester, Mass., lives a little girl named Audrey Santo. On Aug. 9, 1987, at age 3, Audrey drowned in the family pool. After being resuscitated, she was rushed to a hospital, where she was over-medicated with too much Phenobarbital. Little Audrey lapsed into a coma-like state known as Akinetic Mutism.

Therapy worsened her condition. On October 13th, the date of the last apparition at Fatima, she suffered broken legs and a dislocated shoulder. She had to have a tracheotomy. Resisting institutional care, her parents brought their little girl home in the same condtion.

Then, it happened. Audrey's mother, Linda, decided to take her to Medjugorje, the site of the Virgin's apparitions. It was a laborious undertaking. After months of planning, Audrey arrived and several days later, while in the same condition, she was taken to the apparition room. There, when the Virgin appeared, Linda beseeched God for help—or to take her daughter home to heaven.

After a second apparition, Audrey's movements indicated something was happening, but that evening, the little girl lapsed into cardiac arrest. A desperate situation then unfolded. But somehow Audrey survived and was flown back to Massachusetts by a military medical plane. She did not receive what her family requested—instead, something else happened.

Unexpectedly, one month later the wounds of Jesus Christ

appeared on the back of Audrey's hands and later on her right foot, and on Christmas Day 1991, two tears of blood came from each of Audrey's eyes. Then, her mother and nurses observed "whip marks" that appeared and disappeared on Audrey's body.

Little Audrey Santo became a "victim soul," say religious experts who are studying her case. Over the years, her stigmata appeared on certain Holy Days and on Good Friday and thousands now come to see and pray with her.

Some theologians conjecture that while in Medjugorje, Audrey was given a choice, and the little girl chose to suffer in Christ. Physical and spiritual healings through her intercession have also been reported.

In addition, spiritual ties have surfaced, ties that involve the Virgin's previous work in America. Audrey's suffering, some believe, has something to do with America, its past and its future.

This is because it was Aug. 9 at 11:03 a.m. when the first recorded medical entry was made on the day of Audrey Santo's drowning, the exact date and time of another event 42 years before: the atomic bombing of Nagasaki.

While more than 30 reported apparitions attracted attention during the 80's and early 90's in America, by 1998 none had been approved by the Church. And none was close to being approved. Apparently, some say, Mary's messages and apparitions for America were falling victim to confusion and division.

No doubt, many local people have spiritually benefited from these events. And from California to Ohio, Kentucky to Wisconsin, numerous prayer groups were started. Thousands had responded to the events, and not surprisingly, countless reports of miracles and phenomena poured in throughout the country.

But in Arizona, a middle-aged, silver-haired woman seemed to be saying something special. The Virgin, Estela Ruiz declared, was appearing to her and appearing in an incredible fashion. Estela said Mary changed her life and the lives of her entire family. They were radically changed. And this was to be, many believed, an example for all families because it was the only way, the Virgin reportedly told Estela, the world could be saved.

The *family*, Mary insisted to Estela, was the key to America's spiritual survival. Likewise, it was the key to what had gone wrong in the world and the key to what would make it right again.

Indeed, theologians say this all made sense because at Fatima on Oct. 13, 1917, while the 70,000 people witnessed the sun hurtling towards the earth, the children saw other visions. One of the Holy Family. Some Marian experts say this was no accident because the way to stop the fire from the sky is through the survival of the family. The two simultaneous visions presented a choice, the experts say. And soon, very soon, the world may have to decide. The Ruiz apparitions explain this mystery to us better than any other and therefore, they deserve a closer look.

CHAPTER THIRTY

ONE MAN'S PRAYER

"My strength and my courage is the Lord, and He has been my savior. He is my God, I praise Him, the God of my father, I extol him."

—Ex 15:2

Like Biblical characters who are filled with wisdom and led every step by God himself, Estela's husband Reyes Ruiz, personifies a modern-day Abraham. He is many things to many people. Kind. Loving. Honest. Sincere. Hardworking. But most of all, he is prayerful. Always prayerful.

The son and grandson of Mexican farm workers, Reyes Ruiz grew up during the 1930's in Virden, New Mexico. As a young boy, his father's death changed his life. To fill a void, he fell in love, in love with a beautiful lady. A lady from heaven. By age 13, says Reyes, the Virgin Mary was the "love of his life," and his very best friend.

Reyes' other role models had done likewise. The Villalba family, his mother's side, was steeped in generations of devotees to the Virgin of Guadalupe. His great-grandfather, Tifelo Bejarno, committed every waking moment to the Virgin. Tifelo liked to recite Rosaries. Thousands of them. All day. All week. All month. All year. Every year. Until he died at age 87, Tifelo was madly in love with Mary.

But so were all the elders of Reyes' family.

Out in the fields, picking watermelons, cantaloupes, tomatoes, onions, or corn, the field workers would drop to their knees upon approaching images of Mary or Jesus erected at the end of the rows of crops. Not just prayers would flow, but holiness.

While tucked in bed at night, with six or more others, Reyes would often awaken to find his grandfather, Andres Villalba, in prayer, perhaps making up for a few hundred Hail Mary's and Our Father's the old man may have missed that day from his Rosary quota.

Thus, it was no surprise that by age 13, Reyes Ruiz had his priorities set. While others sought success and fortune, fame or families, Reyes was pursuing heaven. He had to get there, he felt, because his love, the Queen of Heaven, was awaiting him.

In 1957, Reyes married Estela, whose maiden name was also Ruiz. From New Mexico, they journeyed to Arizona, where they built a house, had seven kids and settled down to start a normal life.

But it wasn't to be.

Something went wrong. Something that started in the late 60's and 70's. Reyes' oldest son, Isidore, moved to California and left the Church. Two other sons, Armando and Fernando, got involved with politics and seemed to be on the road to power and prominence. But his youngest, Reyes Jr., stumbled onto another path, a path of self-destruction headed toward death.

By age 28, Reyes Jr., known as Little Rey, had done it all. Coke, crack, smack, heroin and crystal meth. Even the gun battles could not cause remorse in him because he wasn't "hooked" on drugs—he was committed to them. As Dad loved the Madonna and made her the center of his life, Reyes Jr. was dedicated to his beloved drugs.

By 1988, Reyes Ruiz, Sr., was desperate for help for his youngest son and for all his family. His wife, Estela, was a committed partner but that was it. Seven kids had taken its toll. Estela was now in her 50's and a successful career woman. Around age 40, she had gone back to school and earned a bachelor's degree and later a master's. After completing her education, she landed a good job, then, a great job.

Earning $40,000 a year and having a reputation for achieving success, Estela Ruiz wanted nothing to do with her husband's quest for heaven. To her, Reyes was a religious kook. Likewise, Mama Ruiz felt she had done all she could for her wayward children. Instead, it was time for a new home. Time to get out of her neighborhood because helicopters and strobe lights, gun shots and crack houses were not her cup of tea. It was South Phoenix of the 80's, a microcosm of America's big cities. Estela wanted out, and by early 1988, she was packing to leave.

But Reyes left first. In September 1988, the family patriarch departed for Medjugorje, Yugoslavia, because he read that his best friend, his Lady from Heaven, was visiting there. With that, he was out the door. His wife, however, rejected his invitation to accompany him, repeating her response daily. "No!" "No!" "No!"

But the truth was that Estela couldn't wait till Reyes was gone because for her, it would be 10 days of freedom, 10 days of peace and reflection, 10 days of no religion.

But that's far from what was to occur. Estela says that she woke one morning several days after Reyes departed. She shuffled to the kitchen to make some coffee. And on the way a voice greeted her, and it wasn't a family member.

"Good morning, Daughter!" the voice said to her.

Estela looked but saw nothing. The voice sounded as if it emanated from a painting her husband had done. No, it couldn't be, she told herself. A painting of the Virgin of Guadalupe. No! She dismissed it. Several days later, it happened again.

"Good morning, Daughter!"

This time, like a reflex, Estela, for some reason, responded. "Good morning, Mother!"

And with that, Estela Ruiz says she almost lost her mind. She knew for sure what she'd heard. She knew it emanated from the location of the painting, and she knew for sure she had replied.

"My God," she thought, "I'm going as crazy as my husband!"

A week later, her husband returned from Medjugorje. Reyes Ruiz came back a new man. Even Estela noticed a change, but she kept quiet because she wanted no one to know what had happened to her.

Soon another strange thing occurred.

Estela had a dream. In it, she says the Virgin appeared as real as could be. Throughout the dream, Estela watched as Mary conversed with her husband as if they were old friends. The dream went on and on. It seemed so lifelike. But more was yet to come.

On Dec. 3, 1988, as Reyes, Estela, and some of their children prayed the Rosary in their bedroom, the supernatural descended on the Ruiz home like a bolt of lightning.

Suddenly, a brilliant light filled the bedroom. Estela says she was taken off guard. Stunned, she was sure everyone else saw it too. But they hadn't.

Next, as if it were a Hollywood movie, Estela reported that she saw a mist-like cloud materialize around a painting of the Virgin. But only Estela could see it.

Not surprisingly, she says her heart raced as the rest of the family continued reciting Hail Mary's, oblivious of what was unfolding in their home.

CHAPTER THIRTY-ONE

OUR LADY OF THE AMERICAS

"Then, Mary said, 'My being proclaims the greatness of the Lord
...'"

—Lk 1:46

As Estela Ruiz was staring at the painting of the Virgin Mary, she says she suddenly spotted Mary herself, suspended in mid-air, surrounded by brilliant light and vapor.

"Oh my God! She's here! You are a beautiful woman!" she exclaimed.

"You are a beautiful woman!" she began to say over and over, as she sat up to better see that Mary was looking directly at her.

With that, the rest of the family realized something outrageous was happening. And Papa Reyes knew what!

After the Madonna completely materialized, she smiled and gazed with her deep blue eyes into Estela's eyes.

"Don't you know I'm going to take care of your children?" she asked Estela.

And then Mary said, **"I'm going to leave now."** With that, the apparition faded and vanished. In just a few minutes, it was over. But in reality it was just the beginning.

From that day forward, Estela was no longer the same person. She was now a "visionary."

Estela says the Virgin Mary quickly began to explain to her how God had a plan to save America and that she had come as "Our Lady of the Americas." Her goal, she told her, was **"to bring the Triumph of the Immaculate Heart into the world."** But it was going to take much work and many apparitions. And time was short.

After her second apparition, Estela says that Mary appeared on an irregular basis not only in the Ruiz home but also in a neighborhood church and a few other places. It was a strictly local affair. Usually, the apparitions took place in the living room or bedroom at various times of the day. But by May 1989, word of the events spread, and people started to come, hundreds then thousands.

By 1990, Estela was still reporting apparitions of Mary, and once a week the Virgin would bring a message for America, a message calling God's people back to Him. As she had done elsewhere, Estela said the Virgin made a strong appeal for prayer and reparation for sin.

But there was also a prophetic content to her messages. As reported in many revelations, the Virgin told Estela that the times were urgent. Estela says that Mary warned over and over that **"destruction"** loomed, and although there was no mention of fire, the implication was clear that change had to come quickly or else the consequences would be grave.

Most of all, the messages reveal that the Virgin spoke strongly to Estela of the fulfillment of her remaining prophecies at Fatima. Yes, nations could still be destroyed, but the Triumph of her Immaculate Heart and the Era of Peace were certain. To prevent disaster, the Virgin kept telling Estela that America needed to look at what it was doing, particularly at what it was doing to the family.

American families, Mary reportedly told Estela, were being destroyed by false teachings, and this in turn was destroying the nation. The abortions, the contraceptives, the divorces, all of this was bringing the country down. Worse yet, America's attempt to export an anti-life philosophy to the rest of the world would cause God to act. America, Estela said she was shown, was following Satan, and this would ultimately bring unfathomable tragedy:

> **Many of God's children have been deceived**
> **by Satan and have come to believe that his evil**
> **ways lead to happiness. Hate, anger, and violence**
> **rule the world, and there is no happiness in that**
> **because they are contrary to the nature of God.**
> **Greed and lust reign supreme and discord has**

separated and pitted brother against brother and children against parents, and Satan has divided and conquered.

Is Satan to remain in control, or are you, my beloved little ones, ready to reject this misery and return to your rightful inheritance, which is to be children of God? Because you were given free will, only you can answer this question, only you, each one of you, can make this decision. Will hate, anger, and confusion continue to reign until humanity is destroyed and extinguished, or are you, the children that God created, ready to change hearts and souls to God's love and peaceful ways? Only time will tell. (Nov. 6, 1993)

The key to change, was a new respect for life, Estela said Mary explained to her. This was crucial. People had to come back to God:

And so today I speak again of God's love for you. I remind you that present times in the world are times of pain and destruction. The signs of the times tell you that the world is in crisis. The greatest offense to God is the lack of respect for life. Yet that is the greatest offense going on in these times. This is done cruelly and without conscience. How can God bless you, His children, if there is no regard for that which He created— life?

During these times, because of His great love for you, and because my Son died for all of you, He can only pour His mercy on you, that you may repent and change the course of destruction to which you in the world are headed.

Listen to my words, my children, hear me! God loves you and does not want to see the destruction of that which He created—you, His children. Allow Him to enter your hearts, that He

may teach you to love, that He may take the hatred from your hearts. He loves you and desires to live in you. I love you and desire that you open your hearts to His love. (July 2, 1994)

In October 1992, Estela Ruiz traveled on a historical pilgrimage to Russia. It was a monumental event, the Virgin reportedly told her, one that would help bring the fulfillment of her prophecy of the Triumph of her Immaculate Heart:

My beloved little ones, you must begin to understand the significance of the event you have been involved in. This event is the spark that ignited the fire that will become a blaze throughout the world of the love of my Immaculate Heart. It is through Russia's conversion that the world will know that these times are truly the reign of my heart and that my love for God and for my earthly children will triumph over evil, so that all nations will know and acknowledge that my Son, Our Lord, Jesus is the King of the world and the hope and salvation of all.

My faithful children, there is much work to do. You who are in the service of my work are being called to do much. Do not linger anymore on past moments, but look to the future and the tremendous amount of work to be done as I call on all of you to move on with me. You have seen many unbelievable events unfold, and you will see many more throughout the world. All of my faithful throughout the world, let us move on to the work at hand. My peace pilgrims, it is only fitting that this event be finalized in Rome, where my beloved son, John Paul, the vicar of my Son, resides. He knows of this event, and in his heart has blessed it. United in love, my Son's most Sacred Heart and my Immaculate Heart have also blessed it. (Oct. 24, 1992)

The Virgin Mary delivered hundreds of messages to Estela Ruiz. Profound revelations. And in 1989, a Church commission investigating the events found nothing contrary to the faith. Although unable to render an affirmative decision on the supernaturalness of the apparitions, the commission permitted the events to continue. By 1998, Mary in many of her messages to Estela, was still pleading, begging the people of America to change—to change before it was too late. As elsewhere, Estela Ruiz's messages spoke with confidence of the coming dawn of a new era. Happily or painfully—either way it was coming, and coming soon.

Indeed, the Ruiz family heard the message, including Reyes Ruiz, Jr., who was miraculously healed of his drug problem. In fact, the entire Ruiz family's change was nothing short of miraculous. But millions more were needed, Estela said Mary told her, because to heal the world, the family had to be healed first.

Perhaps it was a coincidence, perhaps not. This had been Reyes Ruiz's final prayer in Medjugorje in 1988, that somehow, some way, God would change his family. And then America. And then the world.

Mary appeared to Estela Ruiz as, 'Our Lady of the
Americas,' promising to convert America.
The apparitions lasted for ten years. (1988-1998)

CHAPTER THIRTY-TWO

"IT IS THE IMMACULATE ONE"

"And the angel came in and said unto her, 'Hail full of grace, the Lord is with thee, blessed art thou among women.'"

—Lk 1:28

In Ecuador, more than 30 volcanoes tower over valleys and lowlands, their peaks always surrounded by clouds, which at night glow with an eerie orange light reflected from the molten lava in the craters, creating an effect reminiscent of how God was said to signal His presence on Mount Sinai. These are the Andes, for centuries the home of the Incas, who lived there 500 years before the Spanish established a great empire from northern Chile through Peru to Ecuador. To the east, lies Brazil, which stretches to the Atlantic and is a country larger than the United States and as big as all the other South American countries combined. It borders just about every other nation on the continent, Uruguay, Paraguay, Argentina, and Bolivia to the south and west; Guyana, Venezuela, and Colombia to the north. Within it all, dozens of tributaries of the Amazon River wander endlessly across the continent that is considered part of the New World, but which is actually more Old World.

A 100 years before the first settlers came to North America, South American explorers already roamed the continent. Having carved their way south after conquering Montezuma in Mexico, the big push through Central America into South America was at hand. The Europeans brought their civilized ways, their communities, and their hunger for prosperity. Most importantly, they brought their religion.

Through the Portuguese and Spanish, South America was introduced to the Gospel of Jesus Christ. And with Jesus came Mary because the early Europeans always brought the Mother of God to lead the way. Indeed, Columbus himself insisted his ship be called the "Santa Maria."

According to the recorded statements of witnesses, Mary did not totally rely on her devoted followers. Right from the beginning, she is reported to have come herself. A personal mission, here and there to let the people know that heaven had special plans for them. Great plans. For theologians say God was about to free a pagan world from its spiritual slavery.

Like so many accounts in Scripture and Judeo-Christian history, Mary's intersession in this land began with a dream. In 1509, Princess Papantzin lay near death, and in her coma, she reportedly saw a glowing angel with a black cross on his forehead appear to her. The angel led Papantzin to the ocean shore and showed her ships with white sails emblazoned with black crosses sailing to her pagan Aztec nation.

The tyrannical rule of her brother, emperor Montezuma II, would be overthrown, the angel told Papantzin, and her nation would be conquered and brought to the true God. The oppressed Indian people would be liberated, the dream revealed. Liberated by white-skinned invaders. Papantzin awoke and told her brother everything. It is said Montezuma brooded over the news and sullenly awaited his fate.

At that time, Montezuma's reign was one of bloodshed and death, for he and the rulers before him were dedicated to offering as much human blood to their gods as they could—as many as 50,000 victims a year. One in every five children was sacrificed. In 1487, five years before Columbus arrived, 80,000 were offered up in one four-day bloody orgy near Mexico City.

In 1519, the thundering cannons and blazing muskets of the Spaniards left Montezuma believing the invaders were invincible. Within a year, the battle was over. Cortez crushed Montezuma and replaced the Aztec idols with images of Jesus and Mary throughout the land. However, it was not all over for Montezuma's family. A few years later, Princess Papantzin was baptized Catholic, one of the very first, along with a peasant Indian named Juan Diego and his wife, Maria Lucia.

By 1531, Juan Diego was an old 57. He was weary and lonely, for his wife had died and life had not been easy on him. On a cold star-lit December morning, Juan rose early to go to church. It was the Feast of the Immaculate Conception.

As the little Indian approached Tepeyac Hill, the former site of a pagan temple used for sacrifices, he began to hear music. He stopped. The music continued. He heard it clearly now, the sound of what seemed like a choir. It was beautiful, captivating. As his eyes searched for the source, he suddenly spotted a glowing white cloud that gave off a kaleidoscope of colors, which formed a brilliant rainbow. Juan Diego was stunned.

Then, the music stopped, and a voice called to him, a woman's voice that was gentle, yet persuasive.

"Juanito ... Juan Dieguito!" the lady called.

The peasant paused but not out of fear. Racing up a 130-foot summit, he suddenly found himself face to face with an emblazoned woman whose beauty and brilliance were overpowering. The vision, he would later explain, was mesmerizing.

Even though the hill was boulder-strewn and covered with mesquite bushes and prickly plants, all he could see was the lady. Her dress shown like the sun, and she was young, maybe 14 years old.

She beckoned to him. After several steps, Juan fell to his knees, overwhelmed by a feeling of love and peace.

"Juanito, my son, where are you going?"

"Noble lady," he replied, "I am on my way to the church in Tlaltelolco to hear Mass."

She smiled and then told him:

> **Know for certain, dearest of my sons, that I am the perfect and perpetual Virgin Mary, mother of the True God, through whom everything lives, the Lord of all things, who is Master of Heaven and Earth. I ardently desire a teocalli [temple] be built here for me, where I will show and offer all my love, my compassion, my help, and my protection to the people. I am your**

217

merciful mother, the mother of all who live united in this land, and of all mankind, of all those who love me, of those who cry to me, of those who have confidence in me. Here I will hear their weeping and their sorrows, and will remedy and alleviate their sufferings, necessities, and misfortunes. Therefore, in order to realize my intentions, go to the house of the bishop of Mexico City and tell him what you have seen and heard. Be assured that I shall be very grateful and will reward you for doing diligently what I have asked of you. Now that you have heard my words, my son, go and do everything as best as you can.

Juan bowed and replied reverently, "My Holy One, my Lady, I will do all you ask of me."

Hurrying down Tepeyac, Juan raced toward Mexico City. As the peasant arrived at Bishop Zumarraga's house, his worst fear was realized. Physical abuse he could stand, but what would happen if the bishop didn't believe him? And this was exactly what occurred.

Although the bishop eventually received him after hours of waiting, Zumarraga listened and dismissed him. It was too much. The mother of God appearing in Mexico on a hill where a pagan temple once was. Highly unbelievable, the educated bishop concluded, yet curious. He promised Juan he would reflect on his words, but continued to resist, until finally telling Juan to ask the lady for a sign.

And a sign he got.

The Virgin instructed Juan Diego to go to the top of the hill, where he would find a sign for the bishop—flowers, Castilian roses, which were the bishop's favorite.

"Gather them carefully," the Virgin said. **"Assemble them together and then bring them back and show me what you have."**

On the hill, Juan Diego found the flowers—even the roses, which were somehow growing in frozen soil. Not only that. Although it was December, the roses were in full bloom, covered with morning dew. The flowers filled the air with a magnificent fragrance.

Removing his cape, or tilma, Juan filled it with flowers and hurried back to the Virgin. When he returned to her, Mary hastily arranged them with her own hands and gave him his departing orders.

"My little son," she said, **"these varied flowers are the sign which you are to take to the bishop. Tell him in my name that in them he will recognize my will and that he must fulfill it."**

With that Juan Diego was off. The fateful moment had arrived. Again, the little Indian had to argue his way into the bishop's quarters, but he had the required sign. At first, the servants were intent on detaining him, but the sight of the flowers made them change their mind. The bishop emerged from his quarters, and Juan addressed him.

"Your Excellency, I obeyed your instructions; the celestial lady told me to come and see you again," said Juan, explaining all that had happened. Then, he opened his tilma, and the flowers, mingled with Castilian roses, fell to the floor.

Everyone stood stunned and watched in amazement. Juan's tilma, which was woven from cactus fibers, had upon it a beautiful color portrait of the Blessed Virgin Mary. It was breathtaking. The image glowed as if Mary were alive, causing everyone to stand transfixed in wonderment.

"It is the Immaculate One!" exclaimed the bishop.

One by one, they dropped to their knees. Apologetically, the bishop turned to Juan Diego only to find him just as perplexed as they were. What he saw was an exact replica of the celestial lady he encountered on Tepeyac. Her image was now imprinted for all eternity on his tilma. She was, theologians would later say, the woman of Revelation 12:1. And for the Virgin Mary, it was the beginning of a mission that she would later complete at Fatima.

Quickly, a chapel was erected on Tepeyac, and the story spread like wildfire throughout the land. It was discovered later that Mary also appeared to Juan's uncle, Juan Bernadino, giving him the healing she promised his nephew.

Through what historians say were a series of errors and misunderstandings, the Virgin's apparition at Tepeyac became known as the miracle of Guadalupe. However, it appears these errors were intended by God, for the most famous shrine in Spain, where Columbus prayed before his departure, was named "Guadalupe." It was a word thought to be confused with the Aztec word "coatlaxopenh." Thus, the origin of "Our Lady of Guadalupe."

In a few years, 9 million Aztecs were converted to Christianity through the miracle of the apparition, and the Virgin of Guadalupe's image spread throughout Central and South America, converting millions more over the centuries.

Ten years later, in 1541, the Virgin reportedly appeared again to another Indian. This time, she led the visionary to a miraculous spring in Tlaxcala, where the oldest Franciscan monastery in the New World still exists today.

The miracle of Our Lady of Ocotlan, like the miracle of Our Lady of Guadalupe, spread and strengthened even more the faith Native Americans throughout Central and South America would come to have in the Blessed Virgin Mary's power of intercession. Other stories followed.

In the 16th century, Peru's Rosa de Flores, better known today as Saint Rose of Lima, reported apparitions and many mystical experiences, leading to a great spiritual awakening in the land. To this day, she is known as the Patroness of the Americas.

Less than 100 years later, an apparition occurred in Cuba and another in Quito, Ecuador. Like Guadalupe, the apparition in Quito in 1634 was special because theologians say Mary gave a prophetic message about the future, a message that some believe was intended for today.

CHAPTER THIRTY-THREE

DROWNED WITH TRIBULATIONS

"Lo, the Lord empties the land and lays it waste; He turns it upside down, scattering its inhabitants."

— Is 24:1

On February 2, 1634, as Mother Marianna of Jesus Torres prayed before the Blessed Sacrament, the sanctuary light went out, and when the nun tried to light it, a luminous supernatural light filled the church. Out of this light, the Virgin Mary appeared and began to speak to her. It was a message that was quite similar to her words at Fatima, hundreds of years later: **"I wish you to know that my maternal love will always watch over the convents of the entire order of my Immaculate Conception because this order will give me much glory in the holy daughters it will have. The sanctuary lamp burning in front of the Prisoner of Love, which you saw go out has many meanings!"** She then proceeded to give Mother Marianna a prophetic message:

The first is that toward the end of the 19th century and for a large part of the 20th century, various heresies will flourish on this earth, which will have become a free republic. The precious light of the faith will go out in souls because of the almost total moral corruption. In those times, there will be great physical and moral calamities, in private and in public. The little number of souls keeping the faith and practicing the virtues will undergo cruel and unspeakable sufferings. ...

Secondly, meaning: My communities will be abandoned; they will be swamped in a fathomless sea of bitterness and will seemed drowned in tribulations. How many true vocations will be lost for lack of skillful and prudent direction to them! Each mistress of novices will need to be a soul of prayer, knowing how to discern spirits.

Thirdly, meaning: In those times, the air will be filled with the spirit of impurity, which like a deluge of filth will flood the streets, squares, and public places. The licentiousness will be such that there will be no more virgin souls in the world.

The fourth meaning concerns, the power of sects and their ability to penetrate homes and families, thus destroying the beauty of innocence in the hearts of children. The devil will take glory in feeding perfidiously on the hearts of children. The innocence of childhood will almost disappear. Thus priestly vocations will be lost. It will be a real disaster. Priests will abandon their sacred duties and will depart from the path marked for them by God.

Then, the Church will go through a dark night for lack of a prelate and father to watch over it with love, gentleness, strength, and prudence, and numbers of priests will lose the Spirit of God, thus placing their souls in great danger .... Satan will take control of this earth through the fault of faithless men who, like a black cloud, will darken the clear sky of the republic consecrated to the Most Sacred Heart of my Divine Son. This republic, having allowed entry to all the vices, will have to undergo all sorts of chastisements: plagues, famine, war, apostasy, and the loss of souls without

number. And to scatter these black clouds blocking the brilliant dawning of the freedom of the Church, there will be a terrible war in which the blood of priests and of religious will flow. ... That night will be so horrible that wickedness will seem triumphant. Then will come my time: In astounding fashion, I shall destroy Satan's pride, casting him beneath my feet, chaining him up in the depths of hell, leaving Church and country freed at last from his cruel tyranny.

The fifth motive for the extinguishing of the lamp is because men possessing great wealth will look on with indifference while the Church is oppressed, virtue is persecuted, and evil triumphs. They will not use their wealth to fight evil and to reconstruct the faith. The people will come to care nothing for the things of God, will absorb the spirit of evil and will let themselves be swept away by all vices and passions."

As at Guadalupe, miracles followed the Quito apparitions, among the most noteworthy taking place centuries later on April 20, 1906, when an image of Our Lady of Quito wept at the Jesuit school of San Gabriel.

While the Virgin's message to Mother Marianna was profound, it is difficult to deduce what benefit would be gained from warning about events hundreds of years in the future. But this was seen before and mystical events in South America to this day are often looked at in the light of Quito's message.

And indeed, Central and South America today are no different from anywhere else in the world. The Virgin's appearances have been reported everywhere, and this is considered by the people to still be Mary's place, well-prepared over the centuries by her previous appearances.

By the late 1980s, a flood of apparitions was being reported in Central and South America. In Fortaleza and Sao Paulo, Brazil; in Guayaquil, Santo Domingo; Costa Rica; Es Meraldes, Totorillas, and

Port Au Prince, Haiti; Pereira-Risaralda, Colombia; El Huatusco, Panama; Penablanca, Chile; Peru and elsewhere. In Guatemala in 1984, a woman named Carmen claimed apparitions of Mary. Again, the messages warned an "unrepentant world." Likewise, on October 25, 1984, a statue was reported weeping in the Valparaiso area of Chili. Two more statues, Our Lady of La Salette and a Rosa Mystica, also wept there. The eyes were even seen to be swollen on the Rosa Mystica statue.

In Brazil, three different Rosa Mystica statues were reported weeping in 1987, while a corpus of Christ on a crucifix bled on October 20, 1981 in the village of Porta das Caixas, the so-called village of miracles just south of Rio de Janeiro. Many cures were reported as both ecclesiastical and local authorities denied any hoax. At the cathedral in Juiz de Fora, waters miraculously flowed from the walls on June 11th and August 11th and again on August 13th. While on September 15th and 16th, a Rosa Mystica statue wept tears of blood in the home of Mrs. Evepio Orango Cuervo in the village of Los Charcos near Santa Barbara, Columbia.

In Esmeralda, Ecuador, a man named Juan Mariano began having apparitions on August 22, 1987. A strong light preceded the apparitions, Juan reported, and then a young and very beautiful woman full of joy, sweetness and love appeared. Her voice was like music and her words penetrated the heart. Juan said that he saw Heaven, Purgatory, and Hell and that Mary asked for prayer and reparation. He also said that tragedies were coming but the conversion of the world could prevent them.

There were apparitions to a young girl reported in Cuba in 1980 but little information escaped to the free world. But in the fall of 1981, more apparitions offshore were reported in Cuba by exiles fleeing to neighboring Haiti. Mary reportedly appeared as Our Lady of Charity and was suspended above the water off shore of Havana. Dressed in all white, and with the Christ child on her arms, she moved gently about both day and night as she had at Cairo in 1968. Cuban authorities banned the offshore area but the apparition remained visible from other locations. Like at Hrushiv in the Ukraine, there were reports of gun fire by the Communists at the vision. A fifteen year old girl reportedly received a message from Mary that said Cuba would be freed if the people made enough penance and reparation.

Many more reports stood out during the 1980's, but three others are especially worth noting. One apparition was to three children in Terra Blanca, Mexico, in 1987, one to a poor man in Nicaragua, and a series of apparitions in Puerto Rico, that although occurred in 1953, left messages for today.

Terra Blanca, located in the diocese of Queretaro, is a terribly impoverished area, the kind of place where it would be harmful to request people to fast from the little food they had. Instead, during the apparition to the children, Mary reportedly called for a general abstinence from salt. The children were told about her other apparitions throughout the world. This was a revelation that was intriguing because the remoteness and isolation of Terra Blanca left the inhabitants with no knowledge of the world, much less apparitions.

The same thing occurred in Nicaragua, where a 50 year-old peasant claimed Mary visited him in 1980. Bernardo Martinez's account was so improbable and unbelievable that the bishop was convinced of its authenticity. Bishop Vega not only informally approved but even consented to travel with Bernardo as the seer struggled to convey the Virgin's message there. Mary was asking people **"to do more than talk about peace,"** said Bernardo. **"They must make peace."** And he said Mary told him, **"If you do not change your ways, you will provoke a third world war."** Bernardo eventually became a priest.

Not far away, the same message was heard in Sabana Grande, Puerto Rico, where Mary, in her 1953 apparitions, ordered that her seven secret messages be gradually released over a period of decades. By the mid-80's, three messages had been released. In addition, a statue of Our Lady of Sorrows was reported to be weeping in July, 1983, at St. Joseph's Church in Arbonito, Puerto Rico.

But three South American events in the 1980's especially came to the forefront because they were so incredible.

In 1988, in the Andes mountains of Ecuador, a beautiful young fashion model was suddenly visited one night in her bed by the Virgin. Soon, she encountered crying and bleeding statues and began receiving urgent messages.

In San Nicolas, Argentina, Mary came to a humble, lower-class woman in the autumn of 1983. Jesus also reportedly began appearing, and in a short time, she received almost 2,000 messages along with the stigmata. The local bishop approved and a basilica was erected.

And on the outskirts of Caracas, Venezuela, on March 25, 1984, the Virgin was seen by 500 to 1,000 people. Within three years even the bishop ruled that one of Mary's apparitions there was authentic. But one woman had much to tell. She became the voice behind the visions, and like others, she had the wounds of Christ on her body.

All three visionaries gave urgent accounts, and they all spoke of Fatima because their stories related to the future—a future, Mary reportedly said throughout South America, that would be filled with uncertainty and afflicted by tribulations.

CHAPTER THIRTY-FOUR

PACHI

"No one can lay hold on anything unless it is given him from on high."

— Jn: 3:27

Sweet 16. It's an age children look forward to and adults look back at with fond memories or regrets. It's a difficult age. The adult world beckons and everything is within the realm of possibility. For young girls, it's an exciting time.

Beautiful and vibrant, with a radiant glow and a sparkle in her eyes, Patricia Talbot was 16, bored with school and daydreaming about fame and fortune.

Her fantasy was to become a famous model. Those around Patricia didn't doubt she could achieve it. Patricia had always taken to stylish clothes and the things that went with them, often changing three or four times a day. She liked to dance. She liked to go out with her friends. Most of all, she liked to look pretty, and because of her energy and enthusiasm, career opportunities were already opening up.

By 1988, Patricia, or "Pachi" as her friends know her, had joined a group of young girls who modeled clothes designed after the folk dress of her native Ecuador. The girls represented their country by promoting tourism at shows around the world in places like New York, Miami, Costa Rica, and Mexico. For Pachi, at 16, this opportunity was already more than most girls growing up in Ecuador could ever dream possible.

The third oldest child of Fernando Talbot and Carmen Borrero, Pachi lived with her mother, two brothers, and sister. Her parents' divorce caused her much emotional pain, and while her family loved her, no one ever thought she was special.

But then, things started to change.

On Aug. 28, 1988, Sunday, at about 4:30 a.m., Pachi said she suddenly woke from a dream to find her bedroom bathed in a brilliant light. At first, the young woman hid under the covers, but that did no good. The light somehow penetrated through. Her repeated attempts to conceal her eyes and face were unsuccessful. So mustering her courage, she decided to face whatever it was out there. And what was there was unbelievable. In the center of the bright white light was a shining lady. A beautiful lady unlike anyone Pachi had ever seen before. At first, she could only make out the woman's figure because the light was incredibly brilliant, but then, the woman spoke to her.

"Do not be afraid," Pachi said the soft voice told her. **"I am your Mother from Heaven. Fold your hands across your chest and pray. Pray much for peace in the world."**

Pachi was stunned but didn't flee. The figure spoke again, telling her about sin and Satan. The woman requested more prayers. Then, Pachi said the Virgin told her, **"I am the Guardian of the Faith, and I will always be with you."** With that, the apparition vanished, leaving the house filled with the aroma of flowers.

Shortly afterward, more apparitions followed, and in October at the Cathedral in Mexico City before the side altar of Our Lady of Guadalupe, Pachi experienced a stunning visitation. Mary appeared and gave her a vision of naked children of all races. The children were in a big field, and there were flames and smoke everywhere. Then, the Virgin touched Pachi's hands and told her: **"Pray for the peace of the world because it is now that it needs it more than ever."**

The following day outside the Shrine of Our Lady of Guadalupe, before tourists and Pachi's friends, Mary reportedly appeared again. This time the young woman dropped to her knees before the crowd and went into an ecstatic trance with her head tilted back and her hands extended as she stared transfixed into space.

The apparition floated above her. Barefoot and standing on a cloud, Mary wore a blue veil and a crown of twelve stars, Pachi said. Her eyes looked very big, and her hair was the color of honey. In her hands was a Rosary. The apparition left, but minutes later the scene shifted to inside the basilica where Mary reappeared and told Pachi, **"In three days, I will reveal to you a great secret in the sanctuary on Tepeyac Hill."** Of course, this was a special place, for it was there that Juan Diego had encountered the Madonna 300 years before.

Three days later, Pachi reported that Mary revealed a secret to her. Like at Fatima, it was an incredible secret. And as she has done throughout the world, Mary delivered a serious message about the future of the world which would include a **"great trial."**

Months later, parts of the secret were revealed. The Ecuador message was a call to prayer and conversion, and a call to have faith like a "rock." But there was more. A world of decision awaited mankind, Mary reportedly told the girl, and it was serious.

"Children, there is much sorrow in my heart," the Virgin told Pachi, **"for many natural catastrophes and others created by man are coming. Hard times are already taking place. A short decade filled with suffering. The third world war is near. Do not frighten your hearts, because the peace of God is with you."**

The mention of a world war was cause for serious concern. However, Pachi explained, the war was conditional on humanity's conversion. The world had to convert while there was still time. But Fatima's unfulfilled prophecy of the "annihilation of nations" was again seen as real possibility.

"The war is near. It will be started with false peace treaties, treaties in which we should not place our trust," Pachi said she was told by Mary.

And again, Pachi said the Virgin told her that the chastisement could come from the hands of men:

> **Little children, know that all that you do benefits the world. Your prayers, penances, and fasts are helping to prevent the Third World War. Everything is as I have told you. All is in your hands. From you it depends whether the chastisement will be as strong as the pain that my Son feels or that the chastisement be diminished with prayer.**
>
> **You know, my daughter, that the third nuclear war is near. Pray, my children, for China,**

Russia, Czechoslovakia. Pray for the countries from the South. Catastrophes come there. Pray for Panama, Nicaragua, El Salvador. Repent, fast, make penance ... Tell them that I love them so much, all of them.

You have to help very much my little daughter. My daughter is going to suffer very, very much as the time is short. The Third World War is near, natural catastrophes, earthquakes, floods such as humanity has never seen before because of so much sin in the world. You know that you are surrounded by much sin. Convert your heart. Give it to me. Have peace.

Pachi relayed some other serious revelations. If mankind did not convert, there would come days of darkness foretold in the Book of Revelation and by many visionaries. And the earth, Mary revealed, could go out of its orbit for three days. This had been heard before, as there were revelations from some visionaries of the earth's core and axis rotation being affected by underground nuclear testing. There was also talk of chemicals in the atmosphere that would serve as catalysts when ignited by fire, perhaps radioactive fire.

All this, however, was conditional. The Virgin stressed the importance of mankind's conversion. The world, says Pachi, needed a "speedy conversion."

On Jan. 15, 1989, another unusual event occurred. Pictures and statues on Pachi's little altar in her room began to exude oil and tears. Droplets of blood were discovered on a crucifix. Even stamps oozed oil.

A laboratory analysis revealed red corpuscles in the blood and human cells in the oil, but the lab could not identify the kind of oil.

Across Ecuador, about the same time, statues and pictures in other homes began to exude oil and cry tears. A year later, the phenomena were repeated in Cuenca. The Virgin reportedly told Pachi the tears reflected her sorrow for her children, who were **"still so far away from God."**

The apparitions in Ecuador inspired a huge following. In

September 1989, an estimated 100,000 people came to the apparition site, a place known as El Cajas, high in the Andes Mountains outside the city of Cuenca. On Feb. 3, 1990, almost 120,000 gathered for a night of fervent prayer.

One month later, Mary gave to Patricia Talbot her last public apparition and message. Soon after, she was married, and she later traveled to Medjugorje and Rome, where on April 4, 1990, Pachi delivered a small envelope that contained a handwritten, personal message from the Virgin to Pope John Paul II.

"We are together," the Holy Father told her as he accepted the message. It was a response similar to the one that Mary had given Mother Marianna in 1634 in Ecuador. And like then, it had *many possible meanings.*

Our Lady of the Rosary of San Nicolas. Crowds as large as 500,000 would gather to commemorate the 1983 apparitions.

CHAPTER THIRTY-FIVE

A DAWN AWAITING

"And you brought them in and planted them on the mountain of your inheritance, the place where you made your seat, O Lord, the sanctuary, O Lord, which your hands established."

— Ex 15:17

When 120,000 people gather on an Andes mountain to witness an apparition, it is a momentous event. But what do you call crowds of 500,000 and more? Such was the case in nearby San Nicolas, Argentina.

The town of San Nicolas sits on the river Parana, 145 miles north of Buenos Aires, South America's largest city. It was founded as a hamlet in 1608 and declared a city in 1819. Its patron saint is Saint Nicholas de Myra de Barr, who suffered Roman persecution and died in the year 325. Old Saint Nick was known for his work with starving children, and became a holiday fixture in the West. Mary, however, made it clear she hadn't come to Argentina as Santa Claus. Her mission was serious, the messages would disclose, extremely serious.

This time, the Virgin Mary chose a 46-year-old housewife named Gladys Herminia Quiroga de Motta, a humble woman who was an average Christian with solid, practical views. According to friends, Gladys was the type of person who would never draw attention to herself. The mother of two daughters, she was married to a retired metal worker. Like other visionaries, Gladys suffered poor health and had a difficult childhood. She had only four years of elementary school from age 7 to 11. Despite the hardships, Gladys was an optimist. She was a cheery and positive person. A person who enjoyed life. But not a mystic. Not until Sept. 25, 1983.

It began unexpectedly. Gladys says she was praying the Rosary in her room that day, when the Virgin Mary suddenly appeared, wearing a blue dress, with the Christ Child in her arms, and Rosary beads in her hands. Mary stayed briefly, but returned three days later. Both apparitions were short, and the Virgin didn't speak.

On the fourth apparition on Oct. 7, Gladys struck up some nerve, and the stunned woman said she asked the Virgin what she wanted. In response, she received a curious vision of a chapel where Mary disclosed she wished to be with her children.

Then, on October 13th, the anniversary of the last apparition at Fatima, the Virgin addressed Gladys for the first time. Mary reportedly told the visionary she would "travel a long road" and need not fear. The statement was more than accurate.

By mid-November, the apparitions were occurring daily, and in a short time, Gladys received an avalanche of messages and visions. More than 1,800 revelations in all. Soon she reported that Jesus began to speak to her, and on Friday, November 16, 1984, the stigmata appeared on Gladys' wrists.

In Argentina, Gladys Quiroga de Motta became a household name. Word of the events swept the country, and September 25, the initial apparition date, was declared an annual holiday.

The Virgin's messages in Argentina were profound declarations from heaven about an approaching storm, a battle between God and Satan.

Evil was on a rampage, Gladys was told and the world was becoming "corrupt" and "horrifying." Mary added that **"All humanity was contaminated."** And it was an especially dangerous time for the world's youth, who were in "permanent imbalance."

Gladys said Mary told her, **"The majority do not build on truth for failure to know justice. They do not love God. The young people of this world must know that God does not impose anything. God wishes to stay among them. But there is a dawn which is awaiting."**

Gladys received more visions, shocking visions in which she witnessed enormous monsters approaching from every direction like an "avalanche." "They were horrible," she recalled. Some appeared like dinosaurs and others were frightful human beings with huge heads and ears. This was, Mary explained, what Satan does to those who serve him.

In another mystical vision, Gladys saw crawling serpents with large blind eyes, trapped in a green fog as though they were being asphyxiated.

She said Mary explained what it meant: **"The Prince of Evil knows that his kingdom is coming to an end. In this way, he sheds his poison with all his strength. There is only a little time left. His end is approaching."**

The Virgin also told Gladys that mankind was splitting into two divisions. One for God, the other for sensuality and sin. A decisive moment was approaching for everyone.

Psychological and physical exams of Gladys found her to be normal and "in perfect harmony with reality." What seemed abnormal were the crowds flocking to San Nicolas. As in the Andes, on the 25th of each month, more than 50,000 pilgrims converged on the city.

On May 13, 1989, the anniversary of the first apparition at Fatima, the Virgin told Gladys that a climactic moment was approaching for humanity:

> **My daughter, as previously in Fatima, today my visits are renewed on earth. They are more frequent and more prolonged, because humanity is passing through very dramatic times.**
>
> **Has man not understood that he must be uniquely at the service of God? If he resists, his soul is going to perish.**
>
> **Many hearts do not accept my invitation to prayer and to conversion. That is why the work of the devil is growing and is expanding. My dear children, it is only through prayer and conversion that you will return to God. May He not find your hearts dry.**

It was not by accident, Mary told Gladys, that the 13th of each month was chosen for her to manifest herself in such a special way:

Yes, this is my day, Daughter. The thirteenth of each month was chosen by me to leave my messages in Fatima, and the principal cause, the conversion of the poor sinners.

The earth, polluted because of the Evil One, will have to be cleansed by the Grace of God from this day forward. This requires honest attitudes, purity of the heart, and surrender to the Lord and to the mother. It is my Heart that asks, it is my Heart that speaks, and it is my Heart where Jesus wants to see mankind. Cleansed, you will see life. Glory be to the Lord of the Universe (Sept. 13, 1986)!

Outside of Caracas, Venezuela, in a place called Betania, similar events took place in the early 1980s.

There are not enough words to describe the chosen woman, Maria Esperanza, who is a stigmatist, a healer, a mystic, and a prophet. She bilocates. She levitates. She sees visions, and she receives apparitions. People say the scent of roses surrounds Maria and that rose petals fall from the sky when she's near. Most remarkably, on 14 occasions, a living stemmed red rose has reportedly blossomed from the skin of her bosom. The roses, witnesses say, even had dew on them.

CHAPTER THIRTY-SIX

A TEST

*"Remember the deeds that our fathers did in their times, and you
shall win great glory and an everlasting name."*
— 1 Mc 2:51

Maria Esperanza was born on a boat in Barrancos,
Venezuela. During her childhood, she suffered
from sickness and physical disorders, but mystical
events began to occur at an early age. At 5, she reported an apparition
of Saint Therese of Lisieux, and at 12, one of the Virgin Mary. As a
young girl, Maria also witnessed a vision of Christ, His Heart bathed
in light and dripping blood.

By 1954, Maria Esperanza bore the stigmata and received
apparitions of saints like St. John Bosco. On October 13th that year,
on the anniversary of the Fatima miracle, Mary revealed to Maria that
she would be married on December 8th. The Virgin also showed
Maria a vision of a piece of land in Venezuela that included an old
house, a waterfall, and a grotto. She was to obtain this land, the
Virgin said, because it was part of God's plan for the future. After
years of searching, Maria and her husband, Geo, discovered the place
called Finca, Betania.

Situated amid banana farms and tropical mountains, Betania
is 12 miles from a river named Tuy, which is the name of the town in
Spain where Sr. Lucia of Fatima experienced visions in a convent in
1929.

Just as the Virgin foretold Maria, there was an old sugar mill
on the land, a stream, and a waterfall and, not surprising, a grotto that
looked like Lourdes. With that, the stage was set. Soon the Madonna

began to appear regularly in Betania and not just to Maria. Hundreds saw her. Then thousands. Amid the trees and foliage, Mary appeared as the Virgin of the Miraculous Medal, with graces pouring from her hands.

The events quickly caused a stir, and after interviewing hundreds of witnesses, Bishop Ricardo formally approved some of the apparitions in 1987. This approval was restricted to what had occurred on one day, when hundreds testified. Since then, according to Dr. Vinicio Arrieta, more than 10,000 people have seen the Virgin at Betania.

Sightings of Mary there are unpredictable since no one knows when or to whom she will show herself. Formed in a luminous misty light, the Virgin often resembles a living marble statue. The events are so well-known that countless people from the United States go on pilgrimage to Betania, which many suggest is becoming the "Medjugorje" of South America.

Other mystical sights surround the apparitions, people say. Very often, a sparkling radiance descends from the heavens, accompanied by strange lights. A giant cross has also appeared above the mountain, and there have been cures. Many cures. According to Dr. Arrieta, who studied at Harvard, more than 1,000 physical healings have occurred at Betania, including his own from prostate cancer.

Nevertheless, the Virgin's message is the centerpiece of Betania.

"The Virgin comes now," says Maria, "as the Reconciler of Peoples and Nations. For not only are people in the world in danger, but so are entire nations."

Again, Her message is a direct reference to the unfulfilled prophecies of Fatima.

"Mankind," Mary warned Maria, **"is moving toward perdition. If there is no change or improvement of life, you will succumb under fire, war, and death. We want to halt this evil that suffocates you. We want to overcome the spirit of rebellion and darkness of oppression by the enemy. That's why, again in this century, my Divine Son arises."** Mary told Maria this is **"the hour of decision for humanity."** And the world will face **"a very serious moment soon."**

However, the darkness in the world would soon end, and the Era of Peace will come, Mary told Maria. **"A great moment is approaching,"** she said, **"a great day of light."**

However, before this moment dawns, a purification will occur and the intensity of that purification depends on us. It is in our hands, says Maria.

Yes, the unfulfilled prophecies of Fatima have resurfaced in Venezuela, and Maria Esperanza makes it clear that she knows much of what awaits humanity. Something dangerous lies on the horizon, she says, and it involves Russia:

> Be careful especially when all seems to be peaceful and calm. *Russia* may act in a surprising way when you least expect it. I feel a great responsibility right now because something great is coming. Something worldwide. It's a very great responsibility, and you have to pray a lot. I'm not interested in you speaking about Maria Esperanza. It's not being humble. There are small things you can tell, little things, but I don't think the right moment has come yet, the right moment to spread something that doesn't belong to me but is from God.

Maria added, however, that people can't worry about all these things. They need to respond to Mary's requests at Fatima.

"This war has a remedy," she said. "It can be lessened. We need wisdom and humility. People say, 'Oh, this is someone who studied, someone from high society.' And they say, 'What do you think, Maria Esperanza, is the century ending? Do we have ten years left to live?"

"And I think, 'Gosh, the whole thing is that we have to have our feet here on earth.' And to think too much about all these things going on or things that will happen--no, we can't think too much about that. Spiritual things, yes, but the other part, no. We can't spend much time thinking about it."

"The thing about Fatima, when they said, 'Yes, there would be a war,' this was a reality, and okay, it was over with. But now the Lord is giving us opportunities so that man himself will become strong and will see the light and will see that the world is beautiful. It's precious! Not so that you want to get rid of it, but the opposite."

Nevertheless, Maria again indicated something was soon going to happen.

"Pretty soon our Lord is going to give us a test, but it's a good test," she said. "It's not a bad test, and most of us are going to see Him, to see this event, and it's beautiful. I have all the descriptions of this event! And we're going to know it. It's not going to be the end, and it's going to happen pretty soon. It's going to renew us completely. It's going to be a renewal in which we can really place ourselves, and we can really know what we have to do."

What the world has to do, says Maria Esperanza, is convert. It has to change. It has to reject sin and Satan and put God first each day. To all the visionaries in South America and to all the visionaries throughout the world, this message resounds over and over from Mary.

Maria Esperanza may have been one of the last of a chosen group of this era to bring the urgent message of the end times to the world as it rushes toward its destiny.

When one searches for the meaning behind all these revelations, it becomes apparent the "signs of the times" are at hand. From an upheaval in nature to outbreaks of war and violence, from a great apostasy of faith to reports of extraordinary supernatural phenomena in the moon and the sun, the signs are foretelling a dawning moment in history.

Likewise, from visionaries at all the modern apparition sites, we learn it is clear that the decisive moments are at hand. Fatima's two remaining prophecies are said to be near fulfillment, as Pope John Paul II himself has noted. And although the Holy Father has repeatedly proclaimed, like the Virgin Mary, that a great victory for Christianity and a new era of peace await the world, he has also repeatedly warned that a severe test is approaching for the Church and the world. It is a test that may cause "bloodshed" and "suffering," he said.

Tragically, a blind and deaf world has ignored Mary's words at Fatima, where she foretold a second world war and other wars if men failed "to amend their ways."

The evidence is clear. Almost 60 million people perished during World War II, while many millions more died because of Russia's "errors," which spread throughout the world.

But according to the visionaries of the 1980's and 1990's the Virgin Mary has not given up. As we have seen, she continued to proclaim throughout the world that her "Triumph" is coming. But she also continued to warn of dire events in the same way she did at Fatima. On Sept. 27, 1992, Cardinal Jaime Sin of the Philippines was quoted in the *National Catholic Register* as saying the prophecies of Fatima have "come true" and the remaining ones are going to be fulfilled:

> Everything that was foreseen in Fatima is coming true. And there is a growing feeling that the justice of God might fall on humanity at any time. God is merciful, but God wants justice. People are turning to Mary for help. The world has a beginning, and so it will have an end. Maybe Mary has already seen the end and wants to save us. Our Lady has appeared on every continent to touch the lives of all people.

Yes, the Virgin Mary has appeared on every continent and the "signs" of the times are clear. She has spoken and appeared to all her children and people of almost every nationality and religion have reported seeing her, not just Catholics. Indeed, from Buddhists to Hindus, Moslems to atheists, Africans to Americans, the entire world has experienced the apparitional woman from heaven. Mary has come as the Mother of All Mankind with a special mission that she promises will succeed, hopefully with as little suffering, destruction, and death as possible.

But if the half million dead in both Rwanda and Bosnia are any indication of what awaits the world "on every continent" in the remaining years before God's Triumph, the world must take note of the seriousness of the Virgin's messages. Like World War II and the rest of the genocide of this century, an unfathomable series of serious events may come before God's great victory, events said to be part of God's justice.

What exactly are these events? How will they occur? Are these events foretold in the Book of Revelation? What can we still do to prevent them? Certainly an indepth look at these questions is in order and the place to begin has to be with the mystery of Mary's secrets.

PART III

HIDDEN

FROM

THE WISE

"I pray and intercede before my Son, Jesus, so that the dream that your fathers had may be fulfilled."

- The Blessed Virgin Mary
to Maria Lunetti,
Medjugorje, August 25, 1994

CHAPTER THIRTY-SEVEN

SECRETS

"I am sure you heard of the ministry which God in his goodness
gave me in your regard. That is why to me, Paul, a prisoner
for Christ Jesus on behalf of you Gentiles, God's secret
plan as I have briefly described it was revealed."

— Eph 3:1-3

In the evening, when I was in my cell, I saw an angel. The Executor of Divine Wrath. He was clothed in a dazzling robe, his face gloriously bright, a cloud beneath his feet. From the cloud, bolts of thunder and flashes of lightning were springing into his hands, and from his hand they were going forth, and only then were they striking the earth. ... I began to implore the angel to hold off.

-- Sister Faustina Kowalska
Sept. 13, 1935

I then saw the Angel of Wrath, far away in red. Then, there was a black cloud under the Angel of Wrath, with lightning striking out from this cloud of darkness. I could see the Angel of Wrath come forward. In this vision, I would plead with Jesus to drive him back.

-- Christina Gallagher
March 16, 1990

What awaits mankind?

At this moment no one knows for sure. No one could; however, many of the visionaries' messages point to a connection between God's coming triumph and the secret messages given at so many apparition sites.

The basic content of the secrets is known. They concern the signs and times of the tribulation, especially the apostasy. They concern great signs and miracles. And they concern a coming purification, which will bring the world into the new times. Most experts agree, the secrets are very apocalyptical.

As we move through the 1990s and stumble into the future, anyone who is aware of these secrets and their suspected contents, cannot help but wonder what is going to happen or be curious about the fate of the world. But this is normal and has always been part of awaiting the fulfillment of prophecy.

Even in Scripture, the idea of divine secrets is prefigured in St. Paul's epistle to the Ephesians when he speaks of God's "secret" plans. Theologians say that Mary's secrets exist in the same context because they involve what St. Paul declared to be "the Mystery of Christ."

In *The Queen of Peace Visits Medjugorje*, theologian and Mariologist Fr. Joseph Pelletier, A.A., comments on the nature of these mysterious secrets: "The word, 'secret,' has a magical effect on people. It arouses curiosity and stimulates interest. God makes use of this to draw attention to the message he wishes to transmit through his heavenly messenger."

While this may be true, Fr. Slavko Barbaric, OFM, of Medjugorje, says we must benefit from the secrets or Mary wouldn't give them.

"It is certain for us that the secrets of Medjugorje also contain impetus for us," Fr. Barbaric said, "The messages tell us what we have to know for now. The fact of secrets is found again and again in Marian apparitions; obviously they belong to the educational method of the Blessed Mother, which trains one to patience and an ability to wait. We must wait for much until the time for it has come."

Theologian Fr. Rene Laurentin says it is apparent Mary gives secrets to her visionaries because the times are urgent and the future is threatened:

> The secrets then have one function. They
> motivate the urgency for conversion. Their general
> theme is well-known. The world has peacefully

abandoned itself to sin. It has wanted to live joyfully, 'freely,' without God, without faith or love. New-look prophets have announced the death of God, the death of the Father, as good news; and sexual freedom among other things, as good news, but also freedom of the passions and human impulses of violence. The world is destroying itself. It is vehemently preparing its own destruction for having struggled, forgotten, or relegated the essential: God and His law of love, which the messages of Medjugorje recall. The secrets announce, to a large extent, the imminent destructions which are not extrinsic punishments, but imminent justice, the self-destruction of a world which entrusts itself to evil through deviation and frenzy.

But perhaps it is in the simple words of Sr. Lucia of Fatima who wrote in her memoirs that we can find the most profound reason why God used secrets in the life of Mary herself:

> In spite of my good will to be obedient, I trust Your Excellency will permit me to withhold certain matters concerning myself as well as Jacinta, that I would not wish to be read before I enter eternity. You will not find it strange that I should reserve for eternity certain secrets and other matters. After all, is it not the Blessed Virgin herself who sets me the example? Does not the Holy Gospel tell us that Mary kept all things in her heart? And who better than this Immaculate Heart could have revealed to us the secrets of Divine Mercy? Nonetheless, she kept them to herself as in a garden enclosed, and took them with her to the palace of the Divine King.

For the most part, many of the secrets are said to deal with God's plan to end one era and to begin another. But before we try to comprehend some of this, it is important to understand how these secret messages began in the apparitions of the Blessed Virgin Mary. Because from their history, we can better understand their significance.

While Mary has been reportedly appearing since Saragozza, Spain, in the 1st century, it was not until the 19th century at Rue Du Bac, Paris, that the mystery of her secret messages began to unfold. This is where it all started, say theologians. St. Catherine Laboure revealed she had been given secrets, "several things I must not tell."

St. Catherine's revelation is the starting point for this mystery of secrets. But it was with the apparitions of the Blessed Virgin Mary at La Salette in 1846 that this element of the Virgin's revelations emerges as a point of significant interest; not just to the faithful, but to the Church hierarchy investigating the apparition.

Indeed, once the presence of secrets at La Salette were known, public speculation about their content and nature became rampant. Everyone wanted to know if the "special knowledge" concerned them in any way, and if so, what could be done to escape harm. At La Salette, public figures, institutions, different interest groups, members of religious orders, clerics, bishops, cardinals, and even the pope became involved in a drama surrounding the secrets that stretched all the way into the 20th century.

All of this began when the two visionaries, Melanie Calvat and Maximin Geraud, reported that when the Blessed Virgin Mary spoke to them on September 19, 1846, she gave each of them a secret message.

At first, the children apparently made no reference to the secrets in their accounts of the apparition. But upon repeated interrogations during the first week, from September 21-26, Maxamin and then Melanie revealed that personal "secrets" were confided to them. In a letter dated October 12, 1846, Abbe Melin, Cure of Corps, addressed a letter to Victor Rabillou, a librarian at Bourgoin, that briefly noted the existence of the secrets. This was the first document to cite the presence of the secrets. But at this point, the secrets were considered to be of a personal, not public, nature.

The earliest written account of the apparition in mid-October 1846 also disclosed the secrets. This was from the notes of Abbe Louis Perrin, the newly appointed Cure of La Salette, who interviewed the children. According to available documentation, the children initially refrained from even speaking of the secrets for fear of revealing them. But once they were known to exist, an almost ceaseless effort began by an array of investigators to dislodge them. Over time, the children repeatedly out-maneuvered their interrogators, but this did nothing to inhibit the efforts. Threats of punishment and death, bribes, tricks, and pretense all failed to get the children to reveal the secrets. On the positive side, their determination was seen as evidence of their integrity and, therefore, increased the probability that the apparition was authentic.

As the months went by, the pressure on the children continued. When asked if the secrets concerned Heaven, Hell, the world, religion or other matters, Melanie replied, "It concerns that which it concerns; if I tell you this you will know it, and I don't want to tell it."

In the spring of 1847, a report written by Dr. Armand Dumanoir, a Grenoble lawyer, revealed for the first time the possibility the children's secrets were of public relevance. "After these words," wrote Dumanoir, "the Lady gave to each of them a secret which appears to consist in the announcement of a great event, fortunate for some, unfortunate for others."

With this document, a new stage in the mystery of Marian apparitions was upon the world. Church officials now began to intensify their investigation process. The public also started to voice its interest, especially since there was great social and political turmoil in France in 1848. Many began to speculate that the children's secrets were vital for understanding the unfolding contemporary events.

At this time, Church officials also began to write letters of inquiry to the priests involved with the children. By 1849, rumors were running amok, with the contents of the secrets at the center of them. Various scenarios were being outlined, with even "the second coming of Christ" foretold to be at the culmination. Rumors involving Catherine Laboure and then an actual visit by Maximin to the Cure for Ars, Jean Vianny, all contributed to efforts designed to have the children reveal their secrets. But Melanie and Maximin would not budge.

Finally, in June of 1851, Pope Pius IX was informed that the children were willing to transmit their secrets to him. The Pope agreed to the arrangement. On July 2nd, Maximin sat down and recorded his secret. Upon finishing, he reportedly sat up and threw the paper in the air, declaring, "I am unburdened. I no longer have a secret. I am as others! One no longer has any need to ask me anything. One can ask the Pope and he will speak if he wants."

On July 3rd, the next day, Melanie wrote down her secret. Claiming she forgot to write something, she repeated the action on July 6th. The children said that they finally agreed to tell the secrets because they now understood the position of the Pope within the Church. But further information disclosed that both children believed they were graced with special "signs" from heaven that permitted the disclosures.

The secrets of La Salette were then given to Pope Pius IX on July 18, 1851. The Pope opened and read them in the presence of the Grenoble officials. Ironically, this series of events, which finally brought the secrets into the hands of the Pope, also exacerbated speculation that the secrets were apocalyptical in content. Reports and rumors about the audience the conveyors of the secrets had with the Pope further fueled this speculation. Likewise, other reports from a handful of clerics who read the secrets began to emerge. Altogether, the public began to piece together a picture that fit in with their apocalyptic suspicions.

Some of the information was factual. Witnesses who observed the children write their secrets reported the children's facial expressions and other aspects of their behavior. One witness noted that Melanie asked how to spell "antichrist." The length of the texts were noted, as was which of the two secrets was longer.

In addition, Pope Pius IX's reaction upon reading the secrets seemed to convey more information. According to the representatives present, the Pope stated upon reading Maximin's message, "Here is all the candor and simplicity of a child." However, upon reading Melanie's secret, the witnesses said that the Pope's face changed and reflected strong emotion. When he finished, he reportedly stated, "It is necessary that I reread these at more leisure. There are scourges that menace France, but Germany, Italy, all Europe is culpable and merits chastisement. I have less to fear from open impiety, than from indifference and from human respect. It is not without reason that the Church is called militant and you see here the captain."

Afterwards, further comments were attributed to the Pope by respected sources. Cardinal Lambruscini, first minister to Pius IX and Prefect of the Congregation of Rites, reportedly said, "I have known the fact of La Salette for a long time and as a Bishop I believe it. I have preached it in my diocese and I have observed that my discourse made a great impression. Moreover, I know the Secret of La Salette."

Cardinal Fornaric, Nuncio to Paris, said, "I am terrified of these prodigies; we have everything that is needed in our religion for the conversion of sinners, and when Heaven employs such means, the evil must be very great."

Upon returning home from Rome, Abbe Gerin told Melanie that he did not know what she had written, but judging by the Pope's reaction, it wasn't flattering. He then asked Melanie if she knew what the word "flattering" meant. Melanie replied "to give pleasure" and then she added, "But this (the secret) ought to give pleasure to the Pope--a Pope should love to suffer."

Year's later, Father Geraud reportedly stated that in a later audience with Pope Pius IX the Holy Father responded to an inquiry much in the same manner that some contemporary Church leaders have responded today when asked about the third part of the Secret of Fatima. Pope Pius said, "You want to know the secrets of La Salette? Ah, well here are the secrets of La Salette: if you do not do penance, you will all perish."

While the apparitions of the Virgin Mary at La Salette received full approval of the Church, the secrets did not. However, the contents of the secrets continued to be circulated, with eventually Melanie herself releasing a version. This version of Melanie Calvat's secret message is actually what is known today as the Secret of La Salette. This is because Melanie's long secret message contained the apocalyptic references only, not Maximin's. As the years went by, the secrets became irrevocably present in the public realm and this knowledge convinced many Catholics that to know the contents of the secrets of La Salette was crucial to an understanding of the critical times in which they lived. Of course, the teaching authority of the Church established itself as the official guardian of the secrets, and as time went by, the Church moved to silence all versions of the secrets by issuing official Church decrees ordering the faithful to "refrain from treating and discussing the matter under any form." The last decree came in 1923, more than seventy-five years after the apparition at La Salette. But to this day, the secrets still circulate among the faithful.

Most significantly, with the secrets of La Salette, the drama of such prophetic information was permanently introduced into the difficult spectra of understanding the purpose of a reported apparition and its revelations. Why would God choose to reveal something, and then move to inhibit its circulation? Thus, with La Salette a whole new era in Marian prophecy is begun. And besides the confidential aspects of some of the revelation, we also find the elevation of the roles of the visionaries to new heights and mystery.

The Church also now found itself in a most uncomfortable situation after La Salette. While wanting to reap the fruits of authentic events, the presence of secrets placed its very trustworthiness on the line and caused Church officials to be torn between understanding the public's desire to know and its mission to protect sound doctrine from contamination and confusion.

CHAPTER THIRTY-EIGHT

THE PHENOMENA OF SECRETS

"There is nothing concealed that will not be revealed, no secret that will not be known."

— Lk 12:2

There is no limit to the ramifications of what the secrets of La Salette have meant to the drama of many later apparitions, especially to those that have also revealed secrets such as at Fatima and Medjugorje. For as more and more apocalyptical prophecies emerged after La Salette, the secrets of La Salette could not help but be resurrected over and over.

Comparisons, cross-examinations, and new interpretations of the fulfillment of La Salette's secrets are to this day applied to the unfolding of human events, especially major ones. Likewise, the alleged contents of the secrets have already been applied to many world events over the last 150 years, all with the hope of recognizing the complete fulfillment of the more harrowing aspects of La Salette's secrets.

After the apparitions at La Salette in 1846, the phenomena of secrets became more closely linked to Marian apparitions and messages. Almost immediately, because of the secrets of La Salette, the idea that visionaries were receiving secrets, and not the public, began to cause controversy. As a result, some people became suspicious of Marian apparitions. And if not suspicious, at least prudently cautious.

At Lourdes in 1858, the Virgin gave Bernadette Soubirous three secrets she never revealed. Knowledge of the secrets came about after the seventh apparition. According to documents,

Bernadette was returning from the grotto with her mother, her aunts, and some neighbors when she revealed that the Lady had spoken to her about some things that had to remain for herself alone. Bernadette wrote, "In the space of this fortnight, she gave me three secrets." While the contents of the secrets went to the grave with her, her Aunt Basile Castérot said she thought that one of the secrets was sad. "I presume," said her aunt, "that among these secrets their was one which was of a sorrowful nature. For once, when I had caught her crying, I asked her the reason and she answered, "I cannot tell you."

Perhaps because of the secrets of La Salette, efforts to dislodge the secret to see if it involved the nation of France were made. At a hospice, a man named Brother Leonard said that he was talking to Bernadette and said to her, "Has the Lady revealed any secrets to you?" "Yes, brother," said Bernadette. "Do they concern France?," he persisted. "No brother," she replied. Brother Leonard says he persisted and was able to conclude that the secrets were personal. "I know at least one of them;" he said to Bernadette, "it is that you are to become a nun." Bernadette reportedly lowered her head and made no reply. A similar confirmation of the sort was illicited in an interview by the bishop of the diocese, Bishop Forcade, when he asked her if her vocation was foretold at Masabielle. "Ah! My Lord...." Bernadette replied as if to respond, but then assumed an air of mystery and shyness.

A few decades later, the French mystic and stigmatist Marie-Julie Jahenny was told the untellable, "You are sealed with three secrets." At Lepailly, France beginning in 1909, Mary told the visionary Father John Lamy that he was forbidden to speak of the secrets given to him, "except to a few pious souls." In 1911, Jesus reportedly gave Berthe Petit of Brussels, Belgium, many "secret" revelations, of which many have reportedly come true. At Fatima in 1917, the first two parts of the famous Secret of Fatima were not revealed and generally not recognized until the 1940s, but by then, there was a growing understanding of the Virgin's methods. (We will address the Secret of Fatima in its entirety in Chapters 40-41.) While at Portiers, France, in 1920, Sister Josefa Menendez, a nun of the Society of the Sacred Hearts, reportedly went to Rome on Mary's behalf to reveal a secret message to her Mother General.

At Beauraing, Belgium, in 1932, three of the five visionaries claimed they received secrets, secrets they insisted not even the Pope could be told. One of the visionaries, Albert Voisin, upon examination, did say his secret was "sad." Likewise at Banneux in 1933, Mariette Beco was given two secrets she would not reveal during interrogations. Mariette is alleged to have even told her father, while pointing to her chest, "Papa, even if you would place your gun there, I would not tell!" At Heede, Germany (1937-1940), Mary reportedly gave secrets to four little children. Each of them was to confide the secret to the parish priest who was then to convey the messages to the Pope.

At Ille Bouchard, France, in Dec. 1947, four more visionaries claimed to have received secrets, reportedly associated with the revelations at Fatima and said to involve grave dangers and a call for urgent prayers.

After that, at Heroldsbach-Thurn, West Germany, from 1949 to 1952 more secrets were revealed. Some of the secrets were taken to a notary and then sealed with the intention that they would be revealed after the events contained in them began to unfold. Again, following the themes of the Fatima messages, Russia was mentioned as inciting war, and the secrets promised the Virgin's protection. The four visionaries said that on the second day of the apparitions Mary became sad and that she would reveal a secret in three days. But one secret was forbidden then to tell anyone .

Sandra Zimdars-Swartz gives us this account concerning the secrets of Heroldsbach-Thurn in her book *Encountering Mary*:

It is these recorded and notarized secrets that are of particular interest, since they both expressed the children's experiences and helped to shape the way these experiences were subsequently dramatized. On February 10, 1950, in the aftermath of a vision in which the Virgin announced that she would cease appearing to them on February 18th, two eleven year-old girls, Gretl Guegel and her friend Erika, reported that the Virgin had given them two secrets. The girls wrote these down, and when the Virgin appeared to them the next day, she reportedly told Erika that the secrets were not to be made public until the events which they concerned should take place. Several months later, several different seers began to report "Russian Visions," that is, scenes in which they saw battles with Russians or themselves encountered Russians, and apparently described these aloud to the people gathered around them. On May 15, for example, Antonic Saam (age eleven), looked into the sky over some birch woods and reported seeing there a battle with Russians, but she also saw a village over which the Virgin had spread her cloak for protection. The next day, Marian Heilmann (age ten) and Gretl also saw battle scenes, and all four girls reported walking through ruins where they said they encountered Russians, some of whom hit and kicked them, and some of whom were converted when the girls told them they had seen the Virgin. Similar visions were reported the following day, and it seems that at this point the adults, who had been anxiously following the children's visions, determined that something needed to be done. On the following day, May 18th, the secrets of Gretl and Erika were opened, apparently ahead of schedule, and were found to contain a measure of comfort. Gretl's secret, reportedly, was a special promise from the Virgin: **'When the Russians come I will protect Heroldsbach and Thurn. Even the houses will shake when the bombs fall. But I will protect Heroldsbach and Thurn.'** Erika's secrets, it is said, conveyed the same message in similar words.

In 1946, a secret was given to Barbara Reuss at Marinfried Germany. It was never revealed. On April 12, 1947, Mary told Bruno Cornachio at Tre Fontane, Italy a secret. The message was for the Pope and was to be personally delivered. On December 7th and 8th, 1947, Mary gave Pierine Gilli, of the Rosa Mystica apparitions in Montichiari, Italy, two secrets. Once again, the contents remained unknown.

In 1949, in an apparition of the Virgin Mary to Caterina Richero at Balestrino, Italy, Mary conveyed still more secrets which were linked to Fatima. She supposedly disclosed in the secrets that she was the **"Mediatrix of All Graces"** and had come **"to bring Russia to Jesus."** Once again, Zimdars-Swartz gives us this account concerning the secrets of Balestrino:

> Secrets concerning Russia came to expression in a form less vivid but more prolonged, and more directly in accord with the literature concerning the secret of Fatima, in an apparition of the Virgin to Caterina Richero at Balestrino, Italy, which began in 1949 and continued until 1971. Caterina, like many of the more recent seers who claim to have received secrets from the Virgin, understood herself to have a mission to reveal these gradually to the public, as the Virgin gave her permission. On November 5, 1958, for example, she said that the Virgin had told her when she could reveal four secrets that had previously been conveyed to her. On March 5, 1960, in connection with two more secrets she had received, Caterina reported that the Virgin told her, **"At this moment I see before me so many afflicted, weak, and sinful souls. My children, know that I am the Mediatrix of all Graces. Whoever has recourse to me with great faith, nothing will be refused that one. Dear children, today, pray! Because I come to convert and bring Russia to Jesus."** Albert Marty, who collected the messages reported by Caterina and wrote an account of the apparitions through 1971, has understood Caterina's secrets as part of a tradition of more or less orthodox Roman Catholic prophecy stemming from La Salette and Fatima. He suggested, for example, that a secret conveyed to Caterina on 5 October 1961 (to which the other secrets she received were presumably similar) was really identical with the secrets conveyed by the

Virgin at La Salette and Fatima, and also in other more recent Marian apparitions. This secret, he thought, pertained to a variety of chastisements that would strike the world if it did not heed the Virgin's warnings and turn from its evil ways.

At Espes, France, where several visionaries reported apparitions from 1946-1949, more secrets were given. One young boy, 5 year-old Gilles Bourhous, is said to have been taken to Rome where he hand delivered his secret message to Msgr. Montini (the future Pope Paul VI).

At Lipa, in the Philippines in 1949, Mary reportedly gave four (4) secrets to Teresita Castillo. One was for her prioress, one for her community, one for herself and one for China, which had just fallen to communism. The conversion of China would come, Teresita said, but only after "much suffering."

Since 1950's, the presence of secrets appears to especially have added a tantalizing element to the drama in the unfolding mystery involving humanity, heaven, and the Virgin Mary's promise of an Era of Peace.

At Sabanda Grande, Puerto Rico, in 1953, seven secrets were given by Our Lady of the Rosary. These secrets were to be gradually revealed by one of the three children, Juan Angel Collado, over the next five decades. So far, four have been released. Like La Salette and Fatima, they have centered on an apostasy and an approaching time of great evil.

At Eisenburg, Austria, in 1955, Mary told the visionary Oloisia Lex a secret involving an approaching catastrophe. While at Turzovka, Czechoslovakia, in 1958, Mary showed Matous Lasuta several visions that have remained secret. On February 19, 1958, Mary gave a woman name Ida Perleman in Amsterdam a secret message which predicted the death of Pius XII **"at the beginning of October."** Pope Pius XII died on October 9, 1958.

In 1966, Mary gave Enzo Alonci a secret message at Porto San Steffano, Italy. The secret reportedly carried in it the dates of warnings and chastisments. In 1972, secrets were reportedly given at Dozule, France. In 1975, at Bink Loi, Vietnam, Mary gave Stephen Ho Ngor Anh several secrets dealing with the unfolding of future events. Likewise, in Eastern Canada from 1974 to 1987, the Virgin told Brother Joseph Francis three secrets.

Many of the apparitions of the last two decades have contained secret messages. On September 7, 1984, Mary gave a secret to Mirna Nazour, the stigmatist in Damascus, Syria. Jesus delivered three more secrets through Mirna to several priests. In Ireland, the mystic Christina Gallagher received from 1986 to 1992, secrets dealing with the chastisement. Once again, they are not to be revealed. At Litmanova, Czechoslovakia, Mary gave a secret to Ivita Korcakova. Ivita said Mary was "sad" when she revealed it.

At Cuenca, Ecuador (1988-1997), Mary revealed to Patricia Talbott (Pache) a "great secret" This secret was given to her at the shrine of Our Lady of Guadalupe in Mexico City on October 11, 1988. The secret contained three parts, with each involving a coming chastisement of the world. Pachi has said she cannot reveal it entirely because it is "too strong a message and could create panic." But one month "ahead of time," she will be permitted to disclose them. Sister Isabel Bettwy wrote about "The Great Secret" in her book *I Am The Guardian of the Faith*.

The Great Secret

The Holy Virgin gave Patrica the great secret when she appeared to her in the Church of Tepeyac, Guadalupe, Mexico in October, 1988. Our Lady said it corresponds to the one given to other visionaries throughout the world. Patricia was able to tell us, "She gave me the secret that there are bad things going to happen in the world, and what is asked for is conversion. I asked her if I could tell everybody about the secret and the Virgin said, '**No**,' because it was too strong a message to give and it would create panic. And so, I said, I can't just forget about this, and the Virgin said, '**One month ahead of time I'll tell you so you can say**.'" Patricia has not said anymore about the timing of the secret, and since it is part of the secret, she won't talk about it.

At a later time, the Virgin told Patricia certain parts of the secret could be revealed. In fact, the

Great Secret that the Virgin gave Patricia contains three parts. Patricia told us that all three parts have something to do with future events which will be chastisements for our world. Our Lady spoke several times, about the possibility of a third world war, of natural disasters and man-made disasters:

Mary said, **"Great times of tribulation are coming. Natural catastrophes and those created by men, and the third world war are near. You should keep these in you heart. You should pray for the Holy Father, My Pope, My chosen son."**

Finally, from 1985 to 1995, secrets were also reported at Oliveto Citra, Italy, in 1985; at Belpasso in Catania, Italy, in 1986; at Giubiasco, Switzerland, in 1986; at Hrushiv, Ukraine, in 1987; at Inchigela Ireland in 1987; at Santa Maria, Calif., in 1988; at Ontario, Canada, in 1990; at Agoo, Philippines in 1992; and probably at many more lesser-known apparition sites.

CHAPTER THIRTY-NINE

UNFOLDING SECRETS

"Behold, I have told you it beforehand."

— Mt 24:25

The most publicized apparition of the late 20th Century that has dealt with secrets began at Medjugorje in 1981. While the exact prophecies have not been disclosed, their content is said to concern epic events. Events that fulfill possibly some of the 19th and 20th century prophecies, as well as perhaps some biblical prophecies and mysteries. They are events, according to experts, that will bring to fulfillment God's plan of mercy and justice for His people and help to usher in the Era of Peace.

Since a period of time has elapsed since the existence of the secrets was first made known and some of their contents revealed, some experts have revised their earlier apocalyptic interpretations. Nevertheless, there remains a prevailing sense that some, if not all, of these secret events will occur before the end of the 20th century, primarily because the Virgin in her messages insists that her "triumph" is near. Indeed, great events must unfold to bring the Era of Peace to the world that countless visionaries have predicted and some of the secrets are said to contain "great events."

Likewise, many visionaries continue to testify to the urgency of the Virgin's messages. Without hesitation, some also say the events foretold will occur in this decade. Fr. Stefano Gobbi reported an interior locution confirming the coming fulfillment of some secrets before the year 2,000. **"In this period of ten years, (1990-2000) all of the secrets which I have revealed to some of my children will**

come to pass, and all of the events which have been foretold to you by me will take place (Sept. 18, 1988)."

As we have already seen, these secrets involve apostasy, warnings, upheavels in nature, great signs, miracles, conversions, Satan's loss of power and chastisements. And not surprisingly, almost all of these elements already have been given in some degree to many visionaries. Many of the prophecies are more specific and detail the coming of these events against a backdrop of worldwide turmoil that will already be in place. (See *Call of the Ages* by the author.) This turmoil will reportedly arise because of a worldwide economic crisis of unparalled proportions, religous fraticidal conflicts that escalate out of hand, and a global food shortage brought on by drought, natural disasters, and civil wars. New diseases and dangerous dictators also are promised to appear, compounding the confusion and panic that is also promised to arise. Besides the Middle East, one nation is believed to be a pivotal player in it all: Russia.

In Fr. Gobbi's messages, there are descriptive details about a time of apostasy and chaos, a time of cleansing and purification, and a time of renewal and peace. Although no one knows for sure when this will happen, it appears these grave events are drawing near. Mary and Jesus have also reportedly said the same thing to the Irish visionary and stigmatist, Christina Gallagher, who says Mary has spoken to her about "Fatima" and "Medjugorje." Likewise, many writers have openly stated that the message of Akita is the full Secret of Fatima, including the unreleased third part. The urgency sounded in the 1973 message of Akita was more than evident.

This prompts more questions. What exactly are the hidden elements of God's coming purification? Do they involve a nuclear nightmare or some kind of cosmic disaster? Are these same events referred to in the secrets at Fatima, Medjugorje, and the Books of Revelation?

Fr. Michael O'Carroll, C.S.Sp., the Irish theologian, asks us to ponder this mystery in reference to the secrets of Medjugorje:

> What of the secrets? Is it not strange that, with the whole apparatus of Church government publicized as it has never been before with all the public relations, success or failure of Vatican II, with

incessant assemblies, meetings, seminars, renewal courses, committees, and commissions, the Mother of the Church should pick out some unsophisticated children in a remote Yugoslav village to talk to them about matters affecting the future of the whole human race?

There is no time, in passing, to delay over the psychological aspect of this hidden dialogue. In every intelligent plan the parts cohere to produce a final result intended. ... Their secrets are their destiny. Character is destiny and so they are being fashioned day by day for the moment of destiny's fulfillment. They have been faithful thus far to the duty of secrecy. One did divulge something to a medical practitioner who took advantage of her hypnotic state but he feels bound by professional secrecy. The reply given by Marija (Lunetti) to an interviewer from the Canadian paper L'Informateur may be looked at carefully. Asked if there would be a nuclear war, she (Marija) replied that this was "part of the secrets." Something unconsciously given away?

The secrets are a personal matter of conscience for the visionaries. They are also bound by the whole moral program which they teach others in Our Lady's name. Opinions will differ here in the matter of interpretation and scale.

Other theologians have also openly pondered the contents of these secrets. Fr. Robert Faricy, S.J., chairman of mystical theology at the Pontifical Gregorian University in Rome, says that the secret messages are "both prophetic and apocalyptic." Prophetic because "they are telling us what to do" and apocalyptic because "they are telling us what God intends to do." In his book *Mary Among Us, The Apparitions at Oliveto Citra*, Fr. Faricy further describes the Oliveto Citro apparitions and the secrets there:

The events at Oliveto Citra (Italy) have a marked apocalyptic quality. Both in style and in content, the apparitions there have notable apocalyptic aspects. Apocalyptic is a style. It can be a style of writing, as in the New Testament Book of the Apocalypse. Or it can be the style of a situation, of a series of events, as at Oliveto Citra.

The apocalyptic style is characterized by an emphasis on secrets, on hidden things, on the mysterious, and by a stress on divine judgment, on chastisement for sins, on the catastrophic consequences of sinfulness. These factors have their place in the Oliveto Citra apparitions. They give those apparitions, in general, an apocalyptic quality.

The apocalyptic message is a message of hope. Partly because of the apocalyptic aspects, the message of Our Lady at Oliveto Citra is one of hope. God is the Lord of history. History belongs to the Lord. Jesus is victorious over all the forces of evil. And he sends us his mother to call us again to help him, by penance and especially by prayer.

The apocalyptic style and message always contain a prophetic element. In the Old Testament, and also in the New Testament, the prophets call the people to conversion and to greater fidelity to God. Our Lady at Oliveto Citra has a prophetic role in that she speaks to us God's call to conversion, to prayer, and to penance.

French scholar, Fr. Renee Laurentin, considers the timeliness of the secrets:

The messages concerning the future of the world would appear to predict the end of the world. But are these proximate signs or signs of a now distant future? Nobody can answer this with certainty.

From Mary's revealed messages at many of her apparition sites, we know that the miracles, the signs, and wonders alluded to in the secrets will be followed by a short period of grace before there is the time of justice.

At Medjugorje, the visionaries say they can hardly bear what they have been told. Michael Brown, in his book *The Day Will Come*, provides an excellent critique of the overall contents of the Medjugorje secrets:

> Let's be frank. Mirjana says that knowing what she knows would make her "go mad" if she didn't have the consolation of Mary, if the Virgin did not still come to her on occasion. In commenting on the first couple of secrets, when asked if they involved "something like a catastrophe," Mirjana replied, "No. It will not be anything as huge as that. That will come later." She was referring to the final secrets. Mirjana told Fr. Laurentin that the majority of her secrets are "grave, catastrophic."

Brown adds his comments on the gravity of the secrets:

> I can't sugarcoat that. I can't downplay it. If the warnings sound like regional events, these sound like they may involve global circumstances. In 1985 Mirjana reported the Virgin to have said, **"My angel, pray for unbelievers. People will tear their hair, brothers will plead with brothers, they will curse their past lives lived without God. They will repent, but it will be too late. Now is the time for conversion."**
>
> The locutionist Jelena also had a strong message on June 24, 1983, when she quoted the Virgin as saying, **"You cannot imagine what is going to happen nor what the Eternal Father will send to earth. That is why you must be converted! Renounce everything. Do penance. Express my acknowledgment to all my children who have prayed and fasted. I carry all this to my Divine Son in order to obtain an alleviation of His justice against the sins of mankind."**

According to visionaries, this period of divine justice will begin with warnings and even a "global warning" through a miraculous event. This global "warning" will be an *illumination of conscience*, they say. As reportedly prophesied by many seers, this illumination will be in the form of an interior awareness given to each person concerning the state of his or her soul. For many, it will reportedly be a painful experience. Everyone will also be given knowledge that God exists. This internal illumination of the soul, say visionaries, will allow people, all people, to change before it is too late. This prophecy of an inner warning has been foretold for centuries. But many mystics and visionaries have recently repeated the prophecy.

On Pentecost Sunday in 1995, a locution received by Father Gobbi described what this event will hold for all God's people:

> **"Tongues of fire will come down upon you all, my poor children, so ensnared and seduced by Satan and by all the evil spirits who, during these years, have attained their greatest triumph,"** Mary told the priest, **"and thus you will be illuminated by this divine light, and you will see your own selves in the mirror of the truth and the holiness of God. It will be like a judgment in miniature, which will open the door of your heart to receive the great gift of Divine Mercy** (June 4, 1995).

One year later, another message to Father Gobbi revealed again that this event was drawing near: **"Miraculous and spiritual tongues of fire will purify the hearts and souls of all, who will see themselves in the light of God and will be pierced by the keen sword of his Divine Truth** (May 26, 1996)."

Some Marian experts say this prophecy sounds strikingly familiar to Sr. Faustina's predictions that before Judgment Day there would be a period of mercy and "a sign in the heavens and over the earth."

Irish visionary Christina Gallagher agrees: "I can feel it within myself. I can feel it coming at a great speed. After this warning, even atheists will know God exists," she said.

Following the interior warning, there are to be some great miracles, reportedly in the form of permanent signs at places where Mary has truly appeared. These reported prophecies have been recorded at Medjugorje, Hercegovina; El Cajas, Ecuador; Litminova, Slovakia, and other reported apparition sites. This period is then to be followed by a time of purification because everyone will not respond to the warnings and miraculous signs. According to visionaries, many will drift back into sin and this will bring God's justice and the unfolding of the most terrible secrets, perhaps the ones which deal with fire, destruction, and annihilation. These events will reportedly come through nature, perhaps even a cosmic disturbance of some sort, through the hands of man (the nuclear element being the most suspect), and reportedly from God Himself.

One secret especially mentioned the word "annihilation," and a part of that secret has never been revealed. This secret of Mary's has fascinated the world and it is perhaps especially where we should look to better develop our understanding of this mystery. Like most of the other secrets, its contents are curious and controversial. But this is especially true with this secret because it has passed in and out of the hands of five popes. All of whom have chosen not to make it public.

Throughout the world, photographs, icons and statues of Mary weep. Why? Experts say the sins of the world are leading it to a decisive moment of immense danger, and heaven is sending this warning in a graphic and powerful way.

CHAPTER FORTY

THE THIRD SECRET OF FATIMA

"Be on guard, let no one mislead you."
— Mt 24:4

Irish theologian Fr. Michael O'Carroll, C.S.Sp., says, "Fatima has touched the Church at the level of the papacy more than any other event of its kind."

Pope Pius XII, without any public declaration, responded to the request of Our Lady of Fatima when he consecrated the world to her Immaculate Heart on Fatima's silver jubilee in 1942. Pope John XXIII is known to have read the unreleased Third Secret and made a decision to keep its contents hidden.

Pope Paul VI in his apostolic exhortation *Signum Magnum* directed the world to the message of Fatima and to Mary as its "Great Sign." And Pope John Paul II has kept the message of Fatima at the forefront of his pontificate in both word and deed.

Thus, the message of Fatima is truly the best source for what so many visionaries are predicting. Fatima's words, while not as extensive or as detailed as many contemporary private revelations, still represent the essence of almost all 20th century prophecies.

Indeed, if there is ever a great wall in the Vatican covered with paintings depicting 20th century Marian apparitions, those representing Beaurang, Banneux, Akita, and Medjugorje will be displayed prominently on this wall. But Fatima would *be* the wall. In Mary's message at Fatima we can detect where Pope John Paul II and others have taken their direction. Fatima tells us much.

On Sunday, May 13, 1917, Mary first appeared to the three children. After calming their fears, the Virgin said: **"I come from Heaven. I want you to come here at this same hour on the**

thirteenth day of each month until October. Then, I will tell you who I am and what I want."

In June, Mary came again on the 13th. After revealing to the children that **"Francisco and Jacinta would soon leave the world for Heaven,"** the Virgin told Lucia, **"God wishes you to remain in the world for some time because He wants to use you to establish in the world the devotion to my Immaculate Heart. I promise salvation to those who embrace it, and their souls will be loved by God as flowers placed by myself to adorn His throne."**

Finally, in July, Mary gave the visionaries what has come to be known as the Secret of Fatima. Stretching out her arms, the children witnessed a beam of light penetrate into the earth, and they saw a sea of fire and a huge number of damned souls:

> **You have seen hell, where the souls of poor sinners go. To save them, God wishes to establish in the world the devotion to my Immaculate Heart. If people do what I tell you, many souls will be saved and there will be peace.**
>
> **The war [World War I] is going to end. But if people do not stop offending God, another and worse one will begin in the reign of Pius XI. When you shall see a night illuminated by an unknown light [Jan. 25, 1938], know that this is the Great Sign that God gives you that He is going to punish the world for its many crimes by means of war, hunger, and persecution of the Church and the Holy Father.**
>
> **To prevent this, I shall come to ask for the consecration of Russia to my Immaculate Heart and the Communion of Reparation on the five first Saturdays. If my requests are granted, Russia will be converted and there will be peace. If not, she will scatter her errors throughout the world, provoking wars and persecution of the Church. The good will be martyred; the Holy Father will have much to suffer, and various nations will be annihilated. ...**

But in the end, my Immaculate Heart will triumph, the Holy Father will consecrate Russia to me, Russia will be converted, and a certain period of peace will be granted to the world.

The Virgin Mary then asked that this message be kept secret until she gave permission to reveal it, and it is because of this request that Fatima has gained much notoriety. Even though most of the Virgin's messages were eventually disclosed, a portion was not. This part is known as the "Third Secret of Fatima" or more correctly the "Third Part of the Secret of Fatima."

In what *was* released of the secret of July 13, 1917, we find the two most significant revelations that have been consistently reemphasized over the years in many of Mary's messages. These revelations concern the promise of an "Era of Peace," but also the harrowing reminder that before this peace comes, there may be a severe trial leading to the "annihilation of nations."

This prophecy has caused great interest in the Third Secret's contents. Although repeatedly denied by some Fatima authorities, many suspect the unrevealed portion contains specific details of the "annihilation."

Over the decades, the controversy surrounding the Third Secret has escalated, especially since 1960 when Pope John XXIII decided to not reveal its contents. According to Sr. Lucia's memoirs, she did not write down the contents of the Third Secret until late 1943 or early 1944, and they were not necessarily intended to be revealed:

> It may be, Your Excellency, that some people think that I should have made known all this some time ago because they consider that it would have been twice as valuable years beforehand. This would have been the case if God had willed to present me to the world as a prophetess.
>
> But I believe that God had no such intention when He made known these things to me. If that had been the case, I think that in 1917 when He ordered me to keep silent, and this order was confirmed by those who represented Him, He would, on the

contrary, have ordered me to speak. I consider then, Your Excellency, that God willed only to make use of me to remind the world that it is necessary to avoid sin, and to make reparation to an offended God by means of prayer and penance. (Sr. Lucia's memoirs, *In Her Own Words,* by John Haffert)

Responding to concerns about Sr. Lucia's death, Bishop Correia da Silva requested her to write down the Third Secret. Afterwards, she placed the Secret in a sealed envelope and delivered it to Bishop da Silva. On December 8, 1944, the bishop placed the envelope in a larger envelope and instructed that it be given to His Eminence Cardinal Don Manuel, Patriarch of Lisbon "after my death."

While the bishop was given permission by Sr. Lucia to read the Secret's contents, he refrained from doing so because he said it had been addressed to the Holy Father. The envelope was then sent to the Apostolic Nuncio, Msgr. Cento (now Cardinal Cento), who forwarded it to the Sacred Congregation for the Doctrine of the Faith.

Although Pope Pius XII was alive at the time, he reportedly never read the Secret. His successor, Pope John XXIII, read it and reportedly stated the "text did not pertain to his times." He preferred to leave an assessment of its contents to his successors. Pope John XXIII made no public statements about the case.

At that time, it was believed the Secret was to be revealed either in 1960 or upon the death of Sr. Lucia, whichever came first. This allegation has since been denied, as sources close to the Secret have sought to defend Pope John XXIII's decision.

Cardinal Ottaviani, who reportedly also read the Secret, stated, "Yes, the Secret is important; it is important for the Holy Father for whom it was defined. It was addressed to him. And if the one to whom it was addressed has decided not to declare now is the moment to make it known to the world, we should be content with the fact that in his wisdom he wished it to remain a secret."

In 1963, Pope Paul VI succeeded Pope John XXIII and reportedly read the Secret. At the 50th anniversary of Fatima, he reportedly revealed his awareness of the Secret's contents:

The first intention is for the Church; the Church, One, Holy, Catholic and Apostolic. We want to pray, as we have said, for its internal peace. What terrible damage could be provoked by arbitrary interpretations, not authorized by the teaching of the Church, disrupting its traditional and constitutional structure, replacing the theology of the true and great Fathers of the Church with new and peculiar ideologies; interpretations intent upon stripping the norms of faith of that which modern thought, often lacking rational judgment, does not understand and does not like. ... we want to ask of Mary, a living Church, a true Church, a united Church, a holy Church.

While Pope John Paul I met with Sr. Lucia the year before his election, there is no evidence that he had read the Secret before his death. Although it has been written that Sr. Lucia, in this private meeting, reportedly foretold Cardinal Allino Luciani's election to the Chair of Peter and-to Luciani's stunned amazement-his *short* reign.

Pope John Paul II and a statue of Our Lady of Fatima. This statue was given to him by Bishop Paola Hnilica, S.J., on August 22, 1981, just several months after the attempted assassination on his life.

CHAPTER FORTY-ONE

'IF MEN AMEND THEIR LIVES'

*"The distress in the land and the wrath against
the people will be great."*

— Lk 21:23

P ope John Paul II has read the Third Secret of Fatima, and he reportedly made a public comment related to its contents. In an interview from the Oct. 13, 1981 issue of *Stimme des Glaubens*, a German publication, the Holy Father discusses the issues involved in making the Secret known publically:

> On the other hand, it should be sufficient for all Christians to know this much: If there is a message in which it is said that the oceans will flood entire sections of the earth that from one moment to the other millions of people will perish. ... there is no longer any point in really wanting to publish this secret message. ... many want to know merely out of curiosity or because of their tastes for sensationalism, but they forget that to know implies for them a responsibility.

In concluding this interview, the Pope describes future trials for mankind:

> We must be prepared to undergo trials in the not-too-distant future, trials that will require us to be

ready to give up even our lives, and a total gift of self to Christ and for Christ. Through your prayers and mine, it is possible to alleviate this tribulation, but it is only in this way that the Church can be effectively renewed. How many times, indeed, has the renewal of the Church been effected in blood?

This time, again, it will not be otherwise. We must be strong, we must prepare ourselves, we must entrust ourselves to CHRIST and to His Holy Mother, and we must be attentive to the prayer of the Rosary.

Cardinal Ratzinger, the Prefect for the Congregation of the Doctrine of the Faith, has also read the Secret. In his book *The Ratzinger Report*, author Vittorio Messori quotes the Cardinal as having said the Secret contains a serious warning:

A stern warning has been launched from that place [Fatima] that is directed against the prevailing frivolity, a summons to the seriousness of life, of history, to the perils that threaten humanity. It is that which Jesus himself recalls frequently, "unless you repent you will all perish"(Luke 13:3).

Conversion---Fatima fully recalls it to mind--- is a constant demand of Christian life. We should already know from Revelation and also from the Marian apparitions approved by the Church in their known contents, which only reconfirm the URGENCY of penance, conversion, forgiveness, and fasting. To publish the "Third Secret" would mean exposing the Church to the danger of sensationalism, exploitation of the content.

Pope John Paul II's words and Cardinal Ratzinger's statement are intriguing since both add fuel to the debate over the contents of the Secret. The Pope and the Cardinal's words seem to indicate the Secret's contents could be extremely harsh, although there have been statements to the contrary.

Some noted authorities on Fatima have argued that the Secret speaks of an apostasy and nothing else. This is not to de-emphasize the seriousness of such a revelation, but to shift the focus away from apocalyptic interpretations.

In 1984, the Most Rev. Cosme de Amaral, Bishop of Leira-Fatima, stated that the Secret does not concern nuclear issues but, rather, our faith:

> The Secret of Fatima speaks not about the atomic bombs, nor about nuclear warheads, not about SS-20 missiles. It's content concerns our faith. To identify the Secret with a catastrophic announcement or with a nuclear holocaust is to distort the meaning of the message. The loss of faith of a continent is worse that the annihilation of a nation, and it is true that faith is continually diminishing in Europe.

Fr. Joaquin Alonso C.M.F., the official historian of Fatima, concurs, suggesting that the Secret involves a crisis in faith:

> In the period which will precede the great triumph of the Immaculate Heart of Mary, terrible things will occur, and these are the object of the Third Part of the Secret.
>
> What things? If in Portugal, 'the dogma of the faith will always be preserved,' it can be deduced with all clarity that in other parts of the Church these dogmas will be obscured or even lost. It is quite possible that the message not only speaks of a "crisis of faith" in the Church during this period, but also, like the Secret of La Salette, it makes concrete references to internal strife among Catholics and to the deficiencies of priests and religious. It is also possible that this may imply deficiencies even among the upper ranks of the hierarchy.

Perhaps no expert on the contents of the Secret has been quoted more than Fr. Alonso. His statement that the Secret is not about a terrible chastisement is often referenced. However, John

Haffert notes in his extensive writings on Fatima and the meaning of its message that "Fr. Alonso does *not* rule a chastisement out."

While the emphasis on apostasy has been significant, there have been recent messages from the Virgin, as well as other sources, that indicate there is part of the Secret that deals with more than the prediction of an apostasy. Something that perhaps Pope John Paul II was alluding to in the much-publicized interview with *Stimme des Glaubens* in which he hypothetically noted "millions of people will perish."

Over the past 10 years, Fr. Stefano Gobbi has released messages from the Virgin Mary that indicate she specifically stated at Fatima in 1917 that the Third Secret of Fatima also refers to a chastisement.

Although Fr. Gobbi's messages have not yet been approved as worthy of the faith, they have received an imprimatur from both Bishop Donald W. Montrose, D.D., of California and His Eminence, Bernardino Cardinal Echeverria Ruiz, O.F.M., of Ecuador.

Mary has given several messages to Fr. Gobbi concerning the Third Secret of Fatima, but the May 13, 1990, message is the most definitive:

> **I came down from heaven 73 years ago in this Cova da Iria to point out for you the path you should tread in the course of this difficult century of yours. The very painful events which followed have, through their occurrence, given complete fulfillment to the words of my prophecy.**
>
> **Humanity has not accepted my motherly request to return to the Lord along the road of conversion of heart and of life, of prayer and of penance. Thus, it has known the terrible years of the Second World War, which brought about tens of millions of deaths and cast destruction of populace and of nations.**
>
> **Russia has not been consecrated to me by the Pope together with all the bishops and thus she has not received the grace of conversion and has spread her errors throughout all parts of the**

world, provoking wars, violence, bloody revolutions, and persecutions of the Church and of the Holy Father.

Satan has been the uncontested dominator of the events of this century of yours, bringing all humanity to the rejection of God and of His law of love, spreading far and wide division and hatred, immorality and wickedness and legitimating everywhere divorce, abortion, obscenity, homosexuality and recourse to any and all means of obstructing life.

Now, you are beginning the last decade of this century of yours.

I am coming down from Heaven, so that the final secrets may be revealed to you and that I may be able thus to prepare you for what, as of now, you must live through, for the purification of the earth.

My Third Secret, which I revealed here to three little children to whom I appeared and which up to the present has not yet been revealed to you, will be made manifest to all by the very occurrence of the events.

The Church will know the hour of its greatest apostasy. The man of iniquity will penetrate into its interior and will sit in the very Temple of God, while the little remnant which will remain faithful will be subjected to the greatest trials and persecutions.

Humanity will live through the moment of its great chastisement and thus will be made ready to receive the Lord Jesus who will return to you in glory.

For this reason, especially today, I am coming down again from Heaven, through my numerous apparitions; through the messages which I give; and through this extraordinary work of my Marian Movement of Priests, to prepare you

to live through the events which are even now in the process of being fulfilled in order to lead you by the hand to walk along the most difficult and painful segment of this your second advent, and to prepare the minds and the hearts of all to receive Jesus at the closely approaching moment of His glorious return.

Three years later, another message given to Father Gobbi alluded to the contents of the Third Part of the Secret of Fatima. The following is the complete text of that message which was given on May 13, 1993:

By a day-long cenacle at this venerated shrine you, the priests and faithful of my Movement in the region of Lombardy, are today observing the anniversary of my first apparition which took place at Fatima, in the poor Cova da Iria.

You are still in the period described by me in my apparition. Above all, you are in the heart of my message. The struggle between the Woman clothed in the sun and the red dragon has, during these years, reached its highest peak. Satan has set up his kingdom in the world. He is now ruling over you as a sure victor.

The powers which are directing and arranging human events, according to their perverse plans, are the dark and diabolic powers of evil. They have succeeded in bringing all humanity to live without God. They have spread everywhere the error of theoretical and practical atheism. They have built the new idols before which humanity is bowing down in adoration: pleasure, money, pride, impurity, mastery over others, and impiety.

Thus, in these years of yours, violence is spreading more and more. Egoism has made the

hearts of men hard and insensitive. Hatred has blazed up like a scorching fire. Wars have multiplied in every part of the world, and you are now living in the danger of a new terrible world war which will bring destruction to peoples and nations, a war from which no one will emerge victorious.

Satan has succeeded in entering into the Church, the new Israel of God. He has entered there with the smoke of error and sin, of the loss of faith and apostasy, of compromise with the world and the search for pleasure. During these years, he has succeeded in leading astray bishops and priests, religious and faithful.

The forces of Masonry have entered into the Church, in a subtle and hidden way, and have set up their stronghold in the very place where the Vicar of my Son Jesus lives and works.

You are now living *the bloody years of the battle*, because the great trial has now arrived for all.

There is now taking place that which is contained in the third part of my message, which has not yet been revealed to you, but which has now become evident from the events themselves through which you are now living.

To prepare you for them, I have caused my Marian Movement of Priests to spring up in every part of the world. And thus I have chosen this littlest and poorest child of mine, and have brought him everywhere, as an instrument of my motherly plan of salvation and mercy.

By means of him, I have called you from all sides to consecrate yourselves to my Immaculate Heart; to enter, each and all, into the safe refuge which your heavenly Mother has prepared for

you; to multiply the cenacles of prayer as lightning rods which protect you from the fire of chastisement. How many of you have responded to my call with filial love and with great generosity!

My plan is now on the point of being realized, and the task which I have entrusted to this little son of mine is about to be completed. And so today I am looking upon you with the special satisfaction of a Mother who is being consoled and exalted by you.

I urge you to live without fear, but rather with great confidence and trust, *these bloody years of the battle*. From the chalice of sufferings never experienced until now, there will come forth the divine sun of a new era, of a humanity heretofore unknown, of grace and holiness, of love and justice, of joy and peace.

Fr. Gobbi's messages certainly fuel the public debate that still rages over the Third Secret, its contents, and whether or not it was ever intended by Mary to be released. Sister Lucia has repeatedly been quoted as saying the Third Secret was never meant to be released and that the popes have acted in accordance with God's Will. However, the controversy is still alive and Fr. Gobbi's messages have added to it, as have several other of his messages that directly state the consecration of Russia was not completed exactly in accordance with Mary's original request and therefore the danger that still looms over the world, especially through Russia's still prevalent nuclear arsenal, is recognizable. In interviews, Fr. Gobbi has, like Sr. Lucia, acknowledged that in his opinion the 1984 consecration was accepted to a degree and the subsequent changes in the world were a result of the consecration. But the issue appears to still carry some revelance in as far as to why the world is still a powder keg. Some say insufficient reparation is now the real reason (see Chapter 48), while others contend that only by releasing the Third Secret will we understand the existing dangers that still threaten the world with annihilation.

According to the 1995 January-February issue of the

international journal, *The Voice of the Sacred Hearts*, there is another reliable source of information concerning the contents of the Third Secret of Fatima. Howard Dee, a former ambassador of the Philippines to the Holy See wrote a book titled *Mankind's Final Destiny*. In it, Dee discloses that he was told by Cardinal Ratzinger that the Third Secret of Fatima was in essence, the approved message of Akita, a message that foretells an apostasy and a fiery chastisement that could wipe out a significant part of humanity:

> I asked the good Cardinal (Ratzinger) about the correlation of the Fatima and Akita messages. I knew it was a delicate question as his answer might reveal indirectly the content of the Third Secret of Fatima. To my surprise, he confirmed that these two messages were essentially the same.

This statement confirms the opinion of the late Bishop of Akita, John S. Ito, who stated before his death that the message of Akita is the *"full"* message of Fatima, thus implying the Third Secret spoke of a chastisement. Indeed, a great similarity emerges, especially in the revealed texts of both messages, for at Fatima, Mary revealed that **"several entire nations will be annihilated,"** while at Akita, she stated **"fire will fall from the sky; a great part of humanity will be annihilated."**

On the 80 th anniversary (Oct. 13, 1997) apparition of the Virgin Mary at Fatima another uproar over the Third Secret of Fatima was ignited in Rome. The periodical *Inside the Vatican* detailed the controversy in its November, 1997 issue:

> The 80 th anniversary of the last apparition of the Virgin Mary at Fatima (October 13, 1917) sparked controversy in Rome.
> The issue: the famous 'Third Secret' of Fatima. The 'Third Secret' does not predict any 'cataclysmic event,' but a 'spiritual crisis,' apostasy from the faith and grave divisions in the Church the French Mariologist Father Rene Laurentin contended to Italian national television on the evening of

October 12.

'The Virgin was saying: be careful, this Council will be good, but after it there will be a series of deviations and temptations,' Laurentin said. 'This is the last secret. It's too bad they have not made it public. It concerns the Church.' Pope John XXIII committed an 'error' when he decided not to publish the contents of the secret in 1960, since all of these things have come to pass since the Second Vatican Council, Laurentin added.

Laurentin's remarks sparked a flurry of comment.

'I must agree with Rene Laurentin, 'Vittorio Messori, author of book-length interviews with Cardinal Ratzinger and the Pope, wrote in *Corriere della Sera.* 'Evidence confirming this 'ecclesial' reading lies in the one phrase we know from the revelation which has been otherwise kept secret until now: 'Portugal will always hold fast to our dogma.' It seems evident that here a privilege is being announced, in the context of a Church which will not hold fast to that 'dogma.' A further confirmation is that, when Sister Lucia in 1943 sent the text of what she had heard from the Virgin on July 13, 1917 to Rome, she stipulated that the letter not be opened before 1960. 'Because then,' she said, 'everything will be clearer.' Pius XII died in 1958 having respected her wish; the letter was first opened in August 1959 by Pope Roncalli [John XXIII's name]. The previous January he had announced his intention to call the Council that would be called Vatican II.'

Messori concludes that John XXIII, when he read the Fatima secret and saw it conflicted with his policy of 'optimism at all costs,' decided to consign it to the secrecy of the Vatican archives, and that Paul VI and John Paul II have been 'prisoners' of John's decision. 'In fact, how can they admit that, not heeding even divine warnings, Roncalli did not take prudent measures to head off the predicted crisis in the Church?' Messori asks.

But Archbishop Loris Capovilla, 82, John XXIII's personal secretary, who knows the secret's contents, immediately contradicted both Messori and Laurentin. The secret does not concern the Church only, he said, but predicts 'an absolutely exceptional event,' 'a manifestation of the supernatural.' And Cardinal Ratzinger, who also has read the secret, when asked about Laurentin's hypotheses, said: 'They are all fantasies.'

In his message for the 80th anniversary of the last apparition, the Pope made no mention of the secret at all, affirming only that the Madonna of Fatima has helped us to read 'the signs of the times' in this century of 'lights and shadows.'

Meanwhile, at Fatima itself, for the 80th anniversary celebration on October 13, some 500,000 faithful attended a Mass celebrated by the Cardinal Archbishop of Paris, Jean-Marie Lustiger. In his sermon, Lustiger focused on the two principal aspects of the Virgin's message: conversion (in order to live according to God's will) and hope (in the permanent love and protection of Christ and of his Mother.)

Another controversy surrounding the Third Secret of Fatima was reported during this period. On Jan. 13, 1996, the Roman daily *Il Tempo* published an interview with the famous demonologist, Msgr. Conrado Balducci.

Fr. Balducci was straight forward and said he knew the contents of the famous Secret. His words were so shocking that newspapers throughout Europe widely reported the interview.

According to the January-February 1996 issue of *Crusade*, the publication of the American Society for the Defense of Tradition, Family and Property, Fr. Balducci revealed that "the Secret of Fatima speaks about a terrible nuclear conflict that will shake the entire world sometime before the year 2000."

Not surprisingly, some say Fr. Balducci's words are very compatible with Pope John Paul II's comments in *Stimme des*

Glaubens.

"A great chastisement," said Fr. Balducci, formerly a member of the Vatican's Secretariat of State, will fall upon the world, "not tomorrow but in the second half of the 20th century."

"Fire and smoke will fall from the heavens, the water of the oceans will turn to vapor, and the tide will rise and submerge everything. Millions and millions of men will die by the hour, and the living will envy the dead. In every country on all sides, everything will be anguish, ruins and misery."

Fr. Balducci was also asked how Cardinal Ottaviani, the former secretary of the Sacred Congregation of the Holy Office during the pontificate Pope John XXIII reacted to all of this, since he too read the Secret: "When Fr. Cinelli saw me, he told me that I had done well in citing this document. He has had a problem to resolve: another Dominican, whom I also knew, Fr. Mastrocola, director of the Santa Rita Institute, wanted to mail a leaflet containing the text of the Third Part of the Fatima Secret to the 20,000 names in his file. So he went to ask Fr. Cinelli what he thought. Fr. Cinelli told him it was vital to first know Cardinal Ottaviani's opinion on the matter, and the two of them obtained an audience with the cardinal. They were familiar with His Eminence's famed rigidity and skepticism. Great was their surprise when, after they had explained their plan, he exclaimed: 'Go ahead, Father! Publish the text. Distribute it to as many people as you can.'

The interviewer's last question to Fr. Balducci was "Is there hope for humanity?"

The priest's answer was simple and direct, but not optimistic: "If men amend their lives, the conflict can be postponed or lessened in its consequences" (*Crusade* magazine, Jan-Feb. 1996).

Fr. Balducci's reference to fire falling from the sky appears once again to confirm that although God's justice during this period of purification may take many forms, the most often cited is that of fire. Over and over again, the prophecies speak of fire. Therefore, this subject in itself must be examined to separate the truth from any distortions or exaggerations.

The three shepherd children of Fatima. Both Jacinta and Francisco (left and center) died within several years of the apparitions, just as Mary foretold.

Berthe Petit

Padre Pio

Two of the early 20th century's most profound mystics. Both warned of great wars that were coming.

Theresa Neumann

Luisa Piccarreta

The revelations of these two women foresaw a new era coming after a purification of the world.

The five children visionaries at Beuraing, Belgium in 1933.
Beuraing was approved by the Church in 1949.

Sister Josefa Menendez, R.S.C.J

Her powerful account of the existence of Hell and her reported visits
there were considered extraordinary and compatible with the vision
of Hell reported by the children at Fatima around the same time.

The visionaries at Sabana Grande, Puerto Rico today. Juan Collado (on left) is to reveal three secret messages to the world, which he received from Mary in 1953.

An extraordinary photograph of Mary above the Coptic Cathedral in Zeitun, Egypt. The Virgin Mary's appeal to the Muslim people has been well documented. Over 2 million people are said to have seen her at Zeitun.

CHAPTER FORTY-TWO

FIRE FROM THE SKY

"The Lord has spent his anger, poured out his blazing wrath. He has kindled a fire in Zion that has consumed her foundations."
— Lam 4:11

While some revelations have specifically mentioned the consequences of a nuclear exchange and that this would be the source of the prophesied "fire" falling from the sky, most have not.

However, over the past 30 years, there have been numerous reports of "fire" and "fire falling from the sky." It is a universal prophecy, one with many variations. Fire is mentioned 454 times in the Bible.

In the Old Testament, there are references to fire in Genesis, the Psalms, Zechariah, and the Book of Joel, to name a few.

God tells us in the Book of Joel: "I will show wonders in the heavens and on the earth. Blood and fire and pillars of smoke. The sun shall be turned into darkness and the moon into blood before the great and terrible day of the Lord." (Joel 2:28-31)

In the New Testament, St. Paul wrote in the Second Epistle to the Thessalonians: "And to you who are troubled, rest with us when the Lord Jesus shall be revealed from Heaven, with the angels of his power in a flame of fire, giving vengeance to them who know not God, and who obey not the Gospel of Our Lord Jesus Christ" (2 Thes 1:7-8).

St. Peter wrote in his letters: "Know this first of all, that in the last days scoffers will come to scoff, living according to their own desires and saying, 'Where is the promise of his coming?'

From the time when our ancestors fell asleep, everything has remained as it was from the beginning of creation. They deliberately ignore the fact that the heavens existed of old and earth was formed out of water and through water by the Word of God; through these the world that then existed was destroyed, deluged with water. The present heavens and earth have been reserved by the same word for fire, kept for the day of judgment and of destruction of the godless" (2 Peter 3:3-8).

All of these scriptural verses appear to be in reference to a purifying, chastising fire. But there are some who believe Mary's messages about fire, including some of those to Fr. Gobbi, refer to the fire of the Holy Spirit coming down from Heaven to renew the earth. There may be great truth to this opinion, for many revelations indicate that a mystical, sanctifying fire is to come. But regardless of what some messages imply, Mary has also definitely been warning of a physical fire falling from the sky.

Fr. Edward D. O'Connor, C.S.C., a professor of theology at Notre Dame University, addressed these conflicting interpretations in his book *Marian Apparitions Today*:

> Father Gobbi reminded a Japanese audience of the messages given at Akita, about fire falling from heaven. He goes on to reiterate on his own, (that is in the name of Mary) Akita's words: **"Fire will come down from heaven and a great part of humanity will be destroyed. Those who will survive will envy the dead because everywhere there will be desolation, death and ruin."** (Sept. 15,1993)
>
> In the message (to Father Gobbi) of Oct. 13, 1994, Mary said, **"Fire will come down from heaven and humanity will be purified and completely renewed in such a way that it will be ready to receive the glorious Jesus who will return to you in glory."**
>
> Taken by itself, this text might seem to be meant metaphorically; but in view of the messages of Akita, and elsewhere, it is probably to be taken literally.

Indeed, Heaven's numerous messages on this subject have been too graphic to categorize the references to fire as totally symbolic.

Over the last two centuries, there have been many private revelations mentioning fire. From Catherine Emmerich to La Salette, to Akita, the prophecies often mirror each other. But, especially since the late 19th century, the prophecies of fire falling from the sky have increased. In the famous prophecies of La Fraudais, France, visionary and stigmatist Marie-Julie Jahenney's disclosed in 1878, that Jesus told her, **"a rainfall of fire, thunder, and flames, and fire hail ... shall proceed to the earth."** Mary told Marie-Julie, **"The heat from the sky will be so scorching as to be unbearable, even within your closed homes."**

Almost every decade of the 20th century revealed such prophecies. More than a half-century after Janenny's visions, the words sounded the same. A Yugoslavian visionary named Julka saw visions of the air on fire and said, "The whole atmosphere of the earth, from the ground to the sky, was a gigantic flame."

In the 1960s, several Spanish visionaries (children) recounted a terrifying scene of burning fire everywhere. "It would be worse than having fire on top of us, fire under us and fire all around us." One of the visionaries said, "people were throwing themselves into the sea, but instead of dousing the fire, it made them "burn more."

Around the same time, Padre Pio spoke of the world "catching on fire."

In 1968, the Virgin reportedly told Rosa Quattrini in San Damiano, Italy, **"When you see the fire and the whole world burning up, what will become of you who have not listened to my motherly words?"**

In 1976, the Virgin told another Italian visionary and stigmatist, Elena Lombardi, **"An unforeseen fire will descend over the whole earth, and a great part of humanity will be destroyed."** Another Italian visionary and stigmatist, Mother Elena Aiello, reported Mary told her, **"Clouds with lightning, flashes of fire in the sky, and a tempest of fire shall fall upon the world."**

During the mid-80s and early 1990s, these prophecies continued. Almost all contemporary visionaries report receiving messages that mention fire. Josyp Terelya, the Ukrainian visionary, said Mary warned him in 1987 of **"fields aflame, even the air and water burning, smoke and fire everywhere -- rivers of blood."** To Fr. Gobbi, in 1987, a message said, **"Fire will descend from the heavens."** To Amparo Cuervos in Escorial Spain, Mary predicted **"great showers of fire will reduce the world to ashes."** In 1990 at El Cajas, Ecuador, The Virgin told Patricia Talbot, **"The sky will shower fire."** And the Eternal Father told Matthew Kelly on June 21, 1993, **"They will feel the whole force of Heaven against them when fire comes from Heaven, when My Justice comes to those who abuse their freedom ... ."** Many of the visionaries say they have received visions of fire, such as the children in Kibeho who saw "trees of fire and an open abyss."

Not surprisingly, even the Catholic Church has acknowledged this message, in what have become approved apparitions. The La Salette, France, apparition, which was approved in 1851, warned, **"Fire will purge the earth."** Similarly, at Fatima, the promised sign witnessed by 75,000 people on Oct. 13, 1917, was a ball of fire, the sun, hurling towards earth.

Fifty-six years after the Fatima miracle, on Oct. 13, 1973, at Akita, Japan, the Virgin told Sr. Agnes Sassagawa, **"Fire will fall from the sky."** This message was approved by the Church in 1984.

In Betania, Venezuela, where one apparition was approved in 1987, Maria Esperanza said Mary told her, **"Mankind will succumb under fire, war and death."**

Some have questioned whether many of these prophecies are not merely plagiarized old prophecies or reconstituted biblical revelations, but that theory seems to disintegrate by the sheer number, variation, and geographical origin of the modern prophecies.

Striking examples of this are the prophecies emanating from behind what was the Iron Curtain. In Dubovytsa, a village in the Ukraine, The Virgin appeared to a woman named Hanja on the hill of Seredne in 1953, and said, **"Not by flood, but by fire will the destruction come."** She also reportedly told her, **"An immense flood of fire shall destroy nations for sinning before God."** In 1958 in Czechoslovakia, a forester Matus Lasuta reported, "visions of the air and the ground ablaze." While in Hungary a woman named Sr. Maria Natalia revealed she was told much the same. "The Lord showed me how the greater part of the world will become a pile of ruin. I saw the cities, and farms, everything looked like a forest after fire. I saw God's Holy Spirit as a devasting fire inundate the world. The fire did not bring peace, nor mercy but devasting punishment."

A trembling Christina Gallagher says she saw a vision of fire. Then, she saw an L-shaped road filled with "frightened, unprepared people." And, "They all looked as if they were screaming. But I didn't see fire touch anyone."

Again, what will be the cause of this fire? Will it be supernatural? Or will it come from a war?

As nuclear arsenals have grown, the threat of nuclear war has increased. This type of warfare could cause the air, water, and ground to burn by fire through radioactive fallout. Some visionaries have even said an atmospheric accident is going to occur. They say they have been told the air is filled with chemicals, which could create a holocaust when exposed to extreme heat and radiation.

John Haffert in his book *To Prevent This* said that during the Cuban missile crisis, Defense Secretary Robert McNamara insisted that nuclear war would not cause the death of thousands or even millions, but of "nations." This reference to the destruction of nations was an almost haunting reminder of the Virgin's words at Fatima, which prophesied the **"annihilation of nations."** Today's visionaries concur. Often their messages speak specifically of the destruction of nations. The Spanish stigmatist Anparo Cuevos reported that Christ told her, **"Because they have not changed and continue abusing My Mercy...various nations will be destroyed...the judgement of the nations is very near... entire nations will be lost."**

Moreover, while many messages concur with Fatima's foretelling of the annihilation of nations, the revelations of today's visionaries often speak of the great danger *the whole world is approaching*.

"I warn the world," Mary told the stigmatist Glady's Quiroga in Argentina in 1987. To the children in Kibeho, Mary said **"the world's rushing towards its ruin."** While at Olivita Citra in Italy, Mary cautioned that **"the whole world was in danger."**

In 1945 the atomic age began, the age of nuclear weapons, the age of weapons which in 1917 only heaven knew could bring massive fire from the sky that could annihilate nations and affect the whole world. In 1945, President Truman described this new potential as man's capability "to harness the power of the sun." It was literally the power of *fire*.

The approved message at Akita is even more disconcerting because Japan is the only country ever to experience total devastation from nuclear attack. Hiroshima and Nagasaki serve as a testament to the world of how far man will go to annihilate his brother. We have to ask whether Mary gave this message in Japan because of its nuclear history.

On Dec. 26, 1992, Christina Gallagher witnessed another vision with fire. Perhaps it offers a clue to the cause of the chastisements spoken of in Mary's messages to her:

> I had an experience like going to sleep, but it was not sleep, but while I am in this state, it's like living where I'm looking at. I found myself on a cross as has happened before. The pain was awful. I was looking at fire which covered a big area. I could hear people screaming. ... I could see people running out of the fire and they were on fire. I could see the area of fire being surrounded by devils, as if they were delighted and wanted the fire to continue.
>
> Then I saw a number of soldiers marching. I could see them getting into a jeep. There were other jeeps there, but I was taking note of only one. One of the soldiers turned and looked at me. He looked very young, with what looked like Chinese eyes and yellow skin.

A coming war? A war between *China* and *Russia*? A nuclear war that causes fire to fall from the sky?

Christina said this was given to her once before. At the time in 1991, Christina had cautioned, "If another war starts and it's between Russia and China, which I've been led to believe is possible, and if that happens because lack of response in prayer, well, you can be sure a horrific disaster will be the consequence."

The Ukrainian visionary Josyp Terelya reported that in the 1980s, the Virgin showed him a map of Russia with fires burning throughout the country. There were also flames in various parts of the world, and he saw tanks and fire throughout Siberia. The tanks, he said, were "Chinese."

While Mary did say at Medjugorje that Russia **"will become the people who will glorify God the most,"** the role that this country could potentially play as a chastising tool of the Almighty appears to be very much alive, despite the fall of communism and especially because Russia was mentioned more than once by Mary at Fatima. Indeed, if great world unrest does arise, the prophecies appear to indicate that Russia will be at the center of the crisis at some point, whether at the beginning or at the end. And how will the Russian people come to glorify God? Will it be through a great suffering?

Two other respected visionaries, Jim Singer of Ontario and Patricia Talbot of Ecuador, have also indicated there may be a conflict between China and Russia. Moreover, visionary, mystic, and stigmatist Maria Esperanza of Venezuela has stated, the "yellow races will stand up, and that's very serious." And she added, "Russia may act in a surprising way when you least expect it."

If this prophecy of fire is so pervasive and intended for our times, could it be the same fire written of in the Book of Revelation? The Virgin has said we live in the times spoken of in Revelation.

Chapter Eight of the Apocalypse, dealing with the Seventh Seal, offers a vision of fire from the sky during a time of unparalleled tribulation when the earth is ablaze:

> When the lamb opened the seventh seal, there was silence in Heaven for about half an hour. ... Then, I saw the seven angels who stand before God, and another angel came and stood at the altar with a golden censer ... and the smoke of the incense rose with the prayers of the saints from the hand of the angel before God ... Then, the angel took the censer and filled it with fire from the altar and threw it on the earth; and there were peals of thunder, loud noises, flashes of lightning, and an earthquake ... the first angel blew his trumpet, and there followed hail and fire, mixed with blood which fell on the earth; and a third of the earth was burned up ...

On Aug. 20, 1991, Christina Gallagher, received a vision of Jesus holding the globe in His Hands. Suddenly, Christ vanished, and Christina saw the globe being held by a pillar, a pillar that began to crumble. The Virgin told Christina that the pillar was Jesus Christ and that soon the pillar would "fall."

"The world," Mary said, **"will be plunged into the depths of its sin, and drink its bitterness."** With this, Mary instructed Christina to tell her spiritual director, theologian Fr. Gerard McGinnity, to **"read the Seven Seals of God, especially the Seventh Seal."**

Is a great war part of this mystery? Perhaps so. But one man has theorized that there need not be a war to fulfill the prophecies of fire falling from the sky. He contends that an accident could produce this effect. In fact, he theorizes that such an accident would be worse than war and he believes the two great signs prophesied at Fatima were warning of just such a scenario.

CHAPTER FORTY-THREE

INCALCULABLE
SELF DESTRUCTION

*"Then the angel took the censor and filled it with fire from the altar
and threw it on the earth, and there were pearls of thunder,
loud noises, flashes of lightning, and an earthquake ...
the first angel blew his trumpet, and there followed
hail and fire, mixed with blood that fell on the earth;
and a third of the earth was burned up."*

— Rv 8:1-13

As noted, many suspect certain contents of the Third Part of the Secret of Fatima and Mary's foretelling of the "annihilation of nations" in the Second Part of the Secret are both references to a chastisement involving a nuclear dement. Many believe this is apparently the same warning given to so many visionaries and mystics, including those at Akita and Hrushiv.

With the approved revelations of Akita coming from the only nation that has directly experienced the horrors of a nuclear attack, and with Mary mentioning **"fire from the sky"** at Akita, the possibility that this fire will be caused by nuclear warfare is one that should be given serious consideration.

With the massive buildup of nuclear weapons over the last half century, many suspect that such a rain of fire from the sky would probably come from an all-out nuclear war, especially since most prophecies predict the whole world will be affected. But according to some experts, this is not necessarily the case. They say that even a limited nuclear exchange could affect the entire planet, perhaps even one bomb of the right size.

One man has come forward and proposed an even more ghastly scenario. It is a scientific scenario that has been dismissed by some of his colleagues, but one that possibly explains Mary's words at Medjugorje, June 24, 1983: **"You cannot image what is going to happen or what the Eternal Father will send to earth. That is why you must be converted!"** And it would also explain the Virgin's similar words to Irish stigmatist, Christina Gallagher: **"My children, you have not much time until My Son's hand will come over the earth in justice. Convert, I beg you, while you still have time. You do not know what God is going to send to mankind."**

Both messages are staggering in their implications. This is because even though mankind has theorized what the outcome of a total nuclear war might be, Mary appears to warn that the "unimaginable" would take place.

Likewise, it was the unimaginable that Pope John Paul II referred to in his 1984 Act of Consecration when he stated, "deliver us from nuclear war, from INCALCULABLE SELF-DESTRUCTION." Remember that the Holy Father has read the contents of Fatima's Third Secret, which may contain such references.

It is the unimaginable and the incalculable that Professor Rand McNally has postulated in his theory of a "nuclear tornado," which takes the specter of nuclear war to horrifying heights. It is also more than curious how McNally came about his theory while discovering the message of Fatima and its two great signs, which some believe symbolically represent the threat of a nuclear holocaust.

In a paper presented at a spring meeting of the American Physical Society in Washington, D.C., on April 28, 1986, McNally presented his views while calling for an examination of the prophecies of Scripture (McNally specifically cited St. Peter's Second Letter to the Gentiles) and Fatima.

Using these prophecies, McNally outlined his theory about a nuclear tornado, which is based on a mathematical understanding of the dangers of a run away chain reaction. McNally hypothesizes that only one or two of today's super bombs could trigger a thermonuclear reaction in which the atmosphere itself becomes fuel and is ignited by a rapidly moving fire.

This tornado of fire would burn up whole nations, "if not the earth," he warns. Especially troubling is that, according to his theory, there would not have to be an all-out nuclear war, or even a war at all, to cause a worldwide holocaust. One bomb, either deliberately or accidentally exploded, could ignite it. While many believe this theory is objectionable in the framework of Marian apparition and prophecies, the decision to not address it and then suffer the consequences is more objectionable.

This theory is also significant because at several apparition sites there have been statements and/or messages saying there will not be a third world war. As Fr. Edward O'Connor has noted in his book *Marian Apparitions Today*, Conchita Gonzales, a visionary, has repeatedly asserted this view. O'Connor wrote, "Such a prophecy naturally makes us think of nuclear warfare. However, Conchita has repeatedly declared that the Blessed Virgin says there will not be another world war." At Medjugorje, the same disclosure is found. **"The Third World War will not take place**," reported Fr. Rene Laurentin and Rene Lejeune in a message of Mary's published in their 1988 book, *The Messages and Teachings of Mary at Medjugorje*.

In 1952, Dr. Rand McNally first learned of a top-secret lecture by Professor Gregory Breit, a consultant at Los Alamos, the Trinity site of the first atomic bomb test. Since the session had been classified, it could not be discussed. But its implications were horrifying says McNally because it was evident that scientists were considering the possibility of an atmospheric detonation causing a runaway nuclear explosion.

McNally wrote of the possible ignition of the atmosphere in his 1994 article published in *Voice of the Sacred Hearts*:

> According to William J. Broad (*Teller's War*), Dr. J. Robert Oppenheimer called a secret meeting in Berkeley to discuss the A-Bomb Project in the summer of 1942. After treating the primary purpose of the meeting, Edward Teller disclosed his ideas on "the Super" H-Bomb possibilities. Then, he startled the audience with the thought that "the Super" might ignite the atmosphere. Oppenheimer went to Michigan to discuss this with Arthur H. Compton,

who said, "This would be the ultimate catastrophe."

Subsequently, Konopinski and Teller wrote a one-page paper: "Ignition of the Atmosphere" (LAA-01, Dec. 2, 1943), which concluded that the safety factor (bremmstrahlung radiation loss rate/nuclear power production rate) was about 60. Later, after two A-Bombs were dropped on Japan, Konopinski, Maruin, and Teller in a much longer paper concluded the safety factor might be as low as 2.67! (LA-602, Aug. 14, 1946).

Two years later, McNally visited Fatima and became intensely interested in the Virgin's prophecies, the Miracle of the Sun (Oct. 13, 1917), and the prediction of a Great Sign (fulfilled Jan. 25-26, 1938). The second prophecy especially perturbed McNally for it warned **"if men do not amend their lives, various nations will be annihilated."**

He later discovered Sr. Lucia stated after the Jan 25-26 "aurora borealis" that "if scientists would investigate this aurora, they would find in the form in which it appeared, it was not and could not have been an aurora." Sr. Lucia reportedly would later add that some day a scientist would confirm her assertion.

McNally set out to uncover the truth, but it wasn't until 1982 when he discovered that the unusually brilliant 1938 celestial phenomenon had been accompanied by two giant red spots, one being 300 miles or more tall as measured by triangulation methods.

This phenomenon was similar to what had been observed in an August 1958 TEAK fission/fusion bomb test over Johnston Island. In addition, giant red spots were not characteristic of aurorae, which meant the 1958 explosion had apparently produced a "magnetic dynamo" in the upper atmosphere. This seemed to indicate the so-called 1938 aurora borealis was, as Sister Lucia said, not an aurora borealis at all. Possibly, McNally believed, it really was the Great Sign promised by Mary to occur before World War II:

> Should a nuclear tornado triggered by a strong nuclear explosion possess strong enough E x B drive, it might permit the ignition of the atmosphere in a powerful, annihilating nuclear fusion fire which could

burn up whole nations, if not the earth.

The TEAK nuclear explosion of 1958 apparently also produced a magnetic dynamo in the upper atmosphere. And the earth's local magnetic field was disturbed for 10 to 20 minutes! Six minutes after the megaton explosion, the nuclear fireball had lifted and expanded to 200 miles in diameter. It has an accompanying red shock wave 600 miles in diameter. Shades of the great sign of 1938!

McNally contends that atmospheric testing of even 50-megaton bombs could create a disaster. He urged the Soviets to refrain after Premier Khrushchev boasted of a 100-megaton device.

Since then, in repeated letters to scientific organizations, McNally has mathematically outlined the dangers of nuclear testing. and has urged, even begged, for the banning of all nuclear weapons.

In his book, *Energy from Heaven and Earth*, Edward Teller addressed the world's first nuclear test, code-named TRINITY and suggested there were some who said, "Perhaps the explosion will run away."

From what physicists knew at the time, this was not believed possible. However, McNally says, "could there not be other laws of which we are ignorant?"

He also contends that the Miracle of the Sun on Oct. 13, 1917, was a portent of the coming nuclear threat:

The "Miracle" produced "so that all may believe" consisted of what appeared to be the sun "dancing" in the sky above the children, followed by it plummeting toward the ground, generating fear of dying on the part of the many observers, and finally its return to the heavens.

It was seen also in the surrounding countryside to a distance of up to about 30 miles, indicating that its initial altitude may have been only about 700 feet above the assembled crowd of 70,000 people. This suggests that instead of being the sun, it may have been an atmospherically focused real image of the sun or a form of ball lightning."

Of course, only time will tell now and prayer will help, but author Thomas Casaletto in his 1987 novel *A State of Emergency*, attempted to give his readers a fictionalized, yet plausible description of what could happen if a nuclear tornado occurred and spread out of control throughout the world. In an arms negotiation session, a fictional physicist named Alex Carmody presents a computerized simulation of the risk that the United States and the Soviet Union are taking with nuclear atmospheric testing:

> An enormous mushroom cloud swelled, then burst, radiating in every direction, spinning ever outward.
>
> At 't' plus two seconds, a self-feeding nuclear dynamo is generated. Its chain reaction is at this point unstoppable. At 't' plus five seconds, it is moving at close to one hundred miles a minute. In about seven minutes, it reaches the mainland. Leningrad, Helsinki, and Stockholm are vaporized at 't' plus twenty-three minutes.
>
> The video displayed, soundlessly, the disintegration of well-known landmarks of each of the cities mentioned. An inset of contrasting color continuously adjusted the number of fatalities on a kind of odometer of death.
>
> Oslo and Moscow are consumed at 't' plus twenty-five minutes.
>
> Alex deliberately kept his voice subdued. He read the chronicle of catastrophe as though he were listing ingredients for a salad. There was no need to dramatize.
>
> London and Paris are gone eleven minutes later. Twenty-three million people are now dead, but the dynamo is still gathering strength.
>
> A world map appeared on the screen. Devastation spread across it like spilled ink on a blotter.
>
> The holocaust reaches Canada at 't' plus sixty minutes, and the United States, six minutes later.

Boston and New York are incinerated at plus seventy-seven minutes. The death toll is now almost beyond the reach of imagination. Before 't' plus one hour and forty-seven minutes, most of the Northern Hemisphere has been engulfed ... Can we have the lights, please? Dr. Parrish, cut the video there.

There were gasps of relief. It was almost a cause of joy to see the brightly colored images fade, giving way to the chandeliered elegance of the meeting hall.

At this point," Alex continued, "we hope that the nuclear reaction would begin to destabilize and dissipate as the tornado projects itself into outer space. It is equally possible, however, that the reaction would continue until the entire planet is consumed."

Does the fulfillment of the prophecies of fire falling from the sky contain the possible unfolding of such an unpredictable scenario as McNally has outlined? Of course, no one knows for sure and certainly the elements of God's permitted justice must be weighed against the cause - an ocean of sin. Indeed, perhaps, the Ukrainian visionary Josyp Terelya said it best when he revealed that Mary told him the Third Secret of Fatima "**is all around you.**"

But more than that, because of our understanding of such dangers, perhaps the Third Secret has become irrelevant as so many Church authorities have said. This is because, they say, all that is needed to know has been revealed. Therefore, our only concern should be prayer, prayer to prevent such events from coming to fulfillment.

*The official marker at the Trinity Site in New Mexico
where the first atomic bomb was detonated on
July 16, 1945, the feast of Our Lady of Mt. Carmel.
According to some, this was an ominous sign
of the danger that was unfolding here.*

CHAPTER FORTY-FOUR

IS THE THIRD SECRET RELEVANT?

"The coming of the Kingdom of God cannot be observed and no one will announce, Look here it is, There it is."
— Lk 17:21

F r. Conrado Balducci's statement concerning the Third Secret reveals again the deep controversy over its reported contents. Is a portion of the Third Secret apocalyptical in nature or is it not? Perhaps we will never know for sure. But one thing is certain, many who have studied the message of Fatima over the last five decades agree that one of the primary dangers implied in both the second part of the Secret, (**"various nations will be annihilated"**) and the intrinsic symbolism of the two great signs given to the world (Oct. 13, 1917 and Jan. 25-26, 1939) were both in reference to the approaching era of nuclear weapons.

Indeed, many Fatima experts feel that if fire does fall from the sky and if a chastisement does come from the hands of men which "annihilates nations," then this "celestial fire" and this "man-made chastisement" are one and the same thing: a nuclear holocaust of unprecedented ramifications for society, nature, and civilization as we know it.

Just five years after the atomic bomb was dropped on Hiroshima and Nagasaki, the theory that atomic danger was what Mary was warning of at Fatima was already being discerned. In a 1950 article, Bishop Fulton J. Sheen saw the falling sun at Fatima as being filled with atomic energy. He then conjectured that Mary's intervention at Fatima was to halt the fall of atomic bombs at a moment when it appears they are about to destroy the world. (See *Soul* Magazine, March-April 1950, pp.3-4, "The Vision in the Heavens by Bishop Fulton J. Sheen, published by Ave Marie Institute, Washington, New Jersey.)

After many years of studying the message of Fatima, this is also the opinion of John Haffert, the co-founder of the Blue Army. Haffert is the author of over 25 books and perhaps one of the most knowledgeable individuals on the subject of Fatima and its message. His writings are clear; Mary was warning of nuclear danger in the second Part of the Secret and the two great signs foretold at Fatima symbolically conveyed this understanding, too. Furthermore, it may be presumed that this was also the opinion of many of the most authoritative Fatima experts of the last four decades. This is because Haffert, who speaks many languages fluently and was director of the Blue Army for decades, intermingled and conversed during this period with all of the authoritative Fatima figures in the Church, including Sister Lucia, the lone surviving visionary. His views were shaped and formed therefore by the most qualified and respected Fatima authorities in the world.

To emphasize his understanding of Fatima's message, Haffert's most voluminous work is titled *Her Own Words to the Nuclear Age*. It is a title that speaks for itself as far as Mr. Haffert's views are concerned. This book carefully reviews Sr. Lucia's memoirs and concludes that Fatima's message, as revealed in Sister Lucia's memoirs, clearly warns of the danger the world approached when it entered the "atomic age."

In another profound book of his *To Prevent This*, Haffert stated that there are three reasons to believe that the warnings given at Fatima were in reference to a nuclear threat:

> As we have said, of all the warnings given by Our Lady at Fatima only one remains, only one has not yet befallen mankind: several entire nations will be annihilated."
>
> In the past some thought perhaps Ukraine, Byelorussia, Lithuania, Latvia, Estonia, etc., were "annihilated" by being Sovietized. Obviously this is not the case. These nations exist. The word "annihilated" means wiped out, totally destroyed.

Our Lord used the same word in speaking to Lucia in March 1939, in connection with the First Saturday Communions of Reparation: **"The time is coming when the rigor of My Justice will punish the crimes of various nations. Some of them will be annihilated."**

Three reasons cause us to believe these prophecies could mean, that if there are not enough Communions of Reparation, there will be a nuclear holocaust: 1) The Miracle of the Sun; 2) Logic 3) Prophecy of fire.

At Fatima on October 13, 1917, everyone within a radius of several miles thought they were about to be consumed by fire. They thought the ball of fire crashing down upon them was actually the sun. They all believed it was the end of the world.

Why would a merciful Mother terrorize Her children with fire? Why would She have done this unless it were like a warning of what can and will happen if the world does not respond to the message of hope God has sent Her to deliver to us?

In 1917, Her prophecy that 'various nations will be annihilated' caused both wonder and astonishment. Since there would not be another deluge, in what other way could entire nations be annihilated (which means wiped out, made into nothing)?

Then in 1945 it happened. Two cities were wiped out by the first simple atomic bombs. And it is noteworthy that in the very announcement to the world of that annihilation the President of the United States said: 'Man has learned to harness the power of the sun.' At Fatima the tens of thousands of people thought it was the sun itself falling upon them.

The second reason why we may believe that this prophecy of Our Lady refers to a nuclear holocaust is because it seems *logical that man would bring about his chastisement.*

A third reason is the theological principle that

God does not multiply miracles. Since a nuclear holocaust is right at hand, waiting to happen, why would God send some kind of miraculous fire to wipe out entire nations especially in the light of His promise after the deluge?

We cannot overemphasize that in 1973, on the actual anniversary of the miracle which Our Lady performed at Fatima 'so that all may believe,' She appeared in Akita, Japan, and said:

'If men do not repent and better themselves, the Father will inflict a terrible punishment on all humanity. It will be a punishment greater than the deluge...Fire will fall from the sky and will wipe out a great part of humanity...I alone can still save you from calamities which approach.'

This prophecy speaks in almost biblical language. No evil comes from God, but only from sin. But God, seeing the pride and wickedness which had come into the world leading to one global war after another, permitted man to do what President Truman described: 'Harness the power of the sun,' *a power which simply touching the earth can scorch and destroy.*

The famous modern mystic, Marthe Robin (who lived 30 years solely on the Eucharist) remarked with sadness: "This atom bomb! When one thinks that small nations will also have it and only two fools will be needed to ravage everything!

Haffert also revealed an insightful statement given to him by Sister Lucia;

Lucia said the consecration (the 1984 collegial consecration of the world by Pope John Paul II) will have its effects, but it is too late...there has been a tidal wave of evil and a proliferation of nuclear weapons. If we are now to avoid nuclear war, the Blue Army will have much to do. (*Her Own Words to the Nuclear Age*)

Haffert's deductions that Mary's prophesy of the "annihilation of nations" is nuclear related and is still unfulfilled is also well supported by contemporary private revelations, especially as he noted, the approved 1973 message of Akita. The Akita message is the most relevant because numerous Church authorities have supported the message as a reinforcement of Fatima's warning and that it was deliberately given in Japan by Mary because of the two atomic bombings during World War II that occurred there.

There is also much to be found in the words of Pope John Paul II and Cardinal Ratzinger. Pope John Paul II's statement advising that "we must be prepared to undergo trials in the not too distant future, trials that will require us to be ready to give up even our lives" is quite powerful and speculative. While Cardinal Ratzinger's opinion that "a stern warning has been launched from that place (Fatima)" is most compatible with Haffert's interpretation of the message of Fatima. One also has to wonder why Cardinal Ratzinger would state that revealing the Secret of Fatima would "expose the Church to the danger of sensationalism." What is this sensationalism?

Over the years, noted Fatima experts have written similar conclusions concerning the apocalyptical aspects of the message of Fatima. In his book *Fatima, the Great Sign*, Francis Johnston refers to the Fatima message as a "clarion call" to avert mass destruction:

> And who will say that such chastisement may not come when, in the light of Our Lady's warning in 1917 of 'the annihilation of various nations,' if 'men do not stop offending God,' we find ourselves confronted by a world of unprecedented wickedness and possessed of terrifying means of mass destruction? Padre Pio, the famous stigmatist priest, had this to say shortly before his death in 1968: 'I can give you only one piece of advice for today: pray, and get others to pray, for the world is at the threshold of its perdition.'
>
> The message of Our Lady of Fatima is, we repeat once again, a clarion call for the ten just men of this permissive age to stand up and save the city of the world. 'It is no longer time to sleep, but to watch in

order that humanity be saved,' said Padre Pio. 'Help yourselves as much as you can with the arms of faith, with the arms of penance, with the arms of shame. Act now to implore pardon and mercy for all the brutalities of the world. The most Blessed Virgin, compassionate Mother, who sheds tears of blood over today's world, calls all her children to penance and prayer. Let pilgrimages be in a spirit of penance...The time is now the hour of darkness. Therefore, increase Marian pilgrimages to counteract the works of Satan and to prepare for the triumph of the Immaculate Heart of Mary. Let us fear the chastisements of God. Let us give up some elicit pleasures. Let us be like a family which, seeing one of its members dying thinks only of prayers to save it. I speak to you thus, not to make you fear, but so that each one may regulate his own conduct to make the world better. If you do not listen, yours is the responsibility.'

Similarly, Father Luigi Bianchi, a well known Fatima authority, refers to the danger of an atomic apocalypse in his book, *Fatima and Medjugorje*:

The message of Medjugorje is a continuation and a complement of the message of Fatima. It is the extraordinary verification of it in substance. It is the same message of peace for this century of the most dreadful wars in history and of the menace of a fiery deluge of an atomic apocalypse.

Fr. Rene Laurentin and Fr. Ljudevit Rupic, two eminent French theologians of this century, write concerning the meaning of Mary's warnings at Fatima and throughout the world:

The first possibility of self-destruction that comes to mind is that of an atomic war. After a time of detente during the era of Kennedy and Kruschev, aided by John XXIII, the leaders of the world now can only think of safeguarding peace through the balance of terror. This is the formula of those who devise world strategy. In each camp we hear it said: 'Peace can only be maintained by the arms race. If I am the stronger I can assure peace. If I am not, the other side will destroy me. Therefore, I must always be the stronger.' This gives rise to an unbridled escalation which has neither limit nor end, and which has already been able to stock-pile means of destruction which would suffice to annihilate all life on this planet. In her message at Medjugorje. Mary has not insisted much on these obvious facts which are all too clear to everyone.

In 1992, at the Akita International Convention in Japan, dozens of cardinals, bishops, theologians, and laity gathered on the occasion of the 75th anniversary of the Fatima apparitions. The delegates of the convention clarified in their closing resolution that "a definitive danger" and "peace plan" were revealed by Mary at Fatima. This warning and peace plan was then repeated, they concluded, at Akita, Japan, in Mary's 1973 apparitions there. The delegates stated that "the world is heading toward its own destruction and a coming chastisement that could wipe out humanity if men would not repent and amend their ways."

The Akita convention's official statement is at the heart of what almost every pope since the 1940's has stated about Fatima. Pope Pius XII knew of the central theme of Fatima's message and told one visitor, "The pope's thinking is contained in the message of Fatima." Pius was a Marian pope and reportedly resisted all efforts by progressive *"intellegensia"* to get him to say something contrary about Fatima. According to many sources, the only statements he had to make "were positive." Perhaps Fatima's message was the impetus behind his most noted statement, "The world is on the verge of a frightful abyss; men must prepare themselves for suffering such as mankind has never seen." And Pius said, "Next to the Mass, the Fatima devotions are most important."

Other Popes have also understood the gravity of Fatima. They have tried to communicate this understanding in strong, but appropriate language. It is a language that appears to want to reveal without inciting fear or panic or, as Cardinal Ratzinger stated, sensationalism.

On May 13, 1967, Pope Paul VI made a pilgrimage to Fatima to celebrate the 50th anniversary of the apparitions. With Sister Lucia at his side, he delivered his memorable exhortation *Signum Magnum* (The Great Sign). According to some, Pope Paul VI's understanding of the seriousness of the message of Fatima is subtly revealed in the text. The Pope said:

> The world is not happy, not tranquil; that the first cause of it's uneasiness is the difficulty it has to enter into harmonious relationships, it difficulty to follow the path of peace. Everything seems to lead to a world of brotherhood and unity, but instead the heart of mankind still bursts with continuous and tremendous conflicts. Two conditions render this historic moment of mankind difficult. One, the world is full of terrifying and deadly arms, while it has not progressed morally as much as it has scientifically and technically. Two, humanity suffers under a state of need and hunger. While it has been awakened to the disturbing consciousness of its need it is aware of the well-being which surrounds it. Therefore, we say, the world is in danger. For this reason we come to the feet of the Queen of Peace to ask from her the gift of peace. Yes peace, a gift from God, which needs His intervention, gracious, divine, merciful and mysterious.

Seventeen years later, Pope John Paul II traveled to Fatima to give thanksgiving for his life being spared in the attempted assassination on May 13, 1981. In his homily, he voiced an urgent plea that God spare mankind from the devastation warned of in the message of Fatima:

> The successor of Peter presents himself here also as a witness to the immensity of human suffering-a witness to the almost apocalyptic menaces looming over the nations and mankind as a whole.
> In the name of these sufferings and with awareness of the evil that is spreading throughout the

world and menacing the individual human being, the nations, and mankind as a whole, Peter's successor presents himself here with greater *faith in the redemption of the world,* in the saving Love that is always stronger, always more powerful than any evil (May 13, 1982).

In his 1984 consecration of the world to the Immaculate Heart of Mary the Pope specifically noted the nuclear shadow hanging over mankind:

Immaculate Heart! Help us to conquer the menace of evil, which so easily takes root in the heart of the people of today, and whose immeasurable effects already weigh down upon our modern world and seem to block the paths toward the future! From famine and war deliver us. From nuclear wars, from incalculable self-destruction, from every kind of war, deliver us.

Through all of these statements, the complete record becomes clear. Fatima's warnings were directed at the great danger the atomic age would bring with it for the survival of the world. Indeed, there is little doubt that this was at the core of Mary's message at Fatima. It has also been at the core of her "call to conversion" since. Thus, nothing new would be learned with the unveiling of the Third Secret. This is because any apocalyptical contents contained in the Third Secret become irrelevant since the nature of the danger and its consequences to the earth and mankind are understood. In *The Ratzinger Report*, Cardinal Ratzinger notes why the Secret has not been released:

The Holy Father deems it would add nothing to what a Christian must know from Revelation or from the Marian apparitions approved by the Church, which only confirmed the urgency of penance conversion, forgiveness, and fasting.

Indeed, these are the primary elements of the message of the apparations. It is a totally spiritual solution being offered as a remedy to the danger. And it is a call to all mankind, not just Catholics. Every race, every religion, every nation is called to pray for peace.

But this is not to rule out human efforts. In Nicarauga, where the 1980 apparitions to Bernardo Martinez were approved by Bishop Vega on November 13, 1983, Mary said "Do not ask for peace, unless you make peace." With these words, Mary instructed that the world had to let go of its anger and to reach out and make peace happen. Peace, she implied, also required a "human effort" to go with the "spiritual effort."

PART IV

THY

KINGDOM

COME

*"In the end my Immaculate Heart will Triumph...
and an Era of Peace will be granted to the world."*

- The Blessed Virgin Mary
to the three children at Fatima,
Fatima, Portugal, July 13, 1917

CHAPTER FORTY-FIVE

CONFIDENCE IN GOD

*"I know that you can do all things and that
no purpose of yours can be hindered."*

— Jb 42:2

It is difficult to discern the two remaining prophecies of Fatima, both of which foretell extreme consequences for the world. The prophecy of an "Era of Peace" predicts an age of unprecedented bliss and grace while the prophecy of the "annihilation of nations" portends the possibility of a catastrophic event also without human precedent.

Even though both prophecies provoke us to ask countless questions, the Virgin has repeatedly admonished the faithful to restrain their curiosity about the future. Instead, she warns the world that the times ahead are "urgent" and that people must spread her messages "quickly."

Even some Church scholars acknowledge their bewilderment over this apparent paradox. In addition, theologians remind us that the interpretation of apparitions and private revelations is a more complex undertaking than the interpretation of Scripture. Fr. Rene Laurentin, an authority on the subject, says visionaries represent a fragile medium. "Their messages are not the Word of God, and the difference is paramount."

Fr. Laurentin stresses that visionaries are not infallible, and that even with the approved apparitions of Fatima, we encounter difficulty in assessing private revelation.

But, Pope John Paul II continues to point to the message of Fatima, even emphasizing Fatima's remaining prophecies in his book

Crossing the Threshold of Hope. "Mary appeared to the three children at Fatima in Portugal and spoke to them words that now, at the end of this century, seem close to their fulfillment," he wrote.

With these words, the Holy Father encourages the Church and the world to look to Fatima for answers about what lies ahead. The Pope insinuates that some world events which will shape the future will be linked to the remaining prophecies of Fatima, more or less in the sense that they will perhaps be shaped by what degree the world responds to Mary's call to conversion. His writings indicate he foresees both bad and good on the horizon. He, too, chooses to focus on the side of caution and hope rather than to focus on God as the source of impending punishment. Indeed, the Pope calls attention to man's sins as the cause of future calamities if they are to come.

Fr. Laurentin succinctly defines this view when he writes, "The message of the apparitions offers us in the first place a diagnosis: Our modern world has abandoned itself happily and quietly to sin. It is destroying itself. The threats are serious. This is what the apparitions are saying in different ways, sometimes in a language intended to shock, at other times in a secret elliptical language as in the case of Medjugorje, where all that is known are the threats and their causes (sin and forgetfulness of God) and the remedies. Other apparitions allude to the murderous divisions which are tearing Central America apart or, indeed, to the threat of a third world war."

Most importantly, Fr. Laurentin emphasizes a hope that is always present in Scripture and Mary's revelations. He writes that God is good and will not forsake His people. Also certain is that at Fatima, Mary promised a "triumph" and she is repeating her promise at Medjugorje and elsewhere throughout the world today. These promises cannot be truly meaningful if the world is reduced to a burning ash.

"I believe the chastisement can still be prevented," asserted John Haffert at the 1996 Lay Apostolate Foundation's retreat in Washington, N.J.

Haffert's confidence in God, like Fr. Laurentin's, comes from more than his belief that Mary's Triumph cannot be genuine if a great part of humanity is annihilated. Rather, he notes that the sun, during the great miracle of Oct. 13, 1917, returned to its position in the sky at the last moment when thousands believed it was about to strike the earth. Thus, Haffert argues, this was a sign that some day, at the decisive moment, God will spare His people from great suffering if enough persons respond to Mary's requests. And many believe that day is approaching rather than any day of "annihilation."

This also appears to be what the Virgin Mary is saying: Her victory is near; it will come. It will come through her direct intercession, just as it did centuries before at Lepanto. But what is needed is a tremendous amount of prayer and sacrifice, along with consistent and generous acts of reparation as requested at Fatima. In a special letter to Fatima on October 13, 1997, the Pope said that Fatima was one of the greatest signs of our time, not so much because of the miracle, but because "it shows us the alternative" and tells us "the specific response" needed to meet that alternative.

What also may be needed, according to some experts who have studied the many private revelations published over the last seventy years, is for the Church to take several bold and sweeping steps that God is believed to be desirous of receiving at this time in history. Like Mary's request at Fatima for the consecration of Russia to her Immaculate Heart, several important requests from heaven have surfaced in apparitions that the Church has granted approval in one form or another. These are believed by some to be paramount to avoiding or at least mitigating God's justice.

First, and most of all, to hasten and insure God's promised victory the Virgin says she needs a great outpouring of Rosaries, for it is through the Rosary that she will bring the world into the Era of Peace. This need is found in almost all of her apparitions but it is especially noted in her request at Tuy, Spain, to Sister Lucia on June 13, 1929. On that day, Mary requested the faithful participate in the Communion of Reparation (The Rosary plus meditations, confession and Holy Communion) on the first five Saturdays. It is in this manner that Mary says the faithful can best help prevent the "annihilation of nations" and bring the "era of peace." Indeed, in an interview with Cardinal Vidal on October 11, 1993, Sister Lucia said the first Saturday devoton was now "urgent". Thus, both of Fatima's remaining prophecies are connected to this long standing request.

Secondly, is the promulgation by the Holy Father of a fifth and final Marian dogma: the Blessed Virgin Mary as Coredemptrix, Mediatrix and Advocate. The proposed dogma has been recently made more known to many Catholics because of the tremendous amount of publicity which surfaced in Catholic and secular publications during the summer of 1997, While this effort has been embraced by a strong lay movement within the Church, *VOX Populi Marie Mediatrici,* it has roots going back centuries. The urgency for the proclamation of such a definition at this time in history is also voiced by many different visionaries. Contemporary prophets advise that God will bless the world with great graces if and when Mary's final dogma is proclaimed by the Church.

Most prominent of the private revelations surrounding this issue are the messages of the Blessed Virgin Mary to Ida Perleman of Amsterdam in the late 1940's and 1950's. These revelations have recently received a level of approbation by the local bishop of Amsterdam. Mary reportedly told Ida on May 31, 1954, **"When the dogma, the last dogma in Marian history has been proclaimed, the Lady of All Nations would grant peace, genuine peace for the world. ... Then they will experience that the Lady has come as Coredemptrix, Mediatrix, and Advocate."**

Thirdly, a virtually unknown divine request has also come to be understood by some to be of great significance in preventing the chastisement foretold at Fatima and in bringing the era of peace. It is for the Church to proclaim a Feast Day in honour of God Our Father, the Father of All Mankind. This heavenly petition finds its inception in the revelations of God the Father to a French nun in 1932 named Mother Eugenia Ravasio. After ten years of investigation a commission approved her revelations as worthy of the faith. One year later, the local bishop of Grenoble also granted his approbation. According to sources in Rome, the approval was forwarded to Pope Pius XII who found no reason to request another investigation. But because of the tremendous response by the faithful at the time to the Sacred Heart devotions, the matter was reportedly tabled for his successors. In the revelations, the Eternal Father appears to state that the granting of this request will save mankind from the "precipice." However, the Church needed to act in this century, The Father said to Mother Eugenia, for **"fear of having such a grace withdrawn."** Contemporary revelations have echoed this call of the Father and the reported urgency.

A look at all three of these issues is necessary, for in them lies the "secret" of the Triumph and the fulfillment of the remaining prophecies of Fatima.

CHAPTER FORTY-SIX

THE ROSARY

*"Blessed are you, O Lord. Teach me your statutes. With my lips,
I declare all the ordinances of your mouth. In the way of your
decrees I rejoice, as much as in all riches. I will meditate on your
precepts and consider your ways. In your statutes I will delight.
I will not forget your words."*

Ps(s) 119: 12-16

On the wall of the Sistine Chapel, Michelangelo's *Last Judgment* is an awe-inspiring and intimidating painting of the power and glory of God. Completed in 1541 and recently refurbished, the painting projects the story of salvation like no other artwork.

Created during a time of crisis in the Church, the painting was a message from Michelangelo to the bishops and cardinals who met at the Council of Trent in 1545. This council's task it was to initiate the Counter-Reformation that would reaffirm the Church's doctrines and teachings. And in Michelangelo's work, they found the inspiration to do so.

The visual message of *The Last Judgment* preserved the Church doctrines on Mary, the Mother of God, and the honor accorded her.

Michelangelo's great fresco let everyone see for themselves that Mary is forever at the side of her Son, reigning as Heaven's Queen and earth's model of discipleship. And Michelangelo's work was not lacking in depth of meaning, for he painted a huge *Rosary* that hung down over the ramparts of Heaven, a Rosary on which two souls grasp desperately as they pull their way into Paradise.

No word or image tells us better how important the Rosary is to the spiritual lives of the faithful, because for centuries Heaven has been calling souls to this mystery of salvation.

The prayer is said to have slowly evolved in Ireland and over the centuries developed in content and organization. Then, in 1214, the Virgin Mary reportedly appeared to St. Dominic and presented him with the Rosary as a powerful means of converting the Albigensian heretics and other sinners.

The Albigensian heresy rocked the 13th century Church in a frightful way. Tradition tells us that in a forest outside of Toulouse, Mary appeared to St. Dominic after he had been praying for three days and nights. Because of self-mortification, he had lapsed into a coma. At this point, the Virgin appeared and said, **"Dear Dominic, do you know which weapon the Blessed Trinity wants to use to reform the world?"**

"Oh, my Lady," replied St. Dominic, "you know far better than I do because next to your Son, Jesus Christ, you have always been the chief instrument of our salvation."

At this, Mary gave the Rosary to St. Dominic, explaining to him that it was **"the foundation stone of the New Testament."**

The saint returned to Toulouse, where he began to zealously preach the merits of the new prayer. Assisted by angels, he gave a sermon that was accompanied by the roar of heavenly thunder. The sky is said to have darkened, and the earth shook while flashes of lightning laced the heavens. Just as the crowd was overcome with fear, an image of Mary appeared. She raised her arms up and down to Heaven as if to call down God's wrath on the people if they did not convert. After this, townspeople repented and turned back to God, and devotion to the Rosary began to rapidly spread.

St. Dominic preached the spiritual benefits of Rosary for the rest of his life. However, within two centuries the prayer had almost disappeared as a devotion. In 1460, after reportedly receiving a special warning from the Lord, Blessed Alan de la Roche led a crusade to encourage use of the prayer.

Blessed Alan reportedly received a vision that showed how Jesus and Mary had appeared to St. Dominic to help him understand the power of the Rosary. He was told that Heaven wished this prayer to be firmly embraced by the faithful as the preferred weapon to combat evil.

Blessed Alan also received visions of Jesus and Mary and St. Dominic. Through his efforts, the Rosary was firmly reestablished throughout Europe. The faithful were taught how heaven wished souls to survive spiritually in a world besieged by Satan and his followers. Mary revealed that a spiritual war was unfolding, and the Rosary, with the Sacraments, was to be the ultimate weapon during this conflict.

After Blessed Alan restored the prayer in 1460, the Rosary became known as the Psalter of Jesus and Mary because it has the same number of Angelic Salutations as there are Psalms.

In his book, *The Secret of the Rosary*, St. Louis de Montfort explains why the Rosary is so powerful:

> Since simple and uneducated people are not able to say the Psalms of David, the Rosary is held to be just as fruitful for them as David's Psalter is for others.
>
> But the Rosary can be considered to be even more valuable than the latter for three reasons:
>
> 1. Firstly, because the Angelic Psalter bears a nobler fruit, that of the Word Incarnate, whereas David's Psalter only prophecies His (Christ's) coming.
> 2. Secondly, just as the real thing is more important than its prefiguration and as the body is more than its shadow, in the same way the Psalter of Our Lady is greater than David's Psalter which did no more than prefigure it;
> 3. And thirdly, because Our Lady's Psalter (or the Rosary made up of the Our Father and Hail Mary) is the direct work of the Most Blessed Trinity and was not made through a human instrument.

The Virgin Mary's Psalter is divided into three parts of five decades each for the following reasons:

1. To honor the three Persons of the Most Blessed Trinity

2. To honor the life, death, and glory of Jesus Christ

3. To imitate the Church Triumphant, to help the members of the Church Militant, and to lessen the pains of the Church Suffering

4. To imitate the three groups into which the Psalms are divided:

      a) The first being for the purgative life

      b) The second for the illuminative life

      c) The third for the unitive life

5. Finally, to give us graces in abundance during our lifetime, peace at death, and glory in eternity.

The word "Rosary" means "crown of roses," and thus, whenever a person devoutly prays the Rosary, wrote Blessed Alan de la Roche, he or she mystically places a crown of 153 red roses and 16 white roses on the heads of Jesus and Mary.

Blessed Alan taught these mysteries of the Rosary and its promises, and he also began to assemble an association, similar to an army, whose members would pledge to pray the Rosary and spread its devotion.

By the time Blessed Alan de la Roche died on Sept. 8, 1475, more than 100,000 people had joined the *Confraternity of the Rosary*, which he began.

Over the centuries, many great kings, popes, and saints courageously spread the Rosary, often crediting its miraculous power with securing Heaven's favors for both small and great successes.

St. Philip Neri, St. Bernard, St. Robert Bellarmine, St. Francis de Sales, St. Bonaventure, St. Gertrude, St. Ignatius Loyola, St. Teresa of Avila, and St. Louis de Montfort were all champions of the Rosary.

However, it was St. Louis de Montfort who specfically explained and promoted the Rosary's powers and its mysteries. These are the mysteries of Christ's life, death, and resurrection, mysteries that relate to His mother. Most importantly, St. Louis de Montfort tells us in *The Secret of the Rosary* why it is necessary to contemplate the mysteries of the Rosary in order to use the prayer to its fullest potential:

> For, in reality, the Rosary said without meditating on the sacred mysteries of our salvation would be almost like a body without a soul: excellent matter but without the form, which is meditation, this latter being that which sets it apart from all other devotions.
>
> The first part of the Rosary contains five mysteries: the first is the Annunciation of the Archangel St. Gabriel to Our Lady; the second, the Visitation of Our Lady to her cousin St. Elizabeth; the third, the Nativity of Jesus Christ; the fourth, the Presentation of the Child Jesus in the Temple and the Purification of Our Lady; and the fifth, the Finding of Jesus in the Temple among the doctors.
>
> These are called the JOYFUL MYSTERIES because of the joy which they gave to the whole universe. Our Lady and the angels were overwhelmed with joy the moment when the Son of God was incarnate. St. Elizabeth and St. John the Baptist were filled with joy by the visit of Jesus and Mary. Heaven and earth rejoiced at the birth of Our Savior. Holy Simeon felt great consolation and was filled with joy when he took the Holy Child in his arms. The doctors were lost in admiration and wonderment at the answers which Jesus gave, and how could anyone describe the joy of Mary and Joseph when they found the Child Jesus after He has been lost for three days?
>
> The second part of the Rosary is also composed of five mysteries which are called the SORROWFUL MYSTERIES because they show us Our Lord weighed down with sadness, covered with wounds, laden with insults, sufferings, and torments. The first of these mysteries is Jesus' Prayer and

Agony in the Garden of Olives; the second, His scourging; the third, His Crowning with Thorns; the fourth, Jesus carrying His Cross; and the fifth, His Crucifixion and Death on Mount Calvary.

The third part of the Rosary contains five other mysteries, which are called the GLORIOUS MYSTERIES because when we say them, we meditate on Jesus and Mary in their triumph and glory. The first is the Resurrection of Jesus Christ; the second, His Ascension into Heaven; the third, the Descent of the Holy Ghost upon the Apostles; the fourth, Our Lady's glorious Assumption into Heaven; and the fifth, her Crowning in Heaven.

Thus, the prayer of the holy Rosary, together with meditation on its sacred mysteries, is a sacrifice of praise to God in thanksgiving for the great graces of our redemption. It is also, St. Louis de Montfort said, a holy reminder of the sufferings, death, and glory of Jesus Christ, all of which help perfect the spiritual maturity of a soul. Faithfully reciting the Rosary gives a soul the following graces:

1) a perfect knowledge of Jesus Christ
2) a purification of soul and a washing away of sin
3) victory over enemies
4) an increased ease in the practice of virtue
5) a love for Jesus Christ
6) an enrichment in graces and merits
7) the graces necessary to pay all our debts to God and our fellow men

CHAPTER FORTY-SEVEN

THE LADY OF THE ROSARY

"The Mighty one has done great things for me."
— Lk 1: 49

Over the centuries, Mary revealed to visionaries, mystics, and saints how the Rosary melts the most hardened hearts of the greatest sinners. The Rosary creates a fervor for God in us, she said, and produces change in lives. Most of all, it appeases God's justice.

Indeed, it is this need the Virgin often invokes when imploring us to pray the Rosary. Mary pleads for faithful souls and nations to pray her Rosary to restrain the arm of her Son's coming justice.

While some dispute St. Dominic's role in originating the Rosary, five popes have credited him with founding it. Even though its full history remains a mystery, the accounts of its many successes are not.

Just 30 years after the Council of Trent's first session, a greatly outnumbered force of Christian defenders repelled a Turkish invasion on Oct. 7, 1571, off the coast of Greece at the Gulf of Lepanto. It was considered a miraculous victory brought about specifically by the Rosary, when St. Pius V led a Rosary Crusade that united all Europe in prayer. From this, the Feast of the Most Holy Rosary was established in 1573 and is still celebrated to this day on Oct. 7th.

Even before the battle of Lepanto, the Rosary was officially credited with bringing a miraculous victory in 1474 to the city of Cologne, which was under attack by Bergundian troops. After Lepanto, another victory over the Turks came at Peterwardein in

Hungary, by Prince Eugene on Aug. 5, 1716. The Feast of Our Lady of the Snows led Pope Clement XI to extend the Feast of the Most Holy Rosary to the Universal Church.

By the 19th century, so numerous were the miraculous favors credited to the Rosary, that popes began to recognize it as an institution in the Church. During his 25-year reign from 1878 to 1903, Pope Leo XIII wrote 12 encyclical or apostolic letters on the Rosary and its devotion. He attempted to use the Rosary to bring unity to the Church, and his writings "officially" credited the Rosary with the Church's victories of the past.

In *Supremi Apostolatus officio,* Pope Leo XIII began the recognition of October as the month of special devotion to the Rosary. In his letter *Salutaris ille,* published on Dec. 24, 1883, he called on each family to recite the Rosary daily, and in his letter of Sept. 20, 1887, he elevated the feast day to what it is today.

Most significantly, in his September 1892 encyclical, *Magnae Dei Matris,* he stressed the importance of the Rosary as the most appropriate form of prayer to Mary, saying that through the Rosary the great mysteries of our faith can be unlocked. In his 25-year reign, Pope Leo XIII touched on all aspects of the Rosary devotion, elevating it in a landmark way and setting the stage for the 20th century devotion to Mary.

In her last apparition at Fatima, on Oct. 13, 1917, the Virgin Mary told the children that she was "The Lady of the Rosary." Appearing with the Rosary in her right hand and the Brown Scapular in her left, she evoked the memory of what she told St. Dominic centuries before: **"one day the Rosary and the Scapular will save the world."**

According to visionaries and even several popes, that day is today.

Beginning with her apparitions at Rue de Bac, Paris, in 1830, which officially initiated the modern era of Mary, the importance of the "Rosary Crusade" is indisputable.

From Lourdes in 1858, where the Virgin called for penance and the recitation of the Rosary, to Pontmain on Jan. 17, 1871, where the children reported that each time the people prayed the Rosary, the image of Mary in the sky increased in size, the Virgin has continuously invoked this devotion in her apparitions.

When at Fatima she foretold a dangerous future for the world, the Queen of the Most Holy Rosary made it clear this prayer would be the solution to the problems of a world headed into the nuclear age. This is because a critical time in history was coming, a time when "annihilation" would be only moments away. Thefore,the faithful needed to be prepared for those decisive moments.

Pope Paul VI echoed this belief in his encyclical *Signum Magnum,* issued when he visited Fatima on May 13, 1967. And on May 13, 1971, the 25th anniversary of the proclamation of Pope Pius XII, pilgrim statues of Our Lady of Fatima were crowned throughout the world.

Today, visionaries, including Sr. Lucia, say it is evident that Our Lady is winning the war against Satan, and she is winning through the power of the Rosary. It is a power that will bring the final victory foretold at Fatima. Even *The Wall Street Journal* reported this observation in a published report September 27th, one month after the failed coup in the Soviet Union that began on August 17, 1991. It quoted Pope John Paul II as stating, "the collapse of Communism ... compels us to think in a special way about Fatima."

Indeed, Mary's promise of a great victory for God through the Rosary is reaffirmed time and again through historical events. It was reportedly on Oct. 13, 1886, that Pope Leo XIII, the great champion of the Rosary, received his vision of the coming confrontation between Satan and God. And it was in October 1917 that St. Maximilian Kolbe founded the Militia Immaculata, one of the greatest movements ever "to win the world for Mary." The victory would be obtained, Kolbe told his followers, by "fingering the beads of the Rosary."

Once again, we must note that the Jesuit priests were praying the Rosary at Hiroshima on the fateful day of Aug. 6, 1945, when they were spared death from the atomic blast. (August 6th is also the date St. Dominic died [August 6, 1221]). The same thing occurred at Nagasaki, where the Fatima prayers reportedly preserved the lives of a group of friars who were at ground zero of the atomic blast and survived without any radiation effects. It was the Rosary that 70,000 people promised to pray in Austria for seven years before the Soviets departed on May 13, 1955. Furthermore, it was the Rosary that more than 600,000 women in Brazil joined together to pray to derail a communist takeover in Brazil in 1962.

A series of unexplanable events on Fatima anniversary dates involving the Soviet Union surrounds the Cold War era of 1960 through 1990 and must also be noted in recognition of the power of the Rosary, Marian experts say.

On October 12-13, 1960 another major intercession by Mary is believed to have possibly prevented the world from experiencing nuclear destruction. Father Albert Shamon, in his book *The Power of the Rosary*, relays this amazing story:

> *Most of us remember the time when Nikita Khrushchev visited the United Nations in October, 1960 and boasted that "they would bury us" —would annihilate us! And to emphasize his boasting, he took off his shoe and pounded the desk before the horrified world assembly.*
>
> *This was no idle boast. Khrushchev knew his scientists had been working on a nuclear missile and had completed their work and planned in November 1960, the 43rd anniversary of the Bolshevik Revolution, to present it to Khrushchev.*
>
> *But here's what happened. Pope John XXIII had opened and read the Third Fatima Secret given to Sister Lucy. He authorized the Bishop of Leiria (Fatima) to write to all the bishops of the world, inviting them to join with the pilgrims of Fatima on the night of October 12-13, 1960, in prayer and penance for Russia's conversion and consequent world peace.*
>
> *On the night of October 12-13, about a million pilgrims spent the night outdoors in the Cova da Iria at Fatima in prayer and penance before the Blessed Sacrament. They prayed and watched despite a penetrating rain which chilled them to the bone.*
>
> *At the same time at least 300 dioceses throughout the world joined with them. Pope John XXIII sent a special blessing to all taking part in this unprecedented night of reparation.*
>
> *On the night between October 12 and 13,*

right after his shoe-pounding episode, Khrushchev suddenly pulled up stakes and enplaned in all haste for Moscow, cancelling all subsequent engagements. Why?

Marshall Nedelin, the best minds in Russia on nuclear energy, and several government officials were present for the final testing of the missile that was going to be presented to Khrushchev. When countdown was completed, the missile, for some reason or other, did not leave the launch pad. After 15 or 20 minutes, Nedelin and all others came out of the shelter. When they did, the missile exploded killing over 300 people. This set back Russia's nuclear program for 20 years, prevented all-out atomic warfare, the burying of the U.S.-and this happened on the night when the whole Catholic world was on its knees before the Blessed Sacrament, gathered at the feet of our Rosary Queen in Fatima.

On May 13, 1984, as one of the greatest crowds ever to come to Fatima celebrated the anniversary of the Virgin's first apparition there by praying the Rosary, another significant event occurred that would again help "to prevent" nuclear conflict.

On that day, a massive explosion eliminated two-thirds of the surface to air and ship to ship missiles of the Soviet Union's most powerful fleet, the Northern Fleet.

According to *Jane's Defense Weekly* of London, this was "the greatest disaster to occur in the Soviet navy since WW II" Could this have been an accident of great significance? According to Sister Lucia of Fatima, "a nuclear war would have occurred in 1985." (Source: *The Triumphant Queen of the World,* 1995 by Daniel J. Lynch)

Four years later, another event happened. As thousands prayed all night long on May 12, 1988, during the vigil of the anniversary of the apparitions at Fatima, another major explosion shut down the Soviet Union's sole missile motor plant. The Associated Press reported at the time, "A major explosion has shut down the only plant in the Soviet Union that makes the main rocket motors of that country's newest long-range nuclear missile, according to U.S. officials." The Pentagon released a statement noting the accident occurred on May 12th and "destroyed several buildings at a Soviet propellant plant in Paulogriad."

Curiously, just a week before, on May 3, 1988, a similar eruption ripped apart a Nevada facility believed to be handling the ammonium perchlocate used in the main rocket motor for the SS-24.

Since 1989, the Virgin Mary has said repeatedly to visionaries that the Rosary is slowly but surely bringing victory. The peaceful collapse of communism in Eastern Europe, the Soviet Union, Nicaragua, El Salvador, and other Soviet satellite countries is proof, Father Gobbi's messages indicated, along with the relatively peaceful overturning of dictatorships in countries like Panama, Grenada, and the Philippines.

In addition, the end of apartheid and the quick resolution of the Persian Gulf War should also be recognized as evidence, visionaries say, of Mary's mighty intercession for her children through their prayers, especially the Rosary.

We should note what Mary said at Medjugorje on Jan. 25, 1991, days after Iraq President Saddam Hussein flooded the Persian Gulf with oil and ignited the Kuwait oil wells: **"Satan is strong and wishes not only to destroy human life but also nature and the planet ... God sent me so that I can help you ... the Rosary alone can do miracles in the world and in lives!"**

Now visionaries say Mary's triumph will come and it will occur through her intercession and the power of prayer.

Thus, a Rosary crusade is perhaps needed now more than ever. And because of the great danger of our times, it must be a crusade greater than ever before, for it will culminate in Mary's securing her final victory and preventing nuclear disaster. As a message from Mary to Father Gobbi revealed on Oct. 7, 1983, the feast of the Most Holy Rosary: **"Prayer possesses a potent force and starts a chain reaction of good that is far more powerful than any atomic reaction."**

Indeed, visionaries say there can be no doubt that Mary needs people to take action. Estela Ruiz said Mary told her on August 3, 1996: **"To those of you who have heard my call I say this: If you believe that God loves you, and if you love Him, you can no longer sit still and do nothing. You must join forces and fight for** the faith that you have been given. Begin now don't wait any longer. You, my beloved, cannot wait any longer."

Then on Oct. 7th, 1992, the Feast of Our Lady of the Rosary, Fr. Gobbi's received another extraordinary message from Mary about the Rosary. **The Rosary is my prayer; it is the prayer which I came down from Heaven to ask of you because it is the weapon which you must make use of in these times of the great battle, and it is the sign of my assured victory ... . The chain with which the great Dragon is to be bound is made up of prayer made with me and by means of me. This prayer is that of the Holy Rosary."**

"Say the Rosary every day," Mary told the three children at Fatima (at six of the apparitions in 1917), **"to obtain peace for the world."**

On December 10, 1925, and then again on June 13, 1929 Mary appeared to Sister Lucia in a convent in Tuy, Spain, to fulfill her promise of coming to ask for the consecration of Russia to her Immaculate heart and the Communion of Reparation on the five first Saturdays.

In a letter written by Sister Lucia in the 1930's, she makes it clear that reparation to the Immaculate Heart of Mary is necessary and that the practice of reparation is ultimately intended to bring about the true conversion of Russia through the collegial consecration.

Sister Lucia said the Virgin asks the following:

1) **PRAY THE ROSARY**
2) **WEAR THE SCAPULAR** (Mary appeared at Fatima on October 13th in one of the final visions to the children holding a Brown Scapular, the Scapular of Mt. Carmel, in her left hand. The Scapular is considered a sign of consecration to the Immaculate Heart of Mary.)
3) **MAKE THE COMMUNION OF REPARATION OF THE FIRST SATURDAY OF EACH MONTH. THIS INCLUDES CONFESSION,**

COMMUNION, ROSARY, AND SPEND AT LEAST 15 MINUTES IN MEDITATION UPON THE MYSTERIES OF THE ROSARY.

According to many Fatima devotees, the fact that Russia is still not completely converted, an era of peace has not come, and the danger of annihilation still prevails is very much a result of "insufficient reparation" and not the fact that the consecration of Russia was not done in the exact, prescribed manner. This is a very volatile issue, but on March 19, 1939, Sister Lucia wrote concerning the need for the Communion of Reparation devotion in order to prevent another war:

> Whether the world has war or peace depends on the practice of this devotion, along with the consecration to the Immaculate Heart of Mary. This is why I desire its propagation so ardently, especially because this is also the will of our dear Mother in Heaven.

Again on June 20th of the same year, Lucia wrote of the power of this devotion:

> Our Lady promised to put off the scourge of war, if this devotion was propagated and practiced. We see that she will obtain remission of this chastisement to the extent that efforts are made to propagate this devotion; but I fear that we cannot do any more than we are doing and that God, being displeased, will put back the arm of His mercy and let the world be ravaged by this chastisement which will be unlike any other is the past, horrible, horrible.

Two months later, World War II had been declared. Still little had been done to correspond to the requests of Heaven. The bishop of Leiria-Fatima first published the First Saturday devotions on September 21, 1939, granting his imprimatur. Today, the great need for the Communion of Reparation remains as recent interviews with Sister Lucia (October, 1993, and March, 1998) revealed she was still asking for the world to pray, to pray the Rosary.

In an historic interview with Cardinal Vidal of the Phillippines on Oct. 11, 1993, Sister Lucia said:

> All the wars which have occurred could have been avoided through prayer and sacrifice. This is why Our Lady asked for the Communion of Reparation and the Consecration. People expect things to happen immediately within their own time frame. But Fatima is still in its third day. The Triumph is an on going process. We are now in the post consecration period. Fatima has just begun. How can one expect it to be over immediately? The Rosary, which is the most important spiritual weapon in these times, when the devil is so active, is to be recited.

The Cardinal then asked Sr. Lucia whether the (Blue Army) apostolate (with the pledge and the emphasis on first Saturdays) fulfilled Our Lady's requests. Lucia replied:

> I believe so. This movement shows itself to be the fulfillment of what the Virgin asked. To promote the Communion of Reparation is the means to combat atheism... The Virgin is interested in everything, but particularly in the Communion of Reparation.

*The cover of the July, 1981, issue of Life magazine.
One month later, the attempted coup in the Soviet Union
failed, marking the end of communism there. This was a
miracle, Mary said to one visionary, brought about through
her intercession and people's prayers.*

CHAPTER FORTY- EIGHT

A FINAL MARIAN DOGMA?

"Behold from now on all ages will call me blessed."
— Lk 1: 48

Since 1993, a strong lay movement within the Church, Vox Populi Maria Mediatrici (Voice of the People for Mary Mediatrix), has been preparing the way for the Holy Father to make an infallible pronouncement of a fifth and final Marian dogma. Preceded by the dogmas of *Mother of God, Perpetual Virgin, Immaculate Conception, and Assumption into Heaven,* over five million petitions in the last five years have been received encouraging the Holy Father for this final definition. There is even one signed by the late Mother Teresa of Calcutta.

Specifically, Vox Populi has carefully worked to pattern itself on the historical precedents that led to the definition of the Immaculate Conception in 1854 by Pope Pius IX and to the definition of the Assumption in 1950 by Pope Pius XII. Like those definitions, the process for defining an ex-cathedra Marian Dogma rests on three pillars:

1) Theological foundations
2) Episcopal and hierarchical support, and
3) A manifestation of the sensus fidelium.

According to Dr. Mark Miravalle, the founder of VOX Populi and a Professor of Theology at Franciscan University of Steubenville, Ohio, the five million petitions have come from over 150 countries, spanning five continents.

Dr. Miravalle, who has authored two books on the theological foundations of the proposed dogma, reports that although this proposed declaration of Mary's exalted roles as Coredemptrix, Mediatrix, and Advocate appears to sound new, there has already been decades of theological reflection and contribution.

Indeed, beginning with the prophetic call of St. Louis Marie Grignon de Montfort in the 18th Century, a long series of Popes and historic Church figures have prepared the ground for the proposed definition. But according to Miravalle, the 20th century especially reveals the Holy Spirit at work in this process. Starting in the 1920's with Cardinal Mercier and St. Maximillian Kolbe, over 70 years of outstanding and noteworthy episcopal endorsements and exhortations of Mary reveal a doctrinal development from within the Church based upon the sources of Divine Revelation, Scripture and Tradition. But what exactly does this new title mean?

The title *Coredemptrix* is a term that refers to Mary's *unique and intimate cooperation* with her Divine Son in the work of the redemption of the human family. It finds its revealed roots in the book of Genesis where Mary is *prophetically foreshadowed in the promise of victory over the serpent* (Vatican Council II, *Lumen Gentium*, n. 55), as it was God's manifest will that the Women share in the same *enmity* between herself and the serpent as does her redeeming seed (cf. Gen 3:15), Jesus Christ. This great struggle and victory over the serpent foreshadows the divine work of redemption effected by the Saviour of the world, Jesus Christ, *with the Mother of the Redeemer's intimate cooperation in this saving act.*

The prefix *co* in the title, *Coredemptrix,* does not infer an equality with the one Redeemer, Jesus Christ, who alone could reconcile humanity with the Father in his divinity and humanity. Rather, the prefix *co* derives from the Latin word *cum,* which means *with,* and not *equal to.* Jesus as true God and true Man participates with the Divine Redeemer in a completely subordinate and dependent way. Nonetheless, though subordinate and dependent, Mary's human participation remains a uniquely privileged and exalted one, one that was entirely contingent upon her freely and meritoriously uttered *yes* in her words, **"let it be done to me according to your word"** (Lk 1:38).

When the Church invokes Mary under the title, *Mediatrix of all Grace,* it looks back to the Annunciation (Lk 1:38), where Mary's free consent and joyous desire to be the Mother of God brings to the world and thereby *mediates* to the world Jesus Christ, source of all grace. This *maternal mediation,* as our Holy Father likes to call it, fulfills the ancient prophecy of Gen 3:15 as the Women who would bring to the world the seed of victory over Satan, and finds its completeness at the foot of the cross as her dying Son gives Mary as Mother of the human family (cf. Jn 19:26). Mary, Mediatrix of all grace, is in fact a continuation of her role as Coredemptrix. Pope John Paul II tells us, "Mary's role as Coredemptrix did not cease with the glorification of her Son." He is speaking here of a gift from Jesus to Mary, from the Redeemer to the Coredemptrix for her special sharing with her Son in the redemption of the human family, the gift of mediating all the graces obtained from the Cross of her Divine Son. Mary thus becomes *Mediatrix of all graces* for the People of God.

The third title given by Providence to the Mother of Jesus in His gift of universal meditation to her is that of *Advocate for the People of God.* This also is a continuation of her role as Coredemptrix. The early Church manifested its heartfelt belief in the intercessory power of Mary to whom it called for help and protection in the midst of its dangers and trials. The Second Vatican Council confirms this (cf. *Lumen Gentium,* n.66), and also continues this ancient practice of invoking Mary under the title that bespeaks her role as intercessory helper for the People of God in times of peril: "Therefore, the Blessed Virgin is invoked in the Church under the title(s) of Advocate..." (cf. Lumen Gentium,n 62).

Up until the summer of 1997, the awareness of the significance of a new Marian dogma of Mary as Coredemptrix, Mediatrix and Advocate and its relationship to Mary as words at Fatima promising the Triumph of Her Immaculate Heart was restricted to all but the most diehard private revelation followers.

But no more. Since the spring of 1997, a litany of Catholic publications began to focus on this issue to such a degree that even the secular publications could not resist a look. Then, *Newsweek* magazine, one of the two largest American weekly publications, ran a cover story on the questions of the dogma during the week of August 25, 1997. This began an escalation of a debate that has now witnessed commentaries from not only the leadership of the Catholic Church worldwide, but also many other Christian denominations.

The debate takes many forms, but for the most part, it is seen as an internal issue within the Catholic Church. It centers around whether or not Mary needs such a title and whether or not such a declaration would cause confusion and disruption in the ecumenical effort that has picked up some steam in the last couple of decades. Certainly the question also invokes theology and Church history, but for the most part, the most significant aspect of the proclamation of such a dogma, the element of the prophetic importance of such a declaration at this time in history, is neglected or ignored.

But for private revelation experts, the dogma is understood to be of much more significant than any secular journalist can imagine.

Indeed, some of the revelations indicate that, like the consecration of Russia, the Triumph of the Immaculate Heart in the world may be inescapably tied to the proclamation of a final dogma on the Virgin Mary.

While there have been messages given to visionaries, mystics, and saints for quite a while concerning Mary's roles, it is best to focus on what is generally recognized as the beginning of the modern era of Marian devotion — the apparitions to Saint Catherine Laboure in 1830 at Rue du Bac, Paris — to see where all this began in private revelation.

At Paris, Mary proclaimed no titles for herself to saint Catherine, but her actions and words began to reveal more her powerful role as Mediatrix and Advocate.

On the night of July 19, 1930, Our Lady appeared to Catherine and told her to **"Come to the foot of the altar. There graces will be shed upon all, great and little, who ask for them. Graces will be especially shed upon those who ask for them."**

Then Mary told her: **"I particularly love to shed graces upon your community. I love it."** Before she left, the Virgin told St. Catherine, **"I will grant you many graces."** On her next apparition, Saturday, November 27, 1830, Mary appeared standing on a globe, with rays pouring from her fingers. **"The rays,"** Mary told St. Catherine, **"are graces which I give to those who ask for them."**

From this apparition, Saint Catherine was told to have a medal struck showing Mary as Mediatrix of All Grace with rays streaming from her hands. The medal was to bear the words, **"O**

Mary Conceived Without Sin, Pray for Us Who Have Recourse to Thee." These words would be a direct reference to Mary's Immaculate Conception which would be proclaimed as dogma not long afterward in 1854. Indeed, the overall message of this apparition seemed to convey the special role of Mary in the redemption and salvation of mankind. Some writers say that the Two Hearts, on the back of the Miraculous Medal, were to be undisputable evidence of God's plan to bring to the world recognition and devotion to Mary's Immaculate Heart alongside Jesus' Sacred Heart.

The apparitions at La Salette, France (1846), and Lourdes, France (1858), did nothing to diminish recognition to Mary as the source of graces necessary for salvation. Rather, Mary's words and actions in both apparitions reaffirmed Mary's role as Mediatrix and Advocate for her children.

Likewise, two approved apparitions at the end of Nineteenth Century, Pontmain, France (1871) and Knock, Ireland (1879), also seemed to indicate that Mary's Immaculate Heart was to be made known to the world not only as the source for individual graces, but also for nations and suffering peoples.

At Pontmain, Mary told the people to pray and her Son would be moved to help those suffering during the Franco-Prussian War. At Knock her silent, prayerful image depicted her again as Mediatrix of All Graces and Advocate of God's People, especially to her persecuted Catholic children of Ireland.

In the early Twentieth Century, more visionaries and mystics reported messages concerning Mary's roles as Coredemptrix, Mediatrix, and Advocate.

At La Fraudais, France, Marie-Julie Jahenny, the stigmatist of Blain, reported the following message from Jesus concerning Mary's constant intercession:

> **My Mother is untiringly imploring Me, and together with her, a great number of penitent and atoning souls. I cannot deny her anything. Therefore, it is thanks to My Mother and because of My elect that those days are going to be shortened**.

On February 7, 1910, the Belgian stigmatist Berthe Petit also reported that Jesus told her His desires concerning His Mother's recognition in the Redemption:

> **It is in coredemption that My Mother was above-all great. That is why I ask that the invocation, as I have inspired it, should be approved and diffused throughout the whole Church....It has already obtained grace. It will obtain more, until the hour comes when, by Consecration to the Sorrowful and Immaculate Heart of My Mother, the Church shall be uplifted and the world renewed.**

Thus, from the Nineteenth and early Twentieth Century apparitions, Mary's role as Advocate and Mediatrix became clearer. Eminent theologian Father John Lozano writes of this in *Mary, Model of Disciples, Mother of the Lord*:

> **All of the apparitions...involve images and words. The images, especially some of them, are quite expressive in themselves and therefore convey a message all their own. But this message is further explicated in the words that accompany the images. The presence of grace — in these cases, the maternal mediation of the Blessed Virgin.**

At Fatima, Mary's roles as Coredemptrix, Mediatrix and Advocate became more obvious. Her thorn-encircled Heart at Fatima is seen by many Marian writers as a clear sign of her role as Coredemptrix. Likewise, Sister Lucia's report of Mary appearing in the sky on October 13, 1917, as Our Lady of Sorrows has also been seen as a definitive indicator that she be recognized in her role of Coredemption. Indeed, some believe that in the Church's feast of Our Lady of Sorrows on September 15th, we are directed into the mystery of Fatima, the mystery of Coredemption.

In Fatima's message, we also find Mary's role as Mediatrix of All Graces. The best example of this is probably Jacinta's touching words to Lucia, "Tell everyone that Our Lord grants all graces through the Immaculate Heart of Mary, that all must make their petitions to her."

In one noteworthy account, Fatima Bishop Venancio clearly outlines the individual truths contained in the Fatima events and messages concerning Mary's roles. In his report, Bishop Venancio recalled twenty-one truths in the Fatima messages, two of which are most relevant to Mary's roles. In his eighth point, the Bishop seemed to directly reflect upon Mary's role as Coredemptrix. He wrote: "The reality of sin as an offense against God, and by extension, against the pure Heart of His Mother with its true consequences for sinners and for peoples." And in his twelfth point, the Bishop wrote: "The supplicant omnipotence of the Mother of God, as Mediatrix and Dispensatrix of All Graces."

After Fatima, more revelations continued to point to a final dogma, a dogma said and implied in these revelations to be crucial to ushering in the Era of Peace.

At Tuy, Spain in 1929, Mary's exalted status seemed to be given an even clearer endorsement in the words Jesus spoke to Sister Lucia of Fatima.

> **Because I want My entire Church to know that it is through the Immaculate Heart of My Mother that this favor is obtained...so that devotion to her Immaculate Heart may be placed alongside devotion to My own Sacred Heart.**

In a most noteworthy manner, this proclamation by the Lord again brought forth the significance of Mary's words and actions at Rue du Bac where the Two Hearts were engraved together on the back of the Miraculous Medal. Since Fatima, Jesus and Mary have been consistent in Their messages to Their chosen ones that Mary is our Coredemptrix, Mediatrix, and Advocate. At the apparitions of Beauraing, Belgium, in 1933, which received full Chruch approval in 1949, Mary revealed a "Heart of Gold." The old Feast of the Immaculate Heart of Mary, August 22, is also the official Beauraing Feast. While many of her roles were emphasized at Beauraing, Mary's role as Mediatrix was firmly revealed, and the need for the proclamation of this dogma was forwarded. Author Don Sharkey writes of this in the article "The Virgin with the Golden Heart" from the book *A Woman Clothed With the Sun:*

> ...God has entrusted tremendous power to Mary and
> that He refused her nothing. She is the Mediatrix of
> All Graces in the full sense of the term. All our
> prayers and requests go to God through Mary, and she
> distributes all the graces that come from God. Mary's
> Universal Mediation is not yet a dogma of the
> Church, but most theologians accept the idea. It is
> interesting to note that Belgium was the first country
> in the world to have an indult to celebrate a special
> feast in honor of Marys' Mediatrix.

Together with Beauraing, the apparition at Banneux,
Belgium, also in 1933, is seen to be directly responsible for Belgium
being the first country to obtain Holy See permission for the special
liturgical celebration of the Feast of Mary, Mediatrix of All Graces.
At Banneux, Mary came as the Virgin of the Poor. Today, over
500,000 pilgrims a year travel to Banneux, where the Virgin again
demonstrated that she was truly the Mediatrix of All Graces. In his
article, "The Virgin of the Poor" from the book *A Woman Clothed
With the Sun,* author Robert Mally writes that "Banneux is a new
occasion for thankfulness to Almighty God that He has granted us the
Queen of Heaven as the Motherly Mediatrix of His grace."

In the early 1940's, Jesus explicitly told a Poor Clare nun and
victim soul in Jerusalem, Sister Mary of the Trinity that the Virgin
Mary is the Mediatrix of All Graces: **"...You will not understand
until you get to Heaven what you owe to My Mother, and the gift
that was made you when I gave her to you to be your Mother.
How impenetrable is the love of God, Who created for you the
Virgin Mary, "Mediatrix of All Graces."**

Jesus also told Sister Mary of His Mother's Co-Redemption:

> **You do well to feel compassion for My
> Mother. You will never feel too much when you
> think of the Way of the Cross. She shared all My
> sufferings; she drank the bitter chalice to the
> dregs; with Me she worked your Redemption. You**

**must adore rather than seek to understand this
mystery of her cooperation: It is one of the
Father's mercies...** (M.T., no. 469).

Later in the 1940's, Mary and Jesus continued to show Their
desire for Mary to be recognized in her different roles. On June 25,
1946, at Marienfried, Germany, the Virgin declared this to Barbara
Ruess:

**I am the Great Mediatrix of Graces. The
Father wants the world to recognize this rank of
His maidservant. People must believe that I, as the
permanent bride of the Holy Spirit, am the faithful
Mediatrix of All Graces. My sign is emerging.
God wills it thus.**

In 1947 at Montichiari, Italy, (near Brecia, the hometown of
Pope Paul VI), the Virgin appeared to Peirina Gilli requesting
devotion as "Rosa Mystica" and again brought the message to her
children. On October 22, 1947, Mary told Pierina **"I have placed
myself as the Mediatrix between my Divine Son and mankind,
especially for the souls consecrated to God."**

On September 26, 1948, during the last days of the Virgin's
appearances at Lipa in the Philippines, the Virgin told the young
Carmelite Sister Teresita: **"I am Mary, Mediatrix of All Graces."**

But it wasn't until the mid-1950's in Amsterdam, Holland,
that Mary reportedly issued to a woman named Ida Perleman one of
the most prophetic and clear declarations concerning a final dogma
of Mary as Coredemptrix, Mediatrix, and Advocate.

Ida Perleman's messages from the Virgin Mary were many
and often her prophetic utterances were fulfilled. Among them, she
is said to have accurately foretold Vatican II and the exact date of the
death of Pope Pius XII. But it was the explicit and confident
declarations that the Virgin Mary gave her that a final dogma would
be declared, and that this dogma would be crucial for the obtaining
of God's victory in the world, that stood out.

On November 15, 1951, Our Lady reportedly appeared to Ida
standing on the earth with a cross at her back. There were rays
streaming from her hands and a multitude of sheep gathered around

343

the globe. She then said to Ida,

> **The Lady of All Nations is here, standing before the cross of her Son; her feet are placed in the very midst of the world, and the flock of Jesus Christ surrounds her. It is as Coredemptrix and Mediatrix of that I come at these times. I was Coredemptrix from the moment of the Annunciation. This is the meaning: the mother has been constituted Coredemptrix by the will of the Father. Tell this to our theologians. Tell them likewise that this dogma will be the last in Marian history.**

Since then, many more private revelations in support of the title Coredemptrix, Mediatrix, and Advocate have been reported. Such well known stigmatists as Myrna Nazour, Maria Esperanza, Gladys Queroga, Amparo Cueos, Dina Basher, Sister Elena Aiello, and Mother Elena Lombardi have received messages and or visions. Most noteworthy are the interior locutions received by Father Stefano Gobbi, who has repeatedly stated in his messages that Our Lady is Coredemptrix and Mediatrix of all graces. The message of June 14, 1980 is especially seen to indicate the need for the proclamations of the final dogma:

> **Until I am acknowledged there where the Most Holy Trinity has willed me to be, I will not be able to exercise my power fully, in the maternal work of coredemption and of the universal mediation of graces... Sons, let yourselves be transformed by my powerful action as Mother, Mediatrix of Graces, and Coredemptrix** (June 14, 1980).

But the question remains, will this dogma soon be proclaimed?

CHAPTER FORTY-NINE

THE KINGDOM OF THE FATHER

When they had gathered together, they asked him, "Lord,
are you at this time going to restore the kingdom to Israel?"
He answered them, "it is not for you to know the times or seasons
that the Father has established by his own authority."

— Acts 1: 6-7

This book seeks to confront the importance of the remaining prophecies of Fatima. But it does not seek to do so at the expense of Fatima's true and extraordinary message. Fatima was and remains a great message of light and hope for the world. It is a message of peace, prayer, and intercession. At Fatima, the Holy Spirit poured out His graces abundantly and any anxiousness arisen from Fatima's message is due to those who have not taken to heart Fatima's call to conversion. We especially find this with those who still express concern that the unreleased Third Secret of Fatima was apocalyptical and with some of those who say Russia has not been consecrated in the prescribed manner. There is also concern for the many sensational writings associated with Fatima from other private revelations. Like the pseudo versions of the Third Secret, these writings are often filled with mystifications, caricatures, exaggerations, and sensationalism, contributing to an eschatology of calamity. The true and profound message of Fatima points to one thing: God's Love for His people and His desire that their happiness in this world and salvation in the next be obtained.

All of this constitutes the true message of Fatima as it does for all authentic apparitions and revelations. However, the message of Fatima does contain "certain highly dramatic aspects," notes Fr. Joacquin Maria Alonso, C.M.F., the internationally known theologian and expert on Fatima who was appointed by the Bishop of Leiria to prepare the definitive study of Fatima and its message. And it is these aspects that demand attention. "These dramatic aspects were in no way meant to fill us with fear," Fr. Alonso asserted in his writings, but he too noted that they were "deeply serious."

Indeed, the seriousness of Fatima in word and vision is inescapable to anyone who seriously studies its message. And if Fatima's message was serious decades ago, one certainly can see it must be even more serious today. In 1982, Pope John Paul II stated that the message of Fatima was "more urgent now than ever" and that the Church has a "duty" to be mindful of it. "The appeal of the Lady of the message of Fatima is so deeply rooted in the Gospel and the whole of Tradition that the Church feels that the message imposes a commitment upon her (May 13, 1982)."

Sr. Lucia concurs but has also said it may be too late for the world to respond. "The Blessed Virgin is very sad because no one heeds her message, neither the good nor the bad. The good continue in their life of virtue, but without paying attention to the message of Fatima. Sinners keep following the road of evil, because they fail to see the terrible chastisement that is about to befall them. Believe me, Father, God is going to punish the world and very soon. " [Interview with Sister Lucia by Father Fuentes, December 26, 1957; published in *The Secret of Fatima* by Father Joacquin Alonso, Ravengate Press, Cambridge, 1990]. More recent interviews with Sister Lucia disclose her satisfaction that the consecration of 1984 saved the world from nuclear war. But she said that "the devil is rising... and working against God and His creation" (*Christus* magazine, Portugal, March 1998).

Sister Lucia's comments are significant because they address the importance of understanding the remaining prophecies of Fatima. It would be nice to simply extol the pius aspects of Fatima's message and refrain from the serious elements, but the lone surviving visionary of Fatima confronted the reality of the present situation decades ago: "No one heeds her (The Virgin Mary's) message good or bad. ... God is going to punish the world." Not surprisingly, this same assessment is noted by contemporary visionaries. They say the Virgin's efforts are going, for the most part, unheeded. Through her interior locutions to Father Stefano Gobbi, Mary summarized the state of the world and, therefore, its miserable response to her intervention:

> **I am a concerned Mother, because any extraordinary interventions, which I have carried out in order to lead you to conversion and salvation, have been neither accepted nor followed.**
>
> **How can you now save yourselves from the great chastisement which is upon you, if you have refused what the heavenly Mother has offered you for your salvation.** (December 31, 1994)

> **Thus, humanity has arrived at building a civilization without God, has given itself a morality contrary to His Law, has justified every form of evil and sin and has allowed itself to be seduced by materialism, hatred, violence and impurity.** (May 18, 1997)

This reality, that our world is submergered in sin and not responding to Fatima's message, together with the understanding that two of Fatima's prophecies remain unfulfilled, both of which foretell a radical change for the world, brings us to where we are today: at the doorstep of the fulfillment of Fatima's message, and therefore at the doorstep of the Triumph of the Immaculate Heart in the world. This conclusion is more than supposition. Mary has repeatedly stated in contemporary apparitions that her Triumph is imminent and even Pope John Paul II alluded to this in his book *Crossing the Threshold of Hope*: "...Mary appeared to the three children at Fatima in Portugal and spoke to them words that now, at the end of this century, seem close to their fulfillment."

Thus, in a way, we are back at Fatima on October 13, 1917, back to the moments when the great miracle unfolded that day. For it is in those moments that some Fatima experts believe we were symbolically shown what may lie ahead, what our future held, and how God was clearly inviting mankind to return to Him. John Haffert in his book *Now, The Woman Shall Conquer* (1997), perhaps summarized this understanding best:

In most of the books I have written I have stressed the importance of the miracle of Fatima. One cannot know the details well enough or review them too often. Even after I had talked to dozens of witnesses it was many years before I grasped the awesomeness of what happened and came to believe, with the celebrated Jesuit theologian and scientist, Fr. Pio Sciatizzi, S.J., that this was *"the greatest most colossal miracle in history."*

It had been raining heavily before the moment of the miracle. The great hollow of Fatima was a sea of water and mud. But immediately after the miracle (which lasted about 12 minutes) the sea of water and mud had vanished. It was like the miracle of the Red Sea.

The sun itself crashed down upon the earth. It was seen in a radius of 32 miles! It was like the miracle of the sun in the time of Joshua, when the fire of the sun appeared to act *independently* of the sun itself.

It was also like the miracle of Elias, who called fire from the sky so that all would believe that "God is God!...and the fire consumed, not only the sacrifice offered by the prophet, but the water in the trench around it.

Therefore this miracle of Fatima had the elements of the three greatest miracles of the Old Testament. What is more, NEVER BEFORE in history had God, *"so that all may believe,"* performed a miracle at a PREDICTED TIME AND PLACE!

Perhaps the main reason why we feel compelled to look to Fatima as a mystical throne of the Queen of the World is because of the Miracle of the Sun. This unprecedented miracle recalls the description of Our Lady in the Apocalypse. Moreover, the essential power of the sun is atomic power, and the very "annihilation of nations" which Our Lady foretold in Her Fatima apparitions now threatens the world through nuclear weapons. Yet in demonstrating such power, in making such awesome prophecies at Fatima, our Queen could promise "an era of peace to mankind."

Indeed, the clear symbolism in the great miracle of the coming era of nuclear weapons and what this danger would mean to a world that further separated itself from God is well understood. It is the negative consequence of not returning to God, of not responding to Fatima's call. Quite simply, the world was being shown how the heavens could rain fire and destruction, a just punishment imposed upon ourselves. This understanding is reinforced in Lucia's memoirs when she states that of all Mary's words to her during the Fatima apparitions, the words said to her immediately before the great miracle of the sun were most memorable. These words can be understood to be of a "warning" nature and directly connected to the miracle that was about to occur just seconds later:

Now Your Excellency, here we are at the 13th of October (1917).
You already know all that happened on that day. Of all the words spoken at this Apparition, the ones most deeply engraved upon my heart were those of the request made by our heavenly Mother:
"Do not offend Our Lord and God any more, because He is already so much offended!"
How loving a complaint, how tender a request. Who will grant me to make it echo through the whole world, so that all the children of our Mother in heaven may hear the sound of her voice! Then, opening her hands, she made them reflect on the sun.

Lucia writes that the miracle of the sun then began to occur before the stunned onlookers. Researchers say it lasted about ten minutes. During the last phase many believed the sun would strike the earth and the end of the world would occur.

But if God presented in the miracle of the sun the negative consequences of mankind failing to respond to His call, could He perhaps have also symbolically revealed in this same miracle the positive consequences of mankind returning to Him, the deeper meaning of the peace He wished to give to the world.

Indeed, the fact that the sun halted its plunge and returned to its proper position in the sky has been understood to signal that in the end, even if mankind fails to choose to return to Him, God will not permit the evils of the world to bring it to "total" destruction. God will not permit Satan to triumph as Mary so clearly conveyed at Fatima. Therefore, if the terrible symbolism behind the falling sun at Fatima is not to be fulfilled in a negative consequence, then what else may have God been trying to tell us when He chose this miracle to fulfill the Virgin's promise of a "sign"? What other consequence could the falling sun perhaps represent in the great vision witnessed by tens of thousands on that day?

We can search through mountains of revelations since Fatima for greater insight but would probably be faced with attempting to construct a lengthy and hypothetical answer. It is no secret that Our Lady has alluded to intrinsic meanings of what the Triumph of the Immaculate Heart will bring. From crushing Satan's efforts to topple the Church to her direct role in saving mankind from nuclear annihilation, from unifying Christian denominations to bringing the world into a new era, Mary has indicated that the Triumph will mean many good things for the world, especially the Church. But one extraordinary and profound meaning stands out and needs to be pondered. It is one of a definitive nature and is most logical in lieu of Mary's efforts over the last two centuries. It is also an understanding that can be found symbolically in the falling sun, for it is one that is most fitting and appropriate to the reason behind the great miracle at Fatima. And that understanding is this: the miracle of the sun was actually a sign of the coming reunification of God the Father with His creation and with His children. It was a sign of a coming reunification with Him in spirit, in peace and in love, something that our Creator has desired for ages and is spoken of in Scripture. It was a sign of the coming of the restoration of God's Kingdom on earth as the Lord told the Apostles.

Indeed, the restoration of God the Father's Kingdom on earth "as it is in heaven" was at the center of Christ's message. Over and over Christ called our attention to the Father. Scripture prophetically speaks of the Father's Will to come on earth as it is in heaven (Mt

6:10), of the restoration of the Kingdom on earth at a time to be designated by the Father (Acts 1:6), and that the Father's Name, glorified by Christ during His Passion, is to be glorified again (Jn 12:28). A powerful reconnection in spirit with Our Father in heaven is, therefore, an undeniable part of the mission of the Church, although for the past 2,000 years this reunion has not been emphasized. In the past decade, Pope John Paul II has spoken of the "definitive coming of the Kingdom" and several prominent theologians, such as Rev. Bertrand de Margerie, Fr. Renee Laurentin, Fr. Michael O'Carroll, C.S.S.P. and Fr. Jean Galot, S.D., have studied this matter. If we look closely at their writings, we find more and more evidence that perhaps this time, this era of peace, is near.

Fr. Jean Galot S.D. an eminent Biblical scholar and theologian, who teaches at the Pontifical Gregorian University in Rome and is the author of countless books and articles, addressed the issue in his book *Abba Father: We Long to See Your Face* (Alba House, New York, 1992). Fr. Galot went as far as to say that "the answer to *all* our problems is to be found in God the Father:

> Learning to know God our Father is the supreme achievement of theology and, in a more all-embracing way, of all human knowledge. Our intellects are made to know the truth, whose primordial origin is the Father. We can be fully satisfied in our intellectual search for God only when we draw from this primary source which is also the ultimate goal of all human knowledge.
>
> We must admit that until now scholarly effort to understand God our Father has not been as intense as it should have been. The most sublime object of all research and knowledge has not sufficiently challenged the minds of theologians. Our Christian faith has not adequately emphasized the person of God the Father, and liturgical worship has not focussed enough on this divine Person.
>
> Likewise, the kingdom whose coming is desired is the kingdom of the Father. It is, therefore, the reign of a fatherly love that gathers men into one sonship from which the closest brotherhood results.

When Jesus said to "seek his kingdom," he was speaking to his disciples of the kingdom of "your Father" (cf. Lk 12:30-31). The fatherhood of God gives a new meaning to the kingdom.

It this perspective, the words 'on earth as in heaven,' which apply to all three petitions, are given their full significance. The earth must become the image of heaven where there is perfect veneration of the name of the Father, the absolute reign of his paternal love and the complete fulfillment of his Fatherly will. Christians ask that the earthly world be increasingly modeled upon the heavenly realm. The mark of the "new-earth" is that it reflects heaven.

It might surprise us that the building up of the new world is the object of petitions to the Father when it is the Father himself who has the supreme responsibility for his kingdom. Yet here we see a characteristic trait of paternal love. The Father wants his children to collaborate with him in every phase of his work. This collaboration takes the form of prayer first of all, prayer destined to have an impact on the development of the kingdom. The petitions are the means through which Christians can be assured of having a co-responsibility in the work of salvation, a co-responsibility exercised in a spirit of final dependence but guaranteed to have authentic efficacy. In this sense, the "Our Father" contributes to the enhancement of the human personality of its role in the universe.

CHAPTER FIFTY

GOD, FATHER AND CREATOR

*"In just the same way, it is not the will of your heavenly Father
that one of these little ones be lost."*

— Mt 18:14

Mary's words form the core of Fatima's powerful message. But the great miracle of the sun remains the heart of the message, for it was intended to speak to us in a unique and extraordinary way. The sun — can the miracle of the sun be understood in a different way? A way in which the symbolism of the falling sun upon the world changes from a prophetic threat to a wonderful gift to mankind — the reunification of the Father of all mankind with His children? Some believe so.

But before we directly examine this question, let us first briefly examine the history of the symbolism of the sun in religion and in Judeo-Christian writings to see how the sun has often been used as a way to better understand God and our relationship with Him.

There have been numerous sun worshiping religions, especially in ancient times. The Babylonians and the Egyptians are perhaps the best examples. These religions, however, were idolators for the most part. It must be noted that both Hebrews and early Christians were very careful not to confuse God *as* the sun but the sun as a symbol of God. They were quite aware of sun worshipping religions and pagans who thought the sun "was" God. Their writings, therefore, sought to carefully show the sun as only a representation of God and that they did not worship the sun.

However, the story of one sun-worshiping people deserves noting. Between 1372-1354 BC an Egyptian pharaoh named Amenhotep IV, who changed his name to Akhetaton, shook Egyptian civilization to its foundations. Soon after assuming the throne, he swept away ancient Egypt's time-honored gods in favor of one supreme being — Aton, or the disc of the sun. The new religion was made the law of the land. Its tenets of love, peace, forgiveness, and mercy still divide historians over whether or not Akhetaton was an unstable fanatic or a great mystic ahead of his time. Some scholars exalt him as the pioneer of monotheism, history's first great advocate of nonviolence and peace.

Akhetaton refused to defend Egypt against the advancing Hittites because he deplored bloodshed. Curiously, the symbol that converts of the new religion wore was a cross with a loop at the top that symbolized the sun. Akhetaton's wife was known as "Lady of Grace" and all surviving Egyptian images and art depict her at her husband's side, portrayed in domesticate intimacy — playing with their daughters, eating together, riding side by side in the chariot. According to one version of his life, Akhetaton experienced an epiphany moments before he died of poisoning, in which he stated that he realized that the sun (Aton) was really not God, but a "symbol of the one true God who forgave all." Approximately fifty years after Akhetaton, Moses was born.

But the reason this religion and all similar religions were centered around the sun is that their founders came to understand that the sun is inseparably connected to all life. It is the direct source which permits the earth and all forms of life to exist. Its heat and light sustain the planet. Without the sun's existence there would be no life, no creation as we know it.

Of course, we find these same truths in our understanding of God, and especially in what as Christians we know about the First Person of the Holy Trinity, God the Father. The Father, Christ says in Scripture, is the Creator, the source of all life, all energy, all existence. Like the sun, the Father's omnipotence and incomprehensible essence affects and effects all creation. All living beings and creation itself owes it's existence to His eternal presence and sustenance.

Theologians say that although the Eternal Father's personhood is not directly identified until Christ began His ministry, the Triune God, the God of the Old Testament, the God of Abraham, Isaac and Jacob, the God of Moses, is identifiable as a God who is a Father. Pope John Paul II explores this Fatherhood of God in Holy Scripture:

> The mystery of the divine paternity within the Trinity was not yet explicitly revealed in the Old Testament. However, the whole context of the Old Covenant was rich with allusions *to God's Fatherhood* in a moral and analogical sense. *Thus God is revealed as Father of his people*, Israel, when he commands Moses to ask for their liberation from Egypt: 'The Lord says Israel is my first-born son, and I say to you "Let my son go..." Ex 4:22-23).
>
> This is a fatherhood of choice, on the basis of the covenant and is rooted in the mystery of creation. Isaiah wrote: "Yet Lord, you are our Father; we are clay, and you are our potter; we are all the work of your hand" (Is 64:8, 63:16).
>
> This fatherhood does not regard only the chosen people, it reaches every person and surpasses the bond existing with earthly parents. Here are some texts: 'For my father and mother have forsaken me, but the Lord will take me up' (Ps 27:10). 'As a father pities his children, so the Lord pities those who fear him' (Ps 103:13). 'The Lord reproves him whom he loves, as a father the son in whom he delights' (Prov 3:12). The analogical character of the fatherhood of God is evident in the texts just quoted. It is the Lord to whom the prayer is directed. 'O Lord, Father and Ruler of my life, do not abandon me to their counsel, and let me not fall because of them...O Lord, Father and God of my life, do not leave me at the mercy of brazen looks' (Sir 23: 1-4). He again says in the same light: 'If the righteous man is God's son, he will help him, and will deliver him from the hand of his adversaries' (Wis 2:18).
>
> God's Fatherhood is manifested in merciful love, both in regard to Israel and to individuals. We

read for example, in Jeremiah:'With weeping they had departed, and with consolations I will lead them back...for I am a Father to Israel, and Ephraim is my first-born' (Jer 31:9).

Numerous passages in the Old Testament present the merciful love of the God of the covenant:

> 'But you are merciful to all, for you can do all things, and you overlook men's sin, that they may repent.....
> You spare all things, for they are yours,
> O Lord who loves the living:' (Wis 11:23-26).

> 'I have loved you with an everlasting love; therefore I have continued my faithfulness to you' (Jer 31:3).

In Isaiah we meet moving testimonies of care and affection:
> 'But Zion said, "The Lord has forsaken me,
> my Lord has forgotten me."
> Can a woman forget her child...?
> Even if she forget, yet I will not forget you'
> (Is 49:14-15; cf. Also 54:10).

It is significant that in the passages of the prophet Isaiah, God's fatherhood is enriched with allusions inspired by motherhood (cf. *Dives in Misericordia*, note 52).

Jesus frequently announced, in the fullness of the Messianic times, God's fatherhood in regard to humanity by linking it with the numerous expressions contained in the Old Testament. Thus it expresses divine providence in regard to creatures, especially man: "Your heavenly Father feeds them..." (Mt 6:26;

cf. Lk 12:24); "Your heavenly Father knows that you need them all" (Mt 6:32; cf. Lk 12:30). Jesus sought to make the divine mercy understood by presenting as proper to God the welcoming reception of the Father for the prodigal son (cf. Lk 15:11-32). He exhorted those who heard his word "be merciful, even as your Father is merciful" (Lk 6:36).

To conclude, we can say that, through Jesus, God is not only "the Father of Israel, the Father of mankind," but "Our Father."

The omnipotence of Our God, of his "fatherly" presence, is represented in the Old and New Testament in many symbolic ways, but often especially in an analogical relationship with the sun. Psalm 84:11 declares that "the Lord God is a Sun," while Isaiah 19:18 speaks of the "city of the sun", or rather the city of God. God is referred to as the "rising sun" in Isaiah 9. In Luke 1:78, we read that the loving kindness of God is "seen like the sun on high, shining on those who sit in darkness and the shadow of death." The Woman "clothed with the sun" in Rev12:1 has often been cited as Our Lady clothed in God. In Rev 21:23, we find that the sun of the New Jerusalem is now God Himself and the sun, as we know it, is no longer needed. It is especially noted how Christ in Mt 5:45 invokes the sun as His example of the Father's omnipresence over all things, especially His children — both good and bad: "That you may be the children of your Father Who is in heaven, who maketh His sun to rise upon the good and bad, and rainth upon the just and the unjust."

Scripture also refers to the sun in many different passages that, perhaps as occurred at Fatima, are intended to remind us either of the power or presence of God in the events that occur. In 4 King's 20:9-11, God provides a sign of proof to Isaiah that He would prolong Hezechia's life by the retrogression of the sun's shadow, "Lo the sun came back the ten steps it had advanced." While in Joshua 10:11-4, we find perhaps a foreshadowing of the miracle at Fatima, as God prolonged the sun's position in the sky, a "miracle of the sun," in order to enable the Israelites to complete their victory of the land of Canaan. We now know today that in the New Testament, the bright star over Bethlehem was likely a great but distant sun, for all stars are really suns. Likewise, it is

357

especially noted that at the moment Christ died, Scripture says the "sun was darkened" (Lk 23:45). When Mary Magdala and the other women arrived at the tomb to discover that Christ was resurrected "the sun had risen" (Mk 16:2). Were these details symbolic references to God, God the Father, who in this manner was revealing His nearness to all that unfolded during the Nativity, the Crucifiction, and the Ressurection of His only begotten Son?

Our faith presents many other interesting connections to the symbolism of the sun, especially the fact that the new Sabbath for Christians was to be on "Sunday." The term Sunday is often associated with the Bible, but it was probably borrowed from the Chaldeans. The Egyptians and Babylonians then divided the year into weeks of 7 days. The Egyptians named each of the days after one of five planetary bodies (known to them) and after the sun and moon. This was adopted by the Romans:

Sunday = Sun
Monday = Moon
Tuesday = Mars
Wednesday = Mercury
Thursday = Jupiter
Friday = Venus
Saturday = Saturn

The Romans referred to Sunday as the day "called after the Sun." This was later reapplied by early Christians to Jesus Christ, Who is the "Sun of Righteousness" (Mal 4:2 and RV 1:10). From the very beginning of the Church, Christians came together on Sunday to anticipate the second coming of the Lord, to encounter the risen Christ in the Eucharist, and to gratefully recall to mind the death and resurrection of Jesus. Sunday did not arise out of the Jewish Sabbath, because many of the early Christians kept both. The Jew's last day of the week was sacred for the last day of creation. The Christian's first day of the week, Sunday, was sacred because the new day of the new creation (new era) began in the Resurrection of the Lord. Thus, it was the decision of the Fathers of the Church to virilize the symbolism of the Greco-Roman name for this day: DIES SOLIS, Day of the Sun.

This was no accident, for the Fathers of the Church wanted to directly connect the meaning of the day with the faith. St. Justin wrote that "We come together on the day of the sun on which God, changing darkness and matter created the world, and on which Jesus Christ our Savior arose from the dead." Eusebius of Caesarea wrote, "It was on this day that at the time of Creation when God said, "Let there be light, there was light, and on this day also the Sun of Justice (Mal 4:2) arose in our souls." Said St. Jerome, "If it is called the day of the sun by the pagans, we willingly accept the name, for on this day arose the light of the world, on this day shone forth the Sun of Justice in whose rays is health."

As early as the first half of the second century, Christian writers began calling Sunday the "8th Day," the day the Old Testament repeatedly reveals to be the feast day, or day of offering to God. Pseudo-Barnabus uses the expression to indicate the substitution of the New Testament for the Old. He portrays God as resting on the Jewish Sabbath from His Work of Creation, and then accomplishing the New Creation, the Church, on the Eighth Day: "The Sabbaths are not acceptable to Me, only the Sabbath which I have made, in which, after giving rest to all things, I will make the beginning of the eighth day, that is the beginning of another world." Therefore, says Pseudo-Barbabus, "we...celebrate...the 8th day on which Jesus arose from the dead, was made manifest, and ascended into heaven.

The Eschatological symbolism implicit in Pseudo-Barnabus is brought out by Origen: "The number 8, which contains the virtue of the Resurrection, is the figure of the future world." This is concurred by St. Ambrose: He wrote "8=Redemption, the number 8 is the fulfillment of our hope." This fulfillment for Catholics was and continues to be honored in the celebration of the sacrifice of the Mass, a bloodless sacrifice to God Our Father that is required to be attended by all the faithful on Sunday.

All of this is consistent with both the Old and New Testament covenants. The Mosaic circumcision was on the 8th day and Christ arose from the dead on the 8th day (Palm Sunday through Easter Sunday). Patristic writers teach that Sunday represents a definitive stage of creation, which began with the Resurrection, a day taken out of time to emphasize the fact that the events of the Redemption had already initiated for Christians the timeless life of heaven. This is found in Rev 1:10 where "The Lord's Day" [Day of the Lord] "Dies

Dominica" replaced "Dies Solis" [Sun Day] as the legal name of the day.

Sunday was to be joyous in character and penance on Sunday was considered a sin. Emperor Constantine (d. 321 A.D.) converted to Christianity and decreed Sunday to be a day of rest and worship. (The Council of Elvira [A.D. 306] had first encouraged this observation.) Constantine then instituted the first civil legislation regarding Sunday as all work closed on Sunday (except farmers) and it was to be a time for worship. Most significantly, we find Christmas also evolved from this. December 25th had been the Roman feast of "Sol Inictus"(unconquered Sun) until Constantine declared it to be the day of the birth of a new age, the birthday of the "Sun of Righteousness," Jesus Christ (Mal 4:2). Thus, the day of the pagan feast was then celebrated by the Christians and became Christmas. We are reminded, too, that Easter is always celebrated on the Sunday after Passover.

Over the centuries , the role of the sun in many miracles in the lives of the saints, and in great events of the Church are well noted. From Constantine's vision of the cross in the sun to Our Lady of Guadelupe appearing to Juan Diego engulfed in the sun, to the miracles reported at many apparition sites today, God continues to signal the presence of the divine through solar miracles.

At Fatima, Sr. Lucia's states in her memoirs that she was not aware that the promised miracle would come in this manner, by way of the sun. However, Lucia was, she said, interiorly compelled to call attention to the sun:

> Then, opening her hands, she (Mary) made them reflect on the sun, and as she ascended, the reflection of her own light continued to be projected on the sun itself.
>
> Here, Your Excellency, is the reason why I cried out to the people to look at the sun. My aim was not to call their attention to the sun, because I was not even aware of their presence. I was moved to do so under the guidance of an interior impulse.

While the miracle of the sun at Fatima is well known, Our Lady has often spoken of the sun in her apparitions. Like Scripture, these references to God as being "like the sun" in her messages are symbolic of His many attributes. (Highly noted are the writings of Luisa Piccarreta.) An indepth look at all of these messages would not be possible, but at Medjugorje, where Mary said she came to **"fulfill Fatima,"** the Virgin spoke of the sun on April 25, 1998:

> **Dear children! Today I call you, through prayer, to open yourselves to God as a flower opens itself to the rays of the morning sun. Little children, do not be afraid. I am with you and I intercede before God for each of you so that your heart receives the gift of conversion. Only in this way, little children, will you comprehend the importance of grace in these times and God will become nearer to you. (April 25, 1998)**

On the surface this message may not seem to imply anything more than what it says, but a look at a second message given by Our Lady at Medjugorje on January 31, 1985, reveals that Mary appeared to previously define her reference to the sun as being like God the Father, and once again referred to flowers in an analogy to souls:

> **Dear Children! Today I wish to tell you to open your hearts to God like flowers in spring yearning for the sun. I am your mother and I always want you to be closer to the Father, that He will always give abundant gifts to your heart** (January 31, 1985).

These messages, along with Scripture's references to God being like the sun, allow us to understand that if God the Father was represented in the miracle of the sun at Fatima, and if this sign was meant to designate a time in the future when the sun would come close to the earth again, not in a fiery, dangerous way, but in a loving intimate encounter with God the Creator, then Mary's words at Medjugorje on April 25, 1998, indicate this time is near — the time of triumph, the time of the return of God the Father to His creation in a special way as was perhaps symbolized in the great miracle of the sun at Fatima.

In 1932, an extraordinary but almost totally unknown event occurred in Italy that seems to be related to all of this, especially the urgency of Fatima's message. A nun named Mother Eugenia Ravasio reported that the Eternal Father appeared to her in apparitions on July 1, 1932, and again on August 12, 1932.

Mother Eugenia Elisabetta Ravasio was born on September 4, 1907, in San Gervasio d'Adda (now Capriato San Gervasio), a small village in the province of Bergamo, Italy. She came from a peasant background and received only an elementary education. After working several years in a factory, Eugenia entered the Congregation of Our Lady of the Apostles. She was twenty years old. By the age of twenty-five, the young nun was elected Mother General of the Congregation. Mother Eugenia then served in this position from 1935 until 1947. While her spiritual work received the greatest focus, her worldly contributions were also significant. In twelve years of missionary work Mother Eugenia opened seventy relief centers in some of the most distant and removed locations in Asia, Africa and Europe. She is credited with being the first to discover a cure for leprosy, extracting it from the seed of a tropical plant. This process was later advanced at the Pasteur Institute in Paris. She further planned and developed a project for a "Lepers City" at Azopte (Ivory Coast). This center serviced an area of over 200,000 square miles and is still today a leading center for the care of leprosy sufferers. In recognition of this achievement, France conferred upon Mother Eugenia its highest national honor for social work.

But the divine revelations given to Mother Eugenia made her life truly extraordinary. On July 1, 1932, Mother Eugenia reported that she began to hear and see angels which she described as *"the entire Heavenly Court."* According to the book, *God Is Father*, there was beautiful singing, incomprehensible harmony, and then finally the appearance of the Eternal Father Himself. She said God the Father then sat next to her and revealed a profound message of His desires to her. The Eternal Father told her He was now coming among men in order to love them and to help make them know His love. It is also noteworthy that this message was given to Mother Eugenia in Latin, a language totally unknown by her.

The complete revelations to Mother Eugenia can be

characterized as no less than unfathomable. Throughout His message to her, the Eternal Father outlined His plan, a plan that entreats all men and all nations to turn to Him. Most significantly, The Father said He desired mankind to turn to Him not in trepidation, but in total abandonment and love. The Eternal Father also touched on various subjects ranging from the story of His love for men as revealed to Moses and Israel in the Old Testament, to acknowledging the spiritual differences among His present-day children.

The revelations were prophetic and evangelical. As the Eternal Father asserted from the beginning to the saintly nun, the Mystical Body of Jesus Christ, the Catholic Church, truly held within it the supernatural gift and graces which He wanted to give to all mankind. Most significantly, in telling her this, the Eternal Father conveyed to Mother Eugenia that the time of times has come. It was time, He told her, for the fulfillment of His Son's prayer, the *"Our Father."* And that this fulfillment, which would allow Him to be better known, loved and honored, would be best accomplished by a *special feast* in the Church dedicated in His name:

I desire to be known, loved, and honored with a special devotion, I do not ask for anything extraordinary. I desire only this: that one day, or at least a Sunday, be dedicated to honoring Me in a special way under the title of Father of all Mankind. For this feast, I would like a special Mass and Office. It is not difficult to find the texts in the Holy Scriptures. If you prefer to offer Me this special devotion on a Sunday, I choose the first Sunday of August. If you prefer a weekday, I would like it to be always the seventh of that same month.

In 1935, Bishop Alexander Caillot of Grenoble, France, convened a Commission of Inquiry to investigate the reported events. The commission took ten years to complete its work before recommending to the Bishop that he declare his opinion in favor of the apparitions. He did this in 1945. [Note: This decision has never been reversed, but because of events within Mother Eugenia's Order, according to Fr. Rene Laurentin's 1997 investigation, it is difficult to ascertain the complete history of this apparition and why decisions were made to not publicly encourage the spread of the revelations.] The inquiry also discovered, in examining the Father's requests for a feast day, that many of the faithful did not have a good understanding of God the Father. Subsequently, an extensive survey of the faithful revealed that the faithful, across all class lines and even among priests and religious, did not know God the Father. The survey revealed that "few pray to Him" and "nobody thinks of Him." The survey also discovered that many Christians keep distant from the Father, preferring to turn to Jesus because of His Humanity. It even found that many ask Jesus to protect them from the Father's rage. Thus, the commission and the Bishop concluded the request for a feast day by the Eternal Father to Mother Eugenia would effectively reestablish order in many Christian's piety as well as address Christ's words in His prayers concerning the coming of the Father's Kingdom.

Most significantly, the Father specifically told Mother Eugenia during the first apparition that mankind can understand Him better by contemplating the sun: **"My presence among you is like the sun on earth."** The Father said to the nun, **"If you are well disposed to meet Me, I will light you up and warm you with my endless Love."**

The following month, during the second apparition to Mother Eugenia, the Eternal Father again made it clear that indeed, He was like the "sun" in our life, the source of all life and good, and that we should raise our eyes to Him:

> **And you, My children, who have lost your faith and live in the dark, raise your eyes, you will see shining rays coming to illuminate you. I am the Shining Sun, I warm you. Look and you will recognize I am your Creator, your Father, your only and unique God. It is because I love you that I come to make you love Me, so you will all be saved.**

As at Fatima, where the sun moved closer to the earth, so close that many thought it would strike the world in a fiery finale of horror, the Eternal Father told Mother Eugenia that He now moves closer to all mankind, not for Himself, but for His children to know His saving love:

> **I am asking man for what he can give Me, his confidence, his love, and his gratitude. I don't desire to be known, honored and loved just because I need My creature and his adoration; the only reason lies in My Will to save him and make him take part in My Glory. That's why I'm stooping down to him.**

As noted, the primary goal of the revelations given to Mother Eugenia was the Eternal Father's request for a feast day. But this request, for reasons known only by the Father, needed to be fulfilled before the end of the 20th century — or else the grace would be lost:

> **This century is privileged above all others. Do not let this privilege pass, for fear that it might be withdrawn! Souls need a certain divine touch, and time presses; do not be afraid of anything, I am your Father, I will help you in your efforts and your work. ...**
>
> **Time presses. I wish men to know as soon as possible that I love them and that I feel the great happiness in being with them and talking with them, like a father with his children. ...**
>
> **I turn to you, My beloved son, My Vicar, before all others, to place this work in your hands. It should rank first among all your tasks and, because of the fear inspired in men by the devil, it will be accomplished only at this time.**

Was the miracle of the Sun at Fatima on October 13th, 1917, a foreshadowing, symbolic manifestation of this **"stooping down"** of the Father? Was it a symbolic message to the world that only He, the Father of all Mankind, can save us now, at this dangerous time in history. Has Mary been leading the faithful, the Church, and the world to a reunion with its Heavenly Father? Is the final element of

365

the Triumph of the Immaculate Heart, the crowning jewel of Mary's extended era of intercession, the presentation of God's children from the hands of their mother into the loving Arms of their Father?

Mary's message through interior locution to Father Gobbi at Fatima on May 7, 1997, does nothing to discourage this understanding of the fulfillment of the Triumph of the Immaculate Heart:

I have caused to spring up here, for twenty-five years now, my Marian Movement of Priests, so that the message of Fatima, often contested and rejected by many, might in your days come to its complete fulfillment.

Its fulfillment is necessary for you, my children, threatened and stricken, so that you may attain salvation. Its fulfillment is necessary for the Church, so wounded and crucified, so that from its painful and bloody trial, it might emerge all beautiful, without spot or wrinkle, in imitation of its heavenly Mother. Its fulfillment is necessary for all humanity, so that IT MAY RETURN TO THE ARMS OF ITS FATHER and come to know the new times of its full communion of love and of life with its Lord and God.

As of now, this plan of mine is being fulfilled with the Triumph of my Immaculate Heart in the world (May 8, 1997).

Maria Esperanza   *Alophonsine Mumureke*

Maria Esperanza of Venezuela has warned that a 'great event' is near. Alphonsine is one of the visionaries in Rwanda, where Mary warned in 1981 of a coming 'river of blood.' Over a million perished in Rwanda a decade later.

Jacov Colo and Ivan Dragecivic   *Maria Lunetti*

Two of the visionaries at Medjugorje. Jacov received his 10th secret in September, 1998.

The Virgin Mary has given monthly messages to the world for over 12 years through Maria at Medjugorje.

Estela Ruiz, Reyes Ruiz, Emily Petrisko with daughter Maria

*The apparitions to Estela Ruiz in S. Phoenix, Arizona,
ended in December, 1998, but some believe they may
spark a new evangelization of America.*

Georgette Faniel with Dr. Thomas Petrisko

*In Montreal, Georgette Faniel's revelations of God the Father and
how no Church bears His Name moved many people to respond by
building and dedicating chapels to the Eternal Father.*

Sr. Agnes Sasagawa   *Fr. Stefano Gobbi*

The apparitions to Sr. Agnes Sasagawa (Japan) and locutions to Fr. Stefano Gobbi (Italy) both began in 1973, the year of Roe vs. Wade. Both are strongly linked to Fatima and the threat of nuclear 'annihilation', the price, some visionaries say, the world may have to pay for its attack on life through contraception and abortion.

Patricia 'Pachi' Talbot   *Christina Gallagher*

Both Patricia Talbot of Ecuador and Christina Gallagher of Ireland have reported revelations of a coming chastisement. Both have also warned of war and 'fire from the sky.'

Josyp Terelya and Dr. Thomas Petrisko

The author spent 10 days in Ukraine with Josyp in 1994. Here they are in the chapel at Hrushiv, where reportedly 500,000 people saw Mary in the late 1980's.

Pope John Paul II with Sr. Lucia of Fatima

The Pope knows the contents of the Third Secret and publicly prays for 'the definitive coming of the Kingdom.'

John Haffert in Red Square, Moscow

In 1992, hundreds of pilgrims crowned Mary in a spontaneous ceremony outside of Lenin's tomb fulfilling centuries old prophecies.

Little Audrey Santo

The extraordinary child 'victim soul' of Worcester, MA., whose 1987 drowning accident occurred at the exact minute (11:03) and day (August 9th) the A-bomb was dropped on Nagasaki in 1945. Audrey's home reveals dozens of miracles as experts say they believe she suffers to intercede for the prevention of 'annihilation.'

The Eternal Father

Visionaries say the new era will be to some degree the fulfillment of the Lord's prayer, 'Thy Kingdom Come, thy will be done, on earth as it is in heaven.' Will the Church declare a Feast Day for God Our Father, something many believe to be of urgent significance to the fate of the world at this time?

372

CHAPTER FIFTY-ONE

FATIMA LEADS TO ME

"I give praise to you, Father, Lord of heaven and earth,
for although you have hidden these things from the wise
and the learned you have revealed them to the childlike.
Yes, Father, such has been your gracious will."

— Mt 11: 25-26

Perhaps preserved in secrecy by the Will of the Father in order to protect and guide this part of His plan to fruition at a critical, chosen time in salvation history, another extraordinary, prophetic voice has emerged whose revelations further illuminate a great part of the meaning of the Triumph of Mary's Immaculate Heart — the return of God's children to their Father and the beginning of the restoration of His Kingdom on earth.

Barbara Rose Centilli was 44 years of age when she began to record what she believed to be the Voice of the Eternal Father speaking to her in prayer. Prior to this, her life was quite ordinary. Except for a few special experiences she believed to be of God, her life as a mother, grandmother, teacher, and wife were typical of the average American woman of her generation.

Barbara grew up in a small town in Michigan and eventually settled after marriage in a midwestern state. After college she attended graduate school and worked as a teacher from the late 1970's through the early 1990's. During this period she raised four children and became involved with research and educational projects for students with special needs. Beginning in the mid-1990's Barbara began to record in the form of a dialogue her prayerful conversations with God the Father, to whom she had developed a special devotion over her lifetime. These journals were eventually destroyed on the recommendation of a spiritual advisor who told her God does not communicate to people in this manner.

However, in 1996, Barbara again began to record her conversations with the Father. By this time, she noticed the Father's responses to her in prayer were becoming very clear and distinct within her. She could recognize His voice "in her heart and mind" and began to experience visions that sometimes accompanied the Father's Words. Furthermore, as she reconciled and confronted what was happening to her, she became certain her experiences were not self-induced or imaginative but rather something she had no control over within herself.

It would not be possible to fully address the extraordinary contents of the revelations given to this soul. Like Mother Eugenia's revelations, they cover a range of topics and are rich in detail concerning Barbara's interior life with God. However, the essence of the revelations is unmistakable. God the Father was again requesting, as He did with Mother Eugenia, that through His Church all mankind be returned to Him. His Home, He says, is all creation and His children must begin to come home to Him at this time. They must abandon any fear of Him and must know that He is all Love and all Mercy. And again, the Father revealed Himself to Barbara as being in an analogical sense like the "sun" and how His children needed to understand the rich meaning of this symbolism as well as its urgency:

I have shown you this and have shared this with you in our dialogues for many months now. The time has come for you to explain this to My other children. Help them understand that this is the GREATEST HOUR OF MY MERCY. This is the Triumph long awaited for. But so many will be lost without the Light of this loving message.

I am the Father of all mankind. I love each and every one of My children. My heart desires that I live in My children and they in Me. I long to live among My children. The Great Sun amidst so

many stars—all glowing with the Love of God. Such glory. Such power. Such wonders await those children who choose to return home now.

Night falls and the storm approaches. My children need to convert, turn towards their Father, and come home. And when they arrive at the threshold of My loving Arms, they must say "Yes, Father, I will dance with You in the rhythm and harmony of Your Divine Will." In this way they will remain with Me always, — with and in Me. Not outside Me, separated from Me.

It is all quite simple. Before you took refuge in your Mother's Immaculate Heart. She was truly in My Divine Will and so in Me and I in her. Now it is time to recognize that in being safely in her heart, you are in Me, your Father. The process, a roadway leading to Me. Mary, your Mother, is in the Heart of My Son Who is in My Heart — One contained in the Other. How is this possible? Through My Holy Spirit (Sept. 30, 1997).

On November 30, 1997, the Eternal Father revealed to Barbara the meaning of a dream He had given her and why Our Lady communicated to her about this dream in another message:

Where you lay your head is on a bed of roses—each sweet and pure. This pillow of roses is made up of the souls that have sacrificed themselves for the good of all. They have given themselves for this holy purpose. Here you will find your rest, little one.

Roses, roses all, who give themselves to the Father. Each blossoming on the Spring of My Merciful Water. My Water of Love. Each rose watered by My life giving water. The water which proceeds through Me, through the Heart of My Son and the hands of Your Loving Mother— graces to bring you home. This is important. Little time remains before I will come and visit My

Children. I will come to make My abode with them. Prepare them. Make them ready.

A rose must be watered and opens to the Sun. Be beautiful as the rose, My children. Open up to your Father. Be all that you were intended to be. Without My Saving Water, without the warmth and radiance of My Sun, you will wither and perish, never to realize what you could have been—My heirs. Now do you understand, Barbara?

The rose on your pillow was for you—it was your own soul. Opened and blossoming in the Sun, which is the Father. Yes, daughter, even the rose that has bloomed will soon die, and so with all My children. But this is the way it must be. You and so many others will send the sweet scent of your offering and consecration to Me—especially on My Feast Day—to the very heavens. Draw Me with this scent. For soon I will come, as I have planned. Draw down My Mercy, Barbara. Teach all My Children to draw down My Mercy. And I will surely, come. Soon, very soon. Time is but a pane of glass that we look through. It is like a transparent sheet of glass. See Me through it" (Nov. 30, 1997).

The Eternal Father communicated to Barbara that the end of an era is about to dawn upon the world and that these are truly prophetic times. Most significantly, the long awaited Triumph of the Church is about to be fulfilled. This is the "Triumph" Mary promised at Fatima in 1917. And according to the Father's Words to Barbara Centilli, it will be completely fulfilled in accordance with His Will through two means: *individual consecration to God the Father* and by the Catholic Church proclaiming a *Feast Day in His Name*.

Like the revelations to Mother Eugenia, the Father revealed to Barbara that this request needed to be addressed at this time in salvation history, before the end of the 20th century:

Come to Me, My little ones. Come back to

Your Father Who loves you. Night approaches
and surely you will be lost. Approach now while
there is light. Come by the Light. Follow My Son
home. He gathers up My children. The sheep are
being gathered in—as we speak. Do you
understand little one?

The Consecration and Feast Day are the
beacon and the means by which My children may
approach Me and by which I will come to My
children. "THY KINGDOM COME, THY WILL
BE DONE ON EARTH AS IT IS IN HEAVEN."
Your Mother has prepared for this long and many
years. Now is the time. Rest in this knowledge.

FATIMA leads to this time. Fatima leads
to Me. The time of the reverly is over. The time
of rebellion is over. Make My presence known
through the Consecration and Feast Day. I am
coming. Prepare yourselves (November 13, 1997).

On January 12, 1998, the Eternal Father revealed to Barbara
more about the meaning of the Miracle of the Sun at Fatima and how
the miracle illustrated the consequences of choices. Choices mankind
must make at this time:

All around you is in the blaze of a recovery
from sin. The wind blows but the motion of My
Spirit goes undetected. See it in the workings and
phenomenon which surround you—and the world
at large. These are times steeped in treachery and
intrigue. Much is transpiring which My children
cannot and may not see. For it is cloaked behind
a veil of secrecy and sin. There will be a reprieve,
a brief time more before the knowledge of this can
no longer be denied. Pray, pray. Pray with your
whole heart—given to Me in reparation—and for
solace. Understand the gravity of what I say.
Much is transpiring—even now. This time is
decisive. My children must choose; they must
respond now. I weep for them—all the missed

opportunities. Fortify them, daughter, with My Consecration and Feast Day.

All is foretold in the Miracle of the Sun (at Fatima) — The pattern of the fabric I have woven is drawn tighter and the image clearer. Do you understand? All the colored threads of the tapestry which is the story of mankind's salvation history, their journey home to Me, is played out on the diorama that is before you. All the answers are there... Help My children see the grand tapestry which is before them. Watch the threads as they are woven more tightly together. The image comes into clearer focus. The analogy is greater than you thought. Meditate on this. Ponder it in your heart. It (the Miracle of the Sun at Fatima) was more simple than they [My children] thought. A graphic illustration... Why was this shown to My children at that particular time? Meditate on the effects. Harnessing the sun. Harnessing God. For I am energy and light. Consequences - response. Now is the time for choices. Wisely made, based on love. Know Me, My children, before it is too late! I come and I come soon. Know this and be ready. Forgive all those who have offended you. Time is short. And soon petty annoyances, slights, and irritations will no longer matter. I will come to My children in a new way, a powerful way. (Jan. 12, 1998).

Several months later, the Father revealed to Barbara how all of Mary's work has been leading to this moment in time, His return, and how all can be symbolically understood in the Miracle of the Sun on October 13th, 1917 at Fatima:

My daughter, you must realize by now the tightly woven bond which exists between this devotion to Me and the immediate steps leading up to the Triumph of your Mother's Immaculate Heart. Laid out in the scheme of mankind's

Salvation History is the end, the ultimate completion of this journey. Through your Mother's Fiat, her "Yes," My Son Jesus came into the world to redeem My children, all. Now, the time approaches when this final Triumph will be realized. ...

Only when I am recognized, loved, and honored by My children—all—will this triumph be completed. Do you understand?

The return of My children is your mother's triumph. All My children must return unhindered to their one True God and Father. Then My kingdom will have come on earth as it is in heaven.

This process will be gradual, but IT MUST BEGIN NOW....Each of My children has their role to play in My Plan for Mankind....Yours to present to the world—now in this time.

I come to My children as was shown in the MIRACLE OF THE SUN. [at Fatima] I come so close to warm you and fill you with My Light. Why does this frighten My children? Because they are not ready; they are not prepared. They are not able to see beyond their own preconceptions—their constructions of Truth. And the approach of your God without proper preparation as outlined by your Mother is folly indeed. Purification must take place. A cleansing of hearts, bodies, and minds. [I see an image of the Miracle of the Sun—the way the sun's rays seem to color and permeate everything they touch.]

See how I effused all that I touched. See how I chased away the gloom and discomfort. I am Light and Love. And I bring with Me a power that will transform. All will be transformed in the Lord. I WAS PRESENT AT THE MIRACLE OF FATIMA—in graphic depiction of what could have been and what will be yet.

St. Joseph, My good and tender son, represented the Fatherly Arms that hold and behold My Son Jesus—as I desire to hold all of you. **The Spirit, My Spirit, was represented in the rays of the sun penetrating all My Creation. The miracle was not as great as it could have been. I withdrew from My children as they shrank away in terror from the power and glory of their God. Even then many forget the impact of this experience. Yes, daughter, I am represented in the sun as you see clearly in Holy Scripture, My Word. The power of the sun gives life, but it has also been harnessed by man, in aping God, to take life away. LIFE OR CHASTISEMENT. HOW WILL THE POWER OF GOD BE USED?**

I wait patiently, oh, so patiently, to enter you and warm your souls in My Love. But as with all My gifts, even this has been abused and will be again in chastisement if My little ones do not find their way back home to their Father. At FATIMA you saw the options and reactions played out. Approach Me in love and trust and you have nothing to fear. I showed you this at Fatima. See and believe.

I wish mightily for this devotion to be spread swiftly and without hindrance — this Holy Octave of Consecration to God the Father (and Feast Day). Be at peace and know that your Father guides you in your efforts. All you need will be provided in My own way, in My own time. Delight in this gift I give the world. Understand this priceless gift I have placed in your hands. This is what your mother Mary has prepared you for so diligently. The precipice is closer than you think, mankind. Approach your Father who will save you as I have written in 1 Sm 3:21 (March 23, 1998).

[1 Sm 3:21-- "And the Lord appeared again at Shiloh for the Lord revealed himself to Samuel at Shiloh by the word of God." (Central shrine to God at Shiloh; sanctified by the presence of the Ark of the

Covenant. Associated with the Feast of Tabernacles--
8 Day Feast.)]

The Eternal Father's role in Fatima goes beyond discernment of the symbolism of the falling sun and contemporary revelations. Rather, it is the well documented opinion of theologians that the message of Fatima was completed on a Thursday night, December 10, 1929, while Sister Lucia was alone making a holy hour from eleven to midnight in the chapel of the Dorothean convent at Pontevedra, Spain, about 20 miles north of Tuy. On that night, Sr. Lucia received what is referred to as the "Last Vision" of Fatima. While Lucia would continue to receive visions and revelations from Jesus and Mary, this vision is considered the last "public" message of Fatima and from it we understand why the Eternal Father is so much a part of the significance of Fatima.

On that night, Lucia was given to understand the importance of the Communion of Reparation and the Consecration of Russia. But most of all, she was shown a spectacular vision that synthesized Fatima's message in a unique way. The vision revealed the Blessed Trinity, with Jesus hanging on the Cross over an altar, the Holy Spirit (represented as a dove) above His head, and with Mary standing below on the right. Mary's Immaculate Heart was visible as was a Rosary in her right hand. From Jesus' left side came the words "grace" and "mercy".

Most significantly, as so many artistic renditions of the "Last Vision" have portrayed, it is the extraordinary and powerful presence of God the Father, with arms outstretched parallel to His Son's above the cross, that dominates the "Last Vision" of Fatima. In a way that no words could have ever done, this vision, as described by Lucia, indeliby seals the reality of Our Father and His role in the message of Fatima on all who ponder it. And now, with all that has been revealed, we perhaps can better understand why. Likewise, perhaps we can also better understand why Pope John Paul II has repeatly stated that "we approach the millennium in the hope of the definitive coming of the Kingdom." This Kingdom, without a doubt, is none other than that of our heavenly Father's as recalled in the Lord's prayer.

CHAPTER FIFTY-TWO

CONSECRATION TO GOD OUR FATHER

"The hour is coming, and is now here, when true worshippers will worship the Father in spirit and truth; and indeed the Father seeks such people to worship him."

— Jn 4:23

Like Mother Eugenia, who was told by God the Father of His desire for a Feast Day in the Church, the Father revealed to Barbara Centilli this same desire along with His desire that His children be consecrated to Him in a special way.

Based entirely upon Scripture, the Eternal Father revealed to Barbara a consecration to Him known as *The Holy Octave of Consecration to God Our Father and Feast Day of the Father of All Mankind.* This consecration is based upon the traditions of God's people rendering Him honor and gratitude through 8-day feasts as recorded in both the Old and New Testaments. Like in the days of old, the Holy Octave of Consecration to God Our Father is an eight-day consecration to be celebrated as a whole, culminating with a special Feast Day in the Church to honor the Father of All Mankind.

It is especially noted that the Father emphasized to Barbara that there is to be no separation of the two— the Consecration and its Feast day. This is because, the Father revealed, **"the practical purpose of the Feast Day is for My children to consecrate themselves to Me"**.

> **The Feast does not exist for the purpose of providing Me with a Feast Day on the Church Calender. It is what the Feast accomplishes — the return of My children to their Father! This cannot be accomplished with limited temporary honor given Me at one Mass on one Sunday a year. No, this is much greater than one act... this is the final step towards the new era, a new relationship with their Father and God.**

While much can be noted about these revelations, one point must be emphasized. Through the Holy Octave of Consecration and its Feast Day, the Father revealed to Barbara that this involved the fulfillment of what was meant from the beginning. This, He revealed to her, involved to a degree the meaning of the profound words in the Lord's prayer: **"Thy will be done...Thy kingdom come on earth as it is in Heaven."**

The extraordinary revelations given to both Mother Eugenia Ravasio and Barbara Centilli cause us to examine their historical context in relation to the prophecies of Fatima and why there perhaps is an urgency surrounding them. Mary foretold at Fatima that a second world war would erupt under the reign of Pius XI. During the reign of Pius XI, the Eternal Father specifically requested, through Mother Eugenia, that the Feast Day be instituted:

> **I communicated to My Vicar (Pius XI)... a very special predilection for the missionary apostolate in different countries and most of all a great zeal to spread throughout the world devotion to the Sacred Heart of My Son, Jesus. Now I am entrusting Him with the work that this same Jesus came to accomplish, to glorify Me, by making Me known just as I am, telling all men, My creatures and children. THIS CENTURY IS PRIVILEGED ABOVE ALL OTHERS.**

Likewise, on December 13, 1997, The Eternal Father told Barbara Centilli that these were critical times:

THESE ARE MY TIMES, DAUGHTER.
The time in which My children will be offered the
opportunity through the graces given by your
Blessed Mother Mary to return to Me, their God
and Father. This is a time of crucial importance.
THE OPPORTUNITY IS SHORT AND WILL
NOT BE EXTENDED PAST THAT WHICH I
HAVE ORDAINED THROUGH MY DIVINE
WILL. MY PLAN REQUIRES THAT MY
CHILDREN RESPOND TO ME IN THIS TIME.
The ice is melting around the cold heart of this
world. Recognize Me in all My Creation,
especially in each other. For I am here close by,
never abandoning My children. Present this to
those who will listen. The time is short, and I
approach with an expectant and hopeful Heart.
My Arms are open to embrace My children, all.
See clearly in all matters related to this work.
Pray for My Holy Spirit to guide you. Approach
Me through the Sacraments of My Holy Church
and through the special devotion I have given you.

In lieu of all of this, one can't help but examine some of the more critical dates in history that surround this century, especially the 1930's and 1940's. These events have caused some to wonder if God's requests (the Virgin Mary to Sister Lucia) for the consecration of Russia on June 13, 1929, and for His Feast day (God the Father to Mother Eugenia) on July 12, 1932, were not part of a mystical design by heaven to try to help prevent mankind from undergoing the horrors of World War II, especially its "atomic" conclusion. Listed below are some of the critical dates and events of this period:

1929 June 13	Our Lady Tells Sr. Lucia that "The moment has come when God asks the Holy Father, in union with all the bishops of the world, to make the consecration of Russia to My Immaculate Heart, promising to save it by this means."

1930	The Fatima messages are approved by the Church
1932	Mother Eugenia receives her messages on July 12, 1932 and August 12, 1932 during the reign of Pius XI — the Pope of the Fatima messages
1932	James Chadwick discovers neutrons leading to nuclear fusion and the first nuclear reaction.
1934 June	Inquiry begins concerning Mother Eugenia's apparitions.
1934 July 28	Sister Faustina's revelations begin.
1938 January 25	Sister Faustina is given a vision of the anger of God over Poland.
1938 January 25/26	The feast of the conversion of St. Paul. An unknown light is seen over Europe. (Sr. Lucia said, "This was the sign that God used to make me understand that His Justice was ready to deal a blow upon the guilty nations. I do not know, but it seems to me that if they studied it well, they would have realized that owing to the circumstances under which the light appeared, it was not, nor could it have been an aurora borealis.")
1939 February 10	Pius XI dies.
1939 March	Jesus tells Sr. Lucia of Fatima, "The

time is coming when the rigor of My Justice will punish the crimes of various nations. Some of them will be annihilated."

1939 September	WWII breaks out-six months after Pius dies.
1939 October 11	Einstein, Fermi, Szilard, and Wagner send a letter of warning to FDR concerning nuclear danger.
1942	The Manhattan Project begins.
1942	Pius XII's Consecration of the world to the Immaculate Heart of Mary. (This was an incomplete consecration according to Lucia.)
1942 December 2	A chain reaction is sustained. This was the first controlled flow of energy from a source other than the sun.
1945	Mother Eugenia's messages are approved by the Church.
1945 July 16	First nuclear bomb is detonated in New Mexico.
1945 August 5	The first Sunday in August and the first proposed Feast Day for God Our Father in the year of the Commission's approval
1945 August 6	The first atomic bomb is dropped on Hiroshima (This occurred between

two dates requested by God Our
Father for His Feast Day).

1945 August 6	The Feast of the Transfiguration (Great Light)
1945 August 7	The second proposed Feast Day for God the Father.
1945 August 9	The second atomic bomb is dropped on Nagasaki.

Sister Lucia's memoirs during this period as well as Sister Faustina's Diary both contain entries which support the notion that God was attempting to provide special graces. These graces may have helped prevent mankind from crossing the line into a new era of death and destruction, the era of atomic warfare, the ultimate consequence of mankind continuing to choose the Tree of Knowledge over the Tree of Life.

At the beginning of the new millenium, the heavenly requests for a Feast Day for God Our Father appear once again to come at a critical time in history to perhaps offer a solution to the danger Mary has been warning of since Fatima.

The world at the end of the 20th century still faces the threat of nuclear annihilation. The sun (fire from the sky) could still fall and while heaven has indicated it will save the world from total destruction, a great price in death and destruction may still occur. Perhaps this is why the Father must be recognized now, that His Feast Day must be proclaimed. Perhaps it is the fulfillment in our times of the story of the Prodigal Son in Scripture, a son who urgently hastened home to his father in desperation.

Indeed, the world is now in a state of desperation and we, all God's prodigal children, need to return to the safety of Our Father. Perhaps the return of the prodigal children to their Father now comes in the fullness of its meaning, as Our Father races to meet us. And perhaps this truly was what God was showing us in the falling sun at

Fatima — His anxious desire to hurry to us as soon as we turn in His direction. In 1932, God the Father told Mother Eugenia that He desired **"the return of the prodigal sons to their Father's House"** and to Barbara Centilli in 1998, the Father revealed even more of this same understanding; mankind truly *was* represented in this parable, and that the entire story of salvation history as revealed and prophesied in Scripture is related to the parable of the Prodigal Son. In a powerful vision, Barbara was given the following insight concerning this mystery:

> **It was all much simpler than was thought. Man makes the approach to the Creator more difficult than was intended.**
>
> [I see a book of Holy Scripture. It is opened to what seems to be the middle. In the middle is the Parable of the Prodigal Son. As if the book is transparent, I see at the beginning, the first three chapters of the Book of Genesis. At the end, I see the Book of Revelations — the Apocalypse. The Parable of the Prodigal Son is the central focus in what I see with connections to the Book of Genesis and the Book of Revelations.]:
>
> **See the story projected [from The Parable of the Prodigal Son] forward [toward the front of the book] to Genesis and backward [toward the back of the book] to Revelations—all form the Parable of the Prodigal Son. See it this way once more as was given you. [I see it again.] See? So much more will be explained to you now. I bring you all out of bondage. The time has come for the children of God to be reconciled with their Father. Remember, I come as a thief in the night. Be ready. And tell all those you come in contact with that their Father approaches. As My Son Jesus is likened to the Morning Star, so too with the Father—I am the Morning Sun. Remember, I have told you that after the sun sets, it also rises. And so with this time.**

Likewise, everything that will now occur, as with the prodigal son, will be up to the choices that are made. The Father made this clear to Barbara:

The force of My hand will come swiftly and justly—but always, it comes with mercy. Did I not allow My prodigal son to feel the consequences of his choices and actions? And so it will be in these times. There are consequences in the Divine Order that serve as My Justice—but also My Mercy. For in experiencing consequences, My children often see their way clear to come home to their Father. This is not a bad thing, little one. This is My goodness and mercy shining forth to My children.

You have been made to feel the consequences of this culture—in your choices and the choices of those around you. Your life is an intersection of all such choices and consequences.

See the light which appears on the horizon. Be drawn to this light. Be drawn to your God. My Commandments, My Beatitudes provide the outline, the parameter, of My Orderly Will. Within My Will, My children are safe; they are protected under My Heart.

Not surprisingly, this understanding was also somewhat revealed by Mary in a message to Father Gobbi on June 30, 1994:

Let this humanity return, like the Prodigal Son into the Arms of the Heavenly Father, who awaits it with love, so that a new, profound and universal reconciliation may be thus achieved between God and humanity.

There is one more correlating element to all of this. In the parable of the Prodigal Son, the father celebrated his joy over his son's return by proclaiming a feast — a feast in honor of the reunification of father and son. With this understanding we can see why the Feast Day for the Father serves as such an important final step in helping to bring the Triumph of the Immaculate Heart. Indeed, this point must be essential, for the Father says that through a feast, a feast that would celebrate the reunification of God and His children, all can be restored and renewed.

[Note: To learn more about or to obtain the Holy Octave of Consecration to God Our Father and its Feast Day, see the back of the book.]

A rendition of Fatima's 'Last Vision'
as given to Sr. Lucia in 1929.

CHAPTER FIFTY-THREE

THE FEAST OF THE FATHER OF ALL MANKIND

"That you may be children of your heavenly Father."

— Mt 5:45

S o what must be done for the Church to act on this matter? Can a feast day in the Catholic Church be declared for Our Father and why hasn't it been done already?

According to theologians, Christ's resurrection inaugurated new worship which proclaimed that Christ's Father was Our Father. This was in accordance to the risen Savior's words to Mary Magdala, **"I am ascending to My Father and your Father, to My God and your God (Jn 20:17)**. With this, divine worship was to be addressed to the One who is Our Father. Christ's dialogue with the Samaritan woman further established that worship, as the Jews had done, was to change: **"Believe me, woman, the hour is coming when You'll worship the Father neither on this mountain nor in Jerusalem... the hour is coming, and now is when we worshipers will worship the Father in spirit and in truth, for the Father is seeking such people to worship Him" (Jn 4:21-23)**. This worship was to be addressed to the Father, as inspired by the Holy Spirit and carried out in the truth of Jesus Christ. But if all liturgical worship is directed to the Father, should there not be a yearly celebration in His honor?

Such a feast was sought, according to Church documents, as far back as 1657 when a petition was sent from Liege, Belgium, to

Pope Alexander VII, seeking a Divine Office and Mass in honor of the Eternal Father. In 1684, King Charles II of Spain ordered a memorandum to be sent to the Sacred Congregation of Rites. Ten years later the King tried again under the Pontificate of Pope Innocent XII. During this period, discussions went on, but in 1696 the Reporter for the Cause, Cardinal Colloredo, was asked by Msgr. Bottini, the Promotor of the Faith, to cease defending it before the Congregation of Rites. This was because the objections raised were considered serious.

The requests for the establishment of a liturgical feast day for the Eternal Father found their origination in certain places in France and Spain where such a Feast had already developed. The Holy See had approved several congregations established in the name of the Father by granting them indulgences and this devotional movement was thus a normal culmination of what had already developed. However, objections were raised that ranged from opposition to the novelty of such a Mass to several doctrinal concerns that questioned its theological objective. The primary objection was that such a Mass would give distinct veneration to a single divine person in Himself versus Their roles in the mystery of salvation. After much debate, Pope Benedict XII then declared that a liturgical feast must commemorate either a mystery that happened on a specific day or specific divine favor. The Pope concluded after a lengthy argument that such a feast day for the Father would open the door for feast days for the Son and Holy Spirit as single divine persons or for various divine attributes. The Pope concluded, "Let the example of our elders suffice for us. In our worship let us follow the wisdom of the ancients."

Since the 17th century, no serious effort has been attempted to re-open the question of a feast day for the Father. Pope Leo XIII briefly cited the concerns of his predecessor in his encyclical on the Holy Spirit, *Divinum illud,* but raised no new doctrinal objections to the Feast.

The 20th century has witnessed a renewal of interest in the theology surrounding the question of the appropriateness of such a feast for the Father. The objections raised in the 17th century have been responded to through clarification of the purpose of the feast and by a better understanding that in principle, the early objections were not Scripturally sound and were already being practiced by other forms of prayer.

Eminent theologian, Jean Galot, S.J., who has thoroughly confronted this issue, concludes that a feast day should be inaugurated for God the Father:

> The two moments — the beginning and the end — of the work of salvation express the same truth: "God our Father," first in the fundamental intention of the work and then in its ultimate fulfillment. The first moment occurs at the origin of the history of the universe in the divine eternity that precedes creation, and the last moment likewise opens into this eternity into which the entire substance of human history is incorporated. Christ was aware during his earthly life that he came for the Father and was going to the Father (cf. Jn 13: 1-3). The Church likewise must deepen her awareness of having come forth from the Father and of advancing toward him. The liturgical feast of God the Father would express this awareness with greater clarity.

> Such a feast could not be considered an ornamental devotion. It is not a superfluous manifestation of piety, but intrinsic to the liturgical cycle of which this feast is the pinnacle. If we really want to reinstate this cycle in the biblical perspective of the discourse after the Last Supper and of Pauline teaching, we will call for a more explicit proclamation of the mystery of God the Father.

> This proclamation can be celebrated throughout the liturgical year. Yet in order to have its full impact it requires a special day of solemnity reserved for it alone. The purpose of a liturgical feast is to draw attention to a particular person or mystery. The person of God the Father and the mystery of the divine fatherhood deserve more than an implicit veneration or a mere mention in other feasts. We can adequately celebrate and thank God Our Father only with a special

feast in His honor.

Fr. Galot offers strong support for the inauguration of a feast for God Our Father:

> There are sound reasons favoring the inauguration of a feast of God our Father. Above all, there is the capital importance of the Father in the work of our salvation which needs to be given greater recognition in liturgical worship. Only a feast set apart for God the Father can assure the proper veneration of His person and respond to the universal development of His Fatherly love.
>
> This feast would also be most relevant for our time, since it would enhance the nobility of human parenthood and throw light on problems relating to the procreation and education of children. Nor would it be lacking in ecumenical significance.
>
> This feast is therefore to be hoped for. In a more general way, should we not want the prayer of the Church to be more closely modeled on the prayer of Christ through a greater effort to address the Father? Such a way of praying would help us rediscover the spontaneity with which Jesus called his divine Father, *"Abba!"*

Without a doubt, Father Galot's words incite in our own hearts a wrenching call for a feast day for God Our Father to be proclaimed and instituted now.

How many centuries have passed in which the Spirit has moved in this regard? But now, as Fatima's fulfillment stands at the doorstep of the world, the Father Himself appears to us, opens the door, and invites us into His Kingdom to be with Him forever. Mary, the Mother of All Mankind, has escorted her children back to the Father of All Mankind. We need only to open our arms, to embrace Him, and to say to Him, individually and as a Church—as the Mystical Body of His Son— that we, like Christ, love Him with all our hearts and we give ourselves to Him through personal consecration and celebration of His Feast Day.

EPILOGUE

A voice coming from the throne said "Praise our God, all you his servants, [and] you who revere him, small and great."

Then I heard something like the sound of a great multitude or the sound of rushing water or mighty peals of thunder, as they said:

"Alleluia! The Lord has established his reign, [our] God, the Almighty. Let us rejoice and be glad and give him glory. For the wedding day of the Lamb has come, his bride has made herself ready. She was allowed to wear a bright, clean linen garment."

(The linen represents the righteous deeds of the holy ones.)

Then the angel said to me, "Write this: Blessed are those who have been called to the wedding Feast of the Lamb." And he said to me, "These words are true; they come from God."

I fell at his feet to worship him. But he said to me, "Don't! I am a fellow servant of yours and of your brothers who bear witness to Jesus. Worship God. Witness to Jesus is the spirit of prophecy."

Then I saw the heavens opened, and these was a white horse; its rider was [called] "Faithful and True." He judges and wages war in righteousness. His eyes were [like] a fiery flame, and on his head were many diadems. He had a name inscribed that no one knows except himself. He wore a cloak that had been dipped in blood, and his name was called the Word of God. The armies of heaven followed him, mounted on white horses and wearing clean white linen. Out of his mouth came a sharp sword to strike the nations. He will rule them with an iron rod, and he himself will tread out in the wine press the wine of the fury and wrath of God the Almighty. He has a name written on his cloak and on his thigh, "King of kings and Lord of lords."

Then I saw an angel standing on the sun. He cried out [in] a loud voice to all the birds flying high overhead, "Come here. Gather for God's great Feast, to eat the flesh of kings, the flesh of military officers, and the flesh of warriors, the flesh of horses and of their riders, and the flesh of all, free and slave, small and great." Then I saw the beast and the kings of the earth and their armies gathered to fight against the one riding the horse and against his army. The beast was caught and with it the false prophet who had performed in its sight the signs by which he led astray those who had accepted the mark of the beast and those who had worshiped its image. The two were thrown alive into the fiery pool burning with sulfur. The rest were killed by the sword that came out of the mouth of the one riding the horse, and all the birds gorged themselves on their flesh.

Rev 19:5-21

NOTES

INTRODUCTION

The accounts of Saragozza and Le Puy, France are from Michael Brown's book *The Last Secret* which I highly recommend. The following references are all excellent sources for information on documented reports of apparitions: *True and False Apparitions in the Church* by Bernard Billet, *Apparitions* by C.M. Staehlen, *Entu to Sur Les Apparitions De La Vierge* by Yves Chiron, *Religious Apparitions and The Cold War in Southern Europe* by William A. Christian Jr., *Lexicon der Marienerschernungen* by Robert Ernst, *Les Apparitions de La Vierge* by Slyvie Barnay. Barnay's work and Chiron's study are part of the listed apparitions of Dayton University's Marian Research Institute's web page.

The Day Will Come (1996) by Michael Brown, *A Guide to Apparitions of the Blessed Virgin Mary* (1995) by Peter Heinz, and *Erscheinungen und* Borschaften *der Gottesmutler Maria* (1995) are also excellent sources for apparitions. All three works are by lay people.

The quotes by historian Thomas Kselman is from his book *Miracles and Prophecies In Nineteenth Century France,* pages 61 and 62. This book is highly recommended. The quote from Professor David Blackbourn is from his book, *Marpingen*, page 5. Marpingen is also highly recommended and is available at local bookstores.

CHAPTER ONE
SOMETHING IN THE AIR

The information on St. Michael and Fatima comes from the book, *St. Michael and the* Fatima *Connection*, by Carlos Evaristo (available at Fatima). The onset of the Renaissance and its philosophical and political ramifications are discussed in many history books. I used several, most notably *A History of the World* by Hugh Thomas.

CHAPTER TWO
THE FIRST WAVE

The David Blackbourn quote is from his book *Marpingen*, page 20. Tan Books publishes many books about the life and revelations of Anna Catherine Emmerich and is a good source for such information.

Many of the 19th century prophets, prophecies and apparitions cited in this chapter are from Thomas Kselman's book, *Miracles and Prophecies in Nineteenth Century France*, David Blackbourn's *Marpingen*, and *Lexicon, der Marienerschernungen* by Robert Ernst. Michael Brown's *The Last Secret* was also referenced. However, a significant number of apparitions were singled out from dozens of books either read or researched over many years. I have listed them in the bibliography.

The Canori-Mora quote is from author's book *Call of the Ages*. Most of the prophecies can be found in almost any book on Catholic prophecy. The Bishop of Portier's quote is from page 76 of Kselman's, *Miracles and Prophecies of the 19th Century*.

CHAPTER THREE
PRAY FOR THE WORLD

The information and quotes in this chapter on Catherine Labouré are from Joseph Dirvin's book, *Saint Catherine Labouré of the Miraculous Medal*. William Christian Jr's quote is from his highly recommended book *Visionaries, The Spanish Republic and the Reign of Christ* published by the University of California Press at Berkely. (This book is about the apparitions at Ezkioga, Spain in the early 1930's and is outstanding in its scholarly approach).

The information and quotes concerning Bernadette Soubirous in this chapter are from the book *Saint Bernadette Soubirous* by Abbe Francois Trochu (Tan books). Marie Taigi's quote is from the author's book *Call of the Ages*. The story of Father Sauvageaus is from the Thomas Kselman's book *Miracles and Prophecies of the Nineteenth Century.*

Many of the 19th century prophets, prophecies and apparitions cited in this chapter are from Thomas Kselman's book, *Miracles and Prophecies in* Nineteenth *Century France*, David Blackbourn's *Marpingen*, and *Lexicon, der Marienerschernungen* by Robert Ernst. Michael Brown's *The Last Secret* was also referenced. However, a significant number of apparitions were singled out from dozens of books either read or researched over many years. I have listed them in the bibliography.

CHAPTER FOUR
THE APPROACHING STORM

The story of Magdalena Kade is from David Blackbourn's *Marpingen,* pages 13,14,16 and 20. Estele Faquette's story is from the author's *Call of the Ages* and is found in many books on 19th century apparitions, especially Mr. John Haffert's many works. A book on Bartolo Longo is available through Tan Books.

Many of the 19th century prophets, prophecies and apparitions cited in this chapter are from Thomas Kselman's book, *Miracles and Prophecies in Nineteenth Century France.* David Blackbourn's *Marpingen*, and *Lexicon, der Marienerschernungen* by Robert Ernst. Michael Brown's *The Last Secret* was also referenced. However, a significant number of apparitions were singled out from dozens of books either read or researched over many years. I have listed them in the bibliography.

There are many books on Knock and Pontmain. I have listed some of my sources in the bibliography.

CHAPTER FIVE
FORESHADOWING FATIMA

The information on Marie Juli Jahenny's life and revelations comes from *The Prophecies of La Fraudais* by Pierre Roberdel.

Many of the 19th century prophets, prophecies and apparitions cited in this chapter are from Thomas Kselman's book,

Miracles and Prophecies in Nineteenth Century France, David Blackbourn's *Marpingen*, and *Lexicon, der Marienerschernungen* by Robert Ernst. Michael Brown's *The Last Secret* was also referenced. However, a significant number of apparitions were singled out from dozens of books either read or researched over many years. I have listed them in the bibliography.

The secrets of La Salette comes from the booklet *Apparitions of the Virgin Mary on the Mountain of La Salette* published by the Shepherdess of La Salette and printed in America by the Gregorian Press in Berlin, N.J. The story of St. John Vianney is from Tan Books *Cure of Ars* by Father Bartholomew O'Brien. The message of Our Lady of Akita is from *Akita, The Tears and Messages* by Teiji Yasuda O.S.V. Blackbourn's account of Elisa Recktenwald is from his book *Marpingen*, page 326. Kselman's observation is from his book *Miracles and Prophecies in Nineteenth Century, France*, page 122. William A. Christian's quote is from his book *Visionaries, The Spanish Republic and The Reign of Christ*, pages 2 and 3.

The 19th century military facts comes from Hugh Thomas's *A History of the* World.

CHAPTERS SIX AND SEVEN
FLIRTING WITH ANNIHILATION / THE DESTINY OF NATIONS

Many of the 19th century prophets, prophecies and apparitions cited in this chapter are from Thomas Kselman's book *Miracles and Prophecies in Nineteenth Century* France. David Blackbourn's *Marpingen*, and *Lexicon, der Marienerschernungen* by Robert Ernst. Michael Brown's *The Last Secret* was also referenced. However, a significant number of apparitions were singled out from dozens of books either read or researched over many years. I have listed them in the bibliography.

Padre Pio's quotes are from *Padre Pio: The True Story* by C. Bernard Ruffen. I also used *Padre Pio, The Stigmatist* by Rev. Charles Mortimar Carty. Mary's prophecies at Fatima are documented in almost every book written about the apparitions at Fatima. Many such books are in the bibliography. Pope Benedict's XV's quote is from an article by L. Edward Cole in *Soul* Magazine,

Nov.- Dec. 1990. The events of the Bolshevick Revolution were taken primarily from Hugh Thomas's *A History of the World*. Berthe Petit's quote is taken from my book *Call of the Ages*. The Theresa Neuman account is from *Theresa Neuman, Mystic and Stigmatist* by Adalbert Vogl. The Marthe Robin quote is from John Haffert's book *Her Words to the Nuclear Age*. William A. Christian's quote is from his book *Visionaries*, page XX. Sister Consolata Betrone's quoted is from the book *Jesus Appeals To The World* by Lorenzo Sales, I.M.C. (Abba House, New York). Sister Faustina Kowalska's message is from her Diary, *Divine Mercy in My Soul*, page 322, (Stockbridge, Massachusetts, Marian Press 1987).

CHAPTER EIGHT
ARMAGEDDON?

Many of the 19th century prophets, prophecies and apparitions cited in this chapter are from Thomas Kselman's book, *Miracles and Prophecies in Nineteenth Century France*, David Blackbourn's *Marpingen* and *Lexicon, der Marienerschernungen* by Robert Ernst. Michael Brown's *The Last Secret* was also referenced. However, a significant number of apparitions were singled out from dozens of books either read or researched over many years. I have listed them in the bibliography.

Professor's Blackbourn's data is from his book *Marpingen*. The Bruno Cornacchio story comes from Michael Brown's *Final Hour*. The 1980 and 1986 miracles at Tre Fontaine were reported in *The Fatima Crusader*, winter, 1994. The information surrounding the actions of Pope Pius XII comes from the book, *There is Nothing More* published by AMI Press of Washington, N.J.. Pius XII's vision of the miracle of the sun is from Michael Brown's *Final Hour*. Many of the reports of apparitions and weeping statues come from Father Albert Hebert's books: *The Chastisement and the Purification, The Three Days of Darkness, Mary, Why Do You Weep?* and *Signs and Wonders*.

CHAPTER NINE
HER TIME OF VISITATION

The message of Mary on the second page of this chapter is from Father Gobbi's book of messages and was used with permission. General MacArthur's words come from Emmet Culligan's book *The Last World War and the End of Time*.

Many of the reports of apparitions and weeping statues come from Father Albert Hebert's books: *The Chastisement and the Purification, The Three Days* of Darkness, Mary, Why Do You Weep? and Signs and Wonders. Thomas Walsh's interview with Sr. Lucia is from his book, *Our Lady of Fatima*, pages 218-223.

The Fatima information is from many sources. (See bibliography) The story of the August 1931, apparition at Rianjo, Spain comes from the Fatima *Crusader*, Winter 1995. The information from *LeMonde* magazine comes from Michael Brown's *The Last Secret*.

CHAPTER TEN
THE HOUR HAS COME

The information concerning Estela Ruiz came from my book *For the Soul of the Family*, the *Story of the Apparitions of the Blessed Virgin Mary to Estela Ruiz and How One Family Came Back to God*.

The information from the Pontifical Council comes from my book *Call of the Ages*.

The message from Medjugorje is from Michael Brown's *Final Hour*. Glady's Quiroga's message from Mary is from the book, *Messages of Our Lady at San Nicolas*. (published by Faith Publishing). The message of the Virgin Mary at Olivito Citra is from Fr. Robert Faricy's book, *Mary Among Us, The Apparitions of the Blessed Virgin Mary at Olivito Citra*.

CHAPTER ELEVEN
THE SILLY SEASON

The account of the events in Asdee comes from the book, *Warnings, Visions & Messages from Irish Visionaries Today* by Father Albert Herbert. The phenomena reported at Gortnadreda, Bessbrock, Ballenspittle and Melleray comes from the *Queen of Peace* newspaper, Volume I, Pittsburgh Center for Peace (1991). Michael Brown's observations are from his book *Final Hour* as are the *Cork Examiner* quotes and accounts. The accounts of Jim O'herliky and Kevin D. O'Connor are from Fr. Herbert's book *Warnings, Visions and Messages from Irish Visionaries Today*. The accounts of Marie Vaughan and Mrs. Casey come from *Inchilgela, A Call to Prayer*. The story of Mike O'Donnel and Tom and Barry Cliffe comes from *Her Message from Melleray Grotto*. Christina Gallagher's story is from *The Sorrow, the Sacrifice and the Triumph The Apparitions, Visiona and Prophecies of Christina Gallagher* by the author. (published by Simon and Schuster NY, NY).

CHAPTER TWELVE
"THE MOTHER OF GOD IS VISITING EARTH"

The account of the events in Medjugorje come from many sources that I have reviewed and synthesized. The primary source in this chapter was *Spark from Heaven* by Mary Craig, in which the children's "first day" quotes are taken as well as the final quote at the end of the chapter (as noted in the text).

CHAPTER THIRTEEN
THE EPICENTER

The information on Medjugorje comes from many sources, personal notes and experiences. In this chapter, the primary sources quoted or paraphrased come from Michael Brown's *Final Hour*, Dennis Nolan's *A Time for Truth a Time for Action* (The Professor Copelston quote is from this book) and Mary Craig's book, *Spark from Heaven*. Mary's public messages come from Rene Laurentin's and Rene Lejeune's account *Messages* and *Teachings of Mary at Medjugorje, Chronological Corpus of the Messages,* and *Visions of the Children* by Janice T. Connell or *Words From Heaven* (no author, St. James Publishing Co, Birmingham Alabama). These messages also come from Medjugorje directly each month and are available from numerous sources because they are released as public messages.

CHAPTER FOURTEEN
THE FULFILLMENT OF FATIMA

The report sent to Rome by Fr. Tomislav Vlasic is from *Is the Virgin Mary Appearing at Medjugorje?* by Rene Laurentin and Ljudevit Rupic. Mary's message on the first page is from *Words From Heaven* (St. James Publishing). The quoted accounts of the professor from Dusseldorf and the other lay people visiting Medjugorje come from *Is the Virgin Mary Appearing at Medjugorje?* by Rene Laurentin and Ljudevit Rupic and are used with permission.

CHAPTER FIFTEEN
AN APOCALYPTIC MESSAGE

All of the information concerning Father Gobbi and the Marian Movement of Priests, as well as Father Gobbi's interior locution messages, come from book *To the Priest, Our Lady's Beloved Sons* and MMP's periodical newsletters. They are used with the permission of Father Albert Roux, National Director of the Marian Movement of Priests in the United States, headquartered in St. Francis, Maine. All of Fr. Gobbi's messages in this book come from the MMP's book and are used with permission of MMP and are not noted after Chapter 16's notes.

CHAPTER SIXTEEN
A SIGN FOR ALL

All of the information concerning Father Gobbi and the Marian Movement of Priests, as well as Father Gobbi's interior locution messages come from book *To the Priest, Our Lady's*

Beloved Sons and MMP'S periodical newsletters. They are used with the permission of Father Albert Roux, National Director of the Marian Movement of Priests in the United States, headquartered in St. Francis, Maine. All of Fr. Gobbi's messages in this book come from the MMP's book and are used with permission of MMP.

CHAPTER SEVENTEEN
I NEED YOUR PRAYERS

The individual apparitions listed in this chapter are from Bernard's Billet's 1976 study *True and False Apparitions in the Church* or Yves Chiron's work *Entu to Sur Les Apparitions De La Vierge* or the University of Dayton's Marian Library, International Marian Research Center, Web site. Their information was compiled with the help of Fr. Réne Laurentin and Slyvie Barnay and was coordinated by Fr. John Roten.

Some of the apparitions cited came from select, individual texts too numerous to cite here and from the author's personal contacts, experiences, interviews, and knowledge. (These works are listed in the bibliography section).

The account of Amparo Cuevos comes from Rene Laurentin's book, *The Apparitions of the Blessed Virgin Mary Today*. The report on the apparitions at Litminova comes from the Pittsburgh Center for Peace newsletter, *The World Report,* May, 1992 and the booklet, *Wondrous News from* Litminova (no author or publisher listed). The weeping statues in Italy in 1995 were reported in *Inside the Vatican* in its April and May issues of that year. The Cardinal Ratzinger quote was reported in *Inside the Vatican's* June-July 1995 issue. The account of the apparitions at Olvito Citra comes from Fr. Robert Faricy's book *Mary Among Us* and from Réne Laurentin's *The Apparitions of the Blessed Virgin Mary Today*. Bishop Sheen's quote is from *The Sun Danced at Fatima* by Fr. Joseph A. Pellitier, A.P. The Moslem connection to Mary as detailed in the Koran comes from an article by Warren H. Carroll Ph. D., printed in *Soul* Magazine, May-June 1991.

CHAPTER EIGHTEEN
WE BELIEVE IN YOU

The accounts and quotes of the apparitions in Cairo come from *A Lady of Light Appears in Egypt, the Story of Zeitoun* by Youssef G. Kamell and John P. Jackson, *When Millions Saw Mary* by Francis Johnston and *Our Lord's Mother Visit's Egypt in 1968 and 1969* by Pearl Zaki. The quote of St. Louis de Montfort is from *Our Lady Queen of Peace* newspaper, Vol II, The Pittsburgh Center for Peace (1992).

CHAPTER NINETEEN
A RIVER OF BLOOD

The account Sr. Reinolda Mary is from a booklet on her apparitions titled *Our Lady of Ngome, Mary, Tabernacle of the Most High.* No author or publisher was listed. The individual apparitions listed in this chapter are from Bernard's Billets 1976 study, *True and False Apparitions in the Church* or Yves Chiron's work *Entu to Sur Les Apparitions De La Vierge* or the University of Dayton's Marian Library, International Marian Research Center, Web site. This information was compiled with the help of Fr. Réne Laurentin and Slyvie Barnay and was coordinated by Fr. John Roten.

Some of the apparitions cited in this chapter came from select, individual texts too numerous to cite here and from the author's personal contacts, experiences, interviews and knowledge. (These works are listed in the bibliography section).

Some of the contemporary African apparitions were taken from Fr. Réne Laurentin's book *The Apparitions of the Blessed Virgin Mary Today.* The apparitions in Kenya to Sister Anna Ali comes from the book *Thunder of Justice* by Ted and Maureen Flynn.

The account of the apparitions in Rwanda is from several sources, primarily *Our Lady Queen of Peace* newspaper Vol I (1991) and Vol III (1995), and from a paper distributed by the 101 Foundation in Washington, New Jersey. A booklet title *The Apparitions of Our Lady of Kibeho* was helpful as was a book, *Kibeho Rwanda - a Prophecy Fulfilled* by Fr. Gabriel Maindron.

CHAPTER TWENTY
ASIAN WONDERS

The account of the apparitions at Lipa is from the book *Lipa* by June Keithly. The reported apparitions in China comes from the *Washington Post* story and other sources listed. Also helpful were accounts in Michael Brown's *The Day Will Come* and Janice T. Connell's book *Meetings with Mary*.

The individual apparitions listed in this chapter are from Bernard's Billets 1976 study *True and False Apparitions in the Church* or Yves Chiron's work *Entu to Sur Les Apparitions De La Vierge* or the University of Dayton's Marian Library, International Marian Research Center, Web site. This information was compiled with the help of Fr. Réne Laurentin and Slyvie Barnay and was coordinated by Fr. John Roten.

Some of the apparitions came from select, individual texts too numerous to cite here and from the author's personal contacts, experiences, interviews, and knowledge. (Many of these works are listed in the bibliography section).

CHAPTER TWENTY-ONE
MAMA WILL SAVE VIETNAM

The story of Stephen Ho Hgoc Ahn is from the pamphlet *Message of Our Lady of Fatima at Bink Loi* published by the Blue Army in Washington N.J. The story and quote "Mama Will Save Vietnam" is from the *Chastisement and Purification* by Father Albert Hebert. Many of the Ukrainian apparitions come from the book *Witness* by Michael Brown and Josyp Terelya, as did Chornij Zrnovia's account of her experiences in the Soviet Gulag. The story of Dina Basher was given to the author when I served as President of the Pittsburgh Center for Peace (1990-1998). It was published in the center's *World Report* April, 1993. The Nepal account is from a CNS news release in 1992.

The individual apparitions listed in this chapter are from Bernard's Billets 1976 study *True and False Apparitions in the*

Church or Yves Chiron's work *Entu to Sur Les Apparitions De La Vierge* or the University of Dayton's Marian Library, International Marian Research Center, Web site. This information was compiled with the help of Fr. Réne Laurentin and Slyvie Barnay and was coordinated by Fr. John Roten.

Some of the apparitions came from select, individual texts too numerous to cite here and from the author's personal contacts, experiences, interviews, and knowledge. (Many of these works are listed in the bibliography section).

CHAPTER TWENTY-TWO
THE MADONNA OF THE GULAG

The primary source for this account was the book *Witness* by Michael Brown and Josyp Terelya. *In the Kingdom of the Spirit* by Josyp Terelya was also drawn upon as was the author's personal relationship with Josyp Terelya. (I spent 10 days with Josyp in the Ukraine in 1994 and have met with him regularly since then).

The individual apparitions listed in this chapter are from Bernard's Billets 1976 study *True and False Apparitions in the Church* or Yves Chiron's work *Entu to Sur Les Apparitions De La Vierge* or the University of Dayton's Marian Library, International Marian Research Center, Web site. This information was compiled with the help of Fr. Réne Laurentin and Slyvie Barnay and was coordinated by Fr. John Roten.

Some of the apparitions came from select, individual texts too numerous to cite here and from the author's personal contacts, experiences, interviews, and knowledge. (Many of these works are listed in the bibliography section).

CHAPTER TWENTY-THREE
A CHOSEN NATION

The primary source for this account was the book *Witness* by Michael Brown and Josyp Terelya. *In the Kingdom of the Spirit* by Josyp Terelya was also drawn upon as was the author's personal relationship with Josyp Terelya. (I spent 10 days with Josyp in the

Ukraine in 1994 and have met with him regularly since then).

The individual apparitions listed in this chapter are from Bernard's Billets 1976 study *True and False Apparitions in the Church* or Yves Chiron's work *Entu to Sur Les Apparitions De La Vierge* or the University of Dayton's Marian Library, International Marian Research Center, Web site. This information was compiled with the help of Fr. Réne Laurentin and Slyvie Barnay and was coordinated by Fr. John Roten.

Some of the apparitions came from select, individual texts too numerous to cite here and from the author's personal contacts, experiences, interviews, and knowledge. (Many of these works are listed in the bibliography section).

Some related information in the chapter comes from Michael Brown's *Final Hour.*

CHAPTER TWENTY-FOUR
THE CONVERSION OF RUSSIA

The primary source for this account was the book *Witness* by Michael Brown and Josyp Terelya. *In the Kingdom of the Spirit* by Josyp Terelya was also drawn upon as was the author's personal relationship with Josyp Terelya. (I spent 10 days with Josyp in the Ukraine in 1994 and have met with him regularly since then).

The individual apparitions listed in this chapter are from Bernard's Billets 1976 study *True and False Apparitions in the Church* or Yves Chiron's work *Entu to Sur Les Apparitions De La Vierge* or the University of Dayton's Marian Library, International Marian Research Center, Web site. This information was compiled with the help of Fr. Réne Laurentin and Slyvie Barnay and was coordinated by Fr. John Roten.

Some of the apparitions came from select, individual texts too numerous to cite here and from the author's personal contacts, experiences, interviews, and knowledge. (Many of these works are listed in the bibliography section).

Some related information comes from Michael Brown's *Final Hour.*

CHAPTER TWENTY-FIVE
MY GOD: WHAT HAVE WE DONE

The Hiroshima account is from the book *Reader's Digest Illustrated Story of World War II*. The events of Akita come from John Haffert's book The *Meaning of Akita*, Francis Fukushima's book, *Akita: Mother of God as Co-Redemptrix, Modern Miracles of Holy Eucharist* and the book *Akita, The Tears and Message of Mary* by Teiji Yasuda O.S.V. (I also had the opportunity to meet and talk with Mr. Fukushima and Sr. Agnes Sasagawa's spiritual director Father Teiji Yasuda in Rome in June, 1997)

CHAPTER TWENTY-SIX
NO MORE HIROSHIMA'S

The events of Akita come from John Haffert's book *The Meaning of Akita*, Francis Fukushima's book, *Akita: Mother of God as Co-Redemptrix, Modern Miracles of Holy Eucharist* and the book *Akita, The Tears and Message of Mary* by Teiji Yasuda O.S.V. (I also had the opportunity to meet and talk with Mr. Fukushima and Sr. Agnes Sasagawa's spiritual director Father Teiji Yasuda in Rome in June, 1997).

In addition, I used the book, *Resolutions of the Akita International Marian Convention* (1992).

CHAPTER TWENTY-SEVEN
DO MY WILL

The individual apparitions listed in this chapter are from Bernard's Billet's 1976 study, *True and False Apparitions in the Church* or Yves Chiron's work *Entu to Sur Les Apparitions De La Vierge* or the University of Dayton's Marian Library, International Marian Research Center, Web site. This information was compiled with the help of Fr. Réne Laurentin and Slyvie Barnay and was coordinated by Fr. John Roten.

Some of the apparitions came from select, individual texts too numerous to cite here and from the author's personal contacts, experiences, interviews and knowledge. (Many of these works are listed in the bibliography section).

The information on Matthew Kelly comes from the author's personal interview with him in 1994 and from Mr. Kelly's two books, *Words from God* and *Our Father*.

CHAPTER TWENTY-EIGHT
AT THE DOORSTEP OF THE WORLD

The information on Mr. Matthew Kelly comes from the author's personal interview with him in 1994 and from his two books, *Words From God* and *Our Father*.

CHAPTER TWENTY-NINE
A CHOICE

The individual apparitions listed in this chapter are from Bernard's Billet's 1976 study *True and False Apparitions in the Church* or Yves Chiron's work *Entu to Sur Les Apparitions De La Vierge* or the University of Dayton's Marian Library, International Marian Research Center, Web site. This information was compiled with the help of Fr. Réne Laurentin and Slyvie Barnay and was coordinated by Fr. John Roten.

Some of the apparitions came from select, individual texts too numerous to cite here and from the author's personal contacts, experiences, interviews and knowledge. (Many of these works are listed in the bibliography section).

Many of the accounts on bleeding and weeping statues in this chapter come from Fr. Hebert's books *The Chastisement and the Purification, Mary, Why Do you Cry?*, *The Three Days of Darkness* and *Signs and Wonders*. His quote on why Mary cries is also from *Mary, Why Do you Cry?*. The account of little Audrey Santo comes from the author's personal research and interview with the Santo family for my book *In God's Hands, The Miraculous Story of Little Audrey Santo*.

CHAPTER THIRTY
ONE MAN'S PRAYER

All of the information on the Ruiz apparitions come from the author's book *For the Soul of the Family, The Apparitions of the Virgin Mary to Estela Ruiz and How One Family Came Back to God.* The messages to Estela Ruiz are from the book *Our Lady of the Americas* published by the Pittsburgh Center For Peace.

CHAPTER THIRTY-ONE
OUR LADY OF THE AMERICAS

All of the information on the Ruiz apparition comes from the author's book *For the Soul of* the *Family, The Apparitions of the Virgin Mary to Estela Ruiz and How One Family Came Back to God.* The messages to Estela Ruiz are from the book *Our Lady of the Americas* published by the Pittsburgh Center For Peace.

CHAPTER THIRTY-TWO
IT IS THE IMMACULATE ONE

The account of the apparitions of Our Lady of Guadalupe comes from the book *For the Soul of the Family* by the author. (see previous chapter notes)

The individual apparitions listed in this chapter are from Bernard's Billets 1976 study *True and False Apparitions in the Church* or Yves Chiron's work *Entu to Sur Les Apparitions De La Vierge* or the University of Dayton's Marian Library, International Marian Research Center, Web site. This information was compiled with the help of Fr. Réne Laurentin and Slyvie Barnay and was coordinated by Fr. John Roten.

Some of the apparitions came from select, individual texts too numerous to cite here and from the author's personal contacts, experiences, interviews, and knowledge. (Many of these works are listed in the bibliography section).

CHAPTER THIRTY-THREE
DROWNED WITH TRIBULATIONS

The apparition in 1634 to Mother Mariana of Jesus Torres comes from the book *A Spanish Mystic in Ouito, sor Mariana de Jesus Torres.*

The individual apparitions listed in this chapter are from Bernard's Billet's 1976 study *True and False Apparitions in the Church* or Yves Chiron's work *Entu to Sur Les Apparitions De La Vierge* or the University of Dayton's Marian Library, International Marian Research Center, Web site. This information was compiled with the help of Fr. Réne Laurentin and Slyvie Barnay and was coordinated by Fr. John Roten.

Some of the apparitions came from select, individual texts too numerous to cite here and from the author's personal contacts, experiences, interviews, and knowledge. (Many of these works are listed in the bibliography section).

Many of the accounts of weeping statues in South America are from Father Hebert's books *Mary, Why do you Cry, Signs and Wonders, The Chastisement and the Purification and The Three Days of Darkness.*

The story of Bernado Martinez comes from the Our Lady Queen of Peace newspaper Vol I, (1991), published by the Pittsburgh Center for Peace.

CHAPTER THIRTY-FOUR
PACHI

The account of Patricia Talbot's apparitions comes from the book *I am the Guardian of the Faith* by Sr. Isabel Bettwy. The author is also close friends with her and has shared information.

CHAPTER THIRTY-FIVE
A DAWN AWAITING

The account of the apparitions to Gladys Quiroga De Motta comes from Fr. Réne Laurentin's book *An Appeal from Mary in*

Argentina and *Messages of Our Lady of San Nicolas* (Faith Publishing Co.), and from his book, *The Apparitions of The Blessed Virgin Mary Today.*

CHAPTER THIRTY-SIX
A TEST

The account of the events and apparitions in Venezuela to Maria Esperanza comes from the books *Apparitions in Betania, Venezuela* by Sister Margaret Catherine Sims, C.S.J. and *The Bridge to Heaven* by Michael Brown. The author also had the pleasure to meet Maria Esperanza in the United States and to hear her public message. Cardinal Sim's quote is from the *National Catholic Register*, September 27, 1992 issue.

CHAPTER THIRTY-SEVEN
SECRETS

Sister Faustina's quote is from the *Diary of Sister Faustina Kowalska.* Christina Gallagher's quote is from the author's book *The Sorrow, the Sacrifice,* and *the Triumph.* Fr. Pelletier's quote is from his book *The Queen of Peace Visits Medjugorje.* Fr. Slavko Barbaric's quote is from *Medjugorje Gebelsaktion* (see biliography). All of Fr. Réne Laurentin's quotes are from his book *Apparitions of the Blessed Virgin Mary Today* and are used with the author's written permission.

Sister Lucia's quote is from *Fatima, in Lucia's Own Words*, page 19. St. Catherine Labouré's quote is from the book *Saint Catherine Laboure of Sister Mary of the Holy Trinity* by Father Joseph Dirvin (Tan books).

Most of the account of the unfolding of the Secrets of La Salette comes from the book *Encountering Mary* by Sandra L. Zimdars - Swartz, pages 165-189. This book is highly recommended.

CHAPTER THIRTY-EIGHT
THE PHENOMENA OF SECRETS

The account of the secrets given to Bernadette Soubirous at Lourdes comes from the book *Saint Bernadette Soubrous 1844 - 1879* by Abbe Francois Trochu, Chapter 9, Three Secrets, pg 89-100.

Marie Julie-Jahanney account is from the book *The Prophecies of La Fraudais* by Pierre Roberdel.

The presence of secrets in many of the apparitions can be found in the books listed for those apparitions in the bibliography. One particularly helpful source was *A Guide to Apparitions* by Peter Heintz. This book reported on approximately 60 apparitions and specifically cited the presence of any "secret" messages. Likewise, Sandra Zimdars-Swartz book *Encountering Mary* reported on the topic of secrets. (See Chapters 4,5,6). The secrets of Ille Bouchard, Heroldsbach-Thorn and Balestrino are quoted directly from her book in this text.

The "Great Secret" in Ecuador is written of extensively in Sr. Isabel Bettwy's book *I am the Guardian of the Faith* (Franciscan Press, Steubenville University).

Knowledge of many of the secrets came through the author's extensive readings over the years which were not recorded at the time. Recommended texts for this subject, in addition to the books already cited: *The Thunder of Justice* by Ted and Maureen Flynn, *The Day Will Come* and *Final Hour* by Michael Brown, *The Apparitions of the Blessed Virgin Mary Today* by Rene Laurentin and *Call of the Ages* by the author.

CHAPTER THIRTY-NINE
UNFOLDING SECRETS

Fr. Michael O'Carroll's quote comes from his book *Medjugorje:* Facts, Documents, Theology. Fr. Faricy's quotes are from *Mary Among Us, The Apparitions of the Virgin Mary at Olivito Citro.* Fr. Rene Laurentin's quote is from his book *The Apparitions of the Blessed Virgin Mary Today.* Michael Brown's quote is from *The Day Will Come.* For more information on the prophesied "illumination of conscience" (the Warning) see *Call of the Ages* by the author. (I dedicated three entire chapters to this subject in the book and presented many messages from visionaries and mystics). I also suggest *Thunder of Justice* by Ted and Maureen Flynn, *The Warning* by Father Phillip Beebe and the *Final Hour* by Michael Brown. Christina Gallagher's quote is from the author's book, *The Sorrow, the Sacrifice and the Triumph.*

CHAPTER FORTY
THE THIRD SECRET OF FATIMA

Fr. Michael O'Carroll's quote is from his book *Medjugorje; Facts, Documentation and Theology.* The account of the apparitions at Fatima is readily available from many sources. I drew from the *Our Lady Queen of* Peace newspaper, Vol II (1992) by the Pittsburgh Center for Peace and dozens of books on Fatima, especially John Haffert's book *Her Own Words to the Nuclear Age.*

Sister Lucia's quote is from her memoirs published in english under the title *Fatima, In Lucia's Own Words*, distributed by Ravengate Press. The account of the Third Secret comes from an article in *Our Lady Queen of Peace*, newspaper, Vol II, titled *Whatever Happened to the Third Secret of Fatima?* by Anne M. McGlone, (1992).

CHAPTER FORTY-ONE
IF MEN AMEND THEIR LIVES

Pope John Paul II's quote in *Stimmes de Glaubens* has appeared in many books. I used Brown's *Final Hour.* Cardinal Ratzinger is quoted by Vittorio Messori in the *The Ratzinger Report* (1985), pages 109 -112. The Most Rev. Cosme de Amaral, the bishop of Leira - Fatima is quoted from a public statement he made in 1984, excerpted from an article written by Anne M. McGlone titled *Whatever Happened to the 3rd Secret of Fatima?* published in the *Our Lady Queen of Peace Newspaper*, Second Edition II, Spring 1993, Pittsburgh Center for Peace. Father Joaquin Alonso's quote is from the same article and publication. Howard Dee's quote is from his book *Mankind's Final Destiny.* The Akita message is from the book *Akita, Tears and Messages of Mary* by Father John Yasuda O.S.V. *The Inside Vatican* report is from November, 1997 issue. The Msgr. Conrado Balducci quote is from the Jan-Feb issue of *Crusade* magazine, the publication of the American Society for the Defense of Tradition, Family and Property. (This magazine is highly recommended.)

CHAPTER FORTY-TWO
FIRE FROM THE SKY

Fr. Edward O'Conner's quote is from his book *Marian Apparitions Today*, page 24. Marie Jahenny's messages are from the book *The Prophecies of La Fraudais.* Julka's visions and messages comes from the book *Chastisement and Purification* by Rev. Albert Hebert as does the messages to Mother Elena Lombardi and Mother Elena Aillo. Josyp Terelya's message from Mary is from the book *Witness* by Michael Brown and Josyp Terelya. Patricia Talbot's message is from *Guardian of the Faith* by Sr. Isabel Bettwy.

Matthew Kelly's message is from *Words From God,* Sister Agnes Sasagawa's message is from Akita, *The Tears and Message of Mary* by Rev. John Yasuda. The message to Maria Esperanza is from the *Bridge to Heaven* by Michael Brown. Sister Natalie is quoted from the book *The Victorious Queen of the World* (no author). Christina Gallagher's quote is from *The Sorrow, The Sacrifice and the Triumph* by the author. John Haffert's quote is from his book *To Prevent This.* Amparo Cuevos is quoted from an unpublished manuscript of the visions of Amparo Cuevos by Mr. Juan Gonzalez Ph. d., and is used with the permission of the author.

Gladys Quiroga's message comes from the book *The Message of Our Lady of San Nicolas* by Faith Publishing Co. The Virgin's message from Kibeho is from *Our Lady Queen of Peace* Vol I, (1991) The Pittsburgh Center for Peace. The Virgin's message from Olivito Citra is from Fr. Robert Faricy's book, *Mary Among Us, the Apparitions of the Virgin Mary at Olivito Citra.*

Christina Gallagher's visions of a war between China and Russia are from the author's book *The Sorrow, the Sacrifice, and the*

Triumph, Maria Esperanza's quote that "the yellow races will stand up" is from Michael Brown's *Bridge to Heaven.* Josyp Terelya's quotes concerning war are from the *Final Hour* by Michael Brown. Gen. Douglas MacArthur's quote is taken from Emmet Culligan's 1950's classic *World War III and the End of Time.*

CHAPTER FORTY-THREE
INCALCULABLE SELF DESTRUCTION

The contents of this chapter come entirely from a paper by Dr. Rand McNally titled, *The Nuclear Tornado Threat.* Several articles were also referenced: *A Terrible Warning* by John Haffert, *The Story Behind the Film* by Dr. J. Rand McNally Jr. and *The Great Sign,* no author, published in *Soul,* May-June 1984. The unreleased movie *A State of Emergency* was also viewed by the author. Fr. Ed O'Connor is quoted from his book *Marian Apparitions Today.* Dr. McNally is quoted from his article published in a 1994 issue of *Voice of the Sacred Hearts.* *A State of Emergency* by Thomas Lasalette is highly recommend and is quoted at the end of the chapter. It was published in 1987 by Richardson and Steirman, NY, NY.

CHAPTER FORTY-FOUR
IS THE THIRD SECRET RELEVANT

John Haffert's quote is from his book *To Prevent This.* His second quote in this chapter is from his other book *Her Own Words to the Nuclear Age.* Francis Johnston's quote is from his book *Fatima, the Great Sign.* Father Luigi Bianchi's quote is from his book *Fatima and Medjugorje.* Fr. Rene Laurentin and Fr. Ljudent Reupi's quote is from their book - *Is the Virgin Appearing at Medjugorje?*

Pope Pius XII's quotes are from Michael Brown's *Final Hour.* The Akita Convention of 1992 published a book of its resolutions, which is distributed by the Two Hearts Organization of Manilla.

Pope John Paul II's message's at Fatima in 1982 and 1984 are published in their complete text in the book *Fatima, Russia and Pope John Paul II* by Timothy Tindal Robertson.

Cardinal Ratzinger's quote at the end of this chapter is once again from *The Ratzinger Report*, page 110.

CHAPTER FORTY-FIVE
CONFIDENCE IN GOD

All of Father Rene Laurentin's quotes are from his book *The Apparitions of the Blessed Virgin Mary Today*. Pope John Paul II is quoted from his book Crossing *the Threshold of Hope.*, page 221. The quote from Ida Perleman is taken from the book *The Messages of the Lady of All* Nations published by Miriam Verlag.

CHAPTER FORTY-SIX AND FORTY-SEVEN
THE ROSARY / THE LADY OF THE ROSARY

These entire chapters were excerpted from the author's book, *The Last Crusade*. (St. Andrews Productions, McKees Rocks, Pa.)

Sister Lucia's two quotes at the end of chapter forty-seven, come from the *Fatima Crusader*, Winter 1995.

CHAPTER FORTY-EIGHT
A FINAL DOGMA?

This chapter was excerpted and reprinted from an article written by the author for *Our Lady Queen of Peace* newspaperVolume IV, (Eucharist edition) 1997. It was titled, *Mary, Coredemptrix, Mediatrix and Advocate is Mother of the Eucharist*.

The messages of the Virgin Mary concerning the dogma are excerpted from the author's book, *Call of the Ages*, (Part II Chapters 8, 9, 10). These chapters cover almost all of the private revelation surrounding the proposed dogma.

CHAPTER FORTY-NINE
THE KINGDOM OF THE FATHER

Father Alonso's quotes are from his book *The Secret of Fatima, Fact and Legend*. The Pope's words are from his talk at Fatima on May 13, 1982. His quote from chapter forty-five is also repeated here. (*Crossing* the *Threshold of Hope*, page 221.) Sister Lucia's quote is from her well documented interview with Father Augustine Fuentas, December 26, 1957 and published in Fr. Alonso's book *The Secret of Fatima, Fact and Legend*. John Haffert's quotes are from his book *The Woman Shall Conquer Now*. Sr. Lucia's comments on the miracle of the sun are from her memoirs, *Fatima in Lucia's Own Words (Memoirs II and IV)*. Fr. Galot's quote is from his book *Abba Father: We Long to See Your Face, pages 1, 190 and 191*. (This book is highly recommended and available through the Pittsburgh Center for Peace, McKees Rocks, Pa).

CHAPTER FIFTY
GOD, FATHER AND CREATOR

The Story of Akhetaton is from the Reader's Digest Book *Quest for the Past* (pages. 71-72). (The Hollywood motion picture *The Egyptian* conveys this entire story). The writings of Pope John Paul II are taken from the book *God, Father and Creator: A Catechesis on the Creed*, pages 157-159, (highly recommended and published by Pauline Books and Media of Boston). Sister Lucia's quote is from *Fatima, In Lucia's Own Words*, pages 81,82, and 173. The messages of Medjugorje are from *Visions of the Children* (1985 message) by Janice T. Connell and from the regular monthly message (1998) released in the village of Medjugorje on the 25th of each month. The story of Mother Eugenia Ravasio is from the booklet *God is Father*. (no author or publisher was listed). I also obtained considerable information from different sources on Mother Eugenia, most noted is the investigation data shared with me by Father Rene Laurentin from his personal inquiry of 1997-98.

CHAPTER FIFTY-ONE
FATIMA LEADS TO ME

The documentation and messages concerning Barbara Centilli are from my own extensive interviews with her and from the book *Seeing with the Eyes of the Soul* (St. Andrews Productions, McKees Rocks, Pa).

Many Fatima books carry the story of the last vision of Fatima. I have listed some of them in the bibliography.

CHAPTER FIFTY-TWO
CONSECRATION TO GOD OUR FATHER

Once again, the revelations of Barbara Centilli are from the book *Seeing with the Eyes of the Soul*. The author's personal interviews also added to the account. The book *The Holy Octave of Consecration to God Our Father and The Feast of the Father of All Mankind* is the source of the consecration to God Our Father. It is published by The Father of All Mankind Apostolate located in the metropolitian area of Pittsburgh.

CHAPTER FIFTY-THREE
THE FEAST OF THE FATHER OF ALL MANKIND

The information in this chapter comes entirely from Fr. Galot's book *Abba Father, We long to See Your Face*, pages 226 and 233.

Other brief references are made to some of the sources cited in chapters 51 and 52.

SELECTED BIBLIOGRAPHY

—. *Akita International Marian Convention.* Metro Manila, Philippines: Two Hearts Media Organization, Inc., 1993.

Alonzo, Joaquin Maria and Abilio Pina Bibiero. *Fatima Message and Consecration.* Fatima, Portugal Cosolata Missions' Publications.

Alonzo, Joaquin Maria, C.M.F. *The Secret of Fatima Fact and Legend.* Cambridge, Massachusetts: The Ravengate Press, 1990.

Alphonsus, Sister Mary, O.SS.R. *St. Rose of Lima.* Rockford, Illinois: TAN Books and Publishers, Inc., 1982.

—. *Apparition of the Blessed Virgin on the Mountain of La Salette the 19th of September, 1846.* France: Shepherdess of La Salette.

Armstrong, Karen. *A History of God.* New York: Harper and Row, 1989.

—. "As the Third Millennium Draws Near" in *Inside the Vatican.* New Hope, Kentucky: St. Martin de Porres Lay Dominican Community Print Shop, January 1995.

Ashton, Joan. *Mother of All Nations.* New York: Harper and Row, 1989.

Atheran, Robert. *American Today* (Volume 16 of the American Heritage New Illustrated History of the United States). New York: Dell Publishing Co., Inc., 1963.

Bartholomew, Professor Coutenay, M.D. *A Scientist Researches Mary Mother and Coredemptrix.* Asbury, New Jersey: The 101 Foundation, 1998.

Bernstein, Carl and Marco Politi. *His Holiness.* New York, New York: Doubleday, 1996.

Bettwy, Sr. Isabel. *I Am the Guardian of the Faith.* Steubenville, Ohio: Franciscan University Press, 1991.

Biallas, Leonard J. *World Religions A Story Approach.* Mystic, Connecticut: Twenty-Third Publications, 1991.

Blackbourn, David. *Marpingen.* New York: Vintage Books, 1995.

Borelli, Antonio A. and John R. Spann. *Our Lady of Fatima: Prophecies of Tragedy or Hope for America and the World?* United States of America: The American Society for the Defense of Tradition, Family and Property, 1986.

Brown, Michael H. *The Last Secret.* Ann Arbor, Michigan: Servant Publications, 1998.

Brown, Michael H. *The Bridge to Heaven.* Lima, Pennsylvania: Marian Communications, Ltd., 1993.

Brown, Michael H. *The Final Hour.* Milford, Ohio: Faith Publishing Company, 1992.

Brown, Michael H. *The Day Will Come.* Servant Publications: Ann Arbor, Michigan, 1996.

Bunson, Matthew. *Our Sunday Visitor's Encyclopedia of Catholic History.* Huntington, Indiana: Our Sunday Visitor, Inc., 1995.

Cadena Y Almedia, Msgr. Luis E. *Our Blessed Lady is Speaking to You Are You Listening? Her Message from Mellaray Grotto.* W. Deevy, 1986.

Carroll, Warren H. *1917 Red Banners White Mantle.* Front Royal, Virginia: Christendom Publications, 1981.

Carroll, Warren H., Ph.. D. *The Blessed Virgin Mary and the Moslems* in *Soul* Magazine (May, June 1991).

Carty, Rev. Charles Mortimer. *Padre Pio the Stigmatist.* Rockford, Illinois, TAN Books and Publishers, Inc., 1973.

Casalletto, Thomas. *A State of Emergency.* Richardson and Steirman: New York, 1987.

—. *Catechism of the Catholic Church.* New Hope, Kentucky: St. Martin de Porres Community, 1994.

Christian William A. Jr. *Visionaries.* Berkeley, California: University of California Press, 1996.

Cirrincione, Msgr. Joseph A. With Thomas A. Nelson. *The Forgotten Secret of Fatima and the Silent Apostolate.* Rockford, Illinois: TAN Books and Publishers, Inc., 1988.

Cole, L. Edward *Around the World with Our Lady of Fatima on Stamps* in *Soul* Magazine (November, December , 1990).

Collins, Thomas and Thomas W. Petrisko (editors) *Our Lady of the Americas.* McKees Rocks, Pennsylvania: Pittsburgh Center for Peace, 1994.

Connell, Janice T. *The Visions of the Children.* New York: St. Martin's Press, 1992.

Connell, Janice T. *Meetings with Mary, Visions, of the Blessed Mother.* New York: Ballentine Books, 1995.

Connell, Janice. *Queen of the Cosmos.* Orlean, Massachusetts: Paraclete Press, 1990.

Connor, Edward. *Prophecy for Today.* Rockford, Illinois: TAN Books and Publishers, Inc., 1984.

Craig, Mary. *The Mystery of the Madonna of Medjugorje, Spark from Heaven*. Notre Dame, Indiana: Ave Maria Press, 1988.

Croiset, Fr. John, S.J.. *The Devotion of the Sacred Heart of Jesus*. Rockford Illinois: TAN Books and Publishers, Inc., 1988.

Cruz, Joan Carroll. *Miraculous Images of Our Lord*. Rockford, Illinois: TAN Books and Publishers, Inc., 1995.

Cruz, Joan Carroll. *Mysteries Marvels Miracles in the Lives of the Saints*. Rockford, Illinois, TAN Books and Publishers, Inc., 1997.

Culleton, Rev. R. Gerald. *The Prophets and Our Times*. Rockford, Illinois: TAN Books and Publishers, Inc., 1974.

Cullenton, Rev. R. Gerald. *The Reign of Antichrist*. Rockford, Illinois: TAN Books and Publishers, Inc., 1974.

Culligan Emmett. *The Last World War and the End of Time*. (no publisher or date listed).

De Marchi, John. *Fatima From the Beginning*. Portugal: Grafica Almondina Torees Novas, 1994.

de Maria des Agnes, Frere Francois. *Fatima: Prophecies of Tragedy and Triumph*. Frere Francois des Marie des Agnes La Contre-Reforme Catholique, 1991.

de Maria, S. *The Most Holy Virgin at San Damiano*. Hauteville, Switzerland: Editions du Paris.

De Oca, Rev. Fr. V. Montes, C.S.Sp. *More About Fatima*. United States: 1979.

Dennis, Mary Alice. *Melanie*. Rockford, Illinois: TAN Books and Publishers, Inc., 1995.

Dirvin, Fr. Joseph, C.M. *Saint Catherine Laboure of Sister Mary of the Holy Trinity.* Rockford, Illinois: TAN Books and Publishers, Inc., 1987.

—. *Dozule.* France: Nouvelles Editions Latines, 1983.

Dupont, Yves. *Catholic Prophecy.* Rockford, Illinois: TAN Books and Publishers, Inc., 1970.

—. *Elizabeth of the Trinity.* ICA Publications, 1984.

Ernst, Robert. *Lexicon, der Marienersheinungen.* Druck and Verlag: Anton Ruhland, Rudolf-Diesel-Strabe).

Evaristo, Carlos. *Saint Michael and the Fatima Connection.* Codex, Portugal: St. Anne's Oratory, 1996.

Flannery, Austin, O.P. (Editor) *Vatican Council II.* Boston, Massachusetts: St. Paul Editions, 1982.

Faricy, Robert S.J. and Lucy Rooney, S.N.D. *Mary Among Us.* Steubenville, Ohio: Franciscan University Press, 1989.

Flynn, Ted and Maureen. *The Thunder of Justice.* Sterling, Virginia: MaxKol Communications, Inc., 1993.

Foley, Fr. Richard, S.J. *The Drama of Medjugorje.* Dublin, Ireland: Veritas, 1992.

Fox, Rev. Robert J. *Rediscovering Fatima.* Huntington, Indiana: Our Sunday Visitor, Inc., 1982.

Freze, Michael, S.F.O. *Voices Visions and Apparitions.* Huntington, Indiana: Our Sunday Visitor Publishing Division, 1993.

Fukushima, Francis Mursuo. *Akita: Mother of God as Coredemptrix Modern Miracles of Holy Eucharist.* Santa Barbara, California: Queenship Publishing Company, 1994.

—. *Funk and Wagnalls Standard Desk Dictionary (Vol 2)*. New York: Funk and Wagnalls, Inc., 1975.

Galot, Jean SJ. *Abba Father We Long to See Your Face*. New York: Alba House, 1992.

—. *Gebsetsaktion Maria Queen of Peace - Medjugorje*. Vienna, Austria: Gebsetsaktion Maria-Konigin des Friedens-Medjugorje (Editions 1-37).

Girard, Father Guy and Father Armand Girard and Father Janko Bubalo. *Mary Queen of Peace Stay with Us*. Montreal Canada: Editions Pauline, 1988.

Gobbi, Don Stefano. *Our Lady Speaks to Her Beloved Priests*. St. Francis, Maine: The National Headquarters of the Marian Movement of Priests in the United States of America, 1988.

—. *God is Father*. (His Excellency Mons. Caillot's Testimony - no publisher of date listed).

Gouin, Fr. Paul. *Sister Mary of the Cross Shepherdess of La Salette*. Asbury, New Jersey: The 101 Foundation, 1981.

Gottemoller, Father Bartholomew, O.C.S.O. *Words of Love*. Rockford, Illinois: TAN Books and Publishers, Inc., 1985.

Gribble, Richard C.C., *The History and Devotion of the Rosary*, Our Sunday Visitor: Huntington, Indiana, 1992.

Grunner, Father Nicholas et. al. *World Enslavement of Peace... It's Up to the Pope*. Ontario, Canada: The Fatima Crusader.

Grunner, Father Nicholas, S.T. L., S.T.D. "Jesus Said: 'Make it Known to My Ministers...'" in *The Fatima Crusader* Magazine (issue 46, winter 1994).

Haffert, John M. *Her Own Words to the Nuclear Age*. Asbury, New Jersey: Lay Apostalate Foundation, 1993.

Haffert, John M. *The Meaning of Akita*. Asbury, New Jersey: 101 Foundation, Inc., 1989.

Haffert, John M. *To Prevent This*. Asbury, New Jersey: 101 Foundation, Inc., 1993.

Haffert, John M. *Meet the Witnesses*. Fatima, Portugal: AMI International Press, 1961.

Haffert, John M. *Now The Woman Shall Conquer*. Asbury, New Jersey: The 101 Foundation, Inc., 1997.

Hebert, Rev. Albert J., S.M. *Prophecies! The Chastisement and Purification*. Paulina, Louisiana: Hebert, 1986.

Hebert, Rev. Albert J., S.M. *The Tears of Mary and Fatima Why?* Paulina, Louisiana: Hebert, 1989.

Hebert, Albert J., S.M. *The Three Day's Darkness*. Paulina, Louisiana: Hebert, 1986.

Hebert, Albert J., S.M. *Signs Wonders and Response*. Paulina, Louisiana: Hebert, 1988.

Hebert, Albert J., S.M. *Warnings Visions and Messages*. Signs of the Times Apostolate, Inc., 1998.

Heintz, Peter. *A Guide to Apparitions of Our Blessed Virgin Mary*. Sacramento, California: Gabriel Press, 1993.

Hughes, John Jay. *Pontiffs Popes Who Shaped History*. Huntington, Indiana: Our Sunday Visitor, Inc., 1994.

—. *Inchigeela ... A Call to Prayer*. Inchigeela Queen of Peace Group in association with Religious Promotions and Publications, 1989.

—. Interview with Sr. Lucia of Fatima excerpt from Christus magazine March 1998.

Jahenny, Marie-Julie. *Prophecies of La Fraudais*. Montsurs, France: Editions Resiac, 1977.

—. *Jesus and Mary Speak in Ireland* -- Messages to Christina Gallagher. Ireland: 1991.

—. *Jesus Calls Us*. Winterthur, Switzerland: In Waurheit Und Treue, 1988.

John Paul II, Pope. *Crossing the Threshold of Hope*. New York: Alfred A. Knopf, 1994.

John Paul II, Pope. *God Father and Creator Volume One*. Boston, Massachusetts: Pauline Books and Media. 1996.

Johnston, Francis. *The Wonder of Guadalupe*. Rockford, Illinois: TAN Books and Publishers, Inc. 1981.

Johnston, Francis. *Fatima: The Great Sign*. Rockford, Illinois: TAN Books and Publishers, Inc., 1980.

Johnston, Francis. *When Millions Saw Mary*. Chulmeligh, Devon, United Kingdom: Autgustine Publishing Company, 1980.

Josefina, Maria. *"A Pilgrimage to the Heart of Man Through My Mercy"* -- Book II -- in *The Age of the Two Hearts*. (Revelations given to Josefina Maria), Dulles, Virginia: MaxKol Communications, Inc., 1994.

Kamell, Youssef G. and John P. Jackson and Rebecca S. Jackson. *A Lady of Light Appears in Egypt the Story of Zeitoun*. Colorado Spings, Colorado, St. Mark's Avenue Press, 1996.

Keithley, June. *Lipa. Madaluyong*. Metro Manila: Cacho Publishing House, Inc., 1992.

Kelly, Matthew. *Words from God*. Batesman Bay, N.S.W., Australia, 1993.

Keyes, Frances Parkinson. *Bernadette of Lourdes.* Wheathampstead, Hertfordshire: Anthony Clarke, 1975.

—. Kolbe, St. Maximilian, *Aim Higher.* Prow Books/Franciscan Marytown Press: Libertyville, Illinois, 1994.

Knotzinger, Msgr. Dr. Kurt. *"Medjugorje and the Call to New Evangelization"* from *Medjugorje Gebetsaktion, Mary Queen of Peace 27.* Vienna, Austria: Gebetsaktion Maria-Konigin des Freidens 21.

Kondor, Fr. Louis, SVD. (editor) *Fatima in Lucia's Own Words.* Still River, Massachusetts: Marian Helpers, 1991.

Kowalska, Sr. M. Faustina. *Divine Mercy in My Soul. (The Diary of Sister M. Faustina Kowalska),* Stockbridge, Massachusetts: Marian Press, 1987.

Kselman, Thomas A. *Miracles and Prophecies in Nineteenth Century France.* New Brunswick, New Jersey: Rutgers University Press: 1983.

Kunzili, Josef. *The Messages of the Lady of All Nations.* Amsterdam: Miriam-Verlag, 1987.

Langley, Richard. *Signs of the Time ... Apparitions, Visions and Locutions Concerning the Last Times Before the Glorious Return of Our Lord Jesus Christ.* (no publisher given), 1991.

Laurentin, Fr. Rene. *An Appeal from Mary in Argentina: The Apparitions of San Nicolas.* Milford, Ohio: Faith Publishing Company, 1990.

Laurentin, Fr. Rene. *The Apparitions of the Blessed Virgin Mary Today,* Paris France: Veritas Publications 1991.

Laurentin, Fr. Rene and Rupic, Ljudeuit, *Is the Virgin Mary Appearing at Medjugorje?* Washington D.C.: The Word Among Us Press, 1984.

Laurentin, Fr. Rene. *Pilgrimages Sanctuaries Icons Apparitions.* Milford Ohio: The Riehle Foundation, 1994.

Laurentin, Rene and Henri Joyeux. *Scientific and Medical Studies on the Apparitions at Medjugorje.* Dublin, Ireland: Veritas, 1987.

Laurentin, Rene and Rene Lejeune. *Messages and Teachings of Mary at Medjugorje.* Milford, Ohio: The Riehle Foundation, 1988.

—. *Little Nellie of Holy God.* Long Beach, California: Litho Tech Impression, 1993.

Maindron, Fr. Gabriel. *Kibeho Rwanda - A Prophecy Fulfilled the Apparitions of Our Lady at Kibeho.* South Godstone, Surrey: The Marian Spring Centre, 1996.

Manifold, Dierdre. *Fatima and the Great Conspiracy.* United States: The Militia of Our Immaculate Mother, 1992.

—. *Marian Apparitions of the 20th Century.* In the Marian Library International Marian Research Institute, ROTEN@data.lib.udayton.edu.

Martin, Jacov. *Queen of Peace in Medjugorje.* Milford, Ohio: The Riehle Foundation, 1989.

Martin, Malachi. *The Keys of This Blood.* New York: Touchstone - Simon and Schuster, 1990.

McNally, J. Rand, Jr. "The Nuclear Tornado Threat" (Handout [Report] for Spring Meeting, American Physical Society, April 28 - May 1, 1986, Washington, D.C.).

McNally, Dr. J. Rand, Jr. *The Story Behind the Films* in Soul Magazine (January-February, 1987).

Miravalle, Mark, S.T.D. *Heart of the Message of Medjugorje.* Steubenville, Ohio: Franciscan University Press, 1988.

Monsour, Claire and Dr. Antoine. *Our Lady of Soufanieh*. Beverly Hills, California: Mansour, 1991.

—. *Messages of Our Lady at San Nicolas*. Milford, Ohio: Faith Publishing Company, 1991.

Montfort, St. Louis de, *The Secret of the Rosary*, Montfort Publications: Bayshore, N.Y. 1965.

Morse, Joseph Laffan, Sc. B, LL.D. (editor) *The Universal Encyclopedia* (Vols. 1-25). NewYork: Standard Reference Works Publishing Company, Inc., 1956.

Natalia, Sr. Maria. *The Victorious Queen of the World*. (The spiritual diary of a contemporary mystic, St. Natalia of Hungary). Mountain View, California: Queen Publishing, 1993.

Nolan, Denis, *Medjugorje, a Time for Truth, a Time for Action*. Santa Barbara, California: Queenship Publishing, 1993.

O'Brien, Father Bartholomew. *The Cure of Ars*. Rockford, Illinois: TAN Books and Publishers, 1956.

O'Carroll, Michael Cssp. *Medjugorje Facts Documents Theology*. Dubin, Ireland: Veritas, 1989.

O'Connor, Fr. Edward D. C.S.C. *Marian Apparitons Today Why So Many*? Santa Barbara, California: Queenship Publihsing Company, 1996.

O'Dell, Catheine M. *Those Who Saw Her.* Huntington, Indiana: Our Sunday Inc., 1995.

—. *Our Blessed Lady Is Speaking to You: Her Message from Melleray Grotto*. W. Deevy, 1986.

—. *Our Lady of Fatima's Peace Plan from Heaven.* Rockford, Illinois: TAN Books and Publishers, 1983.

—. *"Our Lady of Octolan"* (pamphlet) from *Fatima Family Messenger*. Steubenville, Ohio: Merciful Association, 1992.

Paul VI, Pope and Pope John XXIII and Pope Leo XIII. *17 Papal Documents on the Rosary*. Boston, Massachusetts: St. Paul Editions, 1980.

Pelletier, Joseph A., A.A. *The Sun Danced at Fatima*. Garden City, New York: Image Books, 1983.

Pelletier, Joseph, A., A.A. *The Queen of Peace Visits Medjugorje*. Worcester, Massachusetts: Assumption Publications, 1985.

Petrisko, Thomas W. *Call of the Ages*. Santa Barbara, California: Queenship Publishing Company, 1995.

Petrisko, Thomas W. *For the Soul of the Family*. Santa Barbara, California, Queenship Publishing Company, 1996.

Petrisko, Thomas W. (editor). *Our Lady Queen of Peace* -- Special Edition I. Pittsburgh, Pennsylvania: Pittsburgh Center for Peace, Inc., 1991.

Petrisko, Thomas W. (editor). *Our Lady Queen of Peace* -- Special Edition II. Pittsburgh, Pennsylvania: Pittsburgh Center for Peace, Inc., 1992.

Petrisko, Thomas W. (editor). *Our Lady Queen of Peace* -- Special Edition III. Pittsburgh, Pennsylvania: Pittsburgh Center for Peace, Inc., 1995.

Petrisko, Thomas W. *False Prophets of Today*. McKees Rocks, Pennsylvania: St. Andrews Productions, 1997.

Petrisko, Thomas W. *Mother of the Secret*. Santa Barbara, California: Queenship Publishing Company, 1997.

Petrisko, Thomas W. *The Last Crusade*. McKees Rocks, Pennsylvania: St. Andrew's Productions, 1996.

Petrisko, Thomas W. *The Sorrow, the Sacrifice, and the Triumph: The Apparitions, Visions and Prophecies of Christina Gallagher.* New York: Simon and Schuster, Inc., 1995.

Piccarreta, Luisa. *When the Divine Will Reigns in Souls Book of Heaven.* Jacksonville, Florida: The Luisa Piccaretta Center for the Divine Will, 1995.

Platt, Nathaniel And Mirel Jean Drummon. *Our World Through the Ages*. Englewood Cliffs, New Jersey: Prentice-Hall, Inc., 1954.

—. *Queen of Mercy the Message the Story*. Earth, Texas: Queen of Mercy Center, 1991.

—. *Quest for the Past*. Pleasantville, New York: The Reader's Digest Association, Inc., 1984.

—. *Reader's Digest Illustrated Story of World War II*. Pleasantville, New York: The Reader's Digest Association, Inc., 1969.

Ritchie, Robert E. "The Third Secret of Fatima: Is the Wait Over?" from *Crusade Magazine*. York, Pennsylvania: American Society for the Defense of Tradition, Family and Property (TFP).

Rossman, Doreen Mary. *A Light Shone in the Darkness The Story of the Stigmatist and Mystic Theresa Neumann*. Santa Barbara, California: Queenship Publishing Co., 1997.

Ruffin, C. Bernard Padre Pio: *The True Story*. Huntingdon, Indiana: Our Sunday Visitor, Inc., 1991.

Sales, Lorenzo, I.M.C., *Jesus Appeals to the World*. Staten Island, New York: Alba House, 1955.

Scallan, Dorothy (editor). *The Golden Arrow*. Rockford, Illinois: TAN Books and Publishers, Inc., 1990.

Schmoger, Very Rev. Carl E., C.SS.R. *The Life of Anne Catherine Emmerich* - Volume 1. Rockford, Illinois: TAN Books and Pubishers, Inc., 1976.

Schreck, Alan. *The Compact History of the Catholic Chruch*. Ann Arbor, Michigan: Servant Books, 1987.

Sharkey, Don. *The Woman Shall Conquer*. Libertyville, Illinois: Prow. Franciscan town Press (fourth pringing AMI Press, Washington, New Jersey), 1976.

Shamon, Rev. Albert J.M. *The Power of the Rosary*, Milford, Ohio: The Riehle Foundation, 1990.

Sims, Sr. Margaret Catherine, C.S.J. *Apparitions in Betania, Venezuela*. South Boston, Massachusetts: Star Litho, Inc., 1992.

Sulzberger, C.L. et. Cal. *The American Heritage Picture History of World War II*. American Heritage Publishing Co., Inc.

Szulc, Tad. *Pope John Paul II The Biography*. New York: Scribner, 1995.

Terelya, Josyp with Michael H. Brown. *Witness*. Milford, Ohio: Faith Publishing Company, 1991.

Terelya, Josyp. *In the Kingdom of the Spirit*. Pueblo, Colorado: Abba House, 1995.

—. *The Apparitions of Our Lady of Kibeho* (pamphlet - no publisher or date listed).

—. *The Apostolate of Holy Motherhood*. Milford, Ohio: The Riehle Foundation, 101.

—. *The Great Sign* in Soul Magazine (May, June, 1984).

—. *The Holy Bible* -- Douay Rheims Edition. Rockford, Illinois:

TAN Books and Publishing, Inc.

—. *The New American Bible*, Wichita, Kansas: Catholic Bible Publishers, 1984-1985 Edition.

—. *The Miracle in Naju Korea -- Heaven Speaks to the World.* Gresham, Oregon: Mary's Touch By Mail, 1992.

—. "The Splendor of Truth" in *Inside the Vatican*. New Hope, Kentucky: St. Martin de Porres Lay Dominican Community Print Shop, November 1993.

—. *The Time is Our Time the Messages of The Lady of All Nations A Summary.* Amsterdam: Stichting Vrouwe van alle Volkeren, 1997.

—. *There is Nothing More.* Washington, N.J.: AMI Press.

—. *The Sorrowful and Immaculate Heart of Mary* (Message of Berthe Petit, Franciscan Tertiary). Kenosha, Wisconsin: the Franciscan Marytown Press, 1969.

—. *The Victorious Queen of the World* (The spiritual diary of a contemporary mystic, Sr. Natalia of Hungary). Mountain Veiw, California: Two Hearts Books and Publishers, 1988.

Thomas, Hugh *A History of the World*. New York: Harper and Row, Publishers, 1979.

Thompson, Frank Charles, D.D., Ph. D. (editor). *The Thompson Chain Reference Bible, New International Version*. Indianapolis, Indiana: B.B. Kirkbride Bible Co., Inc., 1991.

Tindal-Robertson, Timothy. *Fatima, Russia and Pope John Paul II*. Still River, Massachusetts: The Ravengate Press, 1992.

Trinite, Bro Michel de la Sainte. *Fatima Revealed.....and Discarded.* Devon: Augustine Pubishing Co., 1988.

Trochu, Abbe Francois. *Saint Bernadette Soubirous*. Rockford, Illinois: TAN Books and Publishers, Inc., 1985.

Vogl, Aldabert Albert. *Theresa Neumann Mystic and Stigmatists*. Rockford, Illinois: TAN Books and Publishers, 1985.

—. *Voice of the Sacred Hearts*. Hawaiian Gardens, California: Two Hearts Media Organization, Jun/Jul/Aug, 1996.

Walsh, William Thomas. *Our Lady of Fatima*. New York: Image Books Doubleday, 1954.

—. *Wars of the 20th Century*. London, England: Bison Books Ltd., 1985.

—. *"Wondorous News From Litmanova"*. (pamphlet -- no date or publisher listed).

Yasuda, Teigi, O.S.V. *Akita --The Tears and Message of Mary*. (English version by John M. Haffert. Asbury, New Jersey: 101 Foundation, Inc., 1991).

Vincent, R. *"Please Come Back to Me and My Son"*. Milford, Co. Armagh, N. Ireland, Milford House, 1992.

Zaki, Pearl. *Our Lord's Mother Visits Egypt in 1968 and 1969*. (Pamphlet - no publisher or date given).

Zimdars-Swartz, Sandra L. *Encountering Mary*. New York: Avon Books-Princton University Press, 191.

INDEX

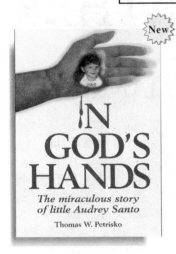
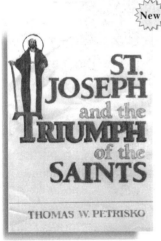

454

False Prophets of Today

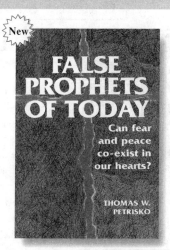

by Dr. Thomas W. Petrisko

'Despise not prophecies, but test all things'
-1Thes. 5:20

The Bible tells us that in the 'end times' many false prophets will arise, spreading messages of confusion and fear throughout the world. Who are these people and how can one determine whether their messages are truly from God? This book will help the reader to exercise discernment in the area of private revelation, so to find peace in the ark of Mary's Immaculate Heart.   84 pages

Only $4.95
ISBN: 1891903020

The Prophecy of Daniel

by Dr. Thomas W. Petrisko

'One day you will see in the holy place he who commits the horrible sacrilege'
-Mt. 24:15

Undoubtedly among the most important of the Old Testament prophecies yet to be fulfilled, it is believed that Daniel foretold the rise of the Antichrist and how this evil ruler would come to commit the 'horrible sacrilege' and 'abolish the daily sacrifice for one thousand two hundred and ninety days.' (Dan. 12:11). Could these be the times of this ancient prophecies fulfillment? 54 pages

Only $4.95
ISBN: 1891903039

455